The Social Psychology
of Group Identity
and Social Conflict

The Social Psychology of Group Identity and Social Conflict

THEORY, APPLICATION, AND PRACTICE

Edited by
Alice H. Eagly
Reuben M. Baron
V. Lee Hamilton

DECADE
of BEHAVIOR
2000-2010

American Psychological Association
Washington, DC

Published by
American Psychological Association
750 First Street, NE
Washington, DC 20002
www.apa.org

To order
APA Order Department
P.O. Box 92984
Washington, DC 20090-2984

Tel: (800) 374-2721; Direct: (202) 336-5510
Fax: (202) 336-5502; TDD/TTY: (202) 336-6123
Online: www.apa.org/books/
E-mail: order@apa.org

In the U.K., Europe, Africa, and the Middle East, copies may be ordered from
American Psychological Association
3 Henrietta Street
Covent Garden, London
WC2E 8LU England

Typeset in Century Schoolbook by Argosy, Waltham, MA

Printer: Sheridan Books, Ann Arbor, MI
Cover Designer: Watermark Design, Alexandria, VA
Project Manager: Argosy, Waltham, MA

The opinions and statements published are the responsibility of the authors, and such opinions and statements do not necessarily represent the policies of the American Psychological Association.

Library of Congress Cataloging-in-Publication Data
The social psychology of group identity and social conflict : theory, application, and practice / edited by Alice H. Eagly, Reuben M. Baron, and V. Lee Hamilton.
    p. cm.—(APA decade of behavior volumes)
    Includes bibliographical references and index.
    ISBN 1-55798-952-4 (alk. paper)
    1. Group identity. 2. Social conflict. 3. Conflict management. I. Eagly, Alice Hendrickson. II. Baron, Reuben M. III. Hamilton, V. Lee. IV. Kelman, Herbert C. V. Series: Decade of behavior.

    HM753 .S623 2004
    302.4—dc22

                                                                    2003017996

British Library Cataloguing-in-Publication Data
A CIP record is available from the British Library.

Printed in the United States of America
First Edition

APA Science Volumes

Attribution and Social Interaction: The Legacy of Edward E. Jones

Best Methods for the Analysis of Change: Recent Advances, Unanswered Questions, Future Directions

Cardiovascular Reactivity to Psychological Stress and Disease

The Challenge in Mathematics and Science Education: Psychology's Response

Changing Employment Relations: Behavioral and Social Perspectives

Children Exposed to Marital Violence: Theory, Research, and Applied Issues

Cognition: Conceptual and Methodological Issues

Cognitive Bases of Musical Communication

Cognitive Dissonance: Progress on a Pivotal Theory in Social Psychology

Conceptualization and Measurement of Organism-Environment Interaction

Converging Operations in the Study of Visual Selective Attention

Creative Thought: An Investigation of Conceptual Structures and Processes

Developmental Psychoacoustics

Diversity in Work Teams: Research Paradigms for a Changing Workplace

Emotion and Culture: Empirical Studies of Mutual Influence

Emotion, Disclosure, and Health

Evolving Explanations of Development: Ecological Approaches to Organism-Environment Systems

Examining Lives in Context: Perspectives on the Ecology of Human Development

Global Prospects for Education: Development, Culture, and Schooling

Hostility, Coping, and Health

Measuring Patient Changes in Mood, Anxiety, and Personality Disorders: Toward a Core Battery

Occasion Setting: Associative Learning and Cognition in Animals

Organ Donation and Transplantation: Psychological and Behavioral Factors

Origins and Development of Schizophrenia: Advances in Experimental Psychopathology

APA Decade of Behavior Volumes

Contents

Contributors

Nancy E. Adler, PhD, Departments of Psychiatry and Pediatrics and Center for Health and Community, University of California, San Francisco

Reuben M. Baron, PhD, Department of Psychology, University of Connecticut, Storrs

Cynthia Chataway, PhD, Department of Psychology, York University, Toronto, Ontario, Canada

Rebecca Dale, MALD, Fletcher School of Law and Diplomacy, Tufts University, Medford, MA

Ann Locke Davidson, PhD, Educational Connections, Portland, OR

Erin Driver-Linn, PhD, Department of Psychology, Harvard University, Cambridge, MA

Alice H. Eagly, PhD, Department of Psychology and Institute for Policy Research, Northwestern University, Evanston, IL

Maria Hadjipavlou, PhD, Department of Social and Political Sciences, University of Cyprus, Nicosia

V. Lee Hamilton, PhD, Duke University Divinity School, Durham, NC

Donna Hicks, PhD, Program on International Conflict Analysis and Resolution, Harvard University, Cambridge, MA

Herbert C. Kelman, PhD, Department of Psychology and Weatherhead Center for International Affairs, Harvard University, Cambridge, MA

Susan H. Korper, MA, Program on International Conflict Analysis and Resolution, Harvard University, Cambridge, MA

Rhoda Margesson, MALD, Congressional Research Service, Library of Congress, Washington, DC

Luc Reychler, PhD, Department of International Relations, Catholic University of Leuven, Belgium

Jennifer A. Richeson, PhD, Department of Psychological and Brain Sciences, Dartmouth College, Hanover, NH

Nadim N. Rouhana, PhD, Departments of Psychology and Sociology, Tel Aviv University, Israel

Janet Ward Schofield, PhD, Department of Psychology, University of Pittsburgh, PA

Jeffrey R. Seul, JD, Groove Networks, Beverly, MA

José R. Torregrosa, PhD, Department of Social Psychology, Universidad Complutense de Madrid, Spain

William Weisberg, PhD, Program on International Conflict Analysis and Resolution, Harvard University, Cambridge, MA

Shoshana Zuboff, PhD, Harvard Business School, Boston, MA

Foreword

In early 1988, the American Psychological Association (APA) Science Director-ate began its sponsorship of what would become an exceptionally successful activity in support of psychological science—the APA Scientific Conferences program. This program has showcased some of the most important topics in psychological science and has provided a forum for collaboration among many leading figures in the field.

The program has inspired a series of books that have presented cutting-edge work in all areas of psychology. At the turn of the millennium, the series was renamed the Decade of Behavior Series to help advance the goals of this important initiative. The Decade of Behavior is a major interdisciplinary campaign designed to promote the contributions of the behavioral and social sciences to our most important societal challenges in the decade leading up to 2010. Although a key goal has been to inform the public about these scientific contributions, other activities have been designed to encourage and further collaboration among scientists. Hence, the series that was the "APA Science Series" has continued as the "Decade of Behavior Series." This represents one element in APA's efforts to promote the Decade of Behavior initiative as one of its endorsing organizations. For additional information about the Decade of Behavior, please visit http://www.decadeofbehavior.org.

During the course of the past years, the Science Conference and Decade of Behavior Series has allowed psychological scientists to share and explore cutting-edge findings in psychology. The APA Science Directorate looks forward to continuing this successful program and to sponsoring other conferences and books in the years ahead. This series has been so successful that we have chosen to extend it to include books that, although they do not arise from conferences, report with the same high quality of scholarship on the latest research.

We are pleased that this important contribution to the literature was supported in part by the Decade of Behavior program. Congratulations to the editors and contributors of this volume on their sterling effort.

Kurt Salzinger, PhD
Executive Director for Science

Virginia E. Holt
Assistant Executive Director
for Science

Preface

As we organized the *Festschrift* conference for Herbert C. Kelman, prepared our presentations, and then delivered them, the world situation that was initiated by the events of September 11, 2001, could not have been imagined. As the millennium was turning, it appeared that the tone of the conference could be one of celebration, an occasion to honor someone whose efforts to establish Israeli–Palestinian peace appeared to have made a major contribution to overcoming decades of conflict and misunderstanding. As we go to press, the Middle East and the wider world face decidedly darker possibilities, with the beginnings of what is described in the West as a war on terrorism. Perhaps peace will still come to the Middle East, but even if it does not in the foreseeable future, no one can gainsay the fact that Herbert Kelman changed many individual Arabs and Israelis toward accepting the goal of peace and dedicating themselves to conflict resolution. This is an extraordinary achievement.

Herbert Kelman's professional career sets before us a model of how one does not have to choose between theory and application or between good science and good deeds. In each phase of his career, Herb has reacted to more than problems disconnected from their context. As he formulated his model of social influence, the United States was being torn by McCarthyism; at the same time, the nation was facing the Korean War, and it was taking steps toward tearing down segregation. Later, out of the atrocities of the Vietnam War came his incisive analysis of sanctioned massacres. In each of these activities, as well as in his specific attention to the role of deception in social psychological research, Herb showed a deep sensitivity to the moral dimensions of whatever challenges he took on. Finally, and in a step that this activist for peace and justice was clearly preparing for all his life, Herb prepared a direct attack on one of humanity's most intractable conflicts—the struggle for the Holy Land between Israelis and Palestinians. In this arena, Herb developed new ways of thinking about the links between self and national identity and new ways of conceptualizing the relation between individual and group processes. The intellectual capstone of these ideas may be the concept of an "uneasy coalition," a construct that resonates with dynamical systems concepts of social psychological phenomena and with the shifting agreements and conflicts in the Middle East.

This volume contains chapters by a number of individuals who studied with Herbert Kelman at various points in his career. The diversity of the content of these essays reflects the several phases of Herb's intellectual progress, as his emphasis shifted from the core of social psychology to the study of peace and conflict resolution. The first group of essays thus considers issues of theoretical foundations that continue to be debated by social psychologists. Reuben M. Baron considers the relation between Herbert Kelman's work and both the classic Lewinian tradition and the contemporary movement toward dynamical systems models. José R. Torregrosa passionately argues that theory and research in social psychology should incorporate more societal considerations—

that is, become more sociological. V. Lee Hamilton considers Herbert Kelman's key concept of identification in relation to contemporary dual-process theories of persuasion and social influence in social psychology. Alice H. Eagly analyzes one of social psychology's core concepts, prejudice, and argues that it must be reformulated in the light of evidence that discrimination is often directed toward groups that people evaluate positively.

The second section of the book contains chapters on applications of social psychology. The first essay, by Nancy E. Adler, illustrates in the area of health psychology the brilliant mix of theory relevance and application that exemplifies Herb's style of research. Janet Ward Schofield and Ann Locke Davidson provide another example of this approach in their analysis of inequalities in students' access to the Internet within schools. Shoshana Zuboff's contribution analyzes business organizations and pinpoints their decline in a pattern of inattention to their context that she terms *organizational narcissism*. Finally, Luc Reychler provides a sophisticated analysis of the conditions that facilitate peace—that is, a *peace architecture*—in situations of long-term conflict.

The third set of chapters concerns social psychological approaches to the practice of conflict resolution. In an essay that considers the conflict in Sri Lanka, Donna Hicks and William Weisberg present an extension of the interactive problem-solving method that Herb Kelman introduced; they argue that participants need to acknowledge deeply rooted injustices and injuries and take responsibility for them. In an essay that gives special attention to the Israeli–Palestinian conflict, Nadim N. Rouhana argues that conflict resolution in long-term national conflicts must involve reconciliation in the sense of achieving a relationship that is based on mutual legitimacy. In a chapter that analyzes the conflict in Cyprus, Maria Hadjipavlou considers the role of bicommunal contacts in building a peaceful civil society. Finally, Cynthia Chataway presents the considerable empirical support that has emerged for the efficacy of interactive problem-solving workshops as a method of conflict resolution.

The first 12 chapters, along with the commentaries on these chapters contributed by recent students of Herbert Kelman, trace the evolution of a scientist and a seeker of peace. In chapter 13, Herb tells his own story of the personal and intellectual journey that took him from his childhood in Europe through the many stages of his varied career as a social psychologist. His students have set forth on many paths, each individual intellectually enriched and personally inspired by this teacher and mentor.

About Herbert C. Kelman

Herbert C. Kelman is the Richard Clarke Cabot Research Professor of Social Ethics at Harvard University and serves as director of the Program on International Conflict Analysis and Resolution at the Weatherhead Center for International Affairs at Harvard. He is renowned for his distinguished career as a social psychologist who is dedicated to reducing social injustice and international conflict. From an intellectual base in the study of attitudes and social influence, he branched out to study ethical issues in research, obedience in the context of authority relationships, nationalism and national identity, and conflict resolution. He was also among the founders of the peace research movement, and in many of his writings he explored the contribution of social psychology to international relations. He also developed a particular method of addressing international and interethnic conflict, known as *interactive problem solving,* and for many years has applied this innovative method in problem-solving workshops between Palestinian and Israeli leaders. In these workshops, influential people from both sides of a conflict meet in an unofficial context in which they can present their views and listen to those of the other side. These workshops helped lay the groundwork for the 1993 Oslo agreement and have provided an instructive model for many scholars and practitioners who are interested in peace building.

Herbert Kelman's personal history began in 1927 in Vienna, Austria. He left Austria with his family to escape the Nazi persecution of the Jews. After spending a year as refugees in Belgium, Herb and his family came to the United States. This early background gave Herb facility in several languages before he learned English. His students were always astonished to find that the meticulous English with which he corrected their written work was not Herb's second language—it was his sixth!

Settling in New York City, Herb completed his secondary education and then attended Brooklyn College, from which he obtained a BA in English and psychology in 1947. He also attended the Seminary College of Jewish Studies, which awarded him a BHL degree in 1947. Graduate work in social psychology proceeded at Yale University, with the PhD awarded in 1951. Herb's intellectual mentors in the study of psychology included Daniel Katz at Brooklyn College and Carl Hovland at Yale.

After serving as a postdoctoral fellow at Johns Hopkins University, spending a year at the Center for Advanced Study in the Behavioral Sciences, and two years as a research psychologist at the National Institute of Mental Health, Herb became a Lecturer in Social Psychology at Harvard University in 1957. During his stay at Hopkins, he developed his influential model of three processes of social influence—compliance, identification, and internalization. In 1962 he was appointed as professor of psychology and research psychologist at the Center for Research on Conflict Resolution at the University of Michigan. He spent a productive period at Michigan and then in 1968 moved back to Harvard, where he has remained.

Herbert Kelman's career is distinguished by many awards, including the American Psychological Association Award for Distinguished Contributions to Psychology in the Public Interest in 1981 and the James McKeen Cattell Award from the American Psychological Society in 2000. Among his many other awards are the Socio-Psychological Prize of the American Association for the Advancement of Science in 1956, the Kurt Lewin Memorial Award of the Society for the Psychological Study of Social Issues in 1973, the New York Academy of Science Award in 1982, the Interamerican Psychology Award in 1983, the Sanford Award of the International Society of Political Psychology in 1983, the Grawemeyer Award for Ideas Improving World Order from the University of Louisville in 1997, the Lifetime Contribution Award of the Division of Peace Psychology of the American Psychological Association in 1997, the Distinguished Service Award from the Society for the Psychological Study of Social Issues in 1998, and the Austrian Medal of Honor for Science and Art, First

Class, 1998. In addition, Kelman received honorary doctorates from Brooklyn College of the City University of New York in 1981, Hofstra University in 1983, and Universidad Complutense of Madrid in 1995. Also, he was named professor honorario of Universidad San Martin de Porres of Lima in 1979. Surely Herbert Kelman is among the most honored of psychologists.

Herbert Kelman has served as president of many organizations. These include two divisions of the American Psychological Association—the Society for the Psychological Study of Social Issues (Division 9) and the Society for Personality and Social Psychology (Division 8). He was also president of the Peace Science Society, the Interamerican Society of Psychology, the International Studies Association, the International Society of Political Psychology, Psychologists for Social Responsibility, and the Division of Political Psychology of the International Association of Applied Psychology. In addition, he also served as chair of the Section on Social Psychology of the American Sociological Association.

Kelman's personal life includes his marriage to Rose Brousman Kelman in 1953, a relationship that has been extremely important to him. Rose has worked closely with Herb and supported all of his endeavors as a social psychologist and activist. Herb also enjoys warm and intellectually fruitful relationships with a wide range of current students, former students, and collaborators.

Herbert Kelman's career illustrates the bridges that can be built between scientific psychology, applied psychology, and psychological practice in conflict situations. He is unique in the importance of his contributions to all of these aspects of psychology.

Part I

Theoretical Foundations

1

The Contributions of Herbert C. Kelman: Reinvigorating Lewin and Anticipating Dynamical Systems Models

Reuben M. Baron

There are many perspectives from which we can appreciate Herbert Kelman's contributions to the theory, application, and practice of social psychology. I have chosen one that is classic—the work of Kurt Lewin—and one that is very contemporary—complex, dynamical systems (Baron, Amazeen, & Beek, 1994; Kelso, 1995; Nowak & Vallacher, 1998). My central argument is that Kelman is one of the most consistently Lewinian social psychologists active today and at the same time a protodynamical systems theorist and practitioner. This happy confluence I propose is, in turn, tied to a higher invariant property shared by Lewin, Kelman, and dynamical systems theory. Specifically, the commitment to the study of change is what ties together these domains. To make this case, I focus on Kelman's model of social influence processes, his dynamical treatment of attitude, and his work on resolving the Israeli–Arab conflict (see, e.g., Kelman, 1958, 1974, 1997a). I situate these efforts between Lewin and current attempts to use principles from complex dynamical systems to reinvigorate social psychology. Finally, with regard to the relationship between Kelman and Lewin, I use differences as well as similarities to elucidate the nature of Kelman's contribution to social psychology.

The Holocaust Connection and World War II

Before discussing specific theoretical and substantive commonalities as well as differences, it is critical to understand that a common influence shaped both Lewin's and Kelman's professional lives, although in somewhat different ways. In a broad sense, both Lewin and Kelman were survivors of the Holocaust in that they fled the onslaught of Nazism. Each had his personal and professional orientation to social psychology shaped by the cauldron of anti-Semitism. At a personal level, both defended their Jewish identities by becoming ardent Zionists (see Kelman, 2001a, and M. Lewin, 1992, for a discussion of these influences). Moreover, each experienced a kind of midcareer shift that directly reflected a commitment to using theory and research in social psychology to solve important social problems. Specifically, Lewin in 1945 founded the Commission on Community Interrelations, and in 1973 Kelman made the Arab–Israeli conflict his "highest priority" (Kelman, 2001a), although the first actual workshop with Israelis and Arabs was conducted in 1971 (Cohen, Kelman, Miller, & Smith, 1977).

Metatheoretically, it can be argued that the Holocaust connection expressed itself most strongly at two levels. At the first level, one common value thread animated both Lewin's and Kelman's applied work—the quest for social justice. Out of this common value matrix, each carried out interventions and wrote theoretically about resolving social conflicts. Second, not too surprisingly, each of them, having personally experienced threats to their Jewish identities, saw "uncertainty of group identity . . . as especially destructive to psychological well being" (Lewin, 1992, p. 26). This theme is elaborated in a number of Kelman's works including one specifically entitled "The Role of National Identity in Conflict Resolution: Experiences from Israeli–Palestinian Problem-Solving Workshops" (Kelman, 2001b).

History as a Source of Differences

In this section it is proposed that history can also be seen as a source of differences between Lewin and Kelman. Here we have to consider differences in their relation to World War II as well as differences in the development of social psychology as an experimental science. One of the major themes of Kelman's work—the ethics of social research—generates a clear division between him and Lewin regarding the ethics of human experimentation. Although Lewin rejected the extreme positivism of the learning theory approach to research, he strongly encouraged human experimentation even though such studies might require some deception. Indeed this side of Lewin (who also endorsed field research) is most strongly exemplified in the work of Leon Festinger, whom he selected to be an instructor at the Center for Group Dynamics at the Massachusetts Institute of Technology. I think part of this difference is historical. Lewin was a pioneer in showing how complex social phenomena could be brought into the laboratory without sacrificing standards of scientific rigor. By the time Kelman received his PhD, this point had pretty much been made, leaving him free to stand back and see the limitations of what Lewin and two generations of Lewinians had wrought.

Note, however, that Kelman has been an excellent experimental social psychologist. Indeed, because I worked closely with him on a series of experimental studies of attitude-discrepant behavior, I can testify to this firsthand. Rather what is at issue, and I only have just begun to understand this, is Kelman's sensitivity to the abuses of power in terms of the "power deficiency of the research participants" (Kelman, 2001a, p. 216). Although other problems exist, such as the invasion of privacy, I believe that the exploitive potential of power differentials is what we need to focus on, particularly because it also is a touchstone for a fundamental difference between Lewin and Kelman with regard to whether one identifies with the majority or minority subcultures (Jewishness aside). Specifically, Lewin likely saw the United States as a bastion of democracy and as such he willingly helped to engineer conformity to the war effort as exemplified in his famous "getting housewives to eat cheap cuts of meat" research (Lewin, 1958). In the terms of Rosenwein and Campbell (1992), Lewin's democratic social engineering and action research amplified the majority position to mobilize the country for collective action. This approach is understandable given that Lewin was rescued from fascism by the United States and that the United States was fighting a "just" war. Kelman's professional and social consciousness has a different historical context: the Korean War, the Cold War, the civil rights movement, and the war in Vietnam. The majority is no longer viewed as uncritically good—the power of the majority culture has proven exploitive of many minorities and had gotten us into an "unjust" war. Out of this political cauldron, Kelman began to question how the Western powers, which social psychologically if not geographically now include Israel, have treated populations deficient in power such as the Palestinian Arabs. Kelman began to relate his out-group experiences to the Palestinian situation, thereby enabling him "to empathize with the Palestinian experiences of displacement, homelessness, statelessness, humiliation" (Kelman, 2001a, p. 214). These experiences, in turn, led Kelman to see Palestinians as victims.

Whether these differences are, as I suspect, a matter of different historical contexts, or reflective of more fundamental value differences, I cannot say, but I am convinced that such differences do exist between the perspectives of Lewin and Kelman. At issue is perhaps what limits there are in trusting the intentions of Western-type democracies when strong power differentials exist between these governments and other national and ethnic groupings in situations that appear to be zero-sum games.

Finally, some of these themes can be seen as being played out at both theoretical and applied levels. For example, Lewin had a more supportive stance toward individualistically focused theoretical formulations than Kelman. However, at the applied level with regard to inducing change, both Kelman and Lewin bucked the tide of individualism in psychology and saw the group as the chief agent of change.

Kelman as a Neo-Lewinian

By citing aspects of Kelman's work on social influence processes, attitudes, and conflict resolution, I try to make the case that no other social psychologist has better practiced Lewin's fundamental axioms that applied work stimulates theory and there is nothing so practical as a good theory (Bargal, Gold, & Lewin, 1992, p. 5). Moreover, although Kelman certainly has not literally used the Lewinian vocabulary, his work—whether we are considering the model of the three processes of social influence (Kelman, 1958), the attitude–action analysis (Kelman, 1974), or workshops to resolve international conflict (Kelman, 1997a)—incorporates Lewin's fundamental concept of the life space that "psychologists would never be able to understand or predict human behavior without making the effort to learn how humans perceive and conceptualize their world" (Bargal et al., 1992, pp. 4–5). More generally, each of their approaches to human nature rejected essentialist models of people having historically fixed properties, favoring instead constructivist and relational models. Indeed, although Lewin's cognitive constructivism was at a more individual level, as in the life space concept (Farr, 1996), I think that his general relational focus would have led him to be very sympathetic to the social constructivism that is reflected in Kelman's (2001b) approach to the negotiation of national identity.

Similarly, Kelman's work in resolving international conflict incorporates many Lewinian principles that recognize the interdependence of the individual and the group, including extensions of Lewin's ideas about group decision making, communication processes, and the "unfreezing" and refreezing of group norms (Lewin, 1958). Indeed, I would claim that it is Kelman's neo-Lewinian slant on "resolving social conflicts" that gives his work a unique blend of depth and breadth, while at the same time separating him from what mainstream social psychologists consider important work in intergroup conflict. Lest this judgment be considered idiosyncratic, I base it on considerations such as the lack of a single reference to Kelman's work in Brewer and Miller's (1996) otherwise excellent analysis of intergroup relations. This omission coincides with the neglect of Lewin in recent versions of *The Handbook of Social Psychology* (Lindzey & Aronson, 1985; see Bargal et al., 1992, for documentation of this claim). I also propose that Kelman's international conflict resolution workshops incorporate aspects of Lewin's approach to action research (Lewin, 1948), involving the importance of establishing a relationship of circular causality between using theory to generate interventions and then using the results of the intervention to "generate new knowledge" (Bargal et al., 1992, p. 8).

Because Kelman's Lewinian cast seems to have influenced his work on social influence, attitudes, and action and on resolving international conflicts, I attempt to demonstrate how in each of these domains Kelman's work can be seen as a reworking and a reinvigoration of the Lewinian heritage.

Compliance, Identification, and Internalization: Three Processes of Attitude Change and Social Influence

The first thing one notices in reviewing Kelman's three-process model is that he motivates his analysis by framing it in terms of Lewin's postulate that nothing is as practical as a good theory. He noted in 1958, for example, that "questions about the nature of attitude change are highly significant for the study of international attitudes" (p. 51). This framing is not too surprising given Kelman's choice of a journal for publishing his early work on the three processes—*Journal of Conflict Resolution*. Conceptually, Kelman's three-process framework is clearly in the tradition of Lewin's treatment of behavior as a function of the relationship between the person and the environment ($P \times E$). In effect, each of the three processes involves an interaction between a person property and an environmental property. Specifically, each of these processes "corresponds to a characteristic pattern of internal responses (thoughts and feelings) in which the individual engages while adopting the induced behavior" (p. 53). The environment in this context is the particular aspect of the source's power that activates the person's motivational processes. For example, in identification, this aspect is the source's attractiveness interacting with the person's desire "to establish or maintain a self-defining relationship to another person or group" (p. 53). Internalization, on the other hand, rests on an interaction between the communicator property of credibility and the motive to adopt behavior that is congruent with the person's salient values. Moreover, this motive of seeking value-consistent information anticipates Festinger's (1957) dissonance motive in certain basic ways.

Kelman goes beyond Lewin in this model by integrating what for Lewin were separate areas—Lewin's tension system view of motives (e.g., the Zeigarnik-effect type of research) and his group process approach to change. For example, Kelman's (1958) analysis of compliance can be viewed as resting on a combination of obedience and conformity pressure, whereas identification clearly integrates individual motives with the desire to build or maintain a relationship. Furthermore, Kelman fleshes out the P × E type of formulation by offering us boundary conditions for the processes that mediate change. Specifically, Kelman stresses the importance of the communicator's control over outcomes, which, in turn, requires surveillance to maintain conformity under compliance conditions. In contradistinction, when the communicator's power is based on attractiveness, the effectiveness of the influence induction depends on the continuing salience of the social relationship for identification to continue. With internalization, environmental moderators such as source credibility become less important in themselves because change under value-congruent conditions is assumed to be intrinsically satisfying.

In summary, Kelman's three processes provide within a single multilevel model two types of elaborations of Lewin's individualist approach to cognitive and motivational processes (Deutsch, 1992): (a) Kelman's constructs show a greater sensitivity to social context and (b) Kelman's constructs may be read as leading to behavioral intentions, whereas Lewin's life space lacks behavioral grounding. In effect, Kelman gives us a social psychological analysis that avoids the standard critique of Lewin's approach that it is "post-perceptual and pre-behavioral" (Gold, 1992, p. 72). Moreover, Kelman's cognitive-motivational concepts are not isolated as an end in themselves; rather, they are immediately situated at the level of social interaction.

Conflict Resolution Workshops

Kelman's workshops to reduce Israeli–Palestinian conflict are neo-Lewinian at a number of levels that draw on both Lewin's founding of group dynamics and his pioneering work in action research. Most basically, Kelman was Lewinian in understanding that a group is more than a collection of individuals with similar interests. Kelman understands Lewin's (1948) important insights that (a) the key aspect of what makes a group is "shared fate" and (b) it is often easier to change a person as part of a group than as a solitary individual. For Kelman (1997a), these insights lead him to treat individuals at the group level as representatives of differing ethnic communities. Specifically, these workshops have two basic purposes:

> First they are designed to produce changes in the workshop participants themselves. . . . These changes at the level of individual participants are a vehicle for promoting change at the policy level. Thus, the second purpose of workshops is to maximize the likelihood that the new insights, ideas, and proposals developed in the course of the interaction are fed back into the political debate and the decision-making process in each community. (Kelman, 1997a, p. 214)

In effect, what Kelman is doing is creating a mutually shared social field (to use Asch's term, 1952, p. 161) or a joint life space (to use Lewin's term) in which both Palestinians and Israelis can share a common identity based on their joint realization that the current situation requires them to share the same small piece of land (Kelman, 1999). The result is socially situated cognitive change based on a sense of shared space. This, in turn, encourages more differentiated images of the other that are anchored in cooperative experiences between interactants who are representing different constituencies. This approach creates a situation in which local, face-to-face changes have potential policy implications that are global. This strategy takes us beyond change being encapsulated in individual life spaces. To paraphrase the title of Kelman's (1974) *American Psychologist* article, life space changes are alive and well and gainfully employed in group-based actions that reduce international conflict.

Kelman's workshops directly incorporate aspects of Lewin's (1958) approach to action research in two critical ways. First, Kelman's research is sensitive to differences in the value systems and power structures of the interactants; indeed, Kelman creates a situation that attenuates power differentials. Second, this research both "solves a problem and generates new knowledge" (Bargal et al., 1992, p. 8). And most broadly like Lewin, Kelman (1997a) simultaneously works at micro and macro levels: "the . . . workshop can be viewed as a microcosm of the larger system" (p. 216). That is, the workshop can "be conceived as a laboratory for producing inputs into the larger system" (p. 216); here psychological social psychology becomes transformed into sociological social psychology (see chap. 2, this volume). Kelman's conflict reduction workshops also draw on two other aspects of Lewin's approach to intergroup relations: (a) A social group's future time perspective is related to its identity and to preservation of its morale and (b) improving the low self-esteem of a minority group is a necessary condition for improving intergroup relations (see Bargal & Bar, 1992, p. 143). Kelman's workshops are structured around principles of equality and reciprocity. Operationally, they provide multiple occasions for the participants to receive mutual reassurance (Kelman, 1997a, p. 219). In Kelman's hands, reciprocity becomes one strategy for reducing the inequality of power that Palestinians and Israelis bring to the table.

Kelman, however, goes beyond Lewin in his treatment of identity at a number of levels. In his work on identity as a collective group-level phenomenon, Kelman is concerned with far more than individual self-esteem. It is the group-level sense of worth that must be negotiated so that each side can feel that the validity of its claims is being recognized at least at the level of this relationship (Kelman, 2001b). The metastrategy that Kelman (1997b) uses is to create a situation in which national identity is not a zero-sum game. The goal of conflict resolution in this context is to focus on doing away with the negative interdependence of separate group identities in the sense that for one group to feel good the other group has to be humiliated or defeated. Kelman tries to do this by emphasizing the common economic interests and historical roots of Palestinians and Israelis. These insights are both consistent with and go beyond how Lewin viewed the role of removing identity threat in resolving conflicts.

Some intriguing overlaps exist, however, between Lewin's (1958) famous formula for group change—*unfreezing, moving,* and *refreezing*—and Kelman's discussion of the stages of conflict resolution. Kelman's suggestion that the process begins with each side gaining an understanding of the other's perspective is likely to "unfreeze" various fears and stereotypes. Kelman's (2001b) second phase focuses on creating "joint thinking about possible solutions," and his third phase involves discussion of the political and psychological "barriers to carrying out ideas for solutions that have been developed in the group" (p. 23). In the context of Lewin's process of *moving,* Kelman's phases provide a process description of how and why moving might occur.

Furthermore, Kelman's (2001b) fourth phase, in which participants are encouraged to come up "with ideas about what their governments, their societies and they themselves" might do to overcome these barriers (p. 200), is important at two levels. First, this phase seems to map well with the Lewinian concept of *refreezing.* Second, it fits Kelman's view of the dual purposes of the change process. That is, Kelman is interested in changing more than the individual participants. He wants changes that transfer into the political process at the levels of both public opinion and decision making. This description of change is both a superb recipe for refreezing and an insightful way to deal with Lewin's consistent attempts to break down the barrier between individual- and group-level change as in the proposition that it is easier to change individuals as part of a group.

Note also that in recent years Kelman has been able to integrate his model of the three processes of social influence with his interpretation of how change occurs within his "peace promoting" workshops. This analysis represents another example of how Kelman has managed to integrate individual- and group-level social psychological processes. Specifically, Kelman (1997b) equated his attempts to induce change based on a "strategy of responsiveness and reciprocity" (p. 208) with change at the level of identification. In particular, he proposes that such strategies will produce private-level change as well as public-level change because creating an atmosphere of reciprocity is likely to produce a relationship of continuing salience. On the other hand, the use of bribes or fear is likely to induce change at the level of compliance, thereby creating relatively unstable change "in public behavior without accompanying change in private beliefs" (Kelman, 1958, p. 52). Furthermore, he proposes that his conflict resolution strategy of "interactive problem solving" has the potential to create change at the level of internalization, where efforts at change are viewed as "congruent with the parties' own values" (Kelman, 1997b, p. 208) and, hence, likely to create change that is private and relatively stable and enduring. Such effects are likely to fall out from Kelman's (1997b) emphasis on creating in the negotiating parties "a sense of ownership and commitment" (p. 208).

As a bridge between this section and the treatment of Kelman as a "protodynamic system theorist," note that both Kelman's three-process model and his view of the stages of conflict resolution strongly implicate a temporal dimension. Specifically, aspects of Kelman's social influence model bring out the dynamical thinking in Lewin by taking some of Lewin's more structural concepts such as life space and behavior as a function of $P \times E$ and giving them a temporal trajectory. A good illustration is the difference between the role of surveillance in compliance and internalization. For change to persist in compliance, where it is induced by external constraints such as reward and punishment, constant monitoring is required. Here effective change is time intensive. Internalization because it is a form of self-persuasion based on a perceived congruency between the content of the change induction and preexisting values results in self-monitoring—a process that frees the temporal agenda of the inducing agent. Furthermore, identification as a mode of social influence is also intrinsically dynamic in that it rests on the continuing salience of the social relationship over time.

In Kelman's hands, life space types of constructs—that is, people's interpretations of social events—are treated in process dynamical terms; internalization, identification, and compliance are meanings the person gives the social influence induction. Such meanings include a temporal dimension as opposed to being a single psychological snapshot. Moreover, because these processes have this property of dynamical mediation, they allow Kelman to make interesting predictions regarding the relationship between public conformity and private acceptance; for example, compliance is limited to public conformity without private acceptance, whereas internalization yields private acceptance. Such analyses provide a functional foundation for many of the types of predictions made by contemporary dual-mode models such as central versus peripheral mediators of change (Petty & Cacioppo, 1986). Furthermore, the very distinction between public and private change is dynamical in the sense that public conformity is likely to have a more limited temporal trajectory than private acceptance. Finally, viewing change as having stages fits very well with the emphasis on qualitative, phase-state changes in the complex dynamical systems model. As noted earlier, a focus on the collective or relationship level is crucial for dynamical interpretations.

Kelman as Protodynamical Systems Theorist

Before presenting citations that support my claim that aspects of Kelman's work anticipate certain key features of the dynamical systems model, I briefly outline some of the key properties of the dynamical systems model.

Order and Chaos

Dynamical systems are poised between order and chaos, thereby creating a situation in which the system can be tipped fairly easily into a new phase state. That is, dynamical systems are in a sense chronically prepared for change. For example, groups by their very structure are always balancing the relative importance of individual-level preexisting goals and values with group-level goals and values. At a collective level, the majority influence creates forces toward order, whereas the minority influence represents possible disorder. It is the ability of a group to balance these opposing forces, however, that allows it to be an open system that is flexible with regard to being open to creative solutions at the intragroup level (as opposed to *groupthink;* Janis, 1972) and to build bridges between groups at the intergroup level. These ideas are somewhat reminiscent of Lewin's (1958) *quasi-stationary equilibrium* concept but are even better captured in Kelman's analysis of *uneasy coalitions* (see Conflict Resolution Workshops section), in which new bonds across groups are delicately balanced by old within-group bonds—for example, ties to doves across groups and hawks within groups must be balanced. One way to describe such groups is to say they are complex in the sense that they can be described by multiple attractors that are in various states of coordination or interdependence.

Attractors and Interdependence

According to Eiser (1994, p. 208), *attractors* are positions or comfort zones in phase space (the site of trajectories of movement) toward which actions appear to be pulled over time and toward which the system returns if perturbed away from the attractor. Furthermore, the attractor may be dominant only over a limited area of the phase space—the basin of attraction (Eiser, 1994, p. 208). A good analogy for the functioning of attractors is what happens to water when a plug is removed from a bathtub or how a set point on a thermostat operates. That is, theorists are trying to specify how behavior is directionally organized over time.

Attractors in this view are intrinsically dynamical, resembling Lewin's gradient of attraction in the sense that distance interacts with strength of motivation. Of particular interest are two other properties of attractors. First, they are defined at a collective level; for example, at the level of a group, an attractor is a collective-level concept, a norm, that is different than summing the goals, values, or attitudes of individual group members. For example, groups are capable of creating genocidal norms that could not be predicted from individual attitudes toward an ethnic group. This property is embedded in Kelman's (1997a) view that change is focused on the relationship or group level. Second, attractors come in different colors that range from acting like a fixed set point on a thermostat (a point attractor) to functioning as periodic attractors that model various shifts in group-level goals. For example, groups might be said to cycle between task and socioemotional attractors, a situation in which different attractors are dominant at different times in a phase space. The quest for peace between Arabs and Israelis may have this character as it vies with the pull of preserving group ethnic identity. It may be argued that Kelman's workshops are sensitive to the periodic character of such attractors because they cycle in and out of salience. Other attractors, called *strange* or *chaotic,* are extremely sensitive to small differences in initial conditions, weather being the classic case. For example, sometimes a slight difference in water temperature can determine whether a given disturbance will become a hurricane. One could perhaps argue that the success or failure of a peace negotiation may have this character.

Indeed, the chaotic character of this negotiation process is indicated by the fact that as of spring 2003 peace talks were in a state of flux and a state of active conflict had resumed, all set off by a single incident—Ariel Sharon visiting a jointly claimed holy site. However, note that this consequence implies a system that was prepared for conflict. Another way to frame the preceding situation is in terms of a breakdown in trust. Such a state of affairs can be modeled dynamically with the concept of hysteresis.

Hysteresis and Trust

In dynamical systems, change or history more generally is irreversible in that a fundamental asymmetry exists between the level of the variable that produces an effect and the levels of that variable needed to restore the original state. For example, if a certain level of trust was needed to create a peace agreement and one or the other side then violated the terms of the agreement, considerably more trust will be required to reinstate the accord (see Baron et al., 1994). Kelman (1993) provided examples in his discussion of the effect for Israel of the Palestinian support for Iraq during the Gulf War and of the Palestinian reaction to the prospect of massive immigration of Soviet Jews in terms of the arousal of Arab fears. In each case situations were created in which the building versus the rebuilding of trust follows a hysteresis-type pattern by which the level of trust needed for peace talks to resume is much greater than the level of trust needed to initiate the peace talks. (A possible analogy is the amount of trust needed to establish a relationship as compared with the level of trust need to restore the relationship after a partner has been unfaithful.)

Based on the events of 2000 through 2003, it appears likely that peace as an attractor was not very strong because, once perturbed, the system did not make a rapid attempt to restore the previous state of affairs in which—at least superficially—peace appeared to be a strong mutual attractor. Indeed, a rapid-phase state change to open hostility occurred instead. How such a situation as this might occur can be modeled by the concept of self-organized criticality in the sense that small changes become amplified when the system approaches a critical threshold.

Dynamical Systems and Processes of Self-Organization

One of the most basic properties of dynamical systems is the idea of self-organization. Self-organization implies that (a) higher order structures emerge bottom-up out of local-level interactions among constituent parts, (b) the global properties that emerge from these interactions cannot be predicted from knowing the local properties of the parts, and (c) self-organized systems show circular causality. Circular causality is a multistep process: (a) Interaction among parts creates a new whole (e.g., individual students form a study group); (b) once the group emerges, its norms and values influence its members through the process of *downward causation* (Campbell, 1990). Analogously, it is proposed that the interdependencies of Israelis and Palestinians lead to interactions that in Kelman's groups create a coalition, which, in turn, changes the participants.

Specifically, Kelman's (1997a) group-based research anticipates dynamical principles such as circular causation with regard to appreciating how interactions among local units can be assembled vis-à-vis self-organization into global structures, such as groups. Such groups then influence the constituent members. Thus, individuals create groups and groups then shape individuals. In effect, I attempt to demonstrate that Kelman's workshops overcome barriers to interaction, thereby allowing the circular causality central to self-organized systems to develop.

Kelman's approach also incorporates another property of complex dynamical systems; namely, certain core configurations such as dyads or coalitions are repeatedly reassembled at various scales of sociality from groups to organizations to society (Caporael & Baron, 1997). At issue here is specifying the dynamical consequences of nested levels of organization for the fate of certain core configurations. For example, Kelman focuses on how, at a small-group level, coalitions between Arabs (e.g., Palestinians) and Israelis can be reassembled at the governmental level. Kelman's approach to training people to be more effective managers of intergroup conflict involves structuring the workshops so as to encourage bottom-up processes of cooperation in the sense that the coalitions are not imposed by the organizers. Such groups may be viewed as self-organizing systems. Within such a framework, people with only moderate motivations for peace can give rise through coordinated interaction to a collective motivation for peace that is stronger than the sum of its parts. I believe that part of the strength of Kelman's approach to conflict resolution is that it intuitively capitalizes on such bottom-up processes in contexts where lower level interactions at the dyadic and small-group level show emergent effects at the organizational intergroup level involving formal peace negotiations. In effect, local coordinations can give rise to structure at a global level.

Another aspect of self-organization—self-organized criticality (Bak, 1996)—can be used to model the collapse of the peace talks and the resumption of violence. Specifically, such systems demonstrate positive feedback in that discrepant inputs—instead of being attenuated—are amplified, thereby allowing small disturbances to create catastrophic effects in systems that are on the edge of chaos. For example, potentially minor disruptions in the peace process can be exaggerated, propelling a prepared system into a critical state in which a small change in the environment can produce a massive change in the state of the system called a *phase-state transition*. The triggering of World War I by a single act of assassination is illustrative in the sense that nations went from an uneasy peace to war.

Conflict-Resolution Workshops

In Kelman's workshops the third party plays "a strictly facilitative role." "The critical work of generating ideas and infusing them into the political process must be done by the participants themselves" (Kelman, 1997a, p. 215). Furthermore, the solutions generated by these groups emerge "out of the interaction between the conflicting parties" (p. 215). This description by Kelman of the process dynamics of the workshops is certainly in the spirit of self-organization. Specifically, these dynamics entail a bottom-up process; local interactions give rise to emergent solutions that could not be predicted from a knowledge of the preinteraction beliefs or attitudes of the conflicting parties. In other contexts, Kelman points out that these solutions will, in turn, influence subsequent political negotiations of the interactants in the manner of circular causality. Specifically, interactants create the solutions or new norms, which, in turn, change the participants' subsequent behavior. Note the similarity of such a process to Sherif's (1936) classic norm formation paradigm, which involves a similar three-step process of (a) local interactions, (b) the emergence of a norm, and (c) the internalization of the norm even when the group is no longer present.

Furthermore, in line with one of the deepest insights of dynamical systems theory, the workshops do not strive to create a highly cohesive group; Kelman (1997a) recognized that "an overly cohesive group would undermine the whole purpose of the enterprise" (p. 219). Thus, Kelman (1992) described a complex, dynamical system that establishes a state of "quasi-stationary equilibrium" by which participants can begin to humanize and trust each other yet not lose "sight of their separate identities and the conflict between their communities" (p. 82). What is created is what Kelman referred to in 1993 as "uneasy coalitions" (p. 242). This situation fits a key aspect of complex dynamical systems; rather than having a single point attractor pushing the system toward equilibrium, such systems of Palestinians and Israelis are multimodal in the sense that they cycle between two or more attractors. For example, in such groups, distal ethnic and religious identities vie with local ties of mutual trust in an ongoing cyclical process.[1]

Dynamical systems are also excellent for dealing with collective properties as a field of interdependency. Elsewhere I (Baron et al., 1994) have used this property in a way that can now be applied to Kelman's approach to the Israeli–Palestinian workshops. Specifically, Kelman's approach to identity negotiation can be modeled in ways analogous to how the logistic equation has been used to model the dynamic interdependence between the size of predator–prey populations (Baron et al., 1994). Kelman's ideas of interdependence could be seen as analogous to the way in which the sizes of predator–prey populations are coupled to maintain reciprocal rates of change. That is, if predators are too successful, they run out of food; if prey are too good at surviving, they overcrowd a niche and run out of food. Such a situation requires long-term coordination.

---

[1]Note also that because Kelman's "uneasy coalitions" approach allows for the existence of dual identities between the conflicting groups, it may appear to be at odds with the common in-group identity model proposed by Gaertner and Dovidio (2000). This model rests on recategorizing in-groups and out-groups to a common higher order identity such as a common humanity or, perhaps more specifically here, the joint descendants of Abraham, which is more inclusive. To reconcile this apparent divergence, two issues need to be considered. First, in naturalistic situations a reentry problem may arise when the existing societal norms do not support the new common identity as is likely in the current Palestinian–Israeli situation. More optimistically, "uneasy consensus" and inclusive group identity may be viewed as differentially appropriate conflict resolution strategies depending on the level of societal readiness for change. That is, "uneasy consensus" may work at lower stages of societal readiness than "inclusive group identity."

I have proposed that majority–minority power relations can be modeled this way. For example, "if majority influence is too strong we get the super conformity of groupthink . . . which undermines the proper functions of the group with regard to error correction and/or accommodating external threats" (Baron et al., 1994, p. 135). If the size of the minority grows too rapidly, the group loses cohesion with global dynamics falling apart as old attractors are annihilated before the minority can grow into a new majority. When this occurs, it can shatter a group into splinter groups with competing attractors (Baron et al., 1994, p. 136). I believe that Kelman, in forming Arab–Israeli coalitions, needs to consider possibilities such as the negotiators becoming too pro-peace too quickly.

As noted earlier, such systems are delicately balanced so that even a small change in the parameters that regulate the system, such as level of trust, can precipitate a large qualitative change, such as a shift in phase state from fear of peace to endorsing peace. As I have discussed, international conflicts are full of negative examples. Such a state of preparedness for change, however, also can produce positive effects. Indeed, perhaps a single shared workshop experience might have helped either precipitate the Oslo peace talks between the Israelis and the Palestinians or trigger the promising agreement that emerged. Thus, "great person effects" and "critical incident effects" may both reflect systems that are already dynamically unstable and thereby susceptible to change that is nonlinear. Such qualitative change is in dynamical terms a *phase transition*. As noted earlier, such systems often demonstrate self-organized criticality (Bak, 1996) in that small deviations from a standard are amplified to precipitate changes. Thus, it could be argued that hawks in both Israeli and Palestinian camps were hard at work all along to prepare the ground for war. What could not be predicted was how close each camp was to a critical state for conflict.

Finally, consistent with Kelman's (1997a, 1997b) attempts to avoid creating too cohesive a group, Baron (2002) has recently proposed that lowering intragroup cohesiveness vis-à-vis encouraging of strong minority influence will increase cooperation between groups. This strategy, in conjunction with the more traditional creation of a superordinate goal, might create stronger intergroup ties.

Kelman's Dynamical Treatment of the Attitude–Behavior Relationship

I propose that Kelman (1974) anticipated in many ways Eiser's (1994) dynamical interpretation of the nature of *attitude–behavior consistency*. In particular, Kelman's analysis fits Eiser's (1994, p. 264) description of attitudes as involving positions in a phase space, with attitude change being described as a trajectory of movement through the attitude space. Specifically, the parallel is striking between Eiser's (1994) statement that attitudes have "a range or repertoire of positions . . . that can be represented by more or less shallow wells of attraction" (p. 211) and Kelman's (1974) proposal that "an attitude indicates a range rather than a point on a scale" and that "any given attitude represents a range of commitment to the attitude object" (p. 321). Moreover, Kelman's further proposal that a person's behavior fluctuates around a modal range of commitment treats the attitude–behavior relation as itself dynamic.

Furthermore, Kelman's (1974) discussion of how a person's latitude of commitment may lead to commitments to a discrepant action that may create the conditions for reassessment and revision of attitudes and thus set a process of attitude change in motion fits nicely with Bak's (1996) idea of self-organized criticality. According to Bak's view, change involves a positive feedback system in which small discrepancies can be amplified rather than corrected as in a negative feedback system. In Kelman's case, people expose themselves to environmental sources or information that is then cognitively amplified. Here change is self-organized in Bak's sense that a situation has been created involving a critical state for which even a minor disturbance may lead to a phase-state change, for example, from a pro to a con attitude. The implication for attitude change, which is implicit in Kelman's approach, is that not all attitude change is smooth; sudden qualitative jumps may occur, such as when a committed communist becomes a committed right-wing conservative. This scenario fits Kelman's 1974 view that by taking action people set in motion a set of forces that help shift them to a new level of commitment (p. 324). Recall also that circular causality is a hallmark of self-organized, dynamical change. In this regard, consider the following statement from Kelman (1974) regarding the nature of the attitude–action relation: "It shows most clearly the engagement of attitude and action in a continuing, reciprocal, circular process" (p. 324).

Conclusion

In summary, I propose that Kelman's contributions can be situated between Lewin's ideas and certain concepts that characterize a dynamical system. With regard to the latter, three underlying properties of Kelman's work support my interpretation: (a) a focus on qualitative change in ways compatible with if not derivable from a dynamical systems approach, (b) the ability to go from an individual to a collective unit of analysis for the understanding of change, and (c) the sensitivity to the significance of unequal relations of power.

The problem of qualitative change is central to Kelman's analysis at many levels ranging from his stage model of social influence to his treatment of attitude as a modal range rather than a single point. Here change itself is not a shift in simple preferences but perhaps a qualitative shift in the relative salience of different attractors such as the relative salience of peace and war. Furthermore, Kelman's treatment of change in his conflict resolution groups provides another kind of dynamic mechanism for qualitative change. Specifically, he focuses on "the occurrence of change and the conditions for promoting further change" as rooted in a kind of "positive self-fulfilling prophecy involving each of the parties' yoked actions" (Kelman, 1996, p. 115). Such an approach is also dynamical in that it captures "escalatory dynamics" (Kelman, 1997a, p. 219) in a way that makes it possible for small positive changes in the negotiation of identities to result in powerful distal effects at the political level. Such changes may be seen to implicate the mechanisms of self-organized criticality (Bak, 1996).

The last aspect of this analysis of Kelman's approach to qualitative change also has implications for the second aspect of Kelman's dynamical tendencies— his use of a collective level of analysis. Specifically, this analysis "give[s] us new insights into how a change at the microlevel can become self-organizing when explicitly fostered and proactively linked to changes in the larger system" (see "Comments on Chapters 1 and 2," this volume). Such an analysis provides a model for how to go from an individual to a collective unit of analysis. In this regard, Kelman in his peace workshops is specifically changing people not as isolated individuals but as members of an ethnic coalition and representatives of broader political constituencies.

It is also possible to use Vygotsky's (1978) zone of proximal development (ZPD) as a way of seeing how relational Kelman's approach is. That is, much as a person can achieve a higher level of cognitive achievement in the context of social support, so can a political attitude become more positive when people are part of a cross-ethnic coalition than would occur without such a context (see Baron & Misovich, 1993, for a ZPD model of attitude and attitude change). This example is, in effect, a new way to spin Lewin's (1948) proposition that it is easier to change a person as part of a group than as an isolated individual.

In effect, it can be argued that an attitude situated in a relationship is different than an attitude viewed at an individual level. This analysis can, in turn, be seen as a type of reframing of Kelman's concept of identification-based attitude change, which rests on the continual salience of that relationship. Viewed in this way, effective attitude change for both Lewin and Kelman is tied to movement at a relational or group level.

The issue of socially grounding change is critical because it provides a way to address one of the holy grails of social psychology—how it is possible for the individual to be in the group and the group in the individual. That is, the person may hold one attitude as an individual and another in a group-constrained role. Kelman's ability to treat the individual–group relation complexity is perhaps best exemplified in his concern with power and its abuse (Kelman, 2001a). This sensitivity to power relations begins with the three-process model, is central to his "crimes of obedience" model, animates his views of the ethics of experimentation, and is, of course, basic to his analysis of the Israeli–Palestinian conflict. More generally, Kelman's complex view of the individual–group relation is central to his attempts to reduce hostility using a strategy that exchanges differences in power for mutual recognition by each side of the legitimacy of the other's right to exist. Power differentials thus become attenuated when reciprocal identity claims are acknowledged.

In a Lewinian context, perhaps the best way to encapsulate Herbert Kelman's contribution is that it adds an ethical dimension to Lewin's maxim that there is "nothing as practical as a good theory" (Bargal et al., 1992, p. 5). Specifically, both practice and theory are harnessed to making the world a better place to live, thereby directly questioning the assumption that good science needs to be (or can be) ethically neutral (Kendler, 1999).

References

Asch, S. E. (1952). *Social psychology*. New York: Prentice Hall.

Bak, P. (1996). *How nature works: The science of self-organized criticality*. New York: Springer-Verlag.

Bargal, D. & Bar, H. (1992). A Lewinian approach to intergroup workshops for Arab–Palestinian and Jewish youth. *Journal of Social Issues, 48*(2), 139–154.

Bargal, D., Gold, M., & Lewin, M. (1992). Introduction: The heritage of Kurt Lewin. *Journal of Social Issues, 48*(2), 3–13.

Baron, R. M. (2002). Exchange and development: A dynamical, complex systems perspective. In B. Laursen & W. Graziano (Eds.), *New directions for child and adolescent development* (pp. 53–71). San Francisco: Jossey-Bass.

Baron, R. M., Amazeen, P. G., & Beek, P. J. (1994). Local and global dynamics for social relations. In R. R. Vallacher & A. Nowak (Eds.), *Dynamical systems in social psychology* (pp. 111–138). San Diego, CA: Academic Press.

Baron, R. M., & Misovich, S. J. (1993). An integration of Gibsonian and Vygotskian perspectives on changing attitudes in-group contexts. *British Journal of Social Psychology, 32*, 53–70.

Brewer, M. B., & Miller, N. (1996). *Intergroup relations.* Pacific Grove, CA: Brooks/Cole.

Campbell, D. T. (1990). Levels of organization, downward causation, and the selection-theory approach to evolutionary epistemology. In G. Greenberg & E. Tobach (Eds.), *Theories of the evolution of knowing* (pp. 1–17). Hillsdale, NJ: Erlbaum.

Caporael, L. R., & Baron, R. M. (1997). Groups as the mind's natural environment. In J. A. Simpson & D. T. Kenrick (Eds.), *Evolutionary social psychology* (pp. 317–344). Mahwah, NJ: Erlbaum.

Cohen, S. P., Kelman, H. C., Miller, F. D., & Smith, B. L. (1977). Evolving intergroup techniques for conflict resolution: An Israel–Palestinian pilot workshop. *Journal of Social Issues, 33*(1), 165–189.

Deutsch, M. (1992). Kurt Lewin: The tough-minded and tenderhearted scientist. *Journal of Social Issues, 48*(2), 31–44.

Eiser, J. R. (1994). Toward a dynamic conception of attitude change. In R. R. Vallacher & A. Nowak (Eds.), *Dynamical systems in social psychology* (pp. 197–218). San Diego, CA: Academic Press.

Farr, R. M. (1996). *The roots of modern social psychology.* Cambridge, MA: Blackwell.

Festinger, L. (1957). *A theory of cognitive dissonance.* Stanford, CA: Stanford University Press.

Gaertner, S., & Dovidio, J. F. (2000). *Reducing intergroup bias: The common ingroup identity model.* New York: Psychology Press.

Gold, M. (1992). Metatheory and field theory in social psychology: Relevance or elegance? *Journal of Social Issues, 48*(2), 67–78.

Janis, I. (1972). *Victims of groupthink.* Boston: Houghton-Mifflin.

Kelman, H. C. (1958). Compliance, identification, and internationalization: Three processes of attitude change. *Journal of Conflict Resolution, 2*, 51–60.

Kelman, H. C. (1974). Attitudes are alive and well and gainfully employed in the sphere of action. *American Psychologist, 29*, 310–324.

Kelman, H. C. (1992). Informal mediation by the scholar/practitioner. In J. Bercovitch & J. Z. Rubin (Eds.), *Mediation in international relations: Multiple approaches to conflict management* (pp. 64–96). New York: St. Martin's Press.

Kelman, H. C. (1993). Coalitions across conflict lines: The interplay of conflicts within and between the Israeli and Palestinian communities. In S. Worchel & J. S. Simpson (Eds.), *Conflict between people and groups* (pp. 236–258). Chicago: Nelson-Hall.

Kelman, H. C. (1996). Negotiation as interactive problem solving. *International Negotiations, 1*, 99–123.

Kelman, H. C. (1997a). Group processes in the resolution of international conflicts: Experiences from the Israeli–Palestinian case. *American Psychologist, 52*, 212–220.

Kelman, H. C. (1997b). Social psychological dimension of international conflict. In I. W. Zartman & J. L. Rasmussen (Eds.), *Peacemaking in international conflict: Methods and techniques* (pp. 191–236). Washington, DC: United States Institute of Peace Press.

Kelman, H. C. (1999). The interdependence of Israel, and Palestinian national identities: The role of the other in existential conflicts. *Journal of Social Issues, 55*, 581–600.

Kelman, H. C. (2001a). Dignity and dehumanization: The impact of the Holocaust on central themes of my work. In P. Suedfeld (Ed.), *Light from the ashes* (pp. 197–220). Ann Arbor: University of Michigan Press.

Kelman, H. C. (2001b). The role of national identity in conflict resolution: Experiences from Israeli–Palestinian problem-solving workshops. In R. D. Ashmore, L. Jussim, & D. Wilder

(Eds.), *Social identity, intergroup conflict, and conflict reduction* (Vol. 3, Rutgers Series on Identity, pp. 187–212). New York: Oxford University Press.

Kelso, J. A. S. (1995). *Dynamic patterns: The self-organization of brain and behavior.* Cambridge, MA: MIT Press.

Kendler, H. H. (1999). The role of value in the world of psychology. *American Psychologist, 54,* 828–835.

Lewin, K. (1948). *Resolving social conflicts.* New York: Harper.

Lewin, K. (1958). Group decision and social change. In E. E. Maccoby, T. M. Newcomb, & E. L. Hartley (Eds.), *Readings in social psychology* (3rd ed., pp. 197–211). New York: Holt, Rinehart, & Winston.

Lewin, M. (1992). The impact of Kurt Lewin's life on the place of social issues in his life. *Journal of Social Issues, 48,* 15–30.

Lindzey, G., & Aronson, E. (Eds.). (1985). *The handbook of social psychology* (3rd ed.,Vols. 1 and 2). New York: Random House.

Nowak, A., & Vallacher, R. R. (1998). *Dynamical social psychology.* New York: Guilford Press.

Petty, R. E., & Cacioppo, J. T. (1986). The elaboration likelihood model of persuasion. In L. Berkowitz (Ed.), *Advances in experimental social psychology* (Vol. 19, pp. 123–205). New York: Academic Press.

Rosenwein, R. E., & Campbell, D. T. (1992). Mobilization to achieve collective action and democratic majority plurality amplification. *Journal of Social Issues, 48*(2), 125–138.

Sherif, M. (1936). *The psychology of social norms.* New York: Harper & Row.

Vygotsky, L. (1978). *Mind in society: The development of higher psychological processes* (M. Cole, V. John-Steiner, S. Scribner, & E. Souberman, Eds. & Trans.). Cambridge, MA: Harvard University Press.

2

Social Psychology: Social or Sociological?

José R. Torregrosa

The title of this chapter has definitional connotations. It is generally assumed that definitions are irrelevant as far as the configuration of a field of knowledge is concerned, given that they are merely intentional or wishful statements and can hardly condense the real scope of what a field of knowledge actually is. It is often said that there are as many definitions as the authors who write in any given field. The fact is that definitions are of much more consequence than scientists generally presume (Sapsford, Still, Miell, Stevens, & Wetherell, 1998). Definitions are what make basic conceptions of a science apparent. They also function as an initial map of the territory encompassed by a field of knowledge. Definitions also legitimize the investigation of certain domains over others. The reader should recognize that to *define* means to fix limits or boundaries. More generally, at a time of thriving nationalisms, disciplinary nationalism also flourishes. Specifically, boundaries and territoriality are at the root of the struggles and conflicts by which the relative status and power of individuals and groups are shaped. Although these disciplinary struggles are discursive and symbolic, this does not prevent them from being very intense.

The major thrust of my analysis is that social psychology, if it is to become a more representative and conceptually specific discipline, has to be not only social but sociological. The sociological dimension is what provides social psychology its specificity with regard to general or basic psychology. That is, in adopting the perspective of sociology, social psychology thereby becomes a part of sociology as well as psychology. This thesis is the connecting thread for the following arguments and observations. For this purpose I first make some historical references that have had a deep impact on the development of psychological social psychology; second, I evaluate briefly the so-called *crisis of social psychology*, a turning point with up-to-date consequences; and third, I describe some viewpoints of European and Latin American social psychology, the writings of which seem to go in the direction I am proposing. I end up with some considerations of Kelman's work and intellectual style, focusing on his conception of the discipline and some of his widely influential contributions in expanding the domain of social psychology.

Historical Antecedents

The expression *social psychology* does not seem to have a clear and explicit meaning beyond the realm of the manifold conceptual and methodological traditions in which it is used. The meaning of the term may vary a great deal depending on what is understood by psychology and, above all, on what meaning is ascribed to the term *social*. On the other hand, what has been the prevalent tendency of academic social psychology would not seem to depart very much from the position maintained by such an influential author as Floyd H. Allport (1924). For him, social psychology is above all psychology and very secondarily social, in whatever way social may be understood. Thus, Allport wrote in a text in which he attempted to specify the basic principles of the field:

> There is no psychology of groups which is not essentially and entirely a psychology of individuals. His biological needs are the end toward which his social behavior is a developed means. Within his organism are provided all the mechanisms by which social behavior is explained. (p. 4)

Or, further on in his famous text, Allport wrote:

> Social psychology has in fact grown up largely through the labors of the sociologists. It is a mistake, however, to suppose, as some have done, that it is a branch of sociology rather than psychology. . . . *In spite of the good offices and interests of the sociologists, the two sciences must remain separate branches of inquiry* [italics added]. (p. 11)

It is beyond the scope of this chapter to undertake a detailed analysis of the implications of programmatic texts of this nature. Other authors have provided such analyses with outstanding insight (Cherry, 1995; Danzinger, 1990; Farr, 1996). However, I would like to emphasize a point related to this scientific *pronunciamiento* that has not yet attracted due attention, at least explicitly. In spite of its obvious conceptual inadequacy and ambiguity, the pronouncement unequivocally conveys a message: Social psychology is *exclusively* psychology. It is so because it deals with the behavior and consciousness of the individual, albeit in his or her social aspects; *malgré tout* [in spite of that], social psychology must be psychology alone. To a very large extent, this position has been maintained and reinforced for decades in the various handbooks of social psychology, which contain chapters by influential authors such as Gordon Allport (1954) and Jones (1985) who expressed these views.

Irrespective of the adequacy of F. H. Allport's conceptual framework for both general psychology and social psychology, it seems obvious that the source of confusion induced by definitions such as his rests to a great extent in the meaning attributed to the terms *social* and *social aspects*. Even without trying to specify the content of those terms, social psychologists may naively ask if a nonsocial or asocial psychology is feasible. Any human psychology—be it individual or collective—has to deal with "social aspects" and, in that sense, it is "social." The expression *social psychology* is therefore somehow tautological, as any psychology is social, in one way or another.

In my opinion, social psychologists will not solve the problem just by stating, as is common practice (even with F. H. Allport), that a psychology is social because it deals with "the social." The subject matter of a science only points to the realm or domain of the reality that it studies or aims to study, but it is not indicative of how it is studied or from what perspective. Paradoxically, social psychology has been very often described as too "individualistic." As Baumeister (1995) has pointed out:

> There is a paradox in the way social psychology is practiced today: It isn't always all that social. Ironically, most social psychologists think of people as largely self-contained units, conceding only that occasionally these units come into contact with each other. (p. 75)

Arguments of similar import have been made by authors of different epistemological orientations (Augoustinos, 1999; Marková, 2000; Osterkamp, 1999; Smith, 1999).

If social psychology is basically the extension of the psychological perspective to "the social," then its "individualistic" bias is hardly surprising, given that the level of analysis of psychological theorizing has usually developed around the personality system or its subsystems. The units of analysis of this psychological theorizing are, from the perspective of other social sciences, rather molecular. If one adds to these analytical stipulations the individualistic ethos of Western culture, one can understand Parsons's (1954) observations about general tendencies of psychological theory:

> 1) Reifying the organism, which by virtue of its genetic constitutions is alleged to provide the "real" basis for the structure of behavior systems; 2) Reifying the "real unit of behavior" which may be either the S-R sequence of the behaviorists, or say the momentary perceptual "gestalt." This then is regarded as the one key to the understanding of all behavior, or; finally, 3) Reifying the individual, the personality in a more or less clearly defined "action" sense. Knowledge of him, independently of his social relationships, current or previous, is alleged to depend on any genuine understanding of how individuals, when put together in societies, will behave. (p. 101)

These observations, made long before social constructionism was fashionable, point not only to the actual difficulties of understanding social behavior by the sole means of the psychological theory in vogue but also to the permanent tension toward a reductionism of "the social" to the individual psychological level or, even further, to the individual biological level. Moscovici (1972) perceptively extended this type of argument to social psychology itself when he attempted to synthesize the implicit assumptions, or postulates, as he calls them, of conventional social psychology:

> The first is that the difference between social and elementary non-social processes is only one of degree and that a hierarchy of phenomena can be established in which they are ordered from simpler to more complex, and from individual to collective. The second postulate is that social processes do not imply the existence of social phenomena governed by their laws, but rather

that they are accounted for by psychological laws, which can at the same time, be based on hypothetical laws of physiology. The final postulate is that there is no difference in kind between social and non-social behaviour: other people intervene only as a part of the general environment. (p. 35)

If the corresponding methodological paradigm of experimentalism is added to these substantive principles, the foundations are laid for establishing the dominant social psychology, as well as for the subsequent counterreactions characteristic of all of the literature that has evolved around the crisis. Such issues are also highlighted in the discipline in what has come to be known as the *European social psychology*, to which I refer later. More recently, a critical social psychology (Fox & Prilleltenski, 1997; Ibáñez & Íñiguez, 1997; Parker & Spears, 1996; Roger, Stenner, Gleeson, & Rogers, 1995; Wexler, 1983) has developed that has clear connections with what is supposed to be a postmodern turn in the discipline (Kvale, 1992), whereby truth is problematic and relative to a particular social position, gender, class, or culture (Kendall & Michael, 1997; Nozick, 2001; Parker, 1998).

These criticisms are usually contested on the grounds that there are at least two social psychologies: one with a psychological orientation and another with a sociological orientation. This distinction implies that both are reductionist with respect to the disciplinary matrix in which they are rooted. In this sense, one might argue that if a psychological bias is noticeable in the psychological social psychology, then there is as well a sociological bias in the sociological social psychology. I believe this type of reciprocal bias argument does not adequately account for the real situation, given that the conceptual framework most representative of sociological social psychology, namely, symbolic interactionism (Mead, 1934), can hardly be labeled "reductionist." Indeed, one of the main achievements of this approach has been to convincingly overcome the old individual–society antinomies, specifying how both realities are constituted through processes of communication and social interaction. This achievement even characterizes the most structural versions, which consider societal norms and roles such as Stryker's (1980) or, in a certain sense, Goffman's (1959).

One of the criticisms that sociologists typically raise against symbolic interactionism is precisely that objective social structure is ignored, thereby reducing sociology to the mentalistic constructions and actions of individuals. On the other hand, I would say that other sociological approaches relevant to social psychology, such as structural-functionalism, which ranges from Parsons (1959) and Inkeles (1963), to Smelser and Smelser (1970), or some of their European colleagues such as Giesen (1987) and Münch (1987), cannot be considered reductionistic. Specifically, their efforts to elucidate the nature of the links between the micro and macro analytical levels—starting with Parsons himself—show their antireductionistic awareness. Also, there have always been "individualistic" traditions within sociological theory that, despite the diversity of their foundations (such as action theory, phenomenology, or exchange theory) exhibit obvious sociopsychological affinities and, in some instances, as in Homans (1967), an explicit psychological reductionism. It would also be difficult to consider such social theorists as Castells (1997), Elias (1987), Giddens (1991), Habermas (1987), or Scheff (1990) as social reductionists when they deal with social psychological problems. Finally, the greater institutional, academic-scientific, and professional recognition of psychology has granted this discipline a higher degree of autonomy than is enjoyed by sociology. The consequence is that psychology has had a greater influence on sociology than sociology has had on psychology (House, 1991).

In the light of these considerations and of others of a more ideological nature, I believe that these two social psychologies, psychological and sociological, cannot be put on the same plane with regard to their respective root disciplines and their theoretical and institutional impact on the development of social psychology as a relatively independent field of inquiry.

The Crisis of Social Psychology and Its Metamorphosis

Regardless of the plausibility of the arguments advanced in the characterization of the discipline from its two main root perspectives, two facts concerning social psychology seem to stand out clearly from the 1950s: On the one hand, we have the hegemonic position of the paradigm of the psychological-individualistic orientation and, on the other, a kind of dissatisfaction aroused by this one-sided hegemony. This dissatisfaction was manifest in the various publications, symposia, and meetings at which social psychologists took stock of the state of the discipline and recommendations were made regarding the necessity of taking into account social variables and the actual context of interaction (e.g., Ring, 1967). The implementation of some "joint programs" by psychology and sociology departments, such as programs at the University of Michigan and Harvard University, might be read as an attempt to bridge the gap between the psychological and sociological leanings. The mid-1960s witnessed their failure in the search for a unitary identity for the discipline as well as the publication of the first texts openly addressing the crisis (Ancona, 1954; Gillin, 1954; Hulett & Stagner, 1952; Kendler, 1981; McGuire, 1999; Newcomb, 1951, 1954; Rohrer & Sherif, 1951; Sarason, 1981; Sherif & Wilson, 1957; Smith, 1974; Tomars, 1957; Westland, 1978).

From the admonitions made by Deutsch and Krauss (1965), Katz (1966), and Ring (1967), to those by Parker and Shotter (1990) or those included in the volume edited by Leary (1989), a substantial amount of literature has accumulated on the frustrating uncertainty and conflict resulting from the nonfulfillment of the scientific advancements predicted by those who, only a few years before, promised great progress, provided that what they considered to be the only truly scientific cannons were strictly observed. Doubts about the consistency, validity, and cumulativeness of scientific findings were raised, as were doubts about their usefulness for the society in which they were produced—not to mention other societies. What started as a matter of internal reflection and debate eventually became an ever-present aspect of any reference dealing with the general problems of the discipline. The confident idea of being on the right path to scientific progress gave way in the 1960s and 1970s to feelings of discouragement and of being at a loss, feelings that were aired frankly by eminent researchers.

In 1963, Berkowitz expressed his confidence about the progressive integration of social psychology within the field of experimental psychology: "Social psychological principles may indeed turn out to be only special cases of more general psychological laws" (p. 378). But in 1972, he observed the following to Brewster Smith:

> Social psychology is now in a "crisis stage," in the sense that Kuhn used this term in his book *The Structure of Scientific Revolutions*. We seem to be somewhat at a loss for important problems to investigate and models to employ in our research and theory. It is certainly time to take stock, to see where we are and where we should go. (as cited in Smith, 1972, p. 86)

Moscovici (1972), from the perspective of what at the time was European social psychology, also pointed out the following:

> It must be admitted that Social Psychology is not truly a science. We wish to give it an appearance of a science by using mathematical reasoning and the refinements of experimental method; but the fact is that Social Psychology cannot be described as a discipline with a unitary field of interest, a systematic framework of criteria and requirements, a coherent body of knowledge or even a set of common perspectives shared by those who practice it. A solid foundation for the future has not been laid. (p. 32) *

A very similar ethos permeates the 1970s works of many authors (Armistead, 1974; Elms, 1975; Gergen, 1973; Harré & Secord, 1972; McGuire, 1973; Smith, 1972; Steiner, 1974). Furthermore, the criticisms of Gergen and of Harré and Secord were accompanied by proposals for alternative paradigms. In the 1980s, though less intensely, this ethos also found its advocates (Bar-Tal & Kruglanski, 1988; Blackler, 1983; Graumann, 1987; Himmelweit & Gaskell, 1990; Leary, 1989; Parker, 1989; Parker & Shotter, 1990; Rosnow, 1981). Indeed, one can observe that this kind of questioning, with different nuances and undertones, persists today (Antaki, 2000; Haslam & McGarty, 2001; Hogg & Grieve, 1999; House, 1991; Kim, 1999; Kruglanski, 2001; Pancer, 1997; Robinson, 2000; Smith, 2000; Wallach & Wallach, 1994).

To call this epistemological uneasiness and relative uncertainty the "crisis of social psychology" might be going too far (Ritzer & Gindoff, 1992). However, if the expression only refers to the psychological social psychology, which adopted the experimental-naturalistic program, then I would say that the word *crisis* is not an overstatement, given the failure by this group of social psychologists to respond to earlier criticisms of that program. Thus, I conclude that there has been no crisis of social psychology as a whole, but rather a crisis of one of its specific perspectives: the experimental-naturalistic-individualistic paradigm, considered as the only possible way toward scientific progress. Moreover, social psychology has found itself to some extent in a situation of uncertainty and malaise similar to the one that exists in the social sciences in general. For example, in 1970 Gouldner announced "the coming crisis of western sociology," with a frontal critique of the then-hegemonic Parsonian structural-functionalism, and provided the conceptual grounds for a more reflexive sociology that questions its own premises. More recently, to explain the "crisis" in sociology, Levine (1995) has underlined external factors, such as the decreasing availability of resources for research or the loss of prestige and status in society at large, as factors that make internal dissent and criticisms more threatening. Horowitz (1993) has emphasized the internal development of unconnected subfields and specialties, with a resulting "decomposition" of the discipline. And Lopreato and Crippen (1999) almost predict the disappearance of sociology as an academic field of knowledge in 25 to 30 years, unless it reconstitutes itself in terms of evolutionary biology.

Viewpoints of European and Latin American Social Psychology

This debate has had far-reaching consequences in social psychology outside the United States, at least in Europe and Latin America. In this sense the interpretation provided by Moghaddam (1987) is interesting. According to him, the so-called *crisis of social psychology* was a consequence of the nonacceptance by European and British social psychologists of the dominant conventional social psychology of the first world, that is, North America. His thesis is that, on the one hand, American social psychologists turned their attention toward intradisciplinary metatheoretical and epistemological problems when faced with those criticisms. On the other hand, European social psychologists seemed to believe that they should generate their own distinctive approach rather than follow the agenda and research programs of American social psychology. This focus on affirming differences, preceded by intense and sometimes heated debates, was in itself a clear refutation of the assumed universal validity of the conventional and hegemonic paradigm.

In the same way, Moghaddam (1987) extends this logic when trying to think about the conditions of the development of social psychology in third world countries. These countries cannot uncritically accept the social and psychological knowledge produced in the most industrialized and rich ones, given their different sociocultural, economic, and political problems and interests. As Jahoda (1983) has pointed out, most current theories in experimental social psychology do not seem to be valid or adequate for the social contexts of third world countries. Therefore, social psychologists in these nations need to construct their own social psychology, not because of more or less intense ideological anticolonialistic attitudes, but because of the scientific requirement of a meaningful justification for all steps of the research process, from concept formation to forms of explanation and interpretation of empirical observations.

The issues dealt with in this review may lack significance in a situation where things are back to "business as usual" and a solid institutional base is well established. However, in other sociocultural contexts for which this institutionalization is more recent or still under way, a good occasion is provided to think about the fundamental problems of the discipline and to learn more about the complexities of its emergence and development. Failure to do this leaves the field open to radical and unjust critical deconstructive metaphors. For example, one critic stated, "Psychology—all of it is a branch of the police; psychodynamic and humanistic psychologies are the secret police" (Richer, 1992, p. 118).

Although talk about the crisis always seems to have negative and problematic connotations, this is not my own attitude. On the contrary, I believe the crisis has had some positive consequences, which are outlined here:

1. *Progressive adoption of a philosophical anthropology or a model of humankind more in accordance with humankind's origins and development.* When this occurs, the constituent ingredients of humanness—symbolism, language, intentionality, agency, and communicative socialized individuality—not only cease to be strange, but are even considered to be objects of study (Hallowell, 1963; Ibáñez, 1989).

2. *An enhanced awareness of temporal specificity or historicity, with respect to the historical condition of the reality that is studied as well as to the psychosociological knowledge itself* (Farr, 1990). For example, what can be known about conformity is specific to a given time period.

3. *The felt need of rethinking and splitting the linear reconstruction of the historical evolution of social psychology and possible cultural and disciplinary diversification of its history.* The criticisms raised about Gordon Allport's (1954) idealized version of "the historical background" of the discipline, leaving aside the problems it may present as an historical interpretation, reopen the question for ongoing investigations of how to establish their historical meaning and their sociocultural anchorage. If those investigations are minimally reflexive or self-critical, researchers will have to rethink their own historical perspective, and, in the last analysis, the definition of its subject matter or the wider tradition in which they are carried out (Graumann, 1987).

4. *Greater awareness of the situated character of psychosociological knowledge itself, as an interactively attained construction in specific contexts and for concrete purposes from which it is not possible to sever its contents of truth, that is, to evaluate its plausibility, adequacy, generativity, or relevance.* I do not think that this more context-dependent notion of social psychological knowledge should be seen as an uncritical acceptance of a relativistic epistemology; rather, what is called for is a broader conception of explanation than is provided in the conventional hypothetico-deductive framework.

5. *Enhanced awareness of the possible ideological functions of social psychology as a provider of categories and methods of interpreting the subjective experience, both individual and collective.* Inasmuch as social psychology has also turned its attention onto itself and therefore has reflexively taken into account the social and existential conditions that may influence its concepts, theories, and methods, a greater transparency may be expected in terms of the relationships between social psychological knowledge and power (social, political, or economic). Specifically, social psychologists need to acknowledge how their work may be a specific case of the more general problem of the knowledge–power relationship. One can ask, for instance, to what use is social psychology in areas such as labor-management relations (industrial, postindustrial, and global), human resources policies, organizational functioning, or mass persuasion in political and economic behavior? Is this knowledge a detached and valid reflection of human

nature or rather a partial account of it, particularly that which is more akin to the dominant ideologies and, therefore, differentially reinforced and accepted, thereby creating in part that human nature as well as explaining it (Heller, 1986; Torregrosa, 1996)?

6. *Enhanced acknowledgment of the legitimacy of a genuine epistemic-methodico-technical pluralism, in which the diverse perspectives may enrich research and extend the field of analysis.* The laboratory opens up its doors to the "natural" contexts of everyday life (Bar-Tal & Bar-Tal, 1988; Munné, 1990).

7. *A sharper and more critical idea of what constitutes scientific progress and cumulativeness, as distinct from a mechanical result of an unceasing process of data gathering and statistical hypothesis testing.* To a large extent, this insight has been possible because the conception of the scientific method—as reconstructed by logical positivism and adopted as a strict (even dogmatic) criterion of what is and is not scientific—has given way to broader conceptions of scientific inquiry in which understanding, intelligibility, and comprehension (i.e., the basis of the hermeneutic-historical paradigm) may be considered as scientific and necessary for the study of human beings as the traditional explanatory-predictive one (Toulmin, 1972). This new philosophy of science seems to narrow the gap between the "two cultures"—that is, the logic of the sciences and the humanities—providing epistemic legitimacy to interpretive methodologies, formerly considered, more or less explicitly, to be inadequate for advancing knowledge about the behavior and experience of human beings. As Fay (1996) wrote:

> The traditional antagonism between nomologicalism and historicism (with all its attendant oppositions) is ill conceived. Each position is one-sided in itself and requires the other as a supplement to achieve a satisfactory account of understanding human beings. Far from being mutually exclusive, both are required to do justice to the richness of social inquiry. (p. 174)

8. *A considerable development toward the applications field, which not only means a differentiation in terms of substantive areas, but also more elaborate conceptions of intervention and practice.*

Delineating the preceding issues, in my opinion, has helped to expand what Katz (1978) called the *second social psychology* (the nonexperimental) and what Himmelweit and Gaskell (1990) have called *societal psychology,* which is becoming more closely related to the other social sciences.

Toward a More Sociological Social Psychology?

Underlying these consequences, I seem to perceive a basic strain: the progressive realization of the need to introduce systematically the sociological point of view in conventional social psychology. That is to say, social psychology, in order to be social, cannot carry on being just social; it has to be sociological. To this end, it should not attempt to reinvent the psychosociological traditions of sociology (for instance, symbolic interactionism and social structure and personality), but should instead assume them explicitly as inherent parts of itself. This critique implies, therefore, that social psychology is, at the same time, psychology and sociology, and that the adoption of both perspectives in the study of human action and interaction constitutes its analytical specificity as a scientific discipline.

My analysis is consistent with the very significant lines of the so-called *European social psychology*, as is the case with the volume edited by Himmelweit and Gaskell (1990). The analyses carried out by Gaskell, Farr, Moscovici, Doise, Deutsch, and Himmelweit and published in that volume are quite revealing. Specifically, these authors invoked perspectives rooted in the classical and more up-to-date sources of sociology and other social sciences, expressing and illustrating the need to consider systematically social organization, institutional structures, ideological and axiological structures (social representations and systems of ideas and beliefs), social movements, and the constructive character of social interaction, all of which presuppose the adoption of a sociological point of view—not merely the psychologization of social reality. The importance of adopting a sociological framework becomes particularly evident in Moscovici's (1972) perspective, whereby to show how societies build and presuppose models of individual subjectivity, self-identities, and moral characters, he claims to rely on data in the tradition of sociological thought. I most certainly share this line of argument. Note, however, that what the tradition of sociological thought affords Moscovici is not data but a way of looking at reality or, in other words, a point of view. This distinction is important if sociological perspectives are to be used effectively and explicitly recognized as an intrinsic component of the social psychological perspective itself.

In 1998 Moscovici seemed to reaffirm his advocacy of the "socialization" of social psychology by stating, "The pre-eminence of the social is more and more recognized in the fields of epistemology, language, and social psychology. Personally I am convinced that this is a tendency which will deepen" (p. 212). This call for the adoption of the sociological point of view similarly permeates the work of Himmelweit (1990). When listing the attributes that a societal psychology ought to take into account, Himmelweit included many items that seem to demand a systematic inclusion of approaches that go beyond a conventional psychological perspective. A detailed analysis of each of the propositions that she stated in her proposal would show that research programs that take them into consideration could not readily be carried out while ignoring the sociological perspective. For this reason, as was the case with Moscovici, I think they point in the right direction, overcoming the contradictions that have traditionally hindered social psychology.

However, the comparison that Himmelweit (1990) draws from sociology and the other social sciences with respect to the closeness of their relationship to social psychology does not seem to be either fair or exact. Economics, politics, anthropology, and sociology cannot be placed on the same plane. The degree of generality of the latter two, as Parsons remarked (1951; Parsons et al., 1962), is much higher than in the first two, which only address one of the general dimensions in terms of which it is possible to contemplate the social system. Production and distribution occur in the case of economics, whereas power characterizes the case of political science. In moving away from this classificatory exercise in social sciences, what needs to be emphasized is that failing to recognize not only a privileged proximity and affinity between social psychology and sociology, but also a partial identity, would be unfair and, moreover, erroneous, both from the standpoint of a historical reconstruction of the discipline and from an exacting logical-systematic approach. One would hardly be likely to find a scientific-academic organization around social psychology in other social sciences, apart from psychology, comparable to the existing one in sociology. It is precisely within the specialty of social psychology that sociologists belonging to the American Sociological Association identify most (Ennis, 1992).

When Moscovici (1972) said that it is paradoxical that, in spite of the great acceptance of Mead's (1934) thought over most social sciences, there is an anti-Mead tendency in social psychology, he expressed only a half-truth. The legacy of Mead's thoughts has continued to the present day as a foundation of the social psychology that is lodged in the disciplinary context of sociology (Joas, 1985; Mead, 1934). To ignore this part of the history and the present day thinking not only implies a biased view of what social psychology has been, is, or should be, but is also rather inconsistent with Moscovici's own tenets. If the two social psychologies must look for ways of coming together and achieving a common identity, as many authors have been postulating for years, then I believe this task calls for an explicit recognition of the fact that both the psychological and sociological points of view ought to be integrated for the sake of the future development of social psychology (House, 1991). The alternative is to follow Allport (1924) and still adhere to the idea that "in spite of the good offices and interests of the sociologists the two sciences must remain separate branches of inquiry" (p. 11). In this case, the perspectives representing contributions and developments of European social psychology, such as those I have just mentioned, would be difficult to implement either in terms of an adequate academic division of labor or in terms of concepts that would establish a clearly distinctive level of analysis. Following Allport's lead would also imply leaving out of the picture the sociological tradition of social psychology (Cook, Fine, & House, 1995; Lindesmith, Strauss, & Denzin, 1999).

Conclusion

Social psychologists have not generally accepted the idea that the two social psychologies should come closer together or merge completely into one single scientific discipline, independent of the two root disciplines, psychology and sociology. For instance, Stryker (1991) argued for the existence and legitimacy of a sociological social psychology. He also maintained that sociology should not be put in the same category as the other social sciences with regard to its relationship with social psychology. Stryker's conceptual strategy is a mixed blessing. On the positive side, it calls for an unrestricted interdisciplinary approach. On the negative side, there is the persistence of those reductionist tendencies that I have been criticizing. This danger was articulated by Parsons (1951):

> There can be no such a thing as a good social psychology without explicit and systematic reference to the sociological aspects of the theory of the social systems. Without that it becomes merely a cover for "psychological bias" in the interpretation of social phenomena. The only alternative to this view is to hold that since all action is "process of the mind" or "behaviour" there is no place for a distinct theory of the social system at all. (p. 553)

This explicitness and systematicity are what I see lacking or even being resisted, at least in the conventional "scientific culture" of European social psychology, whose most representative association marks its distinctive identity with the term *experimental:* European Association of Experimental Social Psychology. Indeed, this collective self-definition does not seem to lend itself to links with the other social sciences, which can hardly be characterized as experimental in the strict sense of the term. Rather, this self-definition seems to reflect the persistent conflict of the two projects of Psychology as Naturwissenschaft (natural science) or as Geistes-Kulturwissenshaft (cultural science) (Jahoda, 1992; Valsiner & van der Veer, 2000).

Some similar considerations can be stated with regard to social psychology in Latin America, where several representative authors have demanded a psychology closer to the other social sciences and more sensitive to concrete realities and to the people. For example, it is indicative of this trend when Montero (1990) tried to justify the usefulness of the concept of ideology, in a more or less Marxist sense, or when she wrote that text production "opened the door to new topics, to new perspectives, and to an increasingly perceptible tendency towards a more sociological social psychology, closer to the theories and perspectives of the social sciences . . ." but "without sacrificing to them its level of analysis and explanation" (Montero, 1994c, p. 19).

Similar implications can be from Martín-Baró's (1990) elaborations on the same concept of ideology:

> Ideology cannot be restricted to a set of ideas and values guiding the life of the person, in a more or less definite way; it must include the system of social forces, which oppress her. . . . Obviously, social forces are historical realities; and it is precisely this "historicity," as an intrinsic determinant of behaviour, that is ignored by the dominant psychosocial analyses. (pp. 94–95)

More generally, what Martín-Baró (1998) offered from his critical psychology of liberation is a social psychology oriented toward social change.

The process of inquiry is always rooted in particular social and cultural traditions. Such an inquiry takes the humans beings themselves as its object and, more specifically, humans as social beings. In this context, those cultural traditions are critical and operate as tacit frameworks whereby the questions that social psychologists ask and attempt to answer become meaningfully grounded. Indeed social science itself has to be considered a very important, enlightening, self-reflexive tradition or even more appropriately viewed as a diversity of traditions with their specific national undertones. There are, however, no easy methodological or ideological gambits such as the advocacy of global pseudo-internationalism that will relieve social psychologists of the critical task of adequately contextualizing the goals and problems of their research programs (Correa & Zaiter, 1996). Such efforts (Martín-Baró, 1983, 1989) toward theoretical criticism and reinterpretation of conventional social psychology have helped people to better understand, explain, and eventually change social psychological processes in Central America. From the beginning Martín-Baró made clear the situated perspective of his inquiry: social psychology from Central America. Although they have a more clearly explicit hermeneutical and discourse-analytic orientation, the collective volumes edited by Montero (1991, 1994a, 1994b) have a similar aim.

More recently, other Latin American social psychologists have expressed their intellectual indebtedness when describing their own work. Lane (1999), a Brazilian social psychologist, writes:

> In traditional social psychological approaches the human being was fragmented through the use of concepts and particular theories, with the hope held out that sometime in the future it would be possible to unify them. Of the main concepts we reviewed "socialization" was the only one which seemed to have some coherence, for it considered the individual as always inserted in a social context. . . . At this point the work of Martín-Baró was of crucial importance to us. . . . [He] left us a testament, a critical revision of the most important contributions from social psychologists in North America and Europe who were searching for a science that would work on behalf of Caribbean people, and of all Latin Americans. (p. 368)

And Dobles (1999), a Costa Rican social psychologist, said:

> Identifying mechanisms by which injustice is legitimized therefore becomes a very important task for a "liberating" psychology. Martín-Baró, who has had such a profound influence in the work of Central American psychologists, wrote about the "deideologization" that psychology had to carry out as major contribution to social justice and the establishment of a real democracy in Latin America as a whole. Specifically, he unmasked many supposed official "truths" in the context of the Salvadorean civil war that had justified foreign intervention and repression by the army. When . . . our psychological work serves the purpose of highlighting and working on existing injustices and oppressions, we feel we are indeed travelling on the road indicated by Martín-Baró, with clear Marxist roots, of deideologization. (p. 409)

In view of what I have written up to this point, it is quite plausible to defend the hypothesis I put forward at the beginning of my argument, namely, that social psychology, if it is to be distinctively social, has to be sociological. To me, this viewpoint seems to be a way of looking at the constitutive ambiguities in the history of the field and the tensions and conflicts manifested during its last three decades. This position also reflects a general underlying trend (one that is not explicitly recognized with regard to the epistemological implications for the discipline) in the development of European and Latin American social psychology. It might be argued, however, that this assessment is biased in overstating the role of the sociological perspective and its traditions in the constitution and development of social psychology, although I disagree with this argument given the excessively individualistic assumptions of general psychology (Sampson, 1999). Additional support for the view that the advocacy of a more sociological social psychology could lead to a productive reorientation of the discipline can be found in the writing of psychologist Farr (1996), an expert on the history of social psychology:

> It is difficult for social psychologists within Psychology . . . to get an adequate appreciation of the distorting effects of the parent discipline. It is prudent to look for other forms of Social Psychology that are not subject to the same distorting influence. There is no need for psychologists to invent new forms of Social Psychology. They already exist—but they do so in disciplines other than Psychology. (p. 131)

This other discipline is, no doubt, sociology. But there is more than one social psychology in sociology: symbolic interactionism (with its diverse developments) and "social structure and personality" or contextual social psychology as Pettigrew (1991) calls it. Searching for a convergence among them and for a more unitary framework with psychological social psychology, Pettigrew has proposed the adoption of Popper's epistemology, which gives more weight to theory construction in the research process than the logical positivist outlook prevailing in experimental social psychology. Though with a different "vision," Kruglanski (2001) has expressed some arguments in the same direction. Following this lead perhaps Popper's "human ontology" should also be taken into account. Because as Popper (1967) has stated:

> We have every reason to believe that man or rather his ancestor was social prior to being human (considering, for example, that language presupposes society). But this implies that social institutions, and with them social regularities or sociological laws, must have existed prior to what some people are pleased to call "human nature," and to human psychology. If a reduction is attempted at all, it would therefore be more hopeful to attempt a reduction or interpretation of psychology in terms of sociology than the other way round. (pp. 111–112)

It is clear that the position I have just described is to a large extent coincident with, and indebted to, the one that Herbert Kelman (1965), early in his academic career, outlined in his book *International Behavior: A Social-Psychological Analysis,* in which he wrote:

> Social psychology—which is a subfield of psychology as well as of sociology—is concerned with the intersection between individual behavior and societal-institutional processes. It follows from this concern that the primary focus for social-psychological analysis is social interaction. (p. 22)

I think that this basic idea of the discipline establishes the framework to which his later intellectual trajectory is linked: a trajectory fruitfully generative of very significant investigations, theoretical and practical.

From an experimental and clinical background, Kelman conceived social psychology in interactionist terms, in accordance with the best theoretical traditions of the discipline, explicitly recognizing the needed convergence between psychological and sociological approaches. In line with this conceptual starting point, it can be said that his work as a whole may be characterized by an interdisciplinary openness that makes clear the deep need for unity of the social sciences, particularly when faced with having to account for complex social phenomena, a situation in which the conceptual frameworks of specific disciplines show their insufficiency. It is this openness and a rigorous style of thinking that allow for the smooth transition between concrete empirical research and a conscious framework of values from which a meaning can be ascribed to research. In this way, as Berlin (1992) has said, "social science knowledge may become ethical wisdom" (p. 22).

With regard to the epistemological disputes that have been taking place in the discipline, and to which I have referred earlier, Kelman has maintained an attitude far away from any methodological dogmatism. Kelman's approach is not an easy or expeditious eclecticism but rather a way of looking at human affairs with the awareness of the complexity of human nature. Furthermore, in unraveling this complexity, Kelman relies more on adequacy, sensibility, and precision of concepts than on methodological and technical virtuosity. Through his investigations, we can observe the primacy of the theoretical moment, the effort at conceptual clarification and construction, and the search for plausible intelligibility. He uses this mode of analysis in those contexts in which the objective is application or the production of change as well as in conflict resolution workshops to improve Palestinian–Israeli relations at both personal and policy levels (Kelman, 1983). These interventions may be taken as instances of the following well-known Lewinian (Lewin, 1964) statement:

> Many psychologists working today in an applied field are keenly aware of the need for close cooperation between theoretical and applied psychology. This can be accomplished . . . if the theorist does not look toward applied problems with highbrow aversion or with a fear of social problems, and if the applied psychologist realizes that there is nothing so practical as a good theory. (p. 169)

Kelman's already classical model of social influence processes has been an alternative approach in the study of attitudes to the more traditional individualistic perspectives of cognitivism. By specifying the motivational bases of attitudes, these processes were anchored more deeply in the personality structure, and the means to induce their change were made explicit. By linking attitude change to specific processes of interaction, the concept of attitude becomes more similar to the meaning with which it is used in the other traditions of the social sciences, as in the theory of social action or the sociology of knowledge. The analytic usefulness of the concept of attitude can then be extended from individual to collective subjectivity. In a certain sense, this type of meaning is what European social psychologists have attempted to convey by the concept of social representations.

In Kelman's study with Hamilton on criminal obedience to authority (Kelman & Hamilton, 1989), the focus is as much on the types of social relationships and their organizational contexts as on the intrapersonal processes of individuals participating in them. This approach, within the frame of Kelman's theory of social influence, allows for the systematic consideration of power, with its correlates such as ideology, interests, and social organization. Destructive or criminal obedient behavior becomes not only the outcome of perverse or irrational dispositions of human nature, but also the way in which people structure their hierarchical relations and the beliefs and the ideologies that legitimate them, as Kelman and Hamilton (1989) wrote:

> The occurrence of sanctioned massacres cannot be adequately explained by the existence of psychological forces—whether these be psychological dispositions to engage in murderous violence or profound hostility against the target—so powerful that they must find expression in violent acts unhampered by moral restraints. Instead, the major instigators for this class of violence derive from the policy process. (p. 15)

These references to the work of Herbert Kelman as well as his explicit recognition of the role of power inequalities in Palestinian–Israeli relations clearly show that his research endeavors and conceptual framework are not confined to the limits of psychological social psychology. Kelman's work can be considered an influential and respected paradigmatic model in which psychological and sociological levels of analysis are meaningfully related.

References

Allport, F. H. (1924). *Social psychology.* Boston: Houghton-Mifflin.

Allport, G. (1954). The historical background of modern social psychology. In G. Lindzey (Ed.), *The handbook of social psychology* (Vol. 1, pp. 3–56). Reading, MA: Addison-Wesley.

Ancona, L. (1954). *La psicologia sociale negli Stati Uniti d'America* [Social psychology in the United States of America]. Milano: Soc. Editrice "Vita e Pensiero."

Antaki, C. (2000). Simulation versus the thing itself: Commentary on Markman and Tetlock. *British Journal of Social Psychology, 39,* 327–331.

Armistead, N. (Ed.). (1974). *Reconstructing social psychology.* Harmondsworth, England: Penguin.

Augoustinos, M. (1999). Ideology, false consciousness and psychology. *Theory and Psychology, 9,* 295–312.

Bar-Tal, D., & Bar-Tal, Y. (1988). A new perspective of social psychology. In D. Bar-Tal & A. W. Kruglanski (Eds.), *The social psychology of knowledge* (pp. 83–108). Cambridge, England: Cambridge University Press.

Bar-Tal, D., & Kruglanski, A. W. (Eds.). (1988). *The social psychology of knowledge.* Cambridge, England: Cambridge University Press.

Baumeister, R. F. (1995). The personal story of an interpersonal psychologist. In G. G. Brannigan & M. R. Merrens (Eds.), *The social psychologists: Research adventures* (pp. 75–96). New York: McGraw-Hill.

Berkowitz, L. (1963). Social psychological theorizing. In G. Marx (Ed.), *Theories in contemporary psychology* (pp. 369–388). New York: Macmillan.

Berlin, I. (1992). *El fuste torcido de la humanidad* [The crooked timber of humanity]. Barcelona, Spain: Ediciones Península. (Original work published 1959)

Blackler, F. (Ed.). (1983). *Social psychology and developing countries.* New York: Wiley.

Castells, M. (1997). *The information age: Economy, society, and culture* (Vol. 2). Cambridge, MA: Blackwell.

Cherry, F. (1995). *The "stubborn particulars" of social psychology.* London: Routledge.

Cook, K. S., Fine, G. A., & House, J. S. (Eds.). (1995). *Sociological perspectives on social psychology.* Boston: Allyn & Bacon.

Correa, N., & Zaiter, J. (1996). Problemas de aplicación e intervención en psicología social [Application and intervention problems in social psychology]. In J. L. Álvaro, A. Garrido, & J. R. Torregrosa (Eds.), *Psicología social aplicada* [Applied social psychology] (pp. 511–517). Madrid, Spain: McGraw-Hill.

Danzinger, K. (1990). *Constructing the subject: Historical origins of psychological research.* Cambridge, England: Cambridge University Press.

Deutsch, M., & Krauss, R. H. (1965). *Theories in social psychology.* New York: Basic Books.

Dobles, I. (1999). Marxism, ideology and psychology. *Theory and Psychology, 9,* 407–410.

Elias, N. (1987). *El proceso de la civilización: Investigaciones sociogenéticas y psicogenéticas* [The civilization process: Sociogenetic and psychogenetic investigations]. México City: Fondo de Cultura Económica.

Elms, A. C. (1975). The crisis of confidence in social psychology. *American Psychologist, 30,* 967–976.

Ennis, J. G. (1992). The social organization of sociological knowledge: Modeling the intersection of specialties. *American Sociological Review, 57,* 259–265.

Farr, R. (1990). Waxing and waning of interest in societal psychology: A historical perspective. In H. T. Himmelweit & G. Gaskell (Eds.), *Societal psychology* (pp. 46–65). London: Sage.

Farr, R. (1996). *The roots of modern social psychology.* Cambridge, England: Blackwell.

Fay, B. (1996). *Contemporary philosophy of social science.* Oxford, England: Blackwell.

Fox, D., & Prilleltenski, I. (Eds.). (1997). *Critical psychology: An introduction.* London: Sage.

Gergen, K. (1973). Social psychology as history. *Journal of Personality and Social Psychology, 26,* 309–320.

Giddens, A. (1991). *Modernity and self-identity: Self and society in late modern age.* Stanford, CA: Stanford University Press.

Giesen, B. (1987). Beyond reductionism: Four models relating micro and macro levels. In J. C. Alexander, B. Giesen, R. Münch, & N. J. Smelser (Eds.), *The micro-macro link* (pp. 337–355). Berkeley: University of California Press.

Gillin, J. (Ed.). (1954). *For a science of social man.* New York: Macmillan.

Goffman, E. (1959). *The presentation of self in everyday life.* Garden City, NY: Doubleday Anchor Books.

Gouldner, A. (1970). *The coming crisis of Western sociology.* New York: Basic Books.

Graumann, C. F. (1987). History as multiple reconstruction: Of mainstreams, tributaries, and undercurrents. In G. R. Semin & B. Krahe (Eds.), *Issues in contemporary German social psychology* (pp. 1–15). New York: Springer-Verlag.

Habermas, J. (1987). *Teoría de la acción comunicativa* [Theory of communicative action]. Madrid, Spain: Editorial Taurus.

Hallowell, A. I. (1963). Personality, culture, and society in behavioral evolution. In S. Koch (Ed.), *Psychology: A study of a science* (Vol. 6, pp. 429–509). New York: McGraw-Hill.

Harré, R., & Secord, P. F. (1972). *The explanation of social behaviour.* Oxford, England: Blackwell.

Haslam, S. A., & McGarty, C. (2001). A 100 years of certitude? Social psychology, the experimental method and the management of scientific uncertainty. *British Journal of Social Psychology, 40,* 1–21.

Heller, F. (Ed.). (1986). *The use and abuse of social science.* London: Sage.

Himmelweit, H. T. (1990). Societal psychology: Implications and scope. In H. T. Himmelweit & G. Gaskell (Eds.), *Societal psychology* (pp. 17–45). London: Sage.

Himmelweit, H. T., & Gaskell G. (Eds.). (1990). *Societal psychology.* London: Sage.

Hogg, M. A., & Grieve, P. (1999). Social identity theory and the crisis of confidence in social psychology: A commentary, and some research on uncertainty. *Asian Journal of Social Psychology, 2,* 79–93.

Homans, G. C. (1967). *The nature of social science.* New York: Harcourt, Brace & World.

Horowitz, I. L. (1993). *The decomposition of sociology.* New York: Oxford University Press.

House, J. S. (1991). Sociology, psychology, and social psychology (and social science). In C. W. Stephan, W. G. Stephan, & T. F. Pettigrew (Eds.), *The future of social psychology* (pp. 45–60). New York: Springer-Verlag.

Hulett, J. E., & Stagner, R. (Eds.) (1952). *Problems in social psychology: An interdisciplinary inquiry.* Urbana: University of Illinois Press.

Ibáñez, T. (Ed.). (1989). *El conocimiento de la realidad social* [The knowledge of social reality]. Barcelona, Spain: Sendai.

Ibáñez, T., & Íñiguez, L. (Eds.). (1997). *Critical social psychology.* London: Sage.

Inkeles, A. (1963). Sociology and psychology. In S. Koch (Ed.), *Psychology: A study of a science* (Vol. 6, pp. 317–387). New York: McGraw-Hill.

Jahoda, G. (1983). Has social psychology a distinctive contribution to make? In F. Blackler (Ed.), *Social psychology in developing countries* (pp. 25–31). New York: Wiley.

Jahoda, G. (1992). *Crossroads between culture and mind: Continuities and change in theories of human nature.* New York: Harvester-Wheatsheaf.

Joas, H. (1985). *George Herbert Mead: A contemporary re-examination of his thought.* Cambridge, England: Polity Press.

Jones, E. E. (1985). Major developments in social psychology during the past five decades. In G. Lindzey & E. Aronson (Eds.), *The handbook of social psychology* (3rd ed., Vol. 1, pp. 1–46). New York: Random House.

Katz, D. (1966). Editorial. *Journal of Personality and Social Psychology, 7,* 341–344.

Katz, D. (1978). Social psychology in relation to the social sciences: The second social psychology. *American Behavioral Scientist, 21,* 779–792.

Kelman, H. C. (Ed.). (1965). *International behavior: A social-psychological analysis.* New York: Holt, Rinehart & Winston.

Kelman, H. C. (1983). Nacionalismo e identidad nacional: Un análisis psicosocial [Nationalism and national identity: A social psychological analysis]. In J. R. Torregrosa & B. Sarabia (Eds.), *Perspectivas y contextos de la psicología social* [Perspectives and contexts of social psychology] (pp. 241–268). Barcelona, Spain: Editorial Hispanoeuropea.

Kelman, H. C., & Hamilton, V. L. (1989). *Crimes of obedience: Toward a social psychology of authority and responsibility.* New Haven, CT: Yale University Press.

Kendall, G., & Michael, M. (1997). Politicizing the politics of postmodern social psychology. *Theory and Psychology, 7,* 7–29.

Kendler, H. H. (1981). *Psychology: A science in conflict.* New York: Oxford University Press.

Kim, U. (1999). After the "crisis" in social psychology: The development of the transactional model of science. *Asian Journal of Social Psychology, 2,* 1–19.

Kruglanski, A. W. (2001). That "vision thing": The state of theory in social and personality psychology at the edge of the new millennium. *Journal of Personality and Social Psychology, 80,* 871–875.

Kvale, S. (1992). *Psychology and postmodernism.* London: Sage.

Lane, S. T. M. (1999). Ideology and consciousness. *Theory and Psychology, 9,* 367–378.

Leary, M. R. (1989). *The state of social psychology.* London: Sage.

Levine, D. N. (1995). *Visions of the sociological tradition.* Chicago: University of Chicago Press.

Lewin, K. (1964). *Field theory in social science: Selected papers* (D. Cartwright, Ed.). New York: Harper Torchbooks. (Original work published 1944)

Lindesmith, A. R., Strauss, A. L., & Denzin, N. K. (1999). *Social psychology* (8th ed.). Thousand Oaks, CA: Sage.

Lopreato, J., & Crippen, T. (1999). *Crisis in sociology: The need for Darwin.* New Brunswick, NJ: Transaction.

Marková, I. (2000). The individual and society in psychological theory. *Theory and Psychology, 10,* 107–116.

Martín-Baró, J. I. (1983). *Acción e ideología: Psicología social desde Centroamérica* [Action and ideology: Social psychology from Central America]. San Salvador, El Salvador: UCA Eds.

Martín-Baró, J. I. (1989). *Sistema, grupo y poder: Psicología social desde Centroamérica* [System, group, and power: Social psychology from Central America]. San Salvador, El Salvador: UCA Eds.

Martín-Baró, J. I. (1990). Religion as an instrument of psychological warfare. *Journal of Social Issues, 46*(3), 93–107.

Martín-Baró, J. I. (1998). *Psicología de la liberación* [Psychology of liberation]. Madrid, Spain: Trotta.

McGuire, W. J. (1973). The yin and yang of progress in social psychology: Seven koan. *Journal of Personality and Social Psychology, 26,* 446–456.

McGuire, W. J. (1999). *Constructing social psychology.* Cambridge, England: Cambridge University Press.

Mead, G. H. (1934). *Mind, self, and society: From the standpoint of a social behaviorist* (C. Morris, Ed.). Chicago: The University of Chicago Press.

Moghaddam, F. M. (1987). Psychology in three worlds: As reflected by the crisis in social psychology and the move towards indigenous third-world psychology. *American Psychologist, 42,* 912–920.

Montero, M. (1990). Ideology and psychosocial research in third world contexts. *Journal of Social Issues, 46*(3), 43–45.

Montero, M. (Ed.). (1991). *Acción y discurso: Problemas de psicología política en América Latina* [Action and discourse: Problems of political psychology in Latin America]. Caracas, Venezuela: Eduven.

Montero, M. (Ed.). (1994a). *Construcción y crítica de la psicología social* [Construction and critique of social psychology]. Barcelona, Spain: Anthropos.

Montero, M. (Ed.). (1994b). *Psicología social comunitaria* [Community social psychology]. Jalisco, Mexico: Publicaciones de la Universidad de Guadalajara.

Montero, M. (1994c). La psicología social en la América Latina [Social psychology in Latin America]. *Anthropos,* Issue 156, pp. 17–23.

Moscovici, S. (1972). Society and theory in social psychology. In J. Israel & H. Tajfel (Eds.), *The context of social psychology: A critical assessment* (pp. 17–68). London: Academic Press.

Moscovici, S. (1998). The history and actuality of social representations. In U. Flick (Ed.), *Defining the social* (pp. 209–273). Cambridge, England: Cambridge University Press.

Münch, R. (1987). The interpenetration of microinteraction and macrostructures in a complex and contingent institutional order. In J. C. Alexander, B. Giesen, R. Münch, & N. J. Smelser (Eds.), *The micro-macro link* (pp. 319–336). Berkeley: University of California Press.

Munné, F. (1990). *Entre el individuo y la sociedad* [Between the individual and society]. Barcelona, Spain: PPU.

Newcomb, T. H. (1951). Social psychological theory: Integrating individual and social approaches. In J. Rohrer & M. Sherif (Eds.), *Social psychology at the crossroads* (pp. 31–49). New York: Harper & Row.

Newcomb, T. H. (1954). Sociology and psychology. In J. Gillin (Ed.), *For a science of social man* (pp. 227–256). New York: Macmillan.

Nozick, R. (2001). *Invariances: The structure of the objective world.* Cambridge, MA: Belknap Press of Harvard University Press.

Osterkamp, U. (1999). On psychology, ideology and individual's societal nature. *Theory and Psychology, 9,* 379–392.

Pancer, S. M. (1997). Social psychology: The crisis continues. In D. Fox & I. Prilleltenski (Eds.), *Critical psychology: An introduction* (pp. 150–165). London: Sage.

Parker, I. (1989). *The crisis in modern social psychology and how to end it.* London: Routledge.

Parker, I. (1998). Against postmodernism: Psychology in cultural context. *Theory and Psychology, 8,* 601–627.

Parker, I., & Shotter, J. (Eds.). (1990). *Deconstructing social psychology.* London: Routledge.

Parker, I., & Spears, R. (Eds.). (1996). *Psychology and society: Radical theory and practice.* London: Pluto Press.

Parsons, T. (1951). *The social system.* Glencoe, IL: Free Press.

Parsons, T. (1954). Psychology and sociology. In J. Gillin (Ed.), *For a science of social man* (pp. 67–101). New York: Macmillan.

Parsons, T. (1959). An approach to psychological theory in terms of the theory of action. In S. Koch (Ed.), *Psychology: A study of a science* (Vol. 3, pp. 612–723). New York: McGraw-Hill.

Parsons, T., Shils, E. A., Allport, G. W., Kluckhohn, C., Murray, H. A., Sears, R. R., et al. (1962). Some fundamental categories of the theory of action: A general statement. In T. Parsons & E. Shils (Eds.), *Toward a general theory of action* (pp. 3–29). New York: Harper Torchbooks. (Original work published 1951)

Pettigrew, T. F. (1991). Toward unity and bold theory: Popperian suggestions for two persistent problems of social psychology. In C. W. Stephan, W. G. Stephan, & T. F. Pettigrew (Eds.), *The future of social psychology* (pp. 13–27). New York: Springer-Verlag.

Popper, K. (1967). *La sociedad abierta y sus enemigos* [The open society and its enemies]. Buenos Aires: Paids. (Original work published 1945)

Richer, P. (1992). An introduction to deconstructionist psychology. In S. Kvale (Ed.), *Psychology and postmodernism* (pp. 110–118). London: Sage.

Ring, K. (1967). Experimental social psychology: Some sober question about some frivolous values. *Journal of Experimental Social Psychology, 3,* 113–123.

Ritzer, G., & Gindoff, P. (1992). Methodological relationism: Lessons for and from social psychology. *Social Psychology Quarterly, 2,* 128–140.

Robinson, D. N. (2000). Paradigms and "the myth of the framework": How science progresses. *Theory and Psychology, 10,* 39–47.

Roger, R. S., Stenner, P., Gleeson, K., & Rogers, W. S. (1995). *Social psychology: A critical agenda.* Cambridge, England: Polity Press.

Rohrer, J., & Sherif, M. (Eds.). (1951). *Social psychology at the crossroads.* New York: Harper.

Rosnow, R. L. (1981). *Paradigms in transition.* New York: Oxford University Press.

Sampson, E. E. (1999). Liberating psychology. In *La psicologia al fin del siglo* [Psychology at the end of the century] (pp. 305–321). Caracas, Venezuela: Sociedad Interamericana de Psicologia.

Sapsford, R., Still, A., Miell, D., Stevens, R., & Wetherell, M. (Eds.). (1998). *Theory and social psychology.* London: Sage.

Sarason, S. B. (1981). *Psychology misdirected.* New York: Free Press.

Scheff, T. J. (1990). *Microsociology: Discourse, emotion, and social structure.* Chicago: University of Chicago Press.

Sherif, M., & Wilson, M. O. (Eds.). (1957). *Emerging problems in social psychology.* Norman: University of Oklahoma Book Exchange.

Smelser, N. J., & Smelser, W. T. (Eds.). (1970). *Personality and social systems.* New York: Wiley.

Smith, J. L. (2000). *The psychology of action.* New York: St. Martin's Press.

Smith, M. B. (1972). Is experimental social psychology advancing? *Journal of Experimental Social Psychology, 8,* 86–96.

Smith, M. B. (1974). *Humanizing social psychology.* San Francisco: Jossey-Bass.

Smith, R. J. (1999). Social/personality psychology in context. *Theory and Psychology, 9,* 769–786.

Steiner, I. D. (1974). Whatever happened to the group in social psychology? *Journal of Experimental Social Psychology, 10,* 94–108.

Stryker, S. (1980). *Symbolic interactionism: A social structural approach.* Menlo Park, CA: Benjamin-Cummings.

Stryker, S. (1991). Consequences of the gap between "the two social psychologies." In C. W. Stephan, W. G. Stephan, & T. F. Pettigrew (Eds.), *The future of social psychology* (pp. 83–97). New York: Springer-Verlag.

Tomars, A. S. (1957). Sociology and interdisciplinary developments. In H. Becker & A. Boskoff (Eds.), *Modern sociological theory* (pp. 501–527). New York: Holt.

Torregrosa, J. R. (1996). Concepciones del aplicar [Conceptions about applying]. In J. L. Alvaro, A. Garrido, & J. R. Torregrosa (Eds.), *Psicología social aplicada* [Applied social psychology] (pp. 39–56). Madrid, Spain: McGraw-Hill.

Toulmin, S. (1972). *Human understanding: The collective use and evolution of concepts.* Princeton, NJ: Princeton University Press.

Valsiner, J., & van der Veer, R. (2000). *The social mind: Construction of the idea.* Cambridge, England: Cambridge University Press.

Wallach, L., & Wallach, M. A. (1994). Gergen versus the mainstream: Are hypotheses in social psychology subject to empirical test? *Journal of Personality and Social Psychology, 67,* 233–242.

Westland, G. (1978). *Current crises of psychology.* London: Heinemann.

Wexler, P. (1983). *Critical social psychology.* London: Routledge.

Comments on Chapters 1 and 2

Susan H. Korper

José Torregrosa's chapter (see chap. 2, this volume) offers a carefully researched yet impassioned argument to social psychologists that the formal definition—of who they are, of what they do, and of what they care about—matters. As he writes, such definitions are not merely "intentional or wishful statements" that are related only vaguely to the legitimacy of the field of knowledge called social psychology. Rather, the definitions are the "initial map of the territory" where, professionally speaking, social psychologists live. This image evokes the ways in which a large-scale geographical map elucidates relationships among various terrains, structures, and empty spaces and reveals the well-known areas and unexplored frontiers. Also displayed are interconnecting highways and byways, some being less traveled trails blazed by a few, some commuter expressways where well-funded, but perhaps narrowly conceived, programs of construction have led to gridlock from the many people going from point A to point B and back again in seemingly endless replications of a familiar commute, having forgotten the possible journeys beyond B.

I also thought of what happens when the drawing of a map is severely constrained by a particular belief. I especially recalled the cover of a *New Yorker* magazine from some years ago that contained an imaginary map of the United States from the perspective of a resident of New York City. The map depicted the major skyscrapers of New York; some uninhabited, barren space; and then San Francisco and the Pacific Ocean. The implication was that New Yorkers do not believe that there is anything worth noting until you cross 3,000 miles and get to San Francisco. The cartoon map was a lighthearted highlighting of the way in which one's selective perception of a terrain, whether from arrogance or merely oblivious self-absorption, can become so distorted that the map itself comes to foil rather than facilitate journeys.

To return more concretely to Torregrosa's discussion in chapter 2 of the problematic consequences of excluding sociological perspectives from the definition of social psychology, "social psychologists will not solve the problem just by stating, as is common practice (even with F. H. Allport), that a psychology is social because it deals with 'the social.'" To act as if that does "solve the problem" is a bit like drawing the attention of those New York residents from the cartoon to the barren space between New York and San Francisco. They can diligently stare at the space but will still be blinded to the richness of that 3,000-mile stretch until their capacity to perceive it is expanded by shaking loose the bias that underlies their selective perception.

In Torregrosa's careful treatment of the historical record of definitions of social psychology from the early Allport *pronunciamento* through "the tensions and conflicts manifested during the last three decades . . . reflects a general underlying trend . . . in the development of European and Latin American social psychology," he has well articulated both the "hegemonic position of the paradigm of the psychological-individualistic orientation" and the voices of those who would shake loose this bias by explicitly integrating, rather than delegitimizing or even denigrating, sociological perspectives in social psychology.

In support of his argument, I offer three additional thoughts. The first relates to Torregrosa's paraphrasing of Jahoda's view that "most current theories in experimental social psychology do not seem to be valid or adequate for the social contexts of third world countries." The implication is that these theories may be "valid" or "adequate" in most social contexts in the United States. I suggest that precisely because the hegemonic individualistic orientation is more entrenched in American social psychology, the proportion of experimental social psychological studies with problematic validity may be even greater in the United States than in other cultural contexts, even if these studies are generalized only to the social contexts within the United States.

Second, I am intrigued by an apparent similarity between some observations Nadim Rouhana and I (1997) have made on asymmetrical power relations in ethnonational conflict and the "disciplinary nationalism" Torregrosa describes. I am referring in particular to his discussion of the more psychological-individualistic orientation of "the dominant conventional social psychology of the first world" (i.e., American social psychology) as compared with the more sociological-group orientation of European and Latin American social psychology. A dominant group is, in general, inclined to focus on an individual level of analysis, presumably because dominant individuals are personally less vulnerable to the consequences of the behavior of members of a minority group. Conversely, members of groups of lesser privilege are more strongly affected by the consequences of the behavior of the dominant group. Presumably for that reason, members of a minority group tend to be more oriented to analyzing structural constraints and to finding group phenomena correspondingly a more salient and appropriate construal of their social reality. It may then be that power asymmetry per se has helped shape the boundaries between schools of thought in social psychology that promote a more individualistic orientation and those that advocate a group or social system orientation.

That said, I would add, third, that the more privileged group is often very insecure about its status. It is my impression that American academic psychologists as a whole suffer the insecurity that they may not be "real scientists." In my view, this insecurity has been dealt with, in many cases and especially in American social psychology, by focusing on making the method of investigation more rigorous. In other words, the method has often come to drive the choice of inquiry, rather than the inquiry driving the choice of method. And the pragmatic fact of the matter is that it is easier to do the kind of rigorous controlled experiments that get published if the focus of the research is on individuals rather than groups.

Returning to my fanciful elaboration of Torregrosa's "initial map," I see Reuben Baron's chapter (see chap. 1, this volume) as illuminating the less-traveled trail blazed by Herbert Kelman, who has resisted the pressures to let method drive inquiry or to allow the micro to subsume the macro. As Baron puts it, Kelman has "bucked the tide of individualism in psychology and saw the group as the chief agent of change." Baron has wonderfully laid out the "happy confluence" of Herbert Kelman as "perhaps the most consistently Lewinian social psychologist active today and at the same time a protodynamic system's theorist and practitioner."

Starting with Kelman's work in compliance, identification, and internalization, Baron locates these processes in the Lewinian tradition of treating behavior "as a function of the relationship between the person and the environment $(P \times E)$" and elucidates how even Kelman's earliest work extended Lewin's model in a variety of ways, some of which foreshadow dynamical systems theory and circular causality in particular. He describes how "Kelman fleshes out the $P \times E$ type of formulation by offering us boundary conditions for the processes that mediate change." For me, this approach is epitomized by Kelman's collaboration with Lee Hamilton in *Crimes of Obedience* (1989), in which they went beyond his already multidimensional model of attitude change, into their rules, roles, and values model.

I find this model to be an extraordinarily sophisticated and complex framework for specifying not only how boundary conditions exist for the processes of social influence but also how in one domain P and E may interact through one process of social influence while simultaneously in another domain interacting through a different process of social influence. This intellectual innovation is well described in Baron's later discussion in chapter 1 of "a key aspect of complex dynamical systems; rather than having a single point attractor pushing the system toward equilibrium . . . [they] are multimodal." His discussion inspired me to notice that the rule, role, and value framework is not only consistent with the Lewinian interdependence of P and E and the dynamical intercausality between the two as they extend in a "temporal trajectory," but it also incorporates the simultaneity of different interdependent and dynamical processes.

In Baron's discussion of how remarkably the dynamical system concepts can be seen in Herbert Kelman's work on the interactive problem-solving workshops, he describes self-organized criticality as involving "a positive feedback such that small discrepancies can be amplified rather than corrected as in a negative feedback system." Thus, in the workshop setting, initially tentative envisionings of a future relationship that is mutually supportive of the human needs of two small groups of enemies can be seen to branch out, as in the graphic generation of a fractal, both within the small groups and beyond to these groups' communities. These small perturbations, with their explicit fostering of norms designed to generate "uneasy coalitions" and to promote interactive problem solving, grow into the beginnings of joint thinking about how to operationalize the early envisioning and how to adjust it so that it is more amenable to operationalizing.

When these cognitive perturbations ripple out to the larger communities, as they are explicitly intended to do, there begins to be a larger system of social support and validation, which then leads to more intensive joint thinking about cognitive and behavioral means to achieve a future that is gradually transformed from a pipe dream into a shared goal. Circular causality occurs whereby the microchanges in the cognitions of the workshop participants about what is possible, acceptable, and necessary to proactively generate a better future gradually cause similar changes in the thinking of people in their larger societies. These changes then create new possibilities (and foreclosures of previously envisioned possibilities) for smaller groups to use when they go back to the drawing board anew. Thus, Baron's analyses of problem-solving workshops in terms of dynamical processes, such as self-organized criticality and circular causality, give us new insights into how a change at the microlevel can become self-organizing when explicitly fostered and proactively linked to changes in the larger system.

Baron further elucidates how the dynamical systems concept of "periodic attractors" helps account for the necessarily "uneasy coalitions" generated in the Kelman problem-solving workshops. The complex nature of this relationship goal is in marked contrast to many models of dialogue groups in which it is hoped that the participants will develop friendships. The Kelman workshops are not designed to generate friendships or even to directly reduce stereotypes. These people are enemies. Changing the affect between them is only a focus insofar as they must have a sufficient level of stereotype reduction and affect moderation to establish sufficient norms of collegiality to be open to hearing the other's needs and claims and to engaging in a process of joint thinking, whether they enjoy the encounters or not. True friendship is a someday thing for enemies in a protracted violent conflict. A goal of creating friendships at this stage is not only not fruitful, but also harmful in that it siphons off the energies and attention from the already draining, often discouraging, and always horrendously difficult work of generating new sociopolitical structures for the intergroup relationship. Such structures, at a minimum, incorporate more justice and less violence and, at best, have embedded within them a process of intergroup reconciliation in which genuine, sustainable interpersonal friendship becomes possible.

References

Kelman, H. C., & Hamilton, V. L. (1989). *Crimes of obedience: Toward a social psychology of authority and responsibility.* New Haven, CT: Yale University Press.

Rouhana, N. R., & Korper, S. H. (1997). Dealing with power asymmetry: Dilemmas of intervention in asymmetric intergroup conflict. *Negotiation Journal, 12,* 315–328.

3

Prejudice: Toward a More Inclusive Understanding

Alice H. Eagly

Studying prejudice is the bread-and-butter of social psychology. The pivotal status of work on prejudice is surely justified because of its potential for exposing the roots of discrimination and social disadvantage. Moreover, to resolve societal conflict and international disputes, which are important endeavors in the work of Herbert Kelman (e.g., 1997), prejudices generally have to be overcome at least to some extent so that the contending parties have sufficient mutual respect that they can work together. It might seem, therefore, that the definition of such a central concept as prejudice would have been agreed on at an early point, to provide long-term guidance. However, this is not the case. As is true of many important concepts in psychology, the understanding of prejudice has matured as the discipline has grown in theoretical sophistication. To further develop a theory about prejudice, I propose that it is time to shift to a more inclusive conceptualization of prejudice, to take account of some important lessons that social scientists have learned about prejudice in recent decades. This new approach treats prejudice as an evaluative reaction—that is, as a negative attitudinal shift—that is elicited at the interface between individual beliefs and a social structure composed of social roles. The view of prejudice in this chapter thus reflects the interdisciplinary tradition whereby social psychology is joined to both psychology and sociology. A similar blending of the social and the individual levels of analysis is manifested in virtually all of the chapters of this volume as well as throughout the work of Herbert Kelman (e.g., Kelman & Warwick, 1973), the teacher and mentor of the authors of these chapters. The approach to prejudice described in this chapter also illustrates a conception of attitudes toward groups as emergents in particular social contexts rather than as context-free evaluations that perceivers transport into social situations. Before introducing this treatment of prejudice, I review classic definitions of the concept with the aim of showing why these approaches are not sufficient to encompass the phenomenon of prejudice.

Traditional Definitions of Prejudice by Social Psychologists

Influential in early discussions of prejudice was Allport's (1954) definition of prejudice as "thinking ill of others without sufficient warrant" (p. 7). Kelman and Pettigrew (1959) suggested that this Allportian definition had become consensual when they wrote that "group prejudice is now commonly viewed as having two components: hostility and misinformation" (p. 436). Subsequent to the 1950s, the main shift in definitions of prejudice consisted of the deletion of the requirement that the beliefs held about a target group are necessarily biased or inaccurate. This change paralleled the removal of inaccuracy from most definitions of stereotype (see Ashmore & Del Boca, 1981). Early theorists had thus included inaccurate perception as one of the defining elements of both prejudice and stereotypes, although they acknowledged that there might be a "kernel of truth" underlying these phenomena (Allport, 1954, p. 190). Given the liberal, social reformist spirit that has guided this research tradition, it is not surprising that early theorists conflated inaccurate perception and negative attitudes and thus reasoned that prejudice is an error contradicting reason and good sense.

Beginning to recognize the complexity inherent in understanding whether the attributes of groups are accurately perceived, social psychologists retained only the negative attitude half of the earlier formulation of prejudice. This minimalist definition as an overall negative attitude toward a group became consensual in social psychology (e.g., Esses, Haddock, & Zanna, 1993). Consistent with contemporary attitude theory (Eagly & Chaiken, 1993), the negative attitude that constitutes prejudice can have various roots in the sense that it can be grounded in beliefs, affects, and representations of behavior, and it can have various consequences in the sense that it can be expressed in beliefs, affects, and behaviors (e.g., Brown, 1995; Duckitt, 1992).

The emphasis on negativity in most treatments of prejudice is not surprising in view of the particular prejudices that received the most attention during the period when theory and research on prejudice and discrimination first developed. Anti-Semitism was an initial focus (Adorno, Frenkel-Brunswik, Levinson, & Sanford, 1950), and in subsequent decades European Americans' prejudices toward African Americans received increasing attention, particularly in their openly hostile forms (Schuman, Steeh, & Bobo, 1985). Somewhat later, prejudice toward other minority groups, including gays and lesbians, became important as well (Herek, 1987). Most often investigated were extreme prejudices that produced outcomes such as the Holocaust, lynchings, and hate crimes.

Two bodies of prejudice research have been decisive in raising doubts about the sufficiency of the negative attitude definition of prejudice that became consensual in social psychology. The first of these research areas pertains to subtle, "modern" prejudices held toward many racial and ethnic minorities. The hallmark of these prejudices is the absence of clear-cut negative content in people's beliefs about the targeted group. The second of these research areas pertains to prejudice toward women, a topic that provides an even greater challenge to the definition of prejudice as a negative attitude. This challenge has arisen because people generally hold positive attitudes toward women, even though they are targets of discrimination in many contexts. As I explain in this chapter, the new knowledge gained about prejudice toward minorities and women surely does not deny that attitudes toward some groups are negative. However, by showing that people can be prejudiced toward many groups despite holding attitudes toward them that are not negative and, indeed, are even positive, the research of the last 20 years has reopened the question of how prejudice should be understood and defined.

Dilemma Posed by Research on Modern Ethnic and Racial Prejudices and Prejudice Toward Women

Modern Ethnic and Racial Prejudices

Research on subtle, modern prejudices began with recognition of a change over time in the attitudes and beliefs that many White people held toward Black people in the United States (McConahay, 1986). Representative national surveys documented a dramatic change from endorsement of racial segregation, discrimination, and the innate inferiority of Black people to rejection of these practices and ideas (Schuman et al., 1985). However, White people nonetheless often endorse a set of beliefs denying that Black people's social and economic problems can be ascribed to external factors such as job discrimination and implicitly ascribing them to internal factors such as lack of motivation. Such beliefs appear in the Modern Racism Scale in the form of statements such as the following: "Discrimination against Blacks is no longer a problem in the United States" and "Over the past few years Blacks have gotten more economically than they deserve" (McConahay, Hardee, & Batts, 1981, pp. 568–570). Although such ideas can foster resentment of policies such as affirmative action that are designed to help disadvantaged minorities, these statements do not directly ascribe negative attributes to them.

This decrease in negativity is evident, not only in racial attitudes and stereotypes, but also in research on various ethnic and national stereotypes held by students in the United States (Madon et al., 2001). Moreover, researchers studying attitudes toward minority groups in European countries have also found it appropriate to design instruments to assess subtle prejudices toward minority groups that are apparently common among citizens of these countries (e.g., Meertens & Pettigrew, 1997). For example, the Subtle Prejudice Scale, which was designed to assess such prejudices, includes items such as the following (here worded to elicit British respondents' reactions to West Indians): "It is just a matter of some people not trying hard enough. If West Indians would only try harder they could be as well off as British people" and "Many other groups have come to Britain and overcome prejudice and worked their way up. West Indians should do the same without special favor" (Meertens & Pettigrew, 1997, p. 69).

The view that contemporary ethnic and racial prejudices generally do not fit the classic negative attitude definition of prejudice has also emerged from work on intergroup relations. In particular, Brewer (1999) argued that out-groups do not typically elicit strong negative sentiments but merely fail to elicit positive sentiments. In her view, much intergroup discrimination arises, not from hostility toward out-group members, but from identification with one's in-group, which fosters preferential treatment of in-group members. Out-groups are variously regarded, sometimes with indifference, sometimes with outright hostility, and under some circumstances even with admiration. However, in

Brewer's view, positive emotions such as sympathy, trust, and loyalty are reserved for the in-group, and in-group identification provides conditions that can degenerate into out-group hate, for example, when groups find themselves in competition for scarce resources.

Prejudice Toward Women

The clearest challenge to the traditional analysis of prejudice derives from research on prejudice toward women because of evidence that women elicit predominantly positive sentiments but are often targets of prejudice. As psychologists began to study attitudes toward women, many believed that these attitudes were negative (e.g., Lips, 1988; Matlin, 1987). However, psychologists' discussions of these presumed negative attitudes generally presented evidence of discrimination against women, not evidence of negative attitudes or stereotypes.

When researchers eventually examined people's evaluations of women and men as social groups, these investigations showed that, on the whole, people do not evaluate women negatively but instead tend to evaluate them positively (see review by Eagly & Mladinic, 1994). For example, research assessing the evaluative content of gender stereotypes indicates that the qualities that people associate with women are on the whole positive and somewhat more positive on the average than the qualities that they associate with men. Of course, people associate both positive and negative qualities with both sexes (Spence, Helmreich, & Holahan, 1979), producing some ambivalence, but this ambivalence appears to be no greater in relation to women than men (Eagly, Mladinic, & Otto, 1991). Also, when standard attitude measures, such as evaluative thermometer ratings or semantic differential ratings, are used to assess attitudes toward women as a social group, they show that on the average people evaluate women positively—in fact, more positively than they evaluate men. My colleagues and I dubbed this especially positive evaluation of women the "women-are-wonderful effect" (Eagly & Mladinic, 1994).

Further illuminating the goodness of the female stereotype is research by Langford and MacKinnon (2000). These investigators assessed gender stereotypes' meaning on the three dimensions of evaluation, potency, and activity, which were established in the work of Osgood and his colleagues on the measurement of meaning (Osgood, Suci, & Tannenbaum, 1957). This method revealed that, when potency and activity were controlled, substantially higher levels of positive evaluation were associated with the traits ascribed to women, especially with communal traits such as gentle and helpful. These results were consistent with analyses in my research showing that the female advantage in evaluation derives from the cluster of positive communal characteristics, which are particularly highly evaluated (Eagly & Mladinic, 1994). These characteristics encompass attributes such as nurturing, supportive, affectionate, sympathetic, gentle, sensitive, kind, and warm. Although some researchers have characterized this aspect of the female stereotype as the ascription of "warmth" to women, reflecting a paternalistic reaction to their lower status (e.g., Fiske, Xu, Cuddy, & Glick, 1999; Jackman, 1994), these communal attributes are considerably broader and more nuanced than mere warmth. Attributes such as nurturant and supportive connote active involvement in caring roles, and attributes such as sensitive, sympathetic, and affectionate connote competence in close relationships.

The apparent goodness of the female stereotype must withstand various challenges to its validity, especially the suspicion that respondents' concerns about social desirability or political correctness might have contaminated these empirical observations. Fortunately, experimental social psychologists have developed useful technologies for circumventing pressures toward social desirability. These methods include implicit attitudinal measures such as the Implicit Association Test, which can assess the strength of association between concepts and positive or negative evaluation (Greenwald, McGhee, & Schwartz, 1998). Research using this method has also obtained more positive evaluation of women than men. Women were thus evaluated more favorably than men in several experiments that assessed the strength of association between male and female category labels and evaluative words (Carpenter, 2000).

Another approach to circumventing social desirability pressures involves disguising the purpose of giving evaluations so that participants are not aware that their gender prejudice is under scrutiny. Illustrating this approach are experiments in the Goldberg paradigm, which is named after Philip Goldberg's (1968) initial experiment involving evaluations of essays ascribed to a woman or man. In such experiments, participants evaluate a product—such as an article or a résumé—that is ascribed to a person who is identified by a masculine or feminine first name and corresponding pronouns. The between-subjects designs that are typically used disguise the fact that other participants receive the same materials but ascribed to a person of the other sex. Meta-analyses of studies that used this paradigm have shown an overall effect that is nearly null. For example, in their meta-analysis of 123 studies in the Goldberg paradigm, Swim, Borgida, Maruyama, and Myers (1989) obtained a only a very slight bias against women—specifically, a mean effect size in the d metric of 0.05 to 0.08. However, Kasof (1993) subsequently showed that the female names that researchers had chosen for Goldberg paradigm studies, compared with the male names, were less attractive and conveyed less intellectual competence as well as older age. He also demonstrated that Goldberg studies showed more negativity toward women to the extent that this naming bias in favor of men was present. In view of this confound between names' gender and their evaluative content, a fair conclusion is that experiments in the Goldberg paradigm have not demonstrated any overall tendency to devalue women or their work. And, as I have already indicated, other paradigms often reveal a bias in favor of women. Thus, the generally positive evaluations of women do not seem to be manifestations of respondents' effort to appear unprejudiced.

One way to allow the finding of a positive attitude toward women to preserve social psychologists' traditional assumptions about prejudice is to regard it as a sign of the waning of prejudice toward women. The idea that attitudes toward women have become more positive is not without merit. However, even the earlier studies, which did not necessarily produce a women-are-wonderful effect, very rarely provided any evidence of a negative attitude toward women (see review by Eagly & Mladinic, 1994). It is also not plausible to interpret this evidence of a positive attitude in studies conducted in the United States as demonstrating that Americans are on the forefront of declining prejudice against women. Instead, evidence of the widespread distribution of positive evaluations of women in world societies emerged in Williams and Best's (1990) cross-national investigation of gender stereotypes. These researchers obtained evaluative ratings of the attributes ascribed to men and women by samples of university students in 25 nations. They found no overall cross-national tendency for the female and the male stereotypes to differ in their favorability, although in some nations the female stereotype was more positive than the male stereotype, and in a few nations (all outside of the Americas and Europe) the male stereotype was more favorable.

Given the lack of evidence that evaluations of women are predominantly negative, it might be tempting to conclude that women are not targets of prejudice after all. However, any such conclusion would be inconsistent with evidence of discrimination against women. For example, economists continue to document a discriminatory wage gap (see Jacobsen, 1998), and psychologists provide evidence that women, more frequently than men, are targets of sexual harassment in the workplace (e.g., Fitzgerald, 1993). In research by Swim, Hyers, Cohen, and Ferguson (2001) on the everyday experience of prejudice, women reported sexist incidents directed toward them at a greater rate than men reported sexist incidents directed toward them. Similarly, in research by Kobrynowicz and Branscombe (1997), women reported personally receiving more gender discrimination than men reported receiving, and both sexes perceived more discrimination directed toward women than men. Therefore, to the extent that such discriminatory behavior reflects prejudice, it is difficult to maintain that women are not targets of prejudice.

Prejudice against women thus appears to be alive and well, despite the lack of evidence that women as a social group are negatively evaluated. If women elicit relatively positive attitudes and many racial and ethnic out-groups fail to elicit clearly negative attitudes, the traditional understanding of prejudice as a negative attitude toward a group is in need of reshaping.

Prejudice at the Intersection of Stereotypes and Social Roles

The best way to broaden the understanding of the nature of prejudice is to take the structure of the social environment into account along with the psychological structure of the individual. A more adequate framework thus retains the classic emphasis on the individual's feelings and beliefs about a social group but also encompasses the social structure that is external to the targeted social group. For purposes of thinking about prejudice, it is useful to regard this environment as an opportunity structure that is composed of social roles. These roles offer opportunities in the form of possibilities for rewarding outcomes such as income, status, respect, admiration, love, knowledge, excitement, and leisure. Of course, some roles can bring unfavorable outcomes such as disrespect, overwork, and boredom, but it is the access of groups to roles with primarily rewarding outcomes that is most relevant to understanding prejudice.

Prejudice often arises at the intersection between beliefs in the form of the attributes ascribed to group members and social roles in the form of their perceived requirements. Thinking about prejudice relationally in terms of the alignment of stereotypic beliefs and role-defined opportunities makes it easy to understand how even favorable beliefs about a social group can have detrimental effects by limiting the group's access to rewarding outcomes. Positive attributes such as kindness or assertiveness, which are stereotypic of some groups, thus are not universally valued in all social roles but are far more appropriate in some roles than others.

The key eliciting condition for prejudice is incongruity between a group's stereotype and the requirements of social roles. Role incongruity in these terms does not in itself produce prejudice but yields a potential for prejudice. This potential exists when social perceivers hold a stereotype about a social group that is inconsistent with the attributes that are required for success in certain classes of social roles. Prejudice is activated when social perceivers consider a group member in the context of an incongruent role. When a stereotyped group member and an incongruent social role become joined in the mind of the perceiver, prejudice is a common outcome. This prejudice consists of a lowering of the evaluation of members of the stereotyped group as occupants of the role, compared with the evaluation of members of groups for whom the role is congruent.

In the face of role incongruity, membership in the stereotyped group causes perceivers to suspect insufficiency in the attributes that are required for success in the role, regardless of whether this insufficiency is actually present in the target group member. This result constitutes prejudice in the form of a less favorable attitude-in-context (or more unfavorable attitude) toward people who are stereotypically mismatched with the requirements of a role, compared with attitudes toward those who are matched. This way of thinking about prejudice is thus consistent with Allport's (1954) view that prejudice occurs when people are placed at some disadvantage that is not warranted by their individual actions or qualifications. This lowered evaluation is the price that members of a stereotyped group ordinarily pay for seeking or occupying incongruent roles. This prejudicially lowered evaluation refers not to the attitude toward the group in general, but to the attitude toward the group members in the role-incongruent context. This attitude can be expressed through downward shifts in beliefs about the members of the target group, affect and emotions held toward them, and behaviors directed toward them.

The unfavorable attitudinal shift that follows from the conjunction of a group's stereotype and the requirements of an incongruent role need not produce a negative attitude toward group members as occupants of the role. If the role in question has high status, the attitude toward the group members as role occupants probably would not be negative but merely less positive than the corresponding attitude toward members of the groups who have historically occupied the role. For example, consider the role incongruity that an African American lawyer might encounter, perhaps being thought to have less technical competence than his or her European American counterpart. The role incongruity that triggers this skepticism would be unlikely to produce a negative attitude toward such a lawyer because the role itself has considerable prestige. Instead, many European Americans would evaluate African American lawyers favorably but, in showing prejudice, would evaluate them somewhat less favorably than their European American counterparts. Discriminatory behavior (e.g., reluctance to become a client of an African American lawyer) is a likely outcome. It is this lowering of the evaluation of members of the target group because of their group membership (e.g., as women, as African Americans) that constitutes role incongruity prejudice.

This decline in evaluation can take place in relation to members of groups whose overall stereotypes are predominantly negative or predominantly positive. Positive stereotypic attributes—for example, the niceness ascribed to women—can thus be perceived as a liability in some social roles. When an evaluatively positive attribute such as niceness is mismatched to the requirements of a role, perceivers suspect that this attribute would foster behavior that is inappropriate to the role. For example, a nice chief executive officer in a competitive industry would be regarded as incompetent if her niceness extended to treating competitors so kindly that the bottom line of the company suffered. Similarly, positive qualities commonly ascribed to men such as independence and assertiveness can be disabling in relation to caring roles requiring interpersonally sensitive and nurturant qualities. These positive qualities then can take on less positive or even negative connotations in the context of incongruent roles.

Research provides many examples of the usefulness of this role incongruity principle in understanding prejudice. Relevant are experiments in the Goldberg (1968) paradigm that require that participants evaluate a man or woman in congruent versus incongruent roles. In their meta-analysis of this research, Swim and her colleagues (1989) discovered that the bias against women was more substantial when the stimuli that participants evaluated were in a masculine or neutral domain rather than a feminine domain. Similarly, a meta-analysis of Goldberg paradigm studies in which the stimuli evaluated were leadership or managerial behaviors ascribed to women or men showed that the devaluation of women, compared with equivalent men, was greater when leaders occupied roles that were especially male dominated and presumably incongruent for women (Eagly, Makhijani, & Klonsky, 1992). Organizational research has confirmed that women who enter nontraditional fields or male-dominated work settings often receive hostile reactions from male colleagues (e.g., Collinson, Knights, & Collinson, 1990; Morrison & Von Glinow, 1990), which can include sexual harassment (Fitzgerald, Drasgow, Hulin, Gelfand, & Magley, 1997). Also, gay men are at risk for prejudiced reactions in domains to which they are stereotypically mismatched—for example, military service (Segal, Gade, & Johnson, 1993). Gay men's relatively effeminate image (e.g., Madon, 1997) is thus incongruent with the tough, masculine role that military organizations construct for soldiers (Goldstein, 2001).

The logic of the role incongruity analysis of prejudice dictates that men, Whites, heterosexuals, and members of other advantaged groups could also be targets of prejudice when their stereotypic attributes are mismatched to role requirements. The most extensive meta-analysis of the subset of Goldberg studies presenting job résumés or applications for evaluation showed precisely this effect for gender discrimination: Women were preferred over equivalent men for jobs rated as female sex typed, and men over equivalent women for jobs rated as male sex typed (Davison & Burke, 2000). It is thus group members' stereotypic mismatch to the requirements of social roles that produces this prejudicial decline in evaluation, regardless of the positive or negative evaluative content of their overall stereotype or of the attitudes commonly held toward the group.

Analysis of inconsistencies between stereotypes and the requirements of roles draws attention to the degree of inconsistency that may be present. Because stereotypes of groups typically encompass a set of attributes, as do the qualities required by social roles, stereotype-role inconsistency can range from nonexistent to mild, moderate, and extreme. For an example of a role that is moderately inconsistent for women, consider the role of physician, which is thought to require not only technical and scientific competence but also communal qualities of sympathy, sensitivity, and nurturance (e.g., Albino, Tedesco, & Shenkle, 1990; Fennema, Meyer, & Owen, 1990). Therefore, women would be generally matched to the physician role on these communal qualities but tend to be mismatched on many of the other qualities. Prejudice against women entering the physician role should therefore be less extreme than it would be if the mismatch were more complete. Moreover, women might be attracted to or channeled into particular types of physician roles for which communal qualities are thought to be especially desirable (e.g., primary care, pediatrics), thereby reducing the inconsistency between the female stereotype and the physician role and reducing the potential for discriminatory treatment (More & Greer, 2000).

The classic emphasis on negative attitudes toward groups as the key to understanding prejudice can be encompassed within this role incongruity analysis by acknowledging that the overall evaluative content of a group's stereotype influences the range of desirable social roles for which group members are thought to be unqualified. If social roles that offer valuable opportunities in terms of prestige, status, income, love, and other outcomes require generally positive attributes, it follows that more negative stereotypes and associated attitudes hinder access to a wider range of desirable roles because role-relevant positive attributes tend to be absent from the stereotype. Groups that are generally devalued or severely stigmatized are in a worse position to attain rewarding roles than groups that are not devalued. The most extreme cases of antipathy toward groups involve the dehumanization that can occur as a concomitant of warfare and extreme intergroup conflict (see Kelman, 1973). If a group is accorded no positive attributes, its members would be ineligible for any desirable roles and, in the extreme, would be thought unworthy of living. The classic treatments of prejudice were tailored to understanding prejudicial reactions to generally devalued groups. Members of such groups suffer from wide-ranging stereotype-role incongruity and have generally reduced access to rewarding roles. However, many, if not most, of the important phenomena of everyday prejudice lie outside of the boundaries of this framing of prejudice.

Origins of Stereotypic Attributes

If stereotypic attributes have the potential to produce prejudice when they are mismatched to the requirements of roles, understanding the origins of these attributes should illuminate the dynamics of prejudice. What accounts for the content of stereotypic beliefs? The most important mechanism of stereotype formation is that perceivers assume correspondence between the types of actions that members of groups typically engage in and their inner dispositions (see Eagly, Wood, & Diekman, 2000; Gilbert, 1998). Social psychologists have interpreted this correspondence tendency as producing error and labeled it the *fundamental attribution error* (Ross, 1977) or *correspondence bias* (Gilbert & Malone, 1995). Regardless of whether inferring people's inner qualities from their actions produces erroneous judgments, correspondent inference is the basic psychological process that produces stereotypes of social groups that mirror the qualities that they play out in their typical social roles. Stereotypes are thus emergents from observed behavior, even though for some groups these observations are mainly indirect, communicated by the media and cultural traditions more generally.

Supporting the principle of correspondent inference, research has demonstrated perceivers' failure to give much weight to the constraints of social roles in inferring role players' dispositions (e.g., Ross, Amabile, & Steinmetz, 1977). In relation to social groups, Schaller (1994; Schaller & O'Brien, 1992) argued that accurate inferences about group members' enduring traits require that perceivers control for situational constraints by using statistical reasoning analogous to an analysis of covariance in which these constraints would function as covariates. Schaller showed that people generally fail to implement such controls. In a similar vein, Hoffman and Hurst (1990) argued that stereotypes function as rationalizations for existing role distributions, as did Jost and Banaji (1994) in their analysis of stereotypes as providing *system justification.*

At least in the eye of the beholder, then, people are what they do, or, as representatives of their social groups, they are what their groups typically do. Whether these correspondent inferences produce error deserves deeper analysis than it has ordinarily received. Although the case for inaccuracy has often been made in laboratory experiments (e.g., Hoffman & Hurst, 1990), in natural settings members of social groups are generally socialized for their futures as adult occupants of the roles that are typical of their group. For example, in virtually all societies, the socialization of girls is arranged to give them practice in child care and nurturing, to ensure their accommodation to mothering as an adult role (Wood & Eagly, 2002). Moreover, engaging in behavior that meets the requirements of adult roles affects inner dispositions, especially through the identification process that Kelman (1961) considered in his three processes of social influence. Identification in turn encompasses more molecular processes such as expectancy confirmation and self-regulation by which people accommodate to their social roles.

In general, groups that are positioned differently in the social structure acquire different characteristics, reflecting their typical life tasks. For example, girls become more nurturant than boys, as assessed by personality tests (see Feingold, 1994), even if they were not intrinsically more nurturant. This reasoning about the power of social roles is consistent with Gilbert's (1998) argument that effects that appear as inferential errors in social psychology experiments do not necessarily have counterparts in natural settings. The errors that are inherent in the inferences that participants in laboratory experiments make about group members' attributes when they reason from their role performances thus may erode in natural settings because of the power of prolonged occupancy of social roles to mold inner dispositions. Consistent with this claim, research within the "accuracy paradigm" in psychology (e.g., Funder, 1995; Lee, Jussim, & McCauley, 1995) has shown that people are often at least moderately accurate in perceiving group members' characteristics at the level of a group average, even for groups that are commonly objects of prejudice (e.g., Ashton & Esses, 1999; Hall & Carter, 1999; Judd & Park, 1993; Swim, 1994). Of course, this moderate accuracy leaves room for a variety of distortions and biases to operate as well (Diekman, Eagly, & Kulesa, 2002).

The idea that stereotypes are grounded in observations of the types of work that are typical of groups of people raises the issue of whether a systematic relation exists between stereotype content and positioning in the social structure. A social role analysis predicts that perceivers accord task-specific attributes to group members based on the work that they typically do. For example, the competence that perceivers accord to women by including traits such as kind and nurturing in the female stereotype reflects a division of labor whereby women take responsibility for domestic work (Eagly et al., 2000). Similarly, in research by Fiske et al. (1999), which defined competence in terms of intelligent, confident, and independent traits, perceivers ascribed such traits to groups that occupy roles in the professions and other well-paid occupations—in other words, high-status roles. In addition, Johannesen-Schmidt and Eagly (2002) found that both positive agentic qualities (e.g., independent, assertive) and negative agentic qualities (i.e., dictatorial, overbearing) were ascribed more strongly to higher income than lower income employees.

Intergroup relationships also shape stereotypes, as many social scientists have maintained (see Bobo, 1999; Fiske et al., 1999). From a social role perspective, this shaping occurs because intergroup relations influence the types of roles in which members of differing groups observe one another. In general, cooperative relationships with another group yield observations of its members engaging in actions that are helpful to one's own group, and competitive relationships yield observations of them engaging in actions that are harmful to one's own group. Stereotype content is therefore shifted in a favorable direction by cooperative relationships and in an unfavorable direction by competitive relationships, with the particular shading of evaluative meaning depending on the particulars of these intergroup relationships. Most dramatically, perceptions of citizens of other nations become more negative as a product of warfare, economic rivalries, and political conflict (Eagly & Kite, 1987; Kelman, 1987; Suedfeld & Tetlock, 1977).

Prejudice as a Social Problem

The principle that social perceivers ascribe attributes to social groups that correspond to their typical role-bound activities helps explain why role incongruity produces downward attitudinal shifts. When group members move into new roles, they are perceived as still adapted to their accustomed social roles and generally seem somewhat unqualified for these new roles. Social perceivers therefore react by lowering their evaluation of these role-incongruent individuals, compared with role-congruent individuals. Despite the usefulness of this model of prejudice, its focus on individual reactions to role incongruity is limiting. Only by also considering the societal context of typical role incongruities can the approach illuminate the conditions under which prejudice gains recognition as a social problem in the sense that racism, sexism, and prejudice against gays and lesbians are commonly acknowledged prejudices in a contemporary context.

To appreciate the variability in the extent to which the public recognizes the existence of prejudice, compare the mismatch between men's stereotypic attributes and many female-dominated occupational roles (e.g., day-care provider) with the mismatch between women's stereotypic attributes and many male-dominated occupational roles (e.g., prosecuting attorney). Agitation and social action have surrounded women's entry into male-dominated occupations but not men's entry into female-dominated occupations. Although people's stereotypic perceptions of men no doubt discourage them from assuming stereotype-incongruent roles that some men may value, discrimination of this sort has surely not become a substantial social issue. Therefore, in both popular and social scientific discourse, *gender prejudice* is ordinarily understood to refer to prejudice against women. Similarly, tension surrounds Blacks' efforts to obtain roles and opportunities that have been dominated by Whites, and the term *racial prejudice* ordinarily refers to prejudice against Blacks.

Importance of Social Change

To represent these asymmetries in the implications of incongruities between groups' stereotypic characteristics and social roles, this social role analysis of prejudice draws attention to groups' effort or lack of effort to gain entry to new roles. Most obviously, groups seldom work to enter roles that offer lower status and fewer privileges than their current roles. Therefore, few men attempt to enter female-dominated roles, and few Whites attempt to enter minority-dominated roles. However, it does not necessarily follow that members of disadvantaged groups attempt to enter roles dominated by members of advantaged groups. Sometimes less privileged groups accept lower status, less income, and exclusion from some social roles, at least for some substantial period of time. For example, most women over long periods of time accepted their inability to hold political offices and vote in elections as well as many other manifestations of patriarchy such as paternalistic definitions of family roles.

It is when social change alters the circumstances of a group that at least a visible subgroup may attempt to gain access to roles that its members have previously not occupied. A group's circumstances change as a result of molar social and economic shifts. For example, critical to change in the status of women is the decline of birth rates in industrialized countries (United Nations, 2001). Relevant to change in African Americans' status is their migration from the rural South to the urban North in the United States (Lemann, 1991). As large numbers of group members react to their changed circumstances by attempting to move from traditional to nontraditional roles, prejudice becomes recognized as a social issue. This awareness arises because members of the group are thought to fit their traditional niche—that is, people believe that they have special qualities that enable them to do the work that their group has always done. For example, 44% of survey respondents in the United States believed that it would be "worse for society" if most primary family providers were women and most of their spouses stayed home to raise children (Roper Center, 2000), presumably because these respondents believed that women are better adapted to child rearing than are men.

The comfortable fit that perceivers assume exists between people's characteristics and their existing social roles becomes problematic when members of a group want to change their roles. Then prejudice becomes the focus of debate and social action. Prejudice is at issue because the group members are inevitably marked by their old social roles, certainly in how they are stereotypically perceived but also to some extent in terms of their actual characteristics due to the processes that have fit them to their typical roles. When they try to move into a different or better position, into work that requires different qualities, they are thought to be relatively unqualified. These newcomers are at risk for having barriers erected to prevent their entry into these roles and for having their work in these new roles devalued, as Eagly and Karau (2002) demonstrated in relation to women's entry into male-dominated leadership roles. Moreover, this devaluation may be fueled by preferences on the part of more privileged groups that members of less privileged groups remain in their traditional social roles and retain their accustomed ways of behaving (Jackman, 1994).

Prejudice becomes an acknowledged social problem when a substantial number of the members of a group aspire to occupy or newly occupy social roles that are inconsistent with their stereotypic attributes. Of course, not all group members desire entry into new roles as a group's status begins to change. For example, a small-scale social movement has developed around the "fascinating womanhood" ideology that features the preservation and veneration of women's time-honored homemaker role (Andelin, 1992). Yet, for prejudice to emerge as an acknowledged social problem, a certain critical mass of group members must agitate for access to incongruent roles. Attitudes toward group members as occupants or potential occupants of new roles then shift downward, compared with attitudes toward the traditional occupants of these roles. Attitudes toward the pathbreakers who seek or attain new roles can also be more negative than attitudes toward the group members who remain in their accustomed roles, as illustrated by the relatively less positive stereotype of feminists compared with housewives (e.g., Haddock & Zanna, 1994) and suggested by national polls showing that more Americans have an unfavorable compared with favorable impression of feminists (Huddy, Neely, & Lafay, 2000). In other words, group members who try to move up in a social hierarchy into new roles are likely to become targets of prejudice.

This insight that prejudice becomes a social problem in the context of group members' attempts to change their social roles is reflected in the measuring instruments that researchers have designed to assess modern prejudices. Typical items assessing modern racial and ethnic prejudices thus express the White majority's resistance to the efforts of Blacks and other minorities to move into new social roles. For example, the Modern Racism Scale includes the item "Blacks are getting too demanding in their push for equal rights" (McConahay et al., 1981, p. 568), and the Subtle Prejudice Scale includes the item "[West Indians] living here should not push themselves where they are not wanted" (Meertens & Pettigrew, 1997, p. 69). Similarly, Glick and Fiske's (1996) Ambivalent Sexism Inventory is built around the principle of resistance to change in women's roles. This instrument defines sexism on a negative dimension (called *hostile sexism*) that assesses predominantly unfavorable reactions to women in nontraditional roles as well as on a positive dimension (called *benevolent sexism*) that assesses predominantly favorable reactions to women in traditional roles.

Debates About the Accuracy of Stereotypes

Social change that has the potential to improve the status of a social group always raises questions about the accuracy of the stereotypes that have characterized them. When the social position of a group undergoes change, its members commonly attack the stereotypes by which they have been described because the new roles that they seek to occupy require characteristics that are different from those contained in the existing stereotype of their group. For example, the role of business executive is thought to require action-oriented, decisive, and competitive qualities that are more stereotypic of men than women (e.g., Martell, Parker, Emrich, & Crawford, 1998). Because change in women's status entails moving up into such positions, existing gender stereotypes are correctly perceived as problematic by many women. The content of such stereotypes is inconsistent with women's emerging social positions and aspirations for social and political equality. Therefore, it is not surprising that eradicating these ideas has been a major focus of the feminist movement.

The group members who are in the forefront of desiring access to new roles are ordinarily somewhat atypical of their group. They are the vanguard or the pathbreakers of their group. They often have the characteristics needed for the new roles that they desire to enter, but they generally find it difficult to be perceived as having them. It is here that the classic notion that inaccurate perceptions accompany prejudice deserves consideration. It is not a misguided idea in the context of role incongruity prejudice. Social perceivers may be skeptical, for example, that a woman is brave enough to be a firefighter or that an African American is intellectually talented enough to be a mathematician or that a Mexican American is ambitious enough to become a Fortune 500 executive. Because members of such groups are prejudged on the basis of their group membership, they are often viewed as unqualified for such roles.

When a group's status is rising, one source of the tension that generally surrounds perceptions of their characteristics is group members' efforts to alter their characteristics as they prepare for and occupy new roles. For example, as Blacks have moved into roles dominated by Whites, these upwardly mobile individuals are sometimes accused of having changed to be like Whites (and they may be labeled with pejorative terms such as *Oreo;* e.g., Willie, 1975). Similarly, in relation to managerial roles that women have entered in large numbers, debates center on whether managerial women should accommodate to the masculine mode of behaving or maintain a more feminine style that some argue is a more effective mode of management (see Eagly & Karau, 2002).

Prejudices of the Disadvantaged Toward the Advantaged

One test of the adequacy of this role congruity approach to understanding prejudice is its ability to encompass the least studied aspect of prejudice—namely, the prejudices that members of subordinated groups may direct toward members of dominant groups. From the role incongruity perspective, the potential for prejudice toward advantaged groups exists when the stereotype commonly held about them contains attributes that are inconsistent with the attributes that would ideally be required by the roles that they typically occupy. In this context, role requirements would function through their injunctive norms— that is, through people's ideas about how roles should be enacted (Cialdini & Trost, 1998). This type of prejudice is activated when the stereotype of an advantaged group comes to mind together with the ideal requirements of the roles that they currently occupy. For example, if men's stereotypic negative agentic characteristics (e.g., egotistical, overbearing) come to mind in the context of their occupancy of leadership roles that are thought to ideally require characteristics such as kindness and concern with subordinates' welfare, the evaluation of these male leaders would shift downward. Similarly, African Americans' view of European Americans as tainted by qualities such as oppressiveness and selfishness can make them seem unworthy to continue to occupy social roles yielding power and wealth (Montieth & Spicer, 2000).

This role incongruity prejudice directed toward members of advantaged groups has limited consequences if only members of relatively powerless groups hold these attitudes. However, in the context of wars and revolutions, less powerful groups can gain power. If one party to a conflict gains sufficient power, its members may displace from their existing social roles those groups that they consider unworthy to occupy these roles. Violent displacements can occur when groups have developed extremely hostile and competitive relationships with one another. Interethnic conflict is rife with examples of such behavior (e.g., ethnic cleansing). The interactive problem-solving workshops pioneered by Herbert Kelman seek to break down the negative stereotyping and prejudice that develop in the wake of such intergroup conflict. The workshops and other conflict resolution methods can establish conditions that favor peaceful transitions rather than violent displacements of groups from their social roles (Rouhana & Kelman, 1994).

Conclusion

In this chapter, I have explained that it is insufficient to view prejudice as a negative attitude toward a group in a general sense. The main flaw in the negative attitude framing derives from the fact that much everyday prejudice consists of the devaluation in specific role contexts of members of a particular group, relative to the evaluation of equivalent members of other groups. Devaluation produces a diminished attitude in context. From this perspective, prejudice remains attitudinal, as in classic definitions, and it can be expressed in beliefs, affects, and behaviors. However, the devaluation—that is, the downward attitudinal shift—does not necessarily produce a negative attitude, nor is the overall context-free attitude toward the target group necessarily negative. The key eliciting condition is the potential entry or actual entry of group members into social roles to which they are stereotypically mismatched. Given this mismatch, even those individuals who actually have the qualities demanded by the new social roles tend to be perceived as somewhat deficient in these qualities because they are stereotypically prejudged. Therefore, prejudice in the form of lowered evaluation is very likely to occur in the specific context of group members' entry into social roles that members of their group previously rarely occupied.

This analysis of prejudice harks back to a point made by Ajzen and Fishbein (1980) about the need for researchers to consider the level of generality or specificity with which they define the targets of attitudes. In the classic attitudinal analysis of prejudice (Allport, 1954), social scientists defined the target of the prejudiced attitude as a social group in general—that is, Jews, African Americans, Latinos, women, and poor people. Studying prejudice at this level has been limiting because most prejudicial phenomena arise in context—in particular, in the context of incongruities between group members' stereotypes and their desired social roles. Therefore, analysis of the conjunction of stereotypes and roles and the resultant attitude-in-context yields a more precise understanding of when group members are targets of prejudice and when they are not (see also Gomez & Trierweiler, 1999). In contrast, treating prejudice in a context-free frame as a negative overall evaluation of a group fails to capture most of the phenomena of everyday prejudices, although the approach does direct attention to the situation of groups that are devalued in a wide range of contexts.

The understanding of prejudice proposed in this chapter also illustrates some of the drawbacks of regarding attitudes as stored evaluations that are transported by perceivers from one setting to another—an approach that is implicit in treatments of prejudice as negative attitudes toward groups. In a new situation a social group becomes, in effect, a new attitude object, or in Asch's terms, perceivers experience not "a change in the judgment of the object but a change in the object of judgment" (Asch, 1940, p. 458). Evaluations of members of social groups are thus context-dependent constructions in the sense that they are labile evaluations, and the valence of these evaluations depends on both the group membership of the target individual and the role context in which that individual is perceived. Even though perceivers possess overall, abstract evaluations of social groups, the evaluation of a target group member that emerges in perceivers' minds in particular situations is not that overall evaluation. Rather, the emergent attitude is dependent on the degree of perceived congruity versus incongruity of the attributes attached to the individual's group and those attached to the role in question. This approach thus has much in common with the attitudes-as-constructions position sometimes advocated by attitude researchers (e.g., Wilson & Hodges, 1992).

In also addressing the conditions under which prejudice becomes an acknowledged social problem, this contextual framework suggests that in times of social stability, although prejudice is present in the beliefs and affects of individual social perceivers, it is unlikely to emerge as an acknowledged social issue because the great majority of group members remain in their traditional social roles. In changing societies, prejudice is an inevitable social problem because it is a concomitant of groups' rise. When social hierarchies are stable, with groups occupying their accustomed social roles, stereotype-role incongruities are so powerful that, when they are activated, they thoroughly dampen people's aspiration for roles that are atypical of their group. Without noticeable aspirations on the part of members of disadvantaged groups, prejudice is not widely discussed or generally acknowledged as a social problem. However, the potential for role incongruity prejudices to emerge as new "isms" lurks in the stereotypes that form around these groups. As visible subgroups from disadvantaged groups attempt to move upward into new, more advantaged roles, prejudice not only becomes more common but also becomes acknowledged and debated. This prejudice dissipates only after considerable social change has occurred whereby large numbers of newcomers prove their success in the new roles and thereby change the stereotype through which they are perceived.

References

Adorno, T. W., Frenkel-Brunswik, E., Levinson, D. J., & Sanford, R. N. (1950). *The authoritarian personality.* New York: Harper & Row.

Ajzen, I., & Fishbein, M. (1980). *Understanding attitudes and predicting social behavior.* Englewood Cliffs, NJ: Prentice Hall.

Albino, J. E., Tedesco, L. A., & Shenkle, C. L. (1990). Images of women: Reflections from the medical care system. In M. A. Paludi & G. A. Streuernagel (Eds.), *Foundations of a feminist restructuring of the academic disciplines* (pp. 225–253). New York: Haworth Press.

Allport, G. W. (1954). *The nature of prejudice.* Reading, MA: Addison-Wesley.

Andelin, H. (1992). *Fascinating womanhood.* New York: Bantam/Fanfare.

Asch, S. E. (1940). Studies in the principles of judgments and attitudes: II. Determination of judgments by group and by ego standards. *Journal of Social Psychology, 12,* 433–465.

Ashmore, R. D., & Del Boca, F. K. (1981). Conceptual approaches to stereotypes and stereotyping. In D. L. Hamilton (Ed.), *Cognitive processes in stereotyping and intergroup behavior* (pp. 1–35). Hillsdale, NJ: Erlbaum.

Ashton, M. C., & Esses, V. M. (1999). Stereotype accuracy: Estimating the academic performance of ethnic groups. *Personality and Social Psychology Bulletin, 25,* 225–236.

Bobo, L. D. (1999). Prejudice as group position: Microfoundations of a sociological approach to racism and race relations. *Journal of Social Issues, 55,* 445–472.

Brewer, M. B. (1999). The psychology of prejudice: Ingroup love or outgroup hate? *Journal of Social Issues, 55,* 429–444.

Brown, R. (1995). *Prejudice: Its social psychology.* Cambridge, MA: Blackwell.

Carpenter, S. J. (2000). *Implicit gender attitudes: Group membership, cultural construal, consistency, and stability.* Unpublished doctoral dissertation, Yale University, New Haven, CT.

Cialdini, R. B., & Trost, M. R. (1998). Social influence: Social norms, conformity, and compliance. In D. T. Gilbert, S. T. Fiske, & G. Lindzey (Eds.), *The handbook of social psychology* (4th ed., Vol. 2, pp. 151–192). Boston: McGraw-Hill.

Collinson, D. L., Knights, D., & Collinson, M. (1990). *Managing to discriminate.* New York: Routledge.

Davison, H. K., & Burke, M. J. (2000). Sex discrimination in simulated employment contexts: A meta-analytic investigation. *Journal of Vocational Behavior, 56*, 225–248.

Diekman, A. B., Eagly, A. H., & Kulesa, P. (2002). Accuracy and bias in stereotypes about the social and political attitudes of women and men. *Journal of Experimental Social Psychology, 38*, 268–282.

Duckitt, J. H. (1992). *The social psychology of prejudice.* New York: Praeger Publishers.

Eagly, A. H., & Chaiken, S. (1993). *The psychology of attitudes.* Fort Worth, TX: Harcourt Brace Jovanovich.

Eagly, A. H., & Karau, S. J. (2002). Role congruity theory of prejudice toward female leaders. *Psychological Review, 109*, 573–598.

Eagly, A. H., & Kite, M. E. (1987). Are stereotypes of nationalities applied to both women and men? *Journal of Personality and Social Psychology, 53*, 451–461.

Eagly, A. H., Makhijani, M. G., & Klonsky, B. G. (1992). Gender and the evaluation of leaders: A meta-analysis. *Psychological Bulletin, 111*, 3–22.

Eagly, A. H., & Mladinic, A. (1994). Are people prejudiced against women? Some answers from research on attitudes, gender stereotypes, and judgments of competence. In W. Stroebe & M. Hewstone (Eds.), *European review of social psychology* (Vol. 5, pp. 1–35). New York: Wiley.

Eagly, A. H., Mladinic, A., & Otto, S. (1991). Are women evaluated more favorably than men? An analysis of attitudes, beliefs, and emotions. *Psychology of Women Quarterly, 15*, 203–216.

Eagly, A. H., Wood, W., & Diekman, A. (2000). Social role theory of sex differences and similarities: A current appraisal. In T. Eckes & H. M. Trautner (Eds.), *The developmental social psychology of gender* (pp. 123–174). Mahwah, NJ: Erlbaum.

Esses, V. M., Haddock, G., & Zanna, M. P. (1993). Values, stereotypes, and emotions as determinants of intergroup attitudes. In D. M. Mackie & D. L. Hamilton (Eds.), *Affect, cognition, and stereotyping: Interactive processes in group perception* (pp. 137–166). San Diego, CA: Academic Press.

Feingold, A. (1994). Gender differences in personality: A meta-analysis. *Psychological Bulletin, 116*, 429–456.

Fennema, K., Meyer, D. L., & Owen, N. (1990). Sex of physician: Patient preferences and stereotypes. *Journal of Family Practice, 30*, 441–446.

Fiske, S. T., Xu, J., Cuddy, A. C., & Glick, P. (1999). (Dis)respecting versus (dis)liking: Status and interdependence predict ambivalent stereotypes of competence and warmth. *Journal of Social Issues, 55*, 473–489.

Fitzgerald, L. F. (1993). Sexual harassment: Violence against women in the workplace. *American Psychologist, 48*, 1070–1076.

Fitzgerald, L. F., Drasgow, F., Hulin, C. L., Gelfand, M. J., & Magley, V. J. (1997). Antecedents and consequences of sexual harassment in organizations: A test of an integrated model. *Journal of Applied Psychology, 82*, 578–589.

Funder, D. C. (1995). On the accuracy of personality judgment: A realistic approach. *Psychological Review, 102*, 652–670.

Gilbert, D. T. (1998). Ordinary personology. In D. T. Gilbert, S. T. Fiske, & G. Lindzey (Eds.), *The handbook of social psychology* (4th ed., Vol. 2, pp. 89–150). Boston: McGraw-Hill.

Gilbert, D. T., & Malone, P. S. (1995). The correspondence bias. *Psychological Bulletin, 117*, 21–38.

Glick, P., & Fiske, S. T. (1996). The Ambivalent Sexism Inventory: Differentiating hostile and benevolent sexism. *Journal of Personality and Social Psychology, 70*, 491–512.

Goldberg, P. (1968). Are women prejudiced against women? *Transaction, 5*, 316–322.

Goldstein, J. S. (2001). *War and gender: How gender shapes the warm system and vice versa.* Cambridge, England: Cambridge University Press.

Gomez, J. P., & Trierweiler, S. J. (1999). Exploring cross-group discrimination: Measuring the dimensions of inferiorization. *Journal of Applied Social Psychology, 29*, 1900–1926.

Greenwald, A. G., McGhee, D. E., & Schwartz, J. L. K. (1998). Measuring individual differences in implicit cognition: The Implicit Association Test. *Journal of Personality and Social Psychology, 74*, 1464–1480.

Haddock, G., & Zanna, M. P. (1994). Preferring "housewives" to "feminists." *Psychology of Women Quarterly, 18*, 25–52.

Hall, J. A., & Carter, J. D. (1999). Gender-stereotype accuracy as an individual difference. *Journal of Personality and Social Psychology, 77*, 350–359.

Herek, G. M. (1987). Can functions be measured? A new perspective on the functional approach to attitudes. *Social Psychology Quarterly, 50*, 285–303.

Hoffman, C., & Hurst, N. (1990). Gender stereotypes: Perception or rationalization? *Journal of Personality and Social Psychology, 58,* 197–208.

Huddy, L., Neely, F. K., & Lafay, M. R. (2000). The polls—trends: Support for the women's movement. *Public Opinion Quarterly, 64,* 309–350.

Jackman, M. R. (1994). *The velvet glove: Paternalism and conflict in gender, class, and race relations.* Berkeley: University of California Press.

Jacobsen, J. P. (1998). *The economics of gender* (2nd ed.). Malden, MA: Blackwell.

Johannesen-Schmidt, M. C., & Eagly, A. H. (2002). Diminishing returns: The effects of income on the content of stereotypes of wage earners. *Personality and Social Psychology Bulletin, 28,* 1538–1545.

Jost, J. T., & Banaji, M. R. (1994). The role of stereotyping in system-justification and the production of false consciousness. *British Journal of Social Psychology, 33,* 1–27.

Judd, C. M., & Park, B. (1993). Definition and assessment of accuracy in social stereotypes. *Psychological Review, 100,* 109–128.

Kasof, J. (1993). Sex bias in the naming of stimulus persons. *Psychological Bulletin, 113,* 140–163.

Kelman, H. C. (1961). Processes of opinion change. *Public Opinion Quarterly, 25,* 57–78.

Kelman, H. C. (1973). Violence without moral restraint: Reflections on the dehumanization of victims and victimizers. *Journal of Social Issues, 29,* 25–61.

Kelman, H. C. (1987). The political psychology of the Israeli–Palestinian conflict: How can we overcome the barriers to a negotiated solution? *Political Psychology, 8,* 347–363.

Kelman, H. C. (1997). Group processes in the resolution of international conflicts: Experiences from the Israeli–Palestinian case. *American Psychologist, 52,* 212–220.

Kelman, H. C., & Pettigrew, T. F. (1959). How to understand prejudice. *Commentary, 28,* 436–441.

Kelman, H. C., & Warwick, D. P. (1973). Bridging micro and macro approaches to social change: A social-psychological perspective. In G. Zaltman (Ed.), *Processes and phenomena of social change* (pp. 13–59). New York: Wiley.

Kobrynowicz, D., & Branscombe, N. R. (1997). Who considers themselves victims of discrimination? Individual difference predictors of perceived gender discrimination in women and men. *Psychology of Women Quarterly, 21,* 347–363.

Langford, T., & MacKinnon, N. J. (2000). The affective bases for the gendering of traits: Comparing the United States and Canada. *Social Psychology Quarterly, 63,* 34–48.

Lee, Y., Jussim, L., & McCauley, C. R. (Eds.). (1995). *Stereotype accuracy: Toward appreciating group differences.* Washington, DC: American Psychological Association.

Lemann, N. (1991). *The promised land: The great Black migration and how it changed America.* New York: Knopf.

Lips, H. M. (1988). *Sex and gender: An introduction.* Mountain View, CA: Mayfield.

Madon, S., (1997). What do people believe about gay males? A study of stereotype content and strength. *Sex Roles, 37,* 663–685.

Madon, S., Guyll, M., Aboufadel, K., Montiel, E., Smith, A., Palumbo, P., et al. (2001). Ethnic and national stereotypes: The Princeton trilogy revisited and revised. *Personality and Social Psychology Bulletin, 27,* 996–1010.

Martell, R. F., Parker, C., Emrich, C. G., & Crawford, M. S. (1998). Sex stereotyping in the executive suite: "Much ado about something." *Journal of Social Behavior and Personality, 13,* 127–138.

Matlin, M. W. (1987). *The psychology of women.* New York: Holt, Rinehart & Winston.

McConahay, J. B. (1986). Modern racism, ambivalence, and the Modern Racism Scale. In G. F. Dovidio & S. L. Gaertner (Eds.), *Prejudice, discrimination, and racism* (pp. 91–125). Orlando, FL: Academic Press.

McConahay, J. B., Hardee, B. B., & Batts, V. (1981). Has racism declined in America? It depends on who is asking and what is asked. *Journal of Conflict Resolution, 25,* 563–579.

Meertens, R. W., & Pettigrew, T. F. (1997). Is subtle prejudice really prejudice? *Public Opinion Quarterly, 61,* 54–71.

Montieth, M. J., & Spicer, C. V. (2000). Contents and correlates of Whites' and Blacks' racial attitudes. *Journal of Experimental Social Psychology, 36,* 125–154.

More, E. S., & Greer, M. J. (2000). American women physicians in 2000: A history in progress. *Journal of the American Medical Women's Association, 55,* 6–9.

Morrison, A. M., & von Glinow, M. A. (1990). Women and minorities in management. *American Psychologist, 45,* 200–208.

Osgood, C. E., Suci, G. J., & Tannenbaum, P. H. (1957). *The measurement of meaning.* Urbana: University of Illinois Press.

Roper Center. (2000). *Women, equality, work, family, men.* Roper Center at University of Connecticut Public Opinion Online. Retrieved on March 2, 2002, from http://web.lexis-nexis.com/universe/document?_m=1483408bb970a78276147e76d331a609&_docnum=13&wchp=dGLSzV-lSlAl&_md5=ad7bc35675d8d5a2cc25dbea0cc4714b

Ross, L. (1977). The intuitive psychologist and his shortcomings. In L. Berkowitz (Ed.), *Advances in experimental social psychology* (Vol. 10, pp. 173–220). New York: Academic Press.

Ross, L., Amabile, T. M., & Steinmetz, J. L. (1977). Social roles, social control, and biases in social-perception processes. *Journal of Personality and Social Psychology, 35,* 485–494.

Rouhana, N. N., & Kelman, H. C. (1994). Promoting joint thinking in international conflicts: An Israeli–Palestinian continuing workshop. *Journal of Social Issues, 50,* 157–178.

Schaller, M. (1994). The role of statistical reasoning in the formation, preservation and prevention of group stereotypes. *British Journal of Social Psychology, 33,* 47–61.

Schaller, M., & O'Brien, M. (1992). "Intuitive analysis of covariance" and group stereotype formation. *Personality and Social Psychology Bulletin, 18,* 776–785.

Schuman, H., Steeh, C., & Bobo, L. (1985). *Racial attitudes in America: Trends and interpretations.* Cambridge, MA: Harvard University Press.

Segal, D. R., Gade, P. A., & Johnson, E. M. (1993). Homosexuals in Western armed forces. *Society, 31,* 37–42.

Spence, J. T., Helmreich, R. L., & Holahan, C. K. (1979). Negative and positive components of psychological masculinity and femininity and their relationships to self-reports of neurotic and acting out behaviors. *Journal of Personality and Social Psychology, 37,* 1673–1682.

Suedfeld, P., & Tetlock, P. (1977). Integrative complexity of communications in international crises. *Journal of Conflict Resolution, 21,* 169–184.

Swim, J., Borgida, E., Maruyama, G., & Myers, D. G. (1989). Joan McKay versus John McKay: Do gender stereotypes bias evaluations? *Psychological Bulletin, 105,* 409–429.

Swim, J. K. (1994). Perceived versus meta-analytic effect sizes: An assessment of the accuracy of gender stereotypes. *Journal of Personality and Social Psychology, 66,* 21–36.

Swim, J. K., Hyers, L. L., Cohen, L. L., & Ferguson, M. J. (2001). Everyday sexism: Evidence for its incidence, nature, and psychological impact from three daily diary studies. *Journal of Social Issues, 57,* 31–53.

United Nations. (2001). *World population prospects: The 2000 revision.* New York: United Nations.

Williams, J. E., & Best, D. L. (1990). *Measuring sex stereotypes: A multination study.* Newbury Park, CA: Sage.

Willie, C. V. (1975). *Oreo: A perspective on race and marginal men and women.* Wakefield, MA: Parameter Press.

Wilson, T. D., & Hodges, S. D. (1992). Attitudes as temporary constructions. In A. Tesser & L. Martin (Eds.), *The construction of social judgment* (pp. 37–65). Hillsdale, NJ: Erlbaum.

Wood, W., & Eagly, A. H. (2002). A cross-cultural analysis of the social roles of women and men: Implications for the origins of sex differences. *Psychological Bulletin, 128,* 699–727.

4

Identification as a Challenge to Dual-Process Theories of Persuasion

V. Lee Hamilton

How shall social psychologists understand the relationship between Kelman's three processes of social influence and dual-process theories of persuasion? This chapter addresses theoretical differences between Kelman's (1958) three processes and the more recent dual-process theories, focusing mainly on the elaboration likelihood model (ELM) of Petty and his colleagues (Petty & Cacioppo, 1981; Petty & Wegener, 1998, 1999). The chapter begins with an overview of the theoretical constructs, turns to a discussion of applications of Kelman's theory, and finally returns to an overview of what has been learned. Throughout, I emphasize one of Kelman's processes—identification—as providing a particularly interesting contrast to dual processing models.

Contrasting the Models

In addressing the relationship—and potential conflict—between the Kelman and dual-process approaches, we must first specify the scope of the theories (Figure 4.1). Kelman's theory pertains to *social influence,* whereby an influencing agent can affect a target either by producing attitude change, which in turn leads to behavior change, or by producing behavior change directly. Dual-process theories, in contrast, refer to *persuasion.* (See, for example, the compendium of these theories gathered by Chaikin & Trope, 1999.) This means that a dual-process theory focuses on attitude change, which may (or may not) lead to behavior change. Viewed from Kelman's perspective, persuasion is a subtype of social influence. Having situated Kelman's three processes within the social influence tradition, we next distinguish among them. In the next subsection I define and discuss Kelman's three processes of social influence: compliance, identification, and internalization. I suggest that part of the difference between the three-process theory and its dual-process competitors lies in the complexity of one of his three processes, identification.

Defining the Three Processes

Kelman's theory has been relatively stable across the decades since he introduced the three processes (see his landmark 1958 and 1961 articles). Somewhat

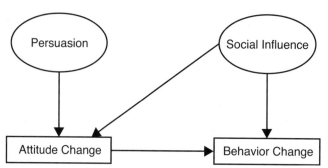

Figure 4.1.   Scope of Kelman's versus dual-process theory: relationship to persuasion and attitude change.

shortened definitions of the processes were provided in a 1963 article and reiterated in a 1974 chapter. In this chapter I use 1961 as the key date for the establishment of Kelman's theory and 1963 for the particular definitions, as cited here:

1. *Compliance* can be said to occur when an individual accepts influence from another person or from a group to attain a favorable reaction from the other, that is, to gain a specific reward or avoid a specific punishment controlled by the other, or to gain approval or avoid disapproval from him.
2. *Identification* can be said to occur when an individual accepts influence from another person or a group to maintain a satisfying self-defining relationship to the other. In contrast to compliance, identification is not primarily concerned with producing a particular effect in the other. Rather, accepting influence through identification is a way of establishing or maintaining a desired relationship to the other, as well as the self-definition that is anchored in this relationship. By accepting influence, the person is able to see himself as similar to the other (as in classical identification) or to see himself as enacting a role reciprocal to that of the other.
3. Finally, *internalization* can be said to occur when an individual accepts influence to maintain the congruence of his actions and beliefs with his value system. Here it is the content of the induced behavior and its relation to the person's value system that are intrinsically satisfying. (Kelman, 1963, p. 400, italics added)

Reading over or hearing these definitions gives an impression that a word count confirms: Identification takes decidedly more words to define. The tallies are 53 words for compliance, 107 words for identification, and 48 words for internalization. I suggest that the sheer length of a definition is one indicator of complexity[1] and hence that something about identification is more complex, harder to define, and tougher to pin down than the other processes of influence. Part of the goal of this chapter is to gain a better sense of what makes identification different.

---

[1]The question of what complexity itself means is, of course, a subject of much modern debate. In this context the larger number of words may be said to reflect the assumption that identification extends into a number of intra- and interpersonal realms, involving both short- and long-term patterns of linkage (a view of complexity elaborated by Nicolis & Prigogene, 1989).

Dual-Process Theories

The recent appearance of a massive collection of extant dual-process theories and related writings edited by Chaikin and Trope (1999) is in itself an indication of the influence currently exercised by these theories within social psychology. Here I concentrate on one of the earliest, and best known, of such theories: the elaboration likelihood model (e.g., Petty & Cacioppo, 1981; Petty & Wegener, 1999). Subsequently I suggest ways in which this model may be the most sharply differentiated from Kelman's three processes of the major dual-process approaches.

The ELM is a theory of persuasion—that is, persuasion leading to attitude change. Its major interest lies in the pathways by which attitude change occurs. According to the ELM, attitudes may change via either *central* or *peripheral* processes. "Central-route attitude changes are those that are based on relatively extensive and effortful information-processing activity. . . . Peripheral-route attitude changes are based on a variety of attitude change processes that typically require less cognitive effort" (Petty & Wegener, 1999, p. 43). To cast these definitions in terms of salient examples: The attitude change that occurs after the introduction of attitude-discrepant information is effortful, involving concentration, and occurring via the central route; in contrast, the attitude change that occurs as a result of picking up cues about a source's attractiveness tends to involve relatively incidental pickup—that is, be peripheral in its route. According to the ELM, a single continuum of attitude change processing exists, whereby at one end of the continuum processing is purely central and at the other it is purely peripheral. A single motive is proposed to drive attitude change: the impulse to have a *correct* attitude, one characterized by accuracy. In the context of attitudes, as Festinger (1954) noted long ago, the search for accuracy is a matter of consensus since there is no objective standard of comparison.

This approach to attitude change is compatible with recent developments in cognitive neuropsychology. For example, Smith and DeCoster (1999, 2000) have proposed that both "fast-learning" and "slow-learning" memory systems are necessary to the human organism. The fast-learning system enables the "rapid learning of new information so that a novel experience can be remembered after a single occurrence" (Smith & DeCoster, 2000, p. 109). The slow-learning system records information "slowly and incrementally" and "matches the typical properties assumed for schema" (Smith & DeCoster, 2000, p. 109). What they term the *associative processing mode* entails retrieval from the slow-learning system, whereas what they term *rule-based processing* is present in both systems; it "uses symbolically represented and intentionally accessed knowledge as rules to guide processing" (Smith & DeCoster, 2000, p. 111). The relevance to the current discussion is the fact that social psychologists are finally discussing underlying physical structures and systems of operation of the brain that might be associated with the ELM's central processes (i.e., Smith and DeCoster's associative processing) and peripheral processes (i.e., some of Smith and DeCoster's rule-based processing). In this development the beginnings of a convergence between the neurological end of cognitive psychology and the cognitive end of social psychology can be seen.

To sum up, the ELM—with its single continuum from central to peripheral, a single motive of correctness, and links to cognitive neuropsychology—

can be contrasted with Kelman's three processes—which stand as qualitatively different, indeed definable in terms of differences in their motives and goals. Thus how can the potential linkages between the ELM and Kelman's processes be conceptualized? Some possible links between the two schemes appear in Figure 4.2. First, it is not clear that compliance is related to either central or peripheral processes, given that it refers to behavior change that may or may not include attitude change. Compliance is an aspect of social influence, not of persuasion per se. Hence, compliance has no necessary link to either central or peripheral processes. Second, Petty and Wegener (1999) explicitly categorize identification as involving peripheral processes. I will return to that assertion later in further analyzing the concept of identification. Finally, internalization as defined by Kelman would appear to involve central processes, predominantly if not entirely. To further elucidate these relationships, I next evaluate how the recent dual-processing literature treats Kelman's three processes; I also take an applied, experiential look at identification. The ultimate question is whether three processes are needed and, if so, for what?

Wood's Resolution of the Debate

Recently, Wood (2000) has written an ambitious, integrative overview of the attitude change and social influence literature. In it she boldly denied the existence of a conflict between Kelman's theory and dual-processing (or other recent) approaches by arguing that no particular mode of processing is necessarily associated with any particular motive or goal. If true, and some recent experimental work suggests that it is the case (e.g., Chen, Schechter, & Chaikin, 1996), this would eradicate those arrows in Figure 4.2 that associated internalization with central processes and identification with peripheral ones.

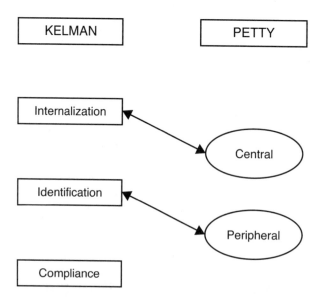

Figure 4.2. Kelman versus ELM: key theoretical constructs and their links.

More important, Wood asserted that numerous theories *call for or require multiple motives*, which she referred to as *normative concerns*. She specified three normative concerns underlying attitude change:

> Attitude change . . . can be motivated by normative concerns for (a) ensuring the coherence and favorable evaluation of the self, and (b) ensuring satisfactory relations with others given the rewards/punishments they can provide, along with an informational concern for (c) understanding the entity or issue featured in influence appeals. (p. 541)

Wood argued that Kelman's three processes and other modern theories of the motives for attitude change converge on a tripartite motive structure (see also Johnson & Eagly's, 1989, meta-analysis of types of involvement). The theories that she saw as paralleling Kelman's include those of Chaikin, Giner-Sorolla, and Chen (1996; see also Chen & Chaikin, 1999); Cialdini and Trost (1998); and Wood's own theory (1999). I have taken Wood's (2000, p. 541) lists of recent sources and concepts and arranged them in tabular form in Table 4.1. Wood's (2000) distinctions appear at the top. The other three theories are then summarized, beginning with Kelman's (1961). I work across the columns from left to right: In Kelman's case, this represents the motives of compliance, identification, and internalization.

Kelman's notion of compliance seems to have both more and less to it than Wood's (2000) idea of "ensuring the coherence and favorable evaluation of the self" (p. 541). It has more in the sense that compliance directly implicates behavior. Furthermore, its motives are rather flexible, restricted only to the extent that they need to be concerned with the seeking of reward and the avoidance of punishment. Compliance need not be connected to the evaluation of the self. Conversely, Kelman's notion of compliance has less to it—that is, it is relatively weak—insofar as links to self-concept and its maintenance are theoretically desirable. Overall, looking down the first column of Table 4.1, each theorist's first motive for persuasion or influence involves concerns with self-defense and impression maintenance *except* Kelman's. And compliance is not always restricted to the first column. For example, in Cialdini and Trost's (1998) discussion, compliance is explicitly viewed as the outgrowth of each—and any—of their three "goals" listed in Table 4.1. One can comply so as to "manage self-concept," "build and maintain social relationships," or "behave effectively." Although their theory is attentive to the notion of compliance and is tripartite in its motivational concerns, there is no straightforward match with Kelman's approach. All the theories may have three aspects or parts, but, at least on this first examination, they do not seem to be the *same* parts.

Probably the closest match among concepts occurs in the middle column of motives. Thus, we see in Table 4.1 that identification parallels Wood's (2000) "ensuring satisfactory relations with others" as well as Chaikin et al.'s (1996) impression-related motives, and Cialdini and Trost's (1998) motive to "build and maintain relationships." Not surprisingly, given the complexity already observed in the definition of Kelman's identification, the other theories' constructs lack some of its elements; they are devoid of the emphasis on the relationship between the parties, and they tend to emphasize the instrumental nature of the act.

Table 4.1. Multiple Theoretical Approaches to Motives for Attitude Change

Author	Process or motive		
Wood (2000)	(a) Coherence and favorable evaluation of the self	(b) Ensuring satisfactory relations with others	(c) Understanding the entity or issue
Kelman (1961)	Compliance	Identification	Internalization
Chaikin et al. (1996)	Ego defensive (to achieve a valued coherent self-identity)	Impression-related (to convey a particular impression)	Validity-seeking (to accurately assess reality)
Cialdini & Trost (1998)	Manage self-concept	Build and maintain relationships	Act effectively

Note. Created from material in "Attitude Change: Persuasion and Social Influence," by W. Wood, 2000, *Annual Review of Psychology,* 51, pp. 539–570.

Finally, turning to the third column, internalization in Kelman's scheme does not necessarily parallel the overarching category of "understanding the entity or issue" introduced by Wood (2000, p. 541). Certainly, Wood's concept of seeking understanding is subsumed by internalization, but the reverse is not the case. Kelman's internalization often refers to values and morals, as well as information and its accuracy. Chaiken et al.'s (1996) theory closely parallels Wood's theory. Cialdini and Trost's (1998) "act effectively" incorporates some of the other theories' emphasis on accuracy, but it is explicitly one of the motives for compliance. Nowhere in Table 4.1 is there a direct parallel to internalization. Internalization contains a broader normative palette than sheer information, and it is anything but a motive for compliance.

The one thing that is certain from Wood's (2000) discussion is that Kelman is in no way isolated from dual-process or other modern theorists. Instead, it is simply not yet clear how and why his concepts link up with theirs. What is also clear, by omission, is that the ELM stands distinct from most of the other dual-process approaches in its reliance on a single motive for attitude change.

Complexity of Identification

To illustrate some of the complexity and richness of the identification concept, I have chosen to provide examples from my own research in field settings and from my experiences with Herbert Kelman. I think the latter is particularly appropriate in discussing a concept whose meaning lies in the relationship between the influencing agent and the influence, especially when the influencing agent in question is the subject of a *Festschrift*.

Identification Among Japanese Schoolchildren

A first example of identification in field settings comes from a research project with Phyllis Blumenfeld, an educational psychologist from the University of

Michigan, and Japanese colleagues Hiroshi Akoh and Kanae Miura of Chiba University. Our topic was how children learn the rules in school. We sampled fifth-grade classrooms: 10 Japanese, 9 American. The N was 184 American and 399 Japanese children, reflecting the typical class size difference between the countries. It was a multimethod study, including observations of teachers and of students, plus experimentally varied questionnaires with children. Details of the material provided here appear in Hamilton, Blumenfeld, Akoh, and Miura (1989).

We asked half of the children "why you think you would follow/not follow" the classroom norms (e.g., do well on a test, study hard). Half were asked why they "would feel good/bad" when they did. The results showed that Japanese children were more internal in their reasons for acting than the Americans. At the same time, especially in their reasons for their feelings, they focused on authorities (teacher, parents) much more. For example, nearly 30% of Japanese children's reasons for their academic performance (*actions*) concerned authority. (*Authority* codes excluded punishment per se. This category meant things like "So my mother will be happy.") Forty percent of their reasons for their *feelings* in this area concerned authority. In no area of classroom life did American children's mention of authority exceed 15% of the total. These results support the role of identification in the shaping of Japanese citizens proposed by some important scholars of Japanese culture (e.g., Doi, 1973; Rohlen, 1989): In their view, identification is a tool used to promote internalization of the rules in schools. Similarly, it appears from our data that Japanese schools purposely harness identification in the service of internalization more than American schools do, at least in the elementary school years.

Note that here we see two phases, or usages, of *internalization*. One needs to *internalize* preferences and values developmentally before one can respond to a social influence attempt via *internalization*. It is internalization in the latter sense—that is, after early socialization has imparted values and attitudes—to which Kelman's theory refers.

Identification Among Russian Army Officers

The next example comes from research in a very different venue: Russian Army officers experiencing downsizing. I have been working with Americans (Robert Caplan, Richard Price, David Segal, Mady Segal, and Amiram Vinokur) and Russians (Gennady Denisovsky, Polina Kozyreva, and the late Mikhail Matskovsky) in this effort.

We adopted a quasi-experimental design in which approximately half of the original sample of officers were slated to lose their jobs within 3 to 6 months. We administered to both officers and their wives an omnibus survey such as that used in American unemployment surveys: first in late 1995, and again 18 months later in 1997. The initial sample consisted of 1,798 officers and 1,609 wives. The N for the second survey was 1,525 officers and 1,490 wives.

In this case the target variable that I see as exemplifying identification is one that is common in studies of business and management: organizational commitment. The items were an abbreviated version of the widely used scale by

Porter, Steers, Mowday, and Boulian (1974), adapted to the army context. As translated back from the Russian, these items were the following: "I am willing to work hard to help the Army fulfill its mission," "I feel very little loyalty to the Army" (reverse scored), "I am proud of serving in the Army," and "I would refuse a higher paying job to remain in the Army." Although short, this four-item scale was adequately reliable (alpha = 0.75).

Theoretically speaking, organizational commitment can be seen as playing a dual role. Recent literature on the justice of downsizing, particularly procedural justice, often adopts organizational commitment as a dependent variable. Procedural injustice in general refers to the extent to which the *process,* rather than the *outcome,* of a decision has been unfair (Lind & Tyler, 1988; Tyler & Lind, 1992, 2001). These process violations include, but are not limited to, such acts as failure to provide the disputant a voice in the decision, failure to apply the rules neutrally, and failure to treat the disputant with respect. A sense that a downsizing event has been unjust is associated with—and presumably causes—a loss of organizational commitment. In turn, I would argue, this indicates a reduced identification with the organization. This relationship is depicted in the top half of Figure 4.3. At the same time, commitment can play a role in shaping one's sense of justice and injustice. As the bottom half of Figure 4.3 shows, a person who is more identified with (committed to) the organization is likely to perceive its actions as more just.

This link between organizational commitment and perceived justice has been explored in two papers (Hamilton, 2000, 2001). As of Wave 1 of the study, officers who were leaving had significantly lower organizational commitment (OC) than those who were staying. A particular variant of justice—interpersonal justice—was significantly linked to OC. Interpersonal justice refers to the manner in which a person is treated, independent of the rules or rewards being administered. For example, the belief that the officer was being treated with respect was a particularly powerful aspect of interpersonal justice for Russian officers. In addition, interpersonal justice interacted with leaver status: The effect of interpersonal justice on OC was stronger (about double) among leavers than among stayers. (This finding also implies an interaction of OC with leaver status in predicting interpersonal justice, if we reverse the arrows.) These results suggest, therefore, that the true relationship between justice percep-

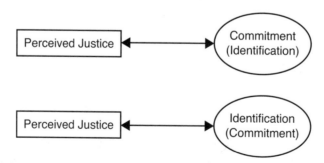

Figure 4.3.   Identification as independent and dependent variable in relation to procedural justice.

tions and organizational commitment (identification) is more complex than Figure 4.3 would have it. In terms of Kelman's three processes, identification is a cause of perceived justice, an effect of perceived justice, and an intertwined interactive force that both shapes the impact of downsizing on the sense of justice and is in turn shaped by that sense of justice.

Identification with Herbert Kelman

To further illustrate the richness and complexity of the notion of identification, consider the reaction that Herbert Kelman's students have to him. First consider the photo of Herb at the front of this book. At the *Festschrift* conference, I showed this photo as part of my paper presentation. Kelman's former students invariably reacted to it with smiles; their identification was a happy one. Now consider Figure 4.4. This photo invariably reminds me of Herb, although not symmetrically: Figure 4.4 always reminds me of Herb's photo, but not the reverse. What is it about memory, and about the reach and power of identification, that produces this linkage?

First, we need to know what Figure 4.4 *is*. It is the entrance to the memorial park and museum in My Lai, Vietnam, photographed in February 2000. At the time, I was teaching at Chinese University in Hong Kong, and our "spring break" was Chinese New Year. The Vietnamese, who also celebrate this holiday, call it Tet. I took the opportunity to go to Vietnam for a week with my husband. After quite a bit of maneuvering and arranging, we managed to get a ride to My Lai on the eve of Tet.

Figure 4.4.   Memorial park and museum at My Lai, Vietnam, in February 2000.

So what is the linkage to Herbert Kelman? It is multifaceted, suggesting to me the richness of identification as a concept. There are not just linkages, but *layers* of linkages involved. First, Herb and I wrote the book *Crimes of Obedience* (1989) in part about, and in reaction to, the 1968 My Lai massacre. One might say I am classically conditioned to link the two concepts of Kelman and My Lai— in ELM terminology, I peripherally connect the two. But identification is more than pure periphery. It is also the case that I looked forward to bringing back photos of My Lai to show Herb and his wife, Rose, and to talking with them about the trip. In terms of identification, one might say I wanted to please them. And as my Japanese research suggests, I believe that identification also links up with internalization. Herb's own prior behavior was an inspiration, as when he was brought to his first meeting with Arafat in the middle of the night in war-torn Beirut decades ago (Kelman, 1983). I remember sitting in the back of the car that was lurching over dirt roads for the four-hour trip to My Lai saying to myself, "If Herb Kelman can meet with Arafat in the middle of the night I can last through a trip on a dirt road to get to My Lai." Identification inspires emulation. I believe that, over time, it also fosters internalization. After all, what I am describing is choosing to visit a massacre site on my vacation, more than 30 years after first meeting Herbert Kelman. I do not believe that purely peripheral processes could produce such effects.

Conclusion

It is time to take stock of what is known and understood about Kelman's three processes and their role in the literature on social influence. This makes me feel a bit like Gertrude Stein who, on her deathbed, asked "What is the answer?" And then asked, thoughtfully, "What is the question?" Perhaps the most important thing to do here is to phrase the question appropriately, because the three processes appear to be answering a different question, or set of questions, from at least some of the dual-process models. Kelman's is a model of social influence, with or without stable attitude change. Indeed, that flexible relation to attitude change is part of the point of the theory.

More specifically, Kelman's approach is a model of motives for behavior change in the face of social influence. The ELM is a model of persuasion and is more closely linked to cognitive processes and memory. It is about attitudes and their accuracy. Kelman's three processes are inherently multimotive (self-interest, connection of the self to another, and the self's values). The ELM is single motive. Thus, it is probably more accurate to say that Kelman's three processes answer different questions from the dual-process models, at least from the ELM. Wood's (2000) recent integrative review suggests that multiple parallels may exist between the three processes and the dual-process school of thought and that motives are precisely the arena of overlap. The contribution that is offered by the three processes involves the extent to which they are dynamic, exciting, and reflective of the processing that goes on in real people. Among Herbert Kelman's three processes, identification stands out as the most complex and potentially most interesting. As an invitation to future research, let me try to summarize the aspects that make identification complex:

1. It addresses social influence at a more affective level than the other processes, perhaps because by definition it involves an emotional tie to another human being. One party wishes to cement a relationship to another.
2. Its effects can be long lasting, probably because of links to internalization, as I have illustrated in my own case.
3. As a result, I earlier facetiously observed that identification takes the largest number of words to define among Kelman's three processes. In this case the number of words is a spurious indicator. Identification is more complex than the other processes, and it takes more words to define; but what both of these things flow from is the fact that identification is more *layered* than the other concepts. It draws together the affective and the cognitive, and it occurs both of its own accord and in the service of another process, internalization. When one has defined *identification,* one has said a great deal.

Having said this much about identification as a concept, let me close by suggesting some future directions for its study. One important set of links to social cognition that remains to be made is the relationship between Kelman's identification and social identity theories (e.g., Brewer & Feinstein, 1999; Tajfel, 1981; Turner, 1987). Social identity theorists have convincingly demonstrated the existence and strength of group-based identities. Yet we know relatively little about what triggers processing in terms of the group rather than the individual identity. It is certainly plausible that identification in Kelman's sense—identification as a motive for acceding to social influence—underlies much of the affective strength of identities as studied by social identity theorists. The study of this link would enable us to come full circle from Herb Kelman's early theoretical contributions to social psychology—his three processes—to his later career in the pursuit of peace.

Research summarized in this paper was supported by National Science Foundation grants SES-8410680, SBR-9402212, SBR-9411755, and SBR-9601760.

References

Brewer, M., & Feinstein, A. S. H. (1999). Dual processes in the cognitive representation of persons and social categories. In S. Chaikin & Y. Trope (Eds.), *Dual-process theories in social psychology* (pp. 255–270). New York: Guilford Press.

Chaikin, S., Giner-Sorolla, R., & Chen, S. (1996). Beyond accuracy: Defense and impression motives in heuristic and systematic information processing. In P. M. Gollwitzer & J. A. Bargh (Eds.), *The psychology of action* (pp. 553–578). New York: Guilford Press.

Chaikin, S., & Trope, Y. (1999). *Dual-process theories in social psychology.* New York: Guilford Press.

Chen, S., & Chaikin, S. (1999). The heuristic-systematic model in its broader context. In S. Chaikin & Y. Trope (Eds.), *Dual-process theories in social psychology* (pp. 73–96). New York: Guilford Press.

Chen, S., Schechter, D., & Chaikin, S. (1996). Getting at the truth or getting along: Accuracy vs. impression-motivated heuristic and systematic information processing. *Journal of Personality and Social Psychology, 71,* 262–275.

Cialdini, R. B., & Trost, M. R. (1998). Social influence: Social norms, conformity, and compliance. In D. T. Gilbert, S. T. Fiske, & G. Lindzey (Eds.), *The handbook of social psychology* (Vol. 2, pp. 151–192). Boston: McGraw-Hill.

Doi, T. (1973). *The anatomy of dependence*. New York: Kodansha.

Festinger, L. (1954). A theory of social comparison processes. *Human Relations, 7*, 117–140.

Hamilton, V. L. (2000). (In)justice in waiting: Russian officers' organizational commitment and mental distress during downsizing. *Journal of Applied Social Psychology, 30*, 1995–2027.

Hamilton, V. L. (2001). Exit ethics: The management of downsizing among the Russian officer corps. In J. Darley, D. Messick, & T. Tyler (Eds.), *Social influences on ethical behavior in organizations* (pp. 89–115). Mahwah, NJ: Erlbaum.

Hamilton, V. L., Blumenfeld, P., Akoh, H., & Miura, K. (1989). Japanese and American children's reasons for the things they do in school. *American Educational Research Journal, 26*, 545–571.

Johnson, B. T., & Eagly, A. H. (1989). The effects of involvement on persuasion: A meta-analysis. *Psychological Bulletin, 106*, 290–314.

Kelman, H. C. (1958). Compliance, identification, and internalization: Three processes of attitude change. *Journal of Conflict Resolution, 2*, 51–60.

Kelman, H. C. (1961). Processes of opinion change. *Public Opinion Quarterly, 25*, 57–78.

Kelman, H. C. (1963). The role of the group in the induction of therapeutic change. *International Journal of Group Psychotherapy, 13*, 399–432.

Kelman, H. C. (1974). Social influence and linkages between the individual and the social system: Further thoughts on the processes of compliance, identification, and internalization. In J. T. Tedeschi (Ed.), *Perspectives on social power* (pp. 125–171). Chicago: Aldine.

Kelman, H. C. (1983). Conversations with Arafat. *American Psychologist, 38*, 203–216.

Kelman, H. C., & Hamilton, V. L. (1989). *Crimes of obedience: Toward a social psychology of authority and responsibility*. New Haven, CT: Yale University Press.

Lind, E. A., & Tyler, T. R. (1988). *The social psychology of procedural justice*. New York: Plenum Press.

Nicolis, B., & Prigogene, I. (1989). *Exploring complexity: An introduction*. New York: Freeman.

Petty, R., & Cacioppo, J. (1981). *Attitudes and persuasion: Classic and contemporary approaches*. Dubuque, IA: William C. Brown Communications.

Petty, R., & Wegener, D. (1998). Attitude change: Multiple roles for persuasion variables. In D. T. Gilbert, S. T. Fiske, & G. Lindzey (Eds.), *The handbook of social psychology* (Vol. 1, pp. 323–390). Boston: McGraw-Hill.

Petty, R., & Wegener, D. (1999). The elaboration likelihood model: Current status and controversies. In S. Chaikin & Y. Trope (Eds.), *Dual-process theories in social psychology* (pp. 41–72). New York: Guilford Press.

Porter, L. W., Steers, R. M., Mowday, R. T., & Boulian, P. V. (1974). Organizational commitment, job satisfaction and turnover among psychiatric technicians. *Journal of Applied Psychology, 59*, 603–609.

Rohlen, T. P. (1989). Order in Japanese society: Attachment, authority, and routine. *Journal of Japanese Studies, 15*, 5–40.

Smith, E., & DeCoster, J. (1999). Associative and rule-based processing: A connectionist interpretation of dual-process models. In S. Chaikin & Y. Trope (Eds.), *Dual-process theories in social psychology* (pp. 323–336). New York: Guilford Press.

Smith, E., & DeCoster, J. (2000). Dual-process models in social and cognitive psychology: Conceptual integration and links to underlying memory systems. *Personality and Social Psychology Review, 4*, 108–131.

Tajfel, H. (1981). *Human groups and social categories*. London: Cambridge University Press.

Turner, J. C. (1987). *Rediscovering the social group*. New York: Basil Blackwell.

Tyler, T. R., & Lind, E. A. (1992). A relational model of authority in groups. In M. Zanna (Ed.), *Advances in experimental social psychology* (Vol. 25, pp. 115–191). New York: Academic Press.

Tyler, T. R., & Lind, E. A. (2001). Procedural justice. In J. Sanders & V. L. Hamilton (Eds.), *Handbook of justice research in law* (pp. 65–92). New York: Kluwer Academic/Plenum Publishers.

Wood, W. (1999). Motives and modes of processing in the social influence of groups. In S. Chaikin & Y. Trope (Eds.), *Dual-process theories in social psychology* (pp. 547–570). New York: Guilford Press.

Wood, W. (2000). Attitude change: Persuasion and social influence. *Annual Review of Psychology, 51*, 539–570.

Comments on Chapters 3 and 4

Erin Driver-Linn

We experience daily showers of influential information bent on persuading us to ends we desire and ends we do not, and these showers saturate us in profound and superficial ways. Inevitable conflicts arise from differences between our private attitudes and those that are socially prescribed. Such conflicts can range from the "growing pains" of change even when we want to be influenced, to the identity challenges involved when unwanted influence is accepted. The psychological negotiation of the conflicts arising from differences between privately held beliefs and external pressures seems thematic to much, if not all, of Professor Kelman's work. Alice Eagly's "Prejudice: Toward a More Inclusive Understanding" (see chap. 3, this volume) and Lee Hamilton's "Identification as a Challenge to Dual-Process Theories of Persuasion" (see chap. 4, this volume) address particular mechanisms involved in conflicts between individual attitudes and social influence. In addressing the mechanisms of this "negotiation process" in their work, both authors reveal what seems to me to be a noble intellectual lineage and inheritance.

Eagly argues for an expanded definition of prejudice, one that emphasizes social roles. She suggests that prejudice arises from the interaction between the consensual beliefs that people hold about a social group and the opportunity structure of a society. More specifically, if there is a mismatch between a stereotype and the requirement of a role, potential prejudice is more likely. This highlights the fundamentally shifting nature of social roles and, in doing so, the fundamentally unstable nature of individual attitudes. In Eagly's "social roles" argument, it is both the targets of prejudice and those who hold prejudicial stereotypes that experience the pressure of external influence acting on privately held beliefs. She concludes that the experience of a mismatch of stereotype and social role, in the context of "opportunity structures" or where social roles have rewards associated with them, is inherently negative or threatening. And it is only when there is stability of stereotypes and social roles—when all roles are prescribed and unchanging—that prejudice will not be activated. In short, changing roles mean changing attitudes, and changing attitudes mean at least temporary instability.

It seems, though, that at least in practice, there are different degrees of instability and different time courses for ensuing social change. For instance, Eagly mentions "ethnic cleansing"—a violent attempt to change social roles. Such violent displacements seem different from other, slower sorts of displacements, such as the experience of African Americans in North America. This raises two questions. First, do these represent different time courses of the same process or two different processes? Second, will fast displacements versus slow displacements result in different degrees of attitude change permanency?

Kelman's work addresses these questions remarkably (although not surprisingly) well. His theory of social influence (1958) suggests that there are in fact qualitatively different processes by which attitude change occurs and, furthermore, that these different processes result in different outcomes. It may be too simplistic to map violent displacements onto compliance-based or identification-based attitude change and slower displacements onto internalization-based attitude change, but to me this seems an intuitively compelling hypothesis.

Hamilton discusses a different mapping of Kelman's (1958) three-process model of influence. She examines the degree to which his three-process model maps onto more current dual-process models of persuasion (specifically, the elaboration likelihood model of Petty & Cacioppo, 1986). In recognizing that these maps are not isomorphic (three and two are not the same, after all, in spite of the ambitious parallels drawn by the cited Wood, 2000), Hamilton disentangles the differences and similarities between these models. She argues that Kelman described an additional, important process of influence—identification—and delineated all of his processes in a more multifaceted manner.

Both the two- and three-process models of influence represent classification schemes for the mechanisms involved when external influences act on privately held attitudes toward changing those attitudes. Hamilton uses several examples from her own work to demonstrate the complexity of identification as a process of influence. In one of these examples, Japanese schoolchildren accept influence through identification with their teachers and parents. In another example, Russian officers accept influence through identification with an organization—the army. Again, this raises a couple of questions related to whether structural differences in the sources of influence result in identifiable differences in the life course of the attitude change that takes place. First, are the effects of identification, in terms of attitude and behavior change, going to be different when a person identifies with a particular individual (such as a teacher or a parent) as opposed to an institution (such as the army)? Second, if so, will the process of change be experienced differently, and will the effects of change have a longer life course (it seems easier to desert the army than to desert one's parents)? Again, Kelman's work provides a cogent answer. He articulated with specificity the process and life course of identification-based attitude change, like the other processes, and this specificity suggests that the life course of attitude change will vary meaningfully as a function of the influencing agent.

These two papers address quite different topics—on one hand, the definition of prejudice, and on the other hand, the overlap of two models of influence. They also address these topics in quite different ways—an expansive and inductively reasoned approach and a humorous, directly comparative approach. They share with one another, however, the aforementioned focus on the mechanisms involved in individuals changing their attitudes as a result of external, social forces—a focus that may be viewed as an inheritance from Professor Kelman. The differences and the common spirit in these two chapters speak to the breadth and focus embodied in Professor Kelman's work. I have known him long enough to recognize and admire his exceptionally great memory, easy laugh, earnest and generous valuations of the world, and rigorous analyses. Thus, it is no surprise that the questions these papers raised for me found their answers in him and his work.

References

Kelman, H. C. (1958). Compliance, identification, and internalization: Three processes of attitude change. *Journal of Conflict Resolution, 2,* 51–60.

Petty, R. E., & Cacioppo, J. T. (1986). *Communication and persuasion: Central and peripheral routes to attitude change.* New York: Springer-Verlag.

Wood, W. (2000). Attitude change: Persuasion and social influence. *Annual Review of Psychology, 50,* 539–570.

Part II

Applications of Social Psychology

5

Rigor and Vigor: Spanning Basic and Applied Research

Nancy E. Adler

In *A Time to Speak,* Herb Kelman (1968) described the tension between "rigor" versus "vigor" within science in general and within social psychology more specifically. He presented the strengths and limitations of each approach and argued that both are needed for social scientists to achieve a complete and systematic understanding of social behavior. Few researchers have been able to incorporate both rigor and vigor into their work as well as has Herb Kelman. His research has involved methodologies ranging from experimental studies to surveys to interventions. This work has been designed to address both basic questions regarding human behavior and applied issues of social concern. In this chapter, I hope to demonstrate how his interest in basic processes in social interaction spawned research that not only informs theory, but also addresses important social problems. This legacy can be seen in my work and in that of many of his students, and it is also reflected in the structure of this volume, which showcases the work that Herb has inspired on theoretical underpinnings, applications of social psychology, and specifically work in the area of conflict resolution.

Kelman's Theory of Responses to Discrepant Action

As a graduate student I felt that I was leading two lives. My academic life was focused on basic theoretical issues in psychology. Outside of my academic work, I was helping a college friend who had established a counseling service for women with unwanted pregnancies. This was in 1970, prior to *Roe v. Wade.* It was illegal to have an abortion in Massachusetts, though legal abortions were available in New York under that state's laws. I was serving as a teaching fellow for Herb and, among other things, teaching about his theory of reactions to discrepant action.

Research on attitude-discrepant behavior had almost universally been conducted to test dissonance theory. This research had demonstrated that when individuals perform an action under conditions of insufficient justification that is contrary to their own beliefs or attitudes, they are likely to change the dissonant beliefs to become more consistent with the action taken (e.g., Brehm &

Cohen, 1962; Festinger & Carlsmith, 1959). Kelman questioned whether all actions would have the same significance to individuals and would result in the same outcomes. He posited that they would not and presented a more elaborate typology of responses to discrepant action (Kelman, 1974). According to that typology, a discrepant action could deviate from societal standards on one of two behavioral dimensions: responsibility or propriety. On either of these dimensions, an action could depart from one of three standards: external rules, role expectations, or values. Kelman predicted specific emotional responses to each of the six resulting types of discrepant action. On the responsibility dimension, the expected emotional response to having taken an action that departs from external rules (compliance based) would be social fear. The response to violating role expectations (identification based) would be guilt, and the response to violating values (internalization based) would be regret. On the dimension of propriety, the comparable predicted reactions to deviant action on the level of rules, roles, and values would be embarrassment, shame, and self-disappointment, respectively.

Not until I began counseling women with unwanted pregnancies did the utility of the model strike me. Many of the women I was counseling experienced abortion as a discrepant action. They were telling me things like "I'm a good Catholic and believe that having an abortion is a sin. Can you tell me where I can have one?" I wondered how these and other women for whom abortion represented a discrepant action would later incorporate and respond to the knowledge that they had terminated their pregnancy. The model presented by Kelman (1974) appeared to be a very appropriate framework for accounting for their responses. Abortion could be discrepant from any of the standards suggested in the theory. Terminating a pregnancy could violate deeply held religious or moral values, a salient role identity (e.g., being a nurse, a mother, or a Catholic), or social norms, particularly because the action might not only engender social disapproval but was also an illegal act in their home state. These are not mutually exclusive, and a woman might be concerned about any or all of these.

Abortion can depart from societal standards in the dimensions of both responsibility and propriety. However, the issues raised most strongly and most frequently about abortion concern the responsibility dimension. Kelman (1974) defined this dimension as involving "actions that cause harm to others or to society in general (e.g., by destroying valuable resources or failing to do productive work)" (p. 153). Many of the moral, theological, and legal arguments about abortion center on harm to the potential child and society's loss of human resources. Although some concerns about abortion reflect issues of propriety as well, the responsibility dimension is far more salient.

The action of having an abortion could potentially deviate from any of the three standards. Take a hypothetical example of a nurse who terminates her pregnancy. At the level of norms she may worry that others in her profession will think less of her if they find out she has had an abortion or (given that abortion was illegal at the time) even that she might lose her job if her abortion were discovered. At the level of identification, she might be concerned that having an abortion violated the expectation that nurses should do whatever they can to preserve life. She might question whether she really is a competent nurse although she performs her duties well. Thus, her anxiety would not derive from concern about what others would think of her as a nurse were they to find out about her action, but about her own evaluation of the adequacy of her fulfillment of this role. At the level of internalization, her concern would be exclusively with the question of taking life. Even though her concern about the value of life may originally have derived from her work or socialization as a nurse, it may have become internalized. If so, her concern would not be about her relationship to her profession; she would still be concerned about taking life even if she were no longer a nurse. A woman could experience the abortion as a discrepant action on any, all, or none of these levels.

Application of Kelman's model of reactions to discrepant action seemed useful as a way to understand the range of responses women could have to abortion. It seemed, equally, a good way to test the theory itself. Although the model was intriguing and built on past research on the three bases of social influence (Kelman, 1958), it had not been empirically tested. Applying it in a real-world setting seemed particularly important in that it provided a more direct, if less controlled, test. Although we might not find as tight a set of results as in the laboratory, the pattern of responses could support or challenge the theory.

Empirical Test of Kelman's Theory

Next I present a brief overview of the findings from testing Kelman's theory in the context of abortion. Not only do these findings illustrate the utility of real-world testing of theory, but they also help me once and for all eliminate a Zeigarnik effect, which has persisted for 28 years. The theoretical part of this research was to appear as a chapter in a book on attitude-discrepant behavior that Herb was editing. However, this was just at the time that he was becoming more involved in conflict resolution, and the book never was published. It is fitting that these data appear as part of his *Festschrift*, and I can now get on with my life.

Behavioral Responses

Based on Kelman's theory of reactions to discrepant action described earlier, I made predictions about behavioral, cognitive, and emotional responses to abortion. Women were recruited and interviewed when they first sought consultation for an unwanted pregnancy, and they were asked to return for a second interview three months after the abortion. At the initial interview they rated the extent to which they were concerned about norms, roles, and values that might conflict with abortion. The compliance-based concern was "whether other people might think less of you or avoid you if they found out that you had an abortion." The identification-based concern was "whether having an abortion is something that a good member of your group (for example, your family, your church, the people you associate with) would do." The internalization-based concern was "whether having an abortion violates your beliefs or values." After rating the extent of her concern about each of the three issues, each woman was then asked to choose the one issue that was of most concern to her about the abortion. The woman's predominant concern about the abortion was taken to be the issue on which rated concern was highest. For those cases in which two or more issues were given equally high ratings, the woman's choice of predominant concern was used, but in some cases no one concern was identified as predominant.

Generally, behavior is the hardest outcome to predict, and in this case there were two relevant behaviors. The first behavior was the act of returning for the follow-up interview. Women who were primarily concerned about norm violation associated with abortion (i.e., those whose concern was compliance based) should be less likely to return for a follow-up interview. Such women would presumably be relatively more concerned about other people finding out about their abortion and disapproving of it. Returning for an interview following the abortion could increase the chances of detection. As a result, I predicted that the women whose predominant concern was compliance based would be more likely to fail to return for the second interview. To test this, women were classified by their predominant concern about abortion beforehand. As can be seen from Table 5.1, the nonreturners were, in fact, more likely to be primarily concerned with compliance. Forty percent of women whose predominant concern was compliance based failed to return for the follow-up interview, compared with 22% of those primarily concerned with issues of internalized values and 10% of those primarily concerned with identification.

A second behavioral indicator was frequency of contact with other people following the abortion. Women concerned about norm violation should be more likely than those not primarily concerned about compliance to try to avoid seeing people who might disapprove of their action, and the degree of avoidance should be greater the more the anticipated disapproval. Avoiding others who are anticipated to disapprove would reduce the possibility that those others would learn about the abortion. Just the opposite prediction would be made for those primarily concerned about identification. Kelman had predicted that individuals concerned with deviation that threatened a role would want to try to reinstate themselves and reestablish their relationship. Given this, it seemed likely that women primarily concerned with identification would increase contact with salient others for whom role relationships might be threatened by the

Table 5.1.   Predominant Concern About Abortion: Returners Versus Nonreturners

Predominant concern	Returners ($n = 69$)	Nonreturners ($n = 25$)
Compliance based	18	12
	(60%)	(40%)
Identification based	9	1
	(90%)	(10%)
Internalization based	42	12
	(78%)	(22%)

Note. $\chi^2 = 4.70$, df $= 2$, $p = .09$. Compliance versus others: $\chi^2 = 4.51$, df $= 1$, $p < .05$.

abortion in order to solidify the role relationship. Thus, for women primarily concerned with identification, there should be greater contact the greater the anticipated disapproval. Internalized concerns, in contrast, should have no impact on behavior one way or the other because this concern is not socially based. Women whose primary concern involved internalization would not be expected to either decrease or increase contact with others.

Prior to the abortion each woman had rated a number of people in terms of how important those people's opinions about abortion were to her and what she thought their opinion would be. Conflict scores were created by multiplying importance by opinion for each person; higher scores indicated greater disapproval by people who were important to the woman. These scores were factor analyzed and formed three factors. One factor consisted of traditional others: neighbors, church members, older people, and clergy. A second consisted of contemporaries: female friend, male friend, and mate. The third was family: father, mother, and relatives. Table 5.2 shows the correlation between the degree of anticipated conflict with members of each group prior to the abortion and the frequency of seeing members of that group following the abortion. The prediction was that for women primarily concerned about compliance, greater conflict would be associated with less frequent contact; that for women primarily concerned about identification, greater conflict would be associated with more frequent contact; and that for women concerned about internalized values, conflict would not affect frequency of contact.

Only two correlations approached or reached statistical significance, and both were in the predicted direction. Conflict was negatively related to contact with traditional others for women primarily concerned about norm violation, whereas conflict was positively related to contact with family for women concerned about identification. These findings suggest that norm violation may have been especially salient in relation to traditional others—particularly clergy and church members. These are also people with whom it may be easier to reduce contact than it would be for family or friends. Role relationships may have been particularly linked to family roles, accounting for the positive correlation between conflict and contact with family members. The numbers of women in each group are small because only some women could be clearly identified in terms of a dominant concern; most of these were concerned with internalized values. However, despite the smaller n for women for whom compliance and identification were the primary concerns, it was in these groups that the

Table 5.2. Correlations Between Conflict and Frequency of Contact for Women Grouped by Predominant Prior Concern

Factors	Predominant prior concern		
	Compliance-based issue ($n = 18$)	Identification-based issue ($n = 11$)	Internalization-based issue ($n = 37$)
Traditional others	−.63**	−.26	.21
Contemporaries	.02	−.32	.05
Family	−.19	.56*	−.09

$* p < .10. ** p < .002.$

correlations were significant. Thus, this pattern of associations is not conclusive but is clearly in the direction predicted by theory.

Emotional Responses

Kelman's model also predicted different emotional responses that should flow from norm, role, or value discrepancy. The predicted compliance-based response, for example, was "worried or nervous that other people would find out that I have had an abortion." I correlated the extent to which the women expressed a prior concern about norms, roles, or values with their endorsement of each response three months postabortion. Because these are not mutually exclusive responses, all women were included for all cells. As shown in Table 5.3, the pattern of responses is not perfectly aligned, but is generally consistent with predictions. The clearest finding is for concern about values; the extent to which women were concerned about value discrepancy before the abortion was significantly correlated only with the internalization-based response. Concern about identification was significantly correlated with the identification-based response, but, though it was weaker, it was also correlated with the compliance-based response. The strength of concern about compliance was correlated with everything and was in fact somewhat higher with the identification-based response than with the compliance-based response.

I also had the women complete ratings of specific emotions, indicating how strongly they had experienced each one following their abortion. Ideally, these would have formed three factors, with emotions associated with compliance, identification, and internalization falling on separate factors, but that was not quite what occurred. Three distinct factors emerged, but they were not perfectly aligned with the three bases of discrepant action. One factor consisted of the two positive emotions: relief and happiness. The negative emotions formed two separate factors. One factor included socially based negative emotions: guilt, shame, and fear of disapproval, which were the emotions predicted for both norm and role violation. The second negative emotion factor reflected more internalized concerns: regret, anxiety, depression, doubt, and anger. Thus, these factors supported a differentiation between internalized responses and socially based responses, but did not show a differentiation between compliance and identification. Correlations between mean emotion scores and the reported concern about norms, roles, and values before the abortion provided some

Table 5.3. Correlations Between Extent of Prior Concern and Strength of Subsequent Response

	Prior concern		
Emotional response	Compliance based	Identification based	Internalization based
Compliance based	.34**	.21*	.15
Identification based	.43**	.38**	.18
Internalization based	.34**	.10	.23*

$*p < .05.$ $**p < .005.$

support that the emotions were reflecting different bases of the discrepancy. As shown in Table 5.4, the strongest correlation was between pre-abortion compliance-based concern and postabortion reports of feelings of shame, guilt, and fear of disapproval. Compliance-based concern was not correlated with either the positive emotions or the internal emotions. The next strongest correlation was between internalization-based concern and the internal emotions, but internalization concern correlated with the social emotions as well. Finally, identification-based concern was related only to the positive emotions.

Although this study was undertaken as a test of theory, over the years it has had substantially more impact in terms of application. Until this study was done, most studies of abortion had been of patients who had sought psychotherapy; clinicians understandably wrote about psychopathology after abortion. They took as their numerator the women they had seen, but they had no sense of the denominator. Though the denominator of women having abortions was actually very large, most clinically based authors did not take this into account. They generalized their findings from a highly self-selected group to all women having abortions. My research represented one of the first studies using a representative sample of women who were undergoing abortion. One of the most striking findings was that the degree of negative emotional response was relatively low. The most strongly felt emotions reported three months after the abortion were the positive emotions; the two negative emotion factors were more weakly endorsed (see Table 5.5). Subsequent studies using representative samples of women following abortion have found the same thing: that positive responses are more strongly experienced following abortion than are negative emotions (e.g., Dagg, 1991; Major et al., 2000; Monsour & Stewart, 1973).

These data have turned out to be important in legal challenges to abortion. Some antiabortion groups promoted the concept of "postabortion trauma syndrome," attempting to limit access to abortion by declaring it a hazard to

Table 5.4. Correlations Between Extent of Prior Concern With Strength of Emotion Factors

	Prior concern		
Emotional factors	Compliance based	Identification based	Internalization based
Positive emotions	−.04	.26*	−.08
Social emotions	.48***	.18	.24**
Internal emotions	.20	−.10	.33**

$* p < .05.$ $** p < .01.$ $*** p < .001.$

Table 5.5. Mean Ratings on Emotions Following Abortion (1–5 Scale)

Emotions	Rating
Positive emotions (relief, happiness)	3.96
Socially based negative emotions (shame, guilt, fear of disapproval)	1.81
Internally based negative emotions (regret, anxiety, depression, doubt, anger)	2.26

women's mental health (e.g., Rue, Speckhard, Rogers, & Franz, 1987). As a result, the psychological effects of abortion became a political and legal issue. In the early 1990s, the American Psychological Association convened an expert panel of psychologists to review the research on the psychological sequelae of abortion. Though there were many articles on abortion, they varied markedly in their scientific merit. When looking only at scientifically valid studies, the results were relatively clear. Data from my sample were consistent with findings from other well-designed studies, showing that abortion posed little hazard to women's mental health. Reports from the expert panel were published in *Science* (Adler et al., 1990) and *American Psychologist* (Adler et al., 1992). In addition, the data have been used in congressional testimony (e.g., Human Resources and Intergovernmental Relations Subcommittee on Government Operations of the U.S. House of Representatives, Washington, D.C., March 16, 1989) and in court cases (e.g., *American Academy of Pediatrics v. Lungren,* 1992; *Planned Parenthood of Central New Jersey v. John J. Farmer, Jr.,* 2000). As one of the relatively few scientifically sound studies of abortion, the findings have had significant social impact despite the fact that the study was designed as a test of theory.

There were other tests of Kelman's theory in my study that I will not detail here, but these were all supportive of the model. The next step in my research, in retrospect, reflects why this presentation is in the "Applications" section of the *Festschrift*. While it is possible for a researcher to have both basic and applied interests, one consideration or the other takes the lead for any given study. For a study whose aim is primarily theoretical, the researcher will search for the right applied situation to test a given hypothesis. In contrast, where the concern is primarily about an applied issue, the researcher starts with the problem and selects a theory that holds promise for improving its understanding. In the former case, one may still contribute to understanding of the problem, and in the latter, one may similarly contribute to improving the theory, but one consideration will take precedence.

Application Requires New Theories

The next step in my research was to follow application rather than theory. Although abortion provided an excellent model for testing reactions to discrepant action, I was troubled by the problem of abortion itself and how to prevent it. I became interested in the question of how the unwanted pregnancy had come about in the first place: Why had these women gotten pregnant and how could these pregnancies have been prevented? In doing this work, a different theoretical perspective was needed. Rational models of choice were being developed which suggested that behaviors followed from a rational evaluation of costs and benefits (Adler, 1979). Could such a rational model account for a seemingly irrational behavior: not using contraception even though you did not want to become pregnant? Even more challenging, could this account for adolescent behavior given that adolescence is generally seen as a life stage where rationality is at low ebb?

Rational Choice Models

Much of my research in the subsequent two decades focused on the application and expansion of rational choice models to adolescent sexual behavior. The first study followed more than 300 sexually active adolescents. The study was designed to test the applicability of the Theory of Reasoned Action, which was at the time a relatively new theory (Fishbein & Ajzen, 1975). I assessed adolescents' beliefs about the likelihood and value of possible consequences of using common methods of contraception, their perceptions of normative expectations regarding contraceptive use, their intention to use contraceptives in the coming year, and their actual use of the methods in the subsequent year.

The findings both provided support for the model and suggested that adolescents were engaging in rational choice even in this highly charged domain (Adler, Kegeles, Irwin, & Wibbelsman, 1990). Their reasoning was consistent in that their intentions regarding contraceptive use followed from their perceptions of outcomes and social norms. And importantly, their intentions predicted their behaviors. The results differed somewhat for male and female adolescents, reflecting gender differences in control over use of available contraceptive methods and in norms for sexual behavior. Female adolescents were more consistent in their reasoning than were male adolescents in that their attitudinal beliefs and normative perceptions were more strongly related to their intentions regarding all methods than was the case for the male adolescents. Female adolescents' intentions regarding use of each of the methods of birth control were significantly related to their subsequent use of the methods. The strongest correlation was for the pill, which is the method over which women have independent control. The reverse was found for male adolescents; intention was significantly correlated with behavior for all methods other than the pill, over which men have relatively little control (Adler et al., 1990).

This research both supported the utility of the rational choice model and told us something about adolescent development. It suggested that even among adolescents, rational models capture important aspects of behavior. The findings were also useful for application. Analysis of specific beliefs associated with intention to use or not use a contraceptive method provided important information regarding ways to intervene. For example, we looked at the beliefs that were associated with condom use (Kegeles, Adler, & Irwin, 1989). Two beliefs that were not related were the belief that condoms would prevent sexually transmitted diseases and the belief that condoms would prevent pregnancy. At first this seems puzzling. Why use condoms except for the fact that they would prevent pregnancy and STDs? Does this undermine the view that adolescents are rational?

On closer look we discovered that beliefs about pregnancy prevention and STD prevention were not associated with intention because there was so little variance. The adolescents almost universally believed that condoms would do these good things. These beliefs were necessary but not sufficient. What seemed to determine condom use were the more social and physical consequences of their use. For both male and female adolescents, the belief that condoms enable sex on the spur of the moment and that condoms are easy to use were associated with intention to use them. In addition, female adolescents who believed that condoms are popular with peers, are clean, do not have side effects, and require the male partner to have self-control were more likely to intend to have their partners use condoms. This last belief surprised us, and it gives some suggestion about the nature of teenage sexuality. It may be that for young women, using a method that slows the process down is positive, and this could be helpful in encouraging condom use.

For male adolescents, those who thought that condoms would not be painful, that condoms could be used without their parents' knowledge, that use would not make them feel guilty, and that condoms would not affect their looks also were more likely to intend to use condoms. The last outcome was unexpected. This outcome had been included because of its relevance for pill use because some young women fear that weight gain associated with pill use could affect their looks. For consistency all outcomes were rated for all methods even though some were not likely outcomes. The male adolescents may have interpreted this outcome in relation to condoms to mean that they would look funny wearing a condom, and it appeared that this belief inhibited their use of them.

Identifying beliefs associated with intentions was informative. Most sex education programs focus solely on the preventive message: The use of condoms will prevent STDs and pregnancy. This is certainly important, but it may not be enough. Programs may be more successful if they also give adolescents information about the popularity of condoms, their lack of side effects, how they can be used to slow sex down and make it more pleasurable, and how men can put a condom on and not look silly.

Limitations of Rational Choice

The completion of this project created a new turning point. The applied road would be to take these findings and create an intervention to test whether addressing the outcome beliefs would modify intentions and behavior. Fortunately, others have done so, because it was not my inclination. Rather, I became interested in the remaining variance in the model. Though we had shown significant associations among components of the rational model, there was a great deal of variance in behavior that was left unexplained. Whereas some of this is due to measurement error, the theory itself may not be sufficiently broad to account for all—or even a major part—of the variance in behavior. The next study expanded on the model by including a measure of motivation. In focusing on contraception we had assumed that the adolescents did not want to get pregnant. Adults use the terms *teen pregnancy* and *unwanted pregnancy* interchangeably, but some teens may want to become pregnant or at least may not be strongly motivated to avoid it. A good deal of debate surrounds the motivation for pregnancy and the extent to which it is a conscious choice or an unconscious wish (e.g., Miller, 1978; Rosenstock, 1980; Swigar, Bowers, & Fleck, 1976; Zabin, Astone, & Emerson, 1993). The Theory of Reasoned Action was developed to account for behavior that is under volitional control and determined by conscious cognitive processes, but it does not give much guidance about what is under volitional control.

In the next study, we supplemented measurement of the components of the Theory of Reasoned Action regarding contraceptive choice with measures tapping both conscious and preconscious motivation for pregnancy (Adler & Tschann, 1993). This study showed that not only did conscious intention regarding pregnancy add to the prediction of contraceptive use above and beyond the beliefs about contraception, but that preconscious motivation also contributed. In terms of theory, these findings suggest that rational considerations are an important determinant of choice, but that factors outside of conscious awareness can also shape behavior. This is not new, but this research both demonstrated it and brought together models that have not been seen as compatible. It also suggested that while educational approaches to teen pregnancy prevention will be useful insofar as these address salient cognitions, approaches that fail to address motivational forces will be limited.

Challenges of Real-World Research

Although testing theory in the context of real-world problems has the potential for advancing science as well as application, there are challenges as well. Real-world tests of theory are more difficult to do well than are controlled studies in the laboratory. For one, it is harder to operationalize variables in a compelling way outside the laboratory; if a variable does not work, it is not clear if the underlying theory is lacking or the operationalization was poor. Although this is also true in laboratory research, there is often more control over operationalization. In the research testing Kelman's model of reactions to discrepant action, it was easier to operationalize discrepancies from norms and values than from roles. The set of relevant norms and values was relatively common among the women, whereas the specific roles that might be jeopardized by their action were more idiosyncratic. In the laboratory, one would test the theory by creating a relevant role disparity, but in the field, the actual variation is more powerful. This may tell us that roles are less salient in people's lives than are norms and values, but it could also mean that I, as a researcher, failed to do it well.

Real-world tests of theory have other complexities as well. In the laboratory, one constrains the choices available, whereas in real life individuals can respond in many ways. A substantial number of women I interviewed following abortion dealt with whatever dissonance was created by their action by avoiding it. Some reported that they simply did not think about it afterwards, whereas others reported actively distracting themselves if they began to think about it. We know from subsequent research on stress and coping that avoidance is one strategy for dealing with a stressor, particularly one that cannot be changed. In the laboratory we do not provide this option. We get a purer test of the effect of a discrepancy in the laboratory, but it may not tell us what will happen when other options are available.

The best test of theory will occur in a program of research that goes back and forth from the laboratory to the field and from the basic to applied. Such a mix will allow for more critical tests of how and when a given theory will hold.

Unfortunately, the balance has been skewed. Much of the effort in psychological research has been understandably focused on internal validity, because that is primary. As a result, most research has been basic laboratory research. We have not given enough attention to external validity and the true functioning of our theories in the outside world. We need to know if our theories work in the real world and within the complexities that occur in people's lives. We should not be surprised or dismayed to find that when we move outside the laboratory and into application, results are generally not neat and rarely account for a substantial part of the overall variance in our outcomes. If one wants to achieve the latter, no one theory is likely to be sufficient. In fact, no one discipline will be sufficient.

This brings me to my current work, in which a focus on application necessitates a broad interdisciplinary approach. I am currently investigating the pathways by which socioeconomic status (SES) influences health. In most industrialized countries, including the United States, a gradient relationship exists between SES and health (Adler et al., 1994). It is not simply that those in poverty have worse health than those above the poverty threshold, but health improves at each step higher in the socioeconomic hierarchy, up to the very top. The usual explanation that health effects are simply due to the extreme deprivation of poverty cannot account for the gradient relationship, nor can the next most common explanation: that the association of SES and health is due to differences in health care; although health care matters, it accounts for relatively little of the SES effect (Adler, Boyce, Chesney, Folkman, & Syme, 1993).

Understanding how socioeconomic status affects health involves social-psychological processes—how does a social variable get under the skin to influence an outcome such as health? Social psychological theories and methods are helpful, but a full explanation of the SES gradient requires an understanding of social environments and biological processes as well as mental and behavioral factors. As of 1997, I have been heading a group of 12 scientists who are examining this question. The disciplines represented range from cultural anthropology and sociology to medicine and neuroscience. We are trying to identify the mechanisms by which SES affects health and each of us brings a different level of analysis and theoretical perspective. For my own part, I have been developing and testing a measure of subjective social status, which has shown to be strongly related to both mental and physical health outcomes (Adler, Epel, Castellazzo, & Ickovics, 2000; Ostrove, Adler, Kuppermann, & Washington, 2000). These data suggest a central role of psychological processes in the interaction of social factors and biological functioning. Some of my colleagues in the network are examining community characteristics such as social cohesion and community resources, others are studying psychological processes associated with exposure to stress, and others have been charting the biological pathways by which stress may result in disease and premature mortality. By putting these together, we hope to have a more complete understanding of the social disparities in health in ways that will better inform policy and intervention (Adler, Marmot, McEwen, & Stewart, 1999). Along the way, there will be opportunities to test theoretical predictions about issues such as social comparison, relative deprivation, stress and coping, social support, and social conflict.

Although the subject matter of these studies has differed, all addressed both basic and applied issues. In each I have struggled with the tension between rigor and vigor about which Herb Kelman has written so eloquently (Kelman, 1968). It is difficult for any one study to capture both. Yet Kelman's career demonstrates that over a lifetime one can conduct research that is both rigorous and vigorous. This is an ideal that I have kept in mind—whatever choice I have made in a given study, whether it was driven by a need to clarify or test theory or to improve the world through application, Kelman has served as a model of one who spans these worlds. He has provided an important guiding image for me and for others represented in this volume.

References

Adler, N. E. (1979). Decision models in population research. *Journal of Population, 2,* 187–202.

Adler, N. E., Boyce, T., Chesney, M., Cohen, S., Folkman, S., Kahn, R., et al. (1994). Socioeconomic status and health: The challenge of the gradient. *American Psychologist, 49,* 15–24.

Adler, N. E., Boyce, W. T., Chesney, M., Folkman, S., & Syme, L. (1993). Socioeconomic inequalities in health: No easy solution. *Journal of the American Medical Association, 269,* 3140–3145.

Adler, N. E., David, H. P., Major, B. N., Roth, S. H., Russo, N. F., & Wyatt, G. E. (1990). Psychological responses after abortion. *Science, 248,* 41–44.

Adler, N. E., David, H. P., Major, B. N., Roth, S. H., Russo, N. F., & Wyatt, G. E. (1992). Psychological factors in abortion: A review. *American Psychologist, 47,* 1194–1204.

Adler, N. E., Epel, E. Castellazzo, G., & Ickovics, J. (2000). Relationship of subjective and objective social status with psychological and physical health in healthy white women. *Health Psychology, 19,* 586–592.

Adler, N. E., Kegeles, S. M., Irwin, C. E., & Wibbelsman, C. (1990). Adolescent contraceptive behavior: An assessment of decision processes. *Journal of Pediatrics, 116,* 463–471.

Adler, N. E., Marmot, M., McEwen, B., & Stewart, J. (1999). *SES & health in industrialized nations.* New York: Annals of the New York Academy of Sciences.

Adler, N. E., & Tschann, J. M. (1993). Conscious and preconscious motivation for pregnancy among female adolescents. In A. Lawson & D. Rhode (Eds.), *The politics of pregnancy: Adolescent sexuality and public policy* (pp. 144–158). New Haven, CT: Yale University Press.

American Academy of Pediatrics v. Lungren, 884–574. Super. Ct. San Francisco (1992).

Brehm, J. W., & Cohen, A. R. (1962). Re-evaluation of choice alternatives as a function of their number and qualitative similarity. *Journal of Abnormal and Social Psychology, 58,* 373–378.

Dagg, P. K. B. (1991). The psychological sequelae of therapeutic abortion—denied and completed. *American Journal of Psychiatry, 148,* 578–585.

Festinger, L., & Carlsmith, J. M. (1959). Cognitive consequences of forced compliance. *Journal of Abnormal and Social Psychology, 58,* 203–210.

Fishbein, M., & Ajzen, I. (1975). *Belief, attitude, intention, and behavior: An introduction to theory and research.* Reading, MA: Addison-Wesley.

Kegeles, S. M., Adler, N. E., & Irwin, C. E. (1989). Adolescents and condoms: Associations of beliefs with intentions to use. *American Journal of Diseases of Children, 143,* 911–915.

Kelman, H. C. (1958). Compliance, identification, and internalization: Three processes of attitude change. *Journal of Conflict Resolution, 2,* 51–60.

Kelman, H. C. (1968). *A time to speak: On human values and social research.* San Francisco: Jossey-Bass.

Kelman, H. C. (1974). Social influence and linkages between the individual and the social system: Further thoughts on the processes of compliance, identification, and internalization. In J. T. Tedeschi (Ed.), *Perspectives on social power* (pp. 125–171). Chicago: Aldine.

Major, B., Cozzarelli, C., Cooper, M. L., Zubek, J., Richards, C., Wilhite, M., et al. (2000). Psychological responses of women after first-trimester abortion. *Archives of General Psychiatry, 57,* 777–784.

Miller, W. B. (1978). The intendedness and wantedness of the first child. In W. B. Miller & L. F. Newman (Eds.), *The first child and family formation* (pp. 209–243). Chapel Hill, NC: Carolina Population Center.

Monsour, K., & Stewart, B. (1973). Abortion and sexual behavior in college women. *American Journal of Orthopsychiatry, 43,* 804–813.

Ostrove, J. M., Adler, N. E., Kuppermann, M., & Washington, A. E. (2000). Resources and rankings: Objective and subjective assessments of socioeconomic status and their relationship to health in an ethnically diverse sample of pregnant women. *Health Psychology, 19,* 613–618.

Planned Parenthood of Central New Jersey v. John J. Farmer, Jr., A-52 Sup. Ct. New Jersey (2000).

Rosenstock, H. (1980). Recognizing the teenager who needs to be pregnant: A clinical perspective. *Southern Medical Journal, 73,* 134–136.

Rue, V., Speckhard, A., Rogers, J., & Franz, W. (1987). *The psychological aftermath of abortion: A white paper.* Testimony presented to the Office of the Surgeon General. Washington, DC: U.S. Department of Health and Human Services.

Swigar, M., Bowers, M. B., & Fleck, S. (1976). Grieving and unplanned pregnancy. *Psychiatry, 39,* 72–80.

Zabin, L. S., Astone, N. M., & Emerson, M. R. (1993). Do adolescents want babies? The relationship between attitudes and behavior. *Journal of Research on Adolescence, 3,* 67–86.

6

Achieving Equality of Student Internet Access Within Schools

Janet Ward Schofield and Ann Locke Davidson

The Internet has moved into schools in the United States at a remarkable rate. Internet connections in schools were virtually unheard of at the beginning of the 1990s. By 1994, a national sample survey reported that 35% of all public schools were connected (Heaviside, Maltitz, & Carpenter, 1995). By the fall of 2001, 99% of all U.S. public schools and 87% of their instructional rooms had access (U.S. Department of Education, 2002).

Many outcomes are expected to emerge from Internet use including decreased isolation of schools from the outside world, increased student learning, and increased equality of educational opportunity (Cummins & Sayers, 1995; Shade, 1999). Indeed, the common belief that Internet use will lead to increased equality of opportunity (Shade, 1999) is epitomized in former President Clinton's (1996) assertion that the Internet will "revolutionize" education since "for the first time in the history of America . . . we can make available the same learning from all over the world at the same level of quality . . . to all our children" (p. 6).

However, Internet use in schools is so new that we know little about whether, how, or under what conditions it will actually affect students. For this reason, the National Science Foundation funded four projects to serve as national testbeds to explore the impact of Internet use on education and to illuminate the kinds of issues that such use raises. This chapter reports some of the results of one of these projects—the Networking for Education Testbed, or NET. Specifically, it deals with the relation between Internet use and the achievement of equality of educational opportunity.

The Internet clearly has the potential to help equalize educational opportunity by making the information and communication resources available to students in all schools more similar than has been the case before. However, prior research on computer use in schools suggests that patterns of technology access and use often mirror and reinforce existing inequalities rather than mitigate them (Becker & Ravitz, 1997; Becker & Sterling, 1987; Schofield, 1995; Shade, 1999; Sutton, 1991). So, it seems utopian to assume, as many do, that Internet access will virtually automatically lead to greater equality of opportunity.

The goal of this chapter is to delineate some of the factors influencing the relation between Internet use in schools and equality of educational opportunity by discussing the issues that arose pertinent to this topic in NET.

However, because this chapter was prepared for this *Festschrift* volume, it is appropriate to point out before proceeding further that the work reported here reflects Herbert Kelman's influence in a variety of ways. First, this chapter reflects a commitment to analyzing social arrangements and policies from the standpoint of what they mean to the individuals affected by them, a focus that Kelman (1968) has explicitly called for and which much of his work exemplifies. Second, more broadly, this research is intended to contribute to understanding ways to foster constructive social change, another characteristic of his work. Third, this research reflects Kelman's (1968) emphasis on selecting the methodological approach appropriate to the questions at hand and his acceptance of naturalistic approaches. Specifically, this research uses qualitative methods that are particularly appropriate for studying topics about which little is known (Heyink & Tymsrra, 1993). Finally, this work has benefited from the model that Kelman provides of the use of data as a stimulus to thought and an aid to conceptualization.

One way to approach the issue of equality of educational opportunity is by focusing on equality of educational inputs—that is, equality of the pertinent physical, financial, and human resources that schools serving various kinds of students have (Good & Brophy, 1986; Harvey & Klein, 1989). This kind of approach locates the analysis within the framework of concerns about inequality of access to technology on the part of U.S. citizens with varying personal characteristics (e.g., minority/majority group membership, gender, socioeconomic status) that has been the focus of considerable attention by policymakers under the rubric of the "digital divide." Concern about this digital divide has stimulated an extraordinary amount of activity within the past several years, ranging from White House press briefings to foundation initiatives to public television programs.

Researchers too have undertaken work related to the digital divide. A substantial amount of attention has been devoted to understanding the extent and nature of this phenomenon in schools, resulting in studies that do things such as compare the availability of Internet access in schools serving poor or minority group students and in those serving affluent or White students (Coley, Cradler, & Engel, 1997; Hoffman & Novak, 1998; U.S. Department of Education, 2002). This work provides very useful information. For example, Anderson and Ronnkvist's (1999) survey of a large sample of schools in the United States concluded that the average household income in the community in which schools are located has a substantial impact on the availability of Internet access. Furthermore, these researchers concluded that schools with higher percentages of minority students have less technology than others, even after controlling for the impact of income. Somewhat more recent research suggests that, although poverty and minority status are no longer connected to school Internet access, they are still associated with lower levels of classroom Internet access (U.S. Department of Education, 2002).

However, in this chapter we take a very different approach to exploring the issue of equality of school-based access to technology for different sectors of the population. Specifically, our work reflects a strong concern that, even if schools with contrasting student profiles have similar technology resources, one cannot assume that equality of access has been attained because social processes within schools may direct technology use in nonrandom ways. Thus, it is important to understand what happens within schools that shapes the use of the computer resources they have and that potentially channels access to that technology toward certain groups of students. Before presenting the study's findings, which suggest that such processes do indeed exist, we very briefly describe the project studied and the methods used in this research.

Networking for Education Testbed and Its District Context

The Networking for Education Testbed is a collaboration among the Waterford Public Schools (WPS), the Wellington Super Computing Center, and the University of Fairfield. NET's primary goal, very simply stated, was to bring Internet access to teachers in the WPS for use in instruction. NET's basic approach was to provide teams of teachers (typically having 6 to 12 members) with the opportunity to write a brief proposal outlining their goals for Internet use and the computer resources they would need to reach these goals. A committee broadly representative of various groups in the WPS selected the most promising proposals submitted to annual competitions. NET staff then provided the participating teams of educators with technological resources and other kinds of support. During its five-year life, NET provided Internet connections, as well as substantial amounts of training and support, to teams of educators at 15 elementary schools, 4 middle schools, and 10 high schools.

The kinds of Internet activities NET fostered, their educational goals, and the computer setups needed to realize these goals varied tremendously. However, teachers typically requested that a small cluster (one to four) of Internet-connected computers be located in team members' classrooms. Projects involving the use of the World Wide Web and e-mail were very common.

The district in which NET was located served a student body that is approximately 55% African American and 45% White. Roughly 60% of its students receive free or reduced-price lunches due to limited family income. On the average, the district's White students come from families of higher socioeconomic status (SES) than its African American students and evidence higher levels of academic achievement. Given the existence of this marked achievement gap, district policymakers were generally quite concerned about issues of equality and equity. The fact that both the school board's president and the head of the board's technology subcommittee were African American contributed to creating a political and policy environment sensitive to such issues.

The issue of educational inputs—of how a potentially valuable resource like the Internet should be allocated between schools serving different kinds of students—arose early in the project and created considerable controversy, because NET did not have enough funds to provide Internet access to every school in the WPS. Indeed, at the end of NET's second year, some members of the school board voiced a strong concern that schools serving poor, heavily African American communities were underrepresented in the set of schools that had received Internet access through NET. Because one of NET's explicit goals was to increase equality of educational opportunity, this charge was particularly disturbing. Thus, NET undertook a number of activities designed specifically to foster Internet access in district schools serving such populations. Although such activities were helpful in ensuring that schools serving poor minority communities were not left out of the project, they did not ensure that *within* participating schools students with different kinds of backgrounds had equal Internet access.

Methods and Data Analysis

The major data-gathering methods used in this research were qualitative observations, semistructured interviews, and the collection of archival material. Repeated observations were conducted in a wide variety of settings. This includes observation of more than 230 class sessions in more than 35 different classrooms in which the Internet was being used. It also includes observation of more than 125 meetings between different groups of teachers involved with the project. Trained observers used the *full field note* method of data collection (Olson, 1976), which involves taking extensive handwritten notes during the events being observed. All notes were made as factual and concretely descriptive as possible.

To gain insight into participants' perspectives, we conducted approximately 400 semistructured open-ended interviews, including more than 170 with teachers, 140 with students, 45 with school district personnel, and 45 with NET educational, technical, and other staff. Such interviews contained numerous specific questions pertinent to the issues discussed here. For example, teachers were asked questions directly related to equality of access, such as how they decided which students would use the Internet, as well as more general but nonetheless pertinent questions, such as whether their actual classroom use of the Internet differed from their planned use of it. Similarly, students were asked both directly pertinent questions, such as those about which students used the Internet in school, and more general but nonetheless potentially relevant questions, such as those about the best and worst things about the way the Internet was used in their schools.

Both field notes and interviews were audiotaped, transcribed, coded, and then analyzed using established qualitative methods (Miles & Huberman, 1984; Taylor & Bogdan, 1998). In the data analysis, the primary emphasis was on the development and systematic application of thematic categories to all data.

Archival materials were another important source of information pertinent to the issues discussed here. With participants' permission, the research team's address was added to virtually all group e-mail lists connected with NET. In addition, account use data for students were collected at 20 schools over a three-year period. Documents, such as the written activity plans of teachers using the Internet, were also systematically collected. The specific analysis method used with archival materials varied, depending on the nature of the information. However, typically these materials were coded thematically, as were the field notes.

Close attention was paid to triangulating data from individuals occupying different roles in the school system as well as data gathered by different methods from individuals occupying similar roles. Furthermore, we specifically made a practice of looking for data that undercut our developing analysis of the situation, because one of the potential pitfalls in this kind of work is a tendency to find what one is looking for and to overlook inconsistent data (Kelman, 1968). Readers desiring more information on data-gathering or analysis procedures should see Schofield and Davidson (2002).

Findings

As previously indicated, NET was sensitive to the importance of fostering participation by schools serving a wide variety of students. This participation facilitated the goal of fostering equality of access that both NET's staff and vocal school board members valued. However, the closely related issue of whether *within-school* or *within-classroom* Internet access was related to student characteristics such as academic achievement or minority group status received essentially no attention in NET, just as it has received very little attention in the existing literature. This issue is important, however, because, even if educational inputs, such as Internet access, are equal at the school level, the question of whether students from different backgrounds actually end up with equal access remains.

Study of NET suggested that inequality of access within specific schools and classrooms did develop. This occurred in two major ways. The first of these, which is discussed next, resulted from decisions that were made about the particular classes within schools that would be provided with Internet access. The second, which is discussed in a subsequent section of this chapter, stemmed from a set of attitudes, practices, and conditions commonly found within NET classrooms

Classes Serving High-Achieving Students Get Disproportionate Internet Access

The large majority of NET activities were located in classrooms serving students not strikingly different in background or in academic achievement from their peers within that school. For example, almost three quarters of the 81 separate projects described by NET teachers participating in a survey about their Internet activities were conducted in classes characterized by the teachers as composed of either average students or an academically heterogeneous group of students. However, it was not unusual for Internet projects to be located in niches of the schools serving unrepresentative samples of students. When this occurred, it was virtually always in programs serving students who were academically stronger than their peers, a finding consistent with Becker and Ravitz's (1997) earlier survey work on Internet use in schools. Differences in the socioeconomic background of White and African American students and the corresponding difference in their average levels of academic achievement often meant that White students had more Internet access than their African American schoolmates.

Almost one quarter of the more than 80 projects described by NET teachers participating in the survey mentioned above involved primarily or exclusively students who were academically advanced compared to other students in their school. So, for example, the NET activity in one school that was 99% African American was located in the honors track, which by definition served the most academically able students. As a group, these students tended to come from families that were somewhat better off than their peers. Similarly, one of the elementary schools participating in NET focused its Internet efforts in its magnet program rather than in its other classrooms, which had a much higher proportion of children with disabilities, limited English proficiency, and other disadvantages. In stark contrast to the substantial proportion of projects located in classrooms serving advanced students, fewer than 4% of the NET projects described by teachers participating in this survey were reported to involve primarily or exclusively lower achieving students.

Interviews with students suggested that they were often well aware that Internet access was not uncommonly channeled to classes containing the academically stronger students. For example, a high school student described the situation in his school this way:

> Mark: The foreign language teachers decide who gets to use the Internet . . . and it's usually on a class basis. Like their higher level classes will use the Internet, whereas the lower level classes won't. And unfortunately it's not very easy for other students to get accounts. . . . I've heard . . . students given the answer that they're not in the foreign language class [that is using the Internet] so they don't really have access to it.

Two factors seemed to contribute importantly to disproportionate Internet access for high-achieving classes. First, because Internet use was seen by most teachers as making their teaching job somewhat more complex, they preferred to use the Internet in classes that were the easiest to teach and to control. Because classes with advanced students were often small and the students in them generally posed relatively few serious classroom management issues, teachers gravitated toward using the Internet with them. Second, interviews with those in the WPS suggested that, because teaching high-achieving students was often seen as desirable by educators, unusually energetic and skilled educators tended disproportionately to find ways to teach such classes. To the extent that such a phenomenon did occur, one might expect the teachers of such classes to be disproportionally likely to submit a proposal to NET and to win in the competitive selection process that NET used.

Student Characteristics Influence Internet Access Within Classrooms

In spite of the tendency just discussed to use the Internet in classes filled with relatively advanced students more than in those serving their academically weaker schoolmates, the majority of NET activities were carried out in academically heterogeneous classes, as indicated in the prior subsection. However, equality issues arose in such cases as well. Specifically, classroom observations suggested that not all students within those classes were equally likely to get Internet access and that students who were advantaged in one way or another were generally the ones to get greater access when there were disparities. We did not see any cases in which teachers blatantly used student characteristics such as race, gender, or socioeconomic status to systematically deny access to any particular group of students within a class. However, more subtle factors, to be discussed shortly, led to high-achieving and advantaged students often obtaining more Internet access than their peers within classrooms with access.

Both teachers and students were quite aware of these patterns of unequal student access within classrooms. For example, in response to interview questions about how they selected students in their classes to use the Internet, teachers ($N = 20$) were more than four times as likely to say that they based their selection on specific student abilities or characteristics as they were to say that all of their students used the Internet (70% vs. 15%), with academic achievement being mentioned more commonly than any other characteristic as a basis for selection. Similarly, of the students ($N = 27$) interviewed on this topic, just 26% reported equal access for all types of students, compared to 74% who perceived unequal access on the basis of one or more student characteristics, again with academic ability being mentioned more frequently than any other single selection criterion.

Several factors appeared to contribute importantly to this disparity in access within heterogeneous classrooms. First, teachers, especially those not working in computer lab settings, tended to see Internet use as a privilege rather than as a basic resource, such as textbooks, to which all students should have access. This view seemed to stem from several sources, including the fact that teachers generally had many more students than Internet access points, which meant that access was a scarce good. As such, it was most easily dealt with as a privilege, rather than something that students should share equally. In addition, work done on the Internet was often seen as enrichment rather than as part of the core curriculum, so that most teachers did not feel a strong responsibility to ensure that all students got to use the Internet. Although this view of Internet work as enrichment was partly due to the relative scarcity of Internet-linked computers, it did not appear to be completely due to this. Rather, teachers had preexisting curriculum materials and accompanying tests that reflected the core of what they expected students to learn. Internet work tended to be added on to this and hence understood as enrichment.

Students' very positive reactions to Internet use reinforced the image of Internet access as a privilege. Most students enjoyed using the Internet, often vociferously asking to be allowed to work on it. (Indeed, disputes even developed between classmates about who would get access.) Teachers were well aware of students' positive reactions to Internet use. In fact, 84% of the teachers ($N = 56$) interviewed on this topic reported positive responses to Internet use on the part of students, saying things like "They love it, and if they could use it all day they would." Observing such behavior tended to reinforce the image of Internet access as a valued privilege in teachers' eyes.

When Internet access was seen as a privilege, the question of which students within a given classroom deserved that privilege arose. Time and time again, a variety of factors conspired to bring greater access to students who were already better off in one regard or another than to their less advantaged classmates. Specifically, teachers frequently used access as a reward for desired behavior, especially strong academic performance. However, it was also awarded for other kinds of desired behavior ranging from paying attention to the teacher, to remembering to bring in homework on time, to appearing to be trustworthy. As one teacher put it:

> Being [there's] only one computer there, I use it as a reward . . . so I think it . . . made it easier to control some . . . not control but . . . to use it as a reward for the kids who are on task and complete their work.

Similarly, behavior of which the teachers disapproved, especially social behavior of this nature, was seen as reason for removal of this privilege or for failure to bestow it. One middle school student captured his understanding of the process this way:

> Interviewer: Could you tell me . . . how it's decided what kids get to use the Internet in your class and what kids don't?
> Tony: Like the kids that behave and . . . get A's and B's [get to use it]. . . . The bad kids . . . sit in their chair [sic] and write.[1]

Even relatively young students understood the link between behavior and Internet access as suggested by the following excerpt from an interview with a teacher who explained what happened when he inquired of a group of fifth graders who were temporarily in his class about why they did not know how to use the Internet, given that their usual classroom had computers with Internet access: [The students said], "Oh, we're not allowed. Well, only certain people are allowed to use it. . . . We're the bad kids, and we're not allowed." (Schofield & Davidson, 2002, p. 111)

Teachers persisted in using Internet access as an incentive and reward for desired behavior in spite of the fact that many of them were aware that this led to negative reactions on the part of some lower achieving students. As one teacher put it:

> Kids who don't have access to it feel as though they're second-rate kids. I mean, they say, "How come those kids get to and we don't?" and I hear it real often. And I don't have an answer. I tell them, "It's because we don't have enough machines. What do you want me to do at this point?"

The tendency to use access as a reward for desired academic and social behavior appeared to be compounded by concerns about the kinds of materials available on the Internet. Teachers believed that students who had shown that they were strongly motivated to achieve by their superior academic performance would be less likely than many of their peers to veer off in noneducational directions or to flout school rules about the kinds of activities they should engage in on the Internet. Similarly, students who showed a general pattern of behavior consistent with school rules were seen as more likely to obey rules

---

[1] From *Bringing the Internet to School: Lessons From an Urban District* (p. 111), by J. W. Schofield and A. Davidson. Copyright © 2002 by John Wiley & Sons. This material is used by permission of John Wiley & Sons, Inc.

regarding appropriate use of Internet access than their peers and hence were viewed as better candidates for the privilege of access. Because constant surveillance was often impractical, teachers felt most comfortable about giving such students access (Schofield & Davidson, 2002).

Interestingly, the teachers' power to decide which students got to use the Internet in class appeared to lead to access functioning not only as a reward for desired behavior that might well have occurred in any event, but also as a mechanism to gain students' compliance with the school's behavioral norms, which other research also suggests tends to happen when access to technology use is conceptualized as a privilege (Martin, 1991). As noted already, access was highly valued by students. Furthermore, many students recognized a direct link between access and behavior, as exemplified by the students quoted previously. Although such compliance-based social influence is fragile in the sense that it is dependent on surveillance by those controlling rewards and punishments (Kelman, 1961), it nonetheless was often useful in the classroom context, as illustrated by one high school teacher's comments on this topic:

> It's a good disciplinary tool. Like, "Okay, you're not quiet. Forget about the Internet. You're not gonna use it. We'll go back to the textbooks and we'll just go back to the transparencies and write stuff on the board."[2]

Thus, educators used the promise of access or the threat of its removal to mold student behavior. The control function was clear in the acceptable use policies developed at NET schools that, like those policies currently used in schools across the country, typically indicated that undesirable behavior on the Internet was reason for removal of access. The control function was also highlighted by the fact that a number of teachers spontaneously characterized Internet use as "a carrot" that they used to shape student behavior. Indeed, one teacher called it "one of the best carrots I've ever found" (Schofield & Davidson, 2002, p. 112).

Teachers' genuine concern about the academic progress of their weaker students also often appeared to contribute to inequality in access. Because Internet usage was generally not conceptualized as the most direct route to helping students master the core curriculum, many teachers believed that weaker students' time was better spent on more traditional activities. These teachers may have been correct, because there is very little hard evidence about the impact of Internet use on students' learning (Schofield & Davidson, 2002). However, inequality in Internet access for weaker students created yet another potentially important dimension on which they were behind others—computer and Internet skills. Furthermore, the stronger students' greater access had the potential to increase any preexisting motivational differences between them and their academically weaker peers because there was widespread agreement that Internet use was motivating (Schofield & Davidson, 2002).

Another factor contributing to disparity in access was that many teachers lacked highly developed knowledge about the Internet and computers more

---

[2] From *Bringing the Internet to School: Lessons From an Urban District* (p. 112), by J. W. Schofield and A. Davidson. Copyright © 2002 by John Wiley & Sons. This material is used by permission of John Wiley & Sons, Inc.

generally (Davidson, Schofield, & Stocks, 2001; Schofield & Davidson, 2002; Schofield, Davidson, Stocks, & Futoran, 1997). This led them to give greater access to students who were already knowledgeable in these areas, since these students could use the Internet most effectively and in a way that made relatively few demands on the teachers' already heavily obligated time. However, such students were disproportionately White, male, and from relatively privileged backgrounds. Enhanced access, in turn, increased and highlighted the knowledge gap between them and their peers with regard to Internet use.

One factor that appeared to contribute to creating the initial gap in expertise between students from different backgrounds was home access. Again and again in interviews, students with advanced computer or Internet skills indicated that home access played an important role in their acquisition of such skills. Previous research suggests that male students are more likely to have home computers and to engage in other computer-related activities, such as attending computer camps, than their female counterparts (Sutton, 1991). It is also clear that those living in affluent households are more likely to have home computers and Internet access than their less well-off peers (U.S. Department of Commerce, 2000). Furthermore, White students are more than twice as likely as African American students to have a computer at home, and adjusting for household income mitigates but does not obliterate this difference (Hoffman & Novak, 1998). Finally, research suggests that, even when the forces that lead to unequal home access to computers on the part of girls or minority group youth are overcome, individuals belonging to these groups may still use that access less than their counterparts and thus have less chance of developing the skills that come from such use (Kraut, Scherlis, Mukhopadhyay, Manning, & Kiesler, 1996). Thus, the differential in computer skills found in NET between male and female students and between students from different backgrounds may well be prevalent elsewhere.

Finally, students' own in-school behavior also tended to reinforce the disproportionate access created by the factors just discussed. For example, male students and students of relatively high socioeconomic status often made disproportionate voluntary use of the Internet before or after school. Similarly, girls were sometimes less assertive than boys in laying claim to computers, reflecting a traditionally feminine style of interaction that served them poorly in the competition for access to this valued resource, a finding consistent with Sadker and Sadker's (1995) work.

Conclusion

In summary, this study suggests that bringing the Internet to schools in a way that provides equal access for all students is likely to be a complex process. First, there is the important issue of whether this educational input will be distributed across schools in ways that exacerbate existing resource inequalities, with richer schools and the students in them having greater access. However, this study suggests that even distribution of access across schools serving different kinds of students does not ensure that all students will have equal access, a fact that points to the importance of reconceptualizing traditional ways of measuring equality of access. Indeed, as this chapter highlights, within any given school access may be located in particular programs or niches that serve specific groups of students. In the case studied here, when such disparities occurred they virtually always favored access for relatively advantaged students. This finding is consistent with the results of a national survey which suggests that teachers who generally teach high-performing students are more likely to use the Internet and to feel it is essential to their work than are teachers of low-achieving students (Becker, 1998). It is also consistent with another survey of more than 300 schools using the Internet to foster educational reform in which it was found that teachers tended to use the Internet more with higher achieving students than with lower achieving ones in classes in which Internet use played a significant role (Becker & Ravitz, 1997).

Even when access is equal for schools serving students from different backgrounds, and when "niche" placement favoring certain kinds of students does not occur, other factors lead to inequality of access. Specifically, the conceptualization of Internet use as a privilege, teachers' view of it as a tool for enrichment rather than as a mechanism for teaching the core curriculum, their concerns about efficient and effective classroom management, their lack of extensive Internet-related knowledge, and differences in students' own behaviors can reinforce existing inequalities with regard to computer and Internet skills by leading to inequality of Internet access. The fact that disparities in access occurred within both a district and a project that evidenced genuine concern about ensuring equal opportunities for students from different backgrounds suggests just how subtle and powerful some of the social processes described in this chapter are.

Finally, before closing, we point out that the significance of the inequalities in access that we document here is heavily dependent on the value of the Internet activities students undertake. There is some reason to think that, like many other computer applications, Internet use may well be motivating to students (Neilsen, 1998; Schofield & Davidson, 2002; Songer, 1998). Furthermore, Internet use may well change classroom roles and relationships in ways that current theory and research suggest are constructive, at least when teachers wish to make such changes (Schofield & Davidson, 2003). Yet, Internet use in schools is so new, and research on its outcomes involves so many potential difficulties and pitfalls, that it is not entirely clear that the Internet, as it is actually used in schools, lives up to the high expectations that many hold for it. Some studies suggest various kinds of positive outcomes for certain kinds of Internet use in schools (Cummins & Sayers, 1995; Davidson & Schofield, 2002; Gallini & Hellman, 1995; Garner & Gillingham, 1996; Schofield & Davidson, 2002). However, others suggest the need for caution (Feldman, Konold, & Coulter, 2000; Wallace, Kupperman, Krajcik, & Soloway, 2000). Thus, we suggest that future research needs both to further elucidate the processes that shape Internet access and use in school and to illuminate the consequences of such access and use for student outcomes.

The research reported here was funded by Contract No. RED-9253452 with the National Science Foundation and Grant No. 42-40-94032 from the U.S. Department of Commerce as well as Grant No. 199800209 from the Spencer Foundation. All opinions expressed herein are solely those of the authors and no endorsement of the conclusions by the National Science Foundation, the U.S. Department of Commerce, or the Spencer Foundation is implied or intended.

References

Anderson, R., & Ronnkvist, A. (1999). The presence of computers in American schools. In *Teaching, learning, and computing: 1998 survey* (Report No. 2). Retrieved September 19, 2003, from the University of California, Irvine, and University of Minnesota's Center for Research on Information Technology and Organizations Web site: http://www.crito.uci.edu/tlc/findings/computers_in_american_schools/

Becker, H. J. (1998). *Internet use by teachers: Conditions of professional use and teacher-directed student use* (Report No. 1). Retrieved September 19, 2003, from the University of California, Irvine, and University of Minnesota's Center for Research on Information Technology and Organizations Web site: http://www.crito.uci.edu/tlc/findings/internet-use/

Becker, H. J., & Ravitz, J. L. (1997, August). The equity threat of promising innovations: The Internet in schools. In P. Bowman (Chair), *Internet and equity in education*. Symposium conducted at the meeting of the American Psychological Association, Chicago, IL.

Becker, H. J., & Sterling, C. W. (1987). Equity in school computer use: National data and neglected considerations. *Journal of Educational Computing Research, 3,* 289–311.

Clinton, W. J. (1996, November 4). *Remarks by the president to the people of the Sioux Falls area*. Retrieved September 19, 2003, from http://clinton6.nara.gov/1996/11/1996-11-04-president-remarks-to-citizens-of-sioux-falls-sd.html

Coley, R. J., Cradler, J., & Engel, P. K. (1997). *Computers and classrooms: The status of technology in U.S. schools* (ITS Policy Information Report). Retrieved September 19, 2003, from ITS Policy Information Center Web site: http://www.ets.org/research/pic/compclass.html

Cummins, J., & Sayers, D. (1995). *Brave new schools: Challenging cultural illiteracy*. New York: St. Martin's Press.

Davidson, A. L., & Schofield, J. W. (2002). Female voices in virtual reality: Drawing young girls into an on line world. In K. A. Renninger & W. Shumar (Eds.), *Building virtual communities: Learning and change in cyberspace* (pp. 34–59). New York: Cambridge University Press.

Davidson, A. L., Schofield, J. W., & Stocks, J. E. (2001). Professional cultures and collaborative efforts: A case study of technologists and educators working for change. *Information Society, 17,* 21–32.

Feldman, A., Konold, C., & Coulter, B. (2000). *Network science a decade later: The Internet and classroom learning*. Mahwah, NJ: Erlbaum.

Gallini, J., & Hellman, K. (1995). Audience awareness in technology-mediated environments. *Educational Computing Research, 13,* 245–261.

Garner, R., & Gillingham, M. (1996). *Internet communication in six classrooms: Conversations across time, space, and culture*. Mahwah, NJ: Erlbaum.

Good, T. L., & Brophy, J. E. (1986). School effects. In M. C. Wittrock (Ed.), *Handbook of research on teaching* (3rd ed., pp. 570–602). New York: Macmillan.

Harvey, G., & Klein, S. (1989). Understanding and measuring equity in education: A conceptual framework. In W. G. Secada (Ed.), *Equity in education* (pp. 43–67). New York: Falmer.

Heaviside, S., Maltitz, G., & Carpenter, J. (1995). *Advanced telecommunications in U.S. public schools, K–12* (NCES Publication No. 95-731). Washington, DC: U.S. Department of Education, Office of Educational Research and Improvement.

Heyink, J. W., & Tymsrra, T. J. (1993). The function of qualitative research. *Social Indicators Research, 29,* 291–305.

Hoffman, D. L., & Novak, T. P. (1998). Bridging the racial divide on the Internet. *Science, 280,* 390–391.

Kelman, H. C. (1961). Processes of opinion change. *Public Opinion Quarterly, 25,* 57–78.

Kelman, H. C. (1968). *A time to speak: On human values and social research*. San Francisco: Jossey-Bass.

Kraut, R., Scherlis, W., Mukhopadhyay, T., Manning, J., & Kiesler, S. (1996). The Homenet field trial of residential Internet services. *Communications of the ACM, 39*(12), 55–63.

Martin, D. (1991). New findings from qualitative data using hypermedia: Microcomputers, control and equity. *Computers and Education, 16,* 219–227.

Miles, M. B., & Huberman, A. M. (1984). *Qualitative data analysis: A source book of new methods*. Beverly Hills, CA: Sage.

Neilsen, L. (1998). Coding the light: Rethinking generational authority in a rural high school tele-communications project. In D. Reinking, M. C. McKenna, L. D. Labbo, & R. D. Kieffer (Eds.), *Handbook of literacy and technology: Transformations in a post-typographic world* (pp. 129–143). Mahwah, NJ: Erlbaum.

Olson, S. (1976). *Ideas and data: Process and practice of social research*. Homewood, IL: Dorsey Press.

Sadker, M., & Sadker, D. (1995). *Failing at fairness: How our schools cheat girls*. New York: Touchstone.

Schofield, J. W. (1995). *Computers and classroom culture*. New York: Cambridge University Press.

Schofield, J. W., & Davidson, A. (2002). *Bringing the Internet to school: Lessons from an urban district*. San Francisco: John Wiley & Sons.

Schofield, J. W., & Davidson, A. (2003). The impact of Internet use on the fourth R—relationship between teachers and students. *Mind, Culture and Activity, 10*, 62-79.

Schofield, J. W., Davidson, A., Stocks, J. E., & Futoran, G. (1997). The Internet in school: A case study of educator demand and its precursors. In S. Kiesler (Ed.), *Culture of the Internet* (pp. 361–181). Mahwah, NJ: Erlbaum.

Shade, L. R. (1999). Net gains: Does access equal equity? *Journal of Information Technology Impact, 1*, 25–42.

Songer, N. B. (1996). Exploring learning opportunities in coordinated network-enhanced classrooms: A case of kids as global scientists. *Journal of Learning Sciences, 5*, 297–328.

Sutton, R. E. (1991). Equity and computers in the schools. *Review of Educational Research, 61*, 475–503.

Taylor, S. J., & Bogdan, R. (1998). *Introduction to qualitative research methods* (3rd ed.). New York: Wiley.

U.S. Department of Commerce. (2000). *Falling through the NET: Toward digital inclusion*. Retrieved September 19, 2003, from Web site: http://www.esa.doc.gov/FallingTroughTheNet.cfm

U.S. Department of Education, National Center for Education Statistics (2002). *Internet access in U.S. public schools and classrooms: 1994–2001* (NCES 2002-018). Washington, DC: Author.

Wallace, R., Kupperman, J., Krajcik, J., & Soloway, E. (2000). Students online in a sixth-grade classroom. *Journal of the Learning Sciences, 9*, 75–104.

Comments on Chapters 5 and 6

Jennifer A. Richeson

In any introductory social psychology course, a student typically spends the first 10 weeks of the semester examining the "basic" theories and classic experiments of the field (e.g., attribution theory, the dissonance paradigm, heuristic processing). Only after being thoroughly grounded in this work are students in the course exposed to what are known as the "applications" of those basics! For example, during the final 2 or 3 weeks of most courses in introductory social psychology, students learn ways in which the basic social psychological principles impact such fields as education, health, and the law. Perhaps because writing this commentary coincides with preparing the syllabus for teaching my first such course, I noticed that these "applications" weeks often cover what I now think of as the "why" of social psychology. In other words, the applications are why social psychology as a discipline is so terribly important. When considered in this manner, it suddenly seems nonsensical to present social psychology as theory separate from its applications.

The chapter offered by Nancy Adler (see chap. 5, this volume) nicely addresses this issue. What is a social psychology that is not applied? Through a poignant narrative of the evolution of some of her own work, she elegantly describes the dialectic between application and theory development. Adler's chapter offers a look into her early life as a researcher, which was primarily motivated by theory refinement, testing, and development, and a later phase more closely tied to a particular question or problem, namely, unwanted pregnancy and abortion. In her early work, Adler examined the predictive value of Herbert Kelman's three responses to discrepant actions (i.e., rule-based fear, role-based guilt, and value-based regret) for the specific case of women who terminated their pregnancies. Kelman's (1974) theory provided clear predictions for how women with rule-, role-, and value-oriented views of abortion would respond to having an abortion. Although the data generated by the study were supportive of the model, Adler faced a critical decision point. Should she pursue the theory, attempting to refine it? Or, should she pursue an understanding of the problem of unwanted pregnancy and abortion? Adler's chapter nicely demonstrates the challenge and conflict that many researchers feel regarding the focus and direction of our work. Is our work too applied? Is it too theoretical? Adler's chapter suggests that it is possible to be both basic and applied in one's research program, but "one consideration will take precedence."

For many of Herbert Kelman's students, the pull between theoretical and applied research is a pressing concern. He demonstrates the ability to be both a scholar and a practitioner and inspires the same ideal in his students. Some of us never imagined ourselves in primarily academic positions when we entered graduate school, whereas many of us never imagined ourselves anywhere other than the academy doing traditional academic work. But, thankfully, somewhere in our training, we bumped into Herbert Kelman, and he prompted us to think differently about our work. He encouraged us to find and highlight the real-world importance of our work—that is, the applications—as well as to fine-tune our methods. In other words, he pushed us to study important problems and to do so rigorously, elegantly, and responsibly.

The chapter by Janet Ward Schofield and Ann Locke Davidson (see chap. 6, this volume) demonstrates research that is important and practical, yet elegant, rigorous, and responsible. The authors describe a large-scale research initiative designed to investigate the practical impact of recent solutions to the "digital divide." The chapter takes a close look at whether increases in the number of Internet-ready computers in public schools have brought widespread and equitable Internet access to students within those schools. The authors present a strong challenge to the assumption and hopeful sentiment that the introduction of the Internet to public schools will level the playing field of educational opportunity. Specifically, Schofield and Davidson's analyses clearly point to a number of potential pitfalls that could undermine solutions to the digital divide that solely involve placing more computers in schools.

Schofield and Davidson describe several factors that occur both within and between schools that undermine equitable access to the Internet and thus support, rather than attenuate, the digital divide. Moreover, their thoughtful examinations of dynamics within schools note several structural, functional, and cognitive factors that thwart equal access to the Internet. For instance, distribution of Internet resources was uneven both within and between classrooms at a number of schools. Students who were in gifted classes and deemed more educationally adept spent more time and had greater access to the Internet than other students. Such discrepancies, among the many factors described in the chapter, contribute to increased Internet access, and, therefore, experience and training, for those most likely to already have advantaged status in schools and greater readiness for demanding endeavors. In other words, widespread access of schools to Internet resources may not necessarily translate into equal opportunity for the students within those schools. Instead, Schofield and Davidson warn, Internet access may even serve to reinforce existing social stratification.

These two chapters nicely represent the responsive, compelling work Herbert Kelman has inspired his students to conduct. The work develops from a model of research wherein the complexities associated with the social context are not brushed under the statistical rug as error variance. Issues of pressing concern such as unwanted pregnancy, consequences of abortion, and the digital divide motivate the research. Thus, the context in which theories are applied is the focus, rather than peripheral noise. In such a model of research, questions are addressed from multiple levels of analysis, using multiple methodologies, with a keen eye to understanding the psychological dynamics associated with a particular problem. The research questions and methods undergo extensive scrutiny. Similarly, the interpretations and the implications of those interpretations are challenged. Furthermore, in Herbert Kelman's model of responsible, ethical research, the core consideration at every stage is how one's work may impact the lives of the individuals studied. The research, therefore, is secondary to the integrity of the process, the context of the sociohistorical moment, and the consideration of the perspectives of the participants.

Herbert Kelman's tradition of social psychological research is illustrated nicely by the Adler chapter and the Schofield and Davidson chapter, as well as all of the work in this *Festschrift*. These two chapters in particular are rooted in, driven by, and attentive to important applications of social psychological theory and methods. However, similar to the typical approach to the teaching of social psychology, the division between basic and applied research runs deep. Many social psychologists at some point grapple with the tension between being a scholar and being a practitioner. Like Herbert Kelman, many of us desire to be both. But it seems increasingly likely, as Nancy Adler asserts, that each researcher at some point will make one or the other a priority. Or, some may move along the continuum from basic research to applied interventions as their work and careers develop. Simultaneous investment in scholarship and intervention, however, is seemingly no longer an option for a social psychologist.

This issue of self-identification as a scholar or a practitioner has far-reaching implications. It suggests not only what approach researchers use to the problems that interest them, but also what problems they examine, which questions they ask, and how they go about obtaining the answers. Thus, whether it is still possible for one to simultaneously be a scholar and practitioner and, if it is possible, what contexts, academic or other, allow for this combined approach are issues that warrant serious consideration. The work included in this *Festschrift* leads one to ponder the future of the scholar-practitioner and, I would argue, the future of social psychology at its best.

Reference

Kelman, H. C. (1974). Social influence and linkages between the individual and the social system: Further thoughts on the processes of compliance, identification, and internalization. In J. T. Tedeschi (Ed.), *Perspectives on social power* (pp. 125–171). Chicago: Aldine.

7

Organizational Narcissism

Shoshana Zuboff

Social Psychology's Middle Kingdom

As a graduate student, the difficult conceptual territory that Herbert Kelman insisted on as the true precinct of social psychology fascinated me. "Our discipline was," he would reiterate at the inception of each seminar, "trained on the intersection of the individual and the larger institutional processes of the society." His approach struck me as classical and different from a good deal of the narrow quantitative work that seemed to be gaining a dominant position in the social psychology of the 1970s. Indeed, the very classicism of Herbert Kelman's vision made it hard to grasp. Where, after all, does one look to observe, and measure, the interaction of individuals and their institutions? This territory is an elusive "middle kingdom" that lies between the individual and the social world. Like the Hebrew God, this place was nameless and formless. Yet its presence seemed undeniable to this believer.

In time, I came to appreciate that the genius behind so many of Herbert Kelman's concepts—as well as those of many of the other classical social psychological thinkers of his generation—lay precisely in their ability to illuminate and chronicle this otherwise invisible territory. I am thinking specifically of Kelman's work on attitudes and modes of linkage to the social system (Kelman, 1961), and, later, his study of Lieutenant Calley and the massacre at My Lai (Kelman & Hamilton, 1989), and, still later, his brilliant work on conflict resolution (Kelman, 1997).

Herbert Kelman is part of a generation for which the relationship between the individual and society had become problematic in ways that had no precedent. As witnesses to the rise of a new mass order, they were shaped by war, by holocaust, and later by a new world of abundance, all of which owed allegiance to the same gods of science, technology, and bureaucracy. In this new order, one's destiny was no longer written in blood. It was no longer sufficient for one to simply be her mother's daughter or his father's son. Instead, all individual human beings had to find new ways to attach themselves to the group and claw their way toward some abiding sense of meaning and purpose. As the 20th century saw the rise of organizations and new mass forms of association, these dramas of connection, belonging, and self-definition came to define the very heart of existence. Before Herbert Kelman and his colleagues trained themselves on this still opaque terrain, there were few ways to comprehend these new human processes. Today, however, as a result of the light they shone, it is now possible to grasp the robustness and explanatory power of social psychology's middle kingdom. Their work reveals an extraordinary fabric so tightly woven that its warp and woof—equally composed of social structure and the predilections of the human heart—can barely be discerned.

This chapter is intended as one contribution to this middle kingdom. In it I explore the chronic distance between producers and consumers and suggest that this distance can be understood as a consequence of the social psychological regularities produced by the efficiency requirements of the organization under managerial capitalism. These reflect the historical conditions in which managerial capitalism was first invented (Kimberly, 1975; Stinchcombe, 1965). These factors reinforce one another to create a powerful centripetal action within organizations. This centripetal action produces an inward focus charged with exclusivity, a phenomenon I name *organizational narcissism*. Organizational narcissism helps to account for what appears to be nonrational, but pervasive, features of managerial behavior. Organizational narcissism is not an economic concept, but a social psychological one. It is intended to illuminate a range of managerial choices and activities that are framed as though they derive exclusively from pragmatic and economic considerations.

The Origins of Organizational Narcissism

It is impossible to imagine managerial capitalism without consumers. It was the new presence of people ready and willing to consume that called this new enterprise logic into existence and sustained it throughout the 20th century. By 1993, nearly two thirds of all jobs in the U.S. economy were directly or indirectly dependent on consumer expenditures, making consumers responsible for more than 79 million jobs that year, a number that is expected to increase to 92 million jobs by 2005 (Pfleeger, 1996). Since the early 1970s, people spent significantly more money on their health, their homes, their computers and other electronic gear, travel, and recreation. Consumer spending generates employment in all but 10 of the 195 industries tracked by the Bureau of Labor Statistics (the 10 are either government related or special industry categories designed for input–output accounting conventions; Pfleeger, 1996). Every one of the 278 occupations used in the bureau's industry-occupation matrix has become more dependent on consumer spending since the mid-20th century. The fastest growing industries have also been those with the highest dependency on consumer spending, such as health care (100%) and educational services (100%). Consumption-related employment growth in computer and data processing services increased by nearly 500% between 1977 and 1997. In management and public relations, that growth was about 250% (Pfleeger, 1996).

From its inception, management has acknowledged this allegiance to consumers. Henry Ford (1922) wrote that mass consumption was the necessary condition for mass production. Has there ever been a chief executive officer who did not repeat this acknowledgment? For decades, public relations, marketing, and advertising staffs have been employed to insist on the claim that the company is devoted to the service of its customers. If that is a universal truth, then so is this: Customers rarely feel well served. The late 20th century has been fertile ground for many forms of managerial innovation geared toward increasing the responsiveness of organizations—from "theory" to participative management, the matrix organization, the quality of work life, the quality movement, reengineering, organizational transformation, mass customization, one-to-one marketing, and, most recently, e-commerce. Each one has followed a familiar and predictable boom and bust cycle of popularity and disillusionment. That is because, I argue, each has sooner or later fallen victim to the centripetal forces of organizational narcissism and its uncanny ability to reproduce the status quo. Even throughout the last decade of the 20th century, after 50 years of business's dedication to management education, consumer ratings of industries declined annually (Fornell, Johnson, Anderson, Cha, & Bryant, 1996).

Structural factors are at work. From the beginning, management defined its project as distinct from its consumers and closed the door on the possibility of formal mechanisms for consumer participation in the production process (Marchand, 1998b, pp. 90–92). Yet even without structurally based power for consumers, there are obvious rational incentives for companies to put consumers first. Instead, the evidence shows that companies put managers first, and consumers are usually last in the parade of claims that shape managerial action. Why is this so?

Sources of Organizational Narcissism

A measure of the distance that separates the firm and its end consumers is the extent to which the modern corporation has developed the behavioral, attitudinal, and financial means to insulate itself from the daily experiences, however painful, and the daily judgments, however damning, of its own end consumers. These powers of self-insulation have their origins in the conditions of production and consumption characteristic of the newly forming mass markets and newly acquired skills of mass production that defined the business environment of the early 20th century. This self-insulating posture is best summarized as an "inward focus," a preoccupation with what is happening in "organization space." The historical factors that originally shaped organizational narcissism have by now produced an elaborate construction of habits, expectations, norms, attitudes, and values that have a life of their own. The inward focus is by now so deeply etched that it is perpetuated outside the awareness of the very people whom it engages. Adults enter these constructed situations and "learn the ropes," accepting them as givens, when in fact they have their origins in very specific historical inventions.

Products First

First and foremost was the preoccupation with the product and its production that characterized the growing complexity of mass-production operations. It was the rigorous attention to innovation in production that made possible the great breakthroughs in increased throughput and lowered unit costs that defined the mass-production marvel. Henry Ford (1922) described it as "modern methods applied in a big way" (p. 75). In fact, the Ford Motor Company was paradigmatic not only in pioneering these modern methods, but in articulating this exclusive focus on the product and translating that inward focus into a new enterprise logic that was widely emulated (Sabel & Zeitlin, 1977; Scranton, 1997). According to James Couzens (1921), one of Ford's early partners, before the era of mass production it was assumed that "selling started with the customer and worked back to the factory—that the factory existed to supply what the customer asked for" (p. 264). But this system frustrated Henry Ford. Satisfying the needs of individual customers made it impossible to achieve the scale and scope that mass production promised. In 1909, as Ford recounted it, his sales force was badgering him for a more diversified product line. "They listened to the 5 per cent," he complained, "the special customers who could say what they wanted, and forgot all about the 95 per cent who just bought without making any fuss" (Ford, 1922, p. 71).

In spite of the pressures to further diversify his range of models, Ford went ahead and announced that rather than increase the product range, he would reduce it, building only one model on only one chassis. The difference in these strategies pivoted on Ford's insight into the true immensity of the mass-market opportunity and what it would mean for production. He stated it clearly in his essay on mass production in the *Encyclopedia Britannica* in 1926: "The necessary, precedent condition of mass production is a capacity, latent or developed, of mass consumption, the ability to absorb large production. The two go together, and in the latter may be traced the reasons for the former" (Ford, 1926, p. 821). While the sales force at Ford Motor Company continued to regard the automobile as a high-priced luxury item whose design should cater to the desires of the wealthy, Ford (1922) anticipated the tidal wave of demand that only mass-produced products would be able to fulfill:

> The selling people could not of course see the advantages that a single model would bring about in production. More than that, they did not particularly care. They thought that our production was good enough as it was and there was a very decided opinion that lowering the sales price would hurt sales. . . . There was very little conception of the motor industry. (p. 72)

The truly profound innovation at the Ford Motor Company was not the moving assembly line, the minute division of labor, or any one of the many production breakthroughs for which his factories became world renown. Henry Ford's single-minded act of brilliance was to take a process that began with the customer and invert it. His unusually canny insight into the then changing structure of consumption, combined with his unique imperviousness to the opinions of others, led to this historic invention: a classic Copernican inversion of periphery and center that would form the template for modern industry in the 20th century. Years later, Couzens (1921) would be the one to state it most clearly: "What the Ford company really did . . . was to reverse the process. We worked out a car and at a price which would meet the largest average need. In effect, we standardized the customer" (p. 131).

Ford's truth would be held as self-evident for decades to come. It lodged in the assumptions and daily practices of managers the world over. It guided textbook writers and chief executives. In 1943 an influential management thinker, Lyndall Urwick, chided his readers:

> To allow the individual idiosyncrasies of a wide range of customers to drive administration away from the principles on which it can manufacture most economically is suicidal—the kind of good intention with which the road to hell or bankruptcy is proverbially paved. (p. 29)

The Politics of the Hierarchy

Ironically, it is that other paradigmatic 20th-century organization, General Motors, that best illustrates a second factor—the politics of the professional managerial hierarchy. Whereas Ford invented the enterprise logic that laid the basis for the new economies of scale and scope, he eschewed the kind of management infrastructure that would be necessary to coordinate and control complexity on this grand scale. As far as he was concerned, it was the product and its production that should command everyone's full attention, not organizational structure or career advancement. Ford (1922) complained, "To my mind there is no bent of mind more dangerous than that which is sometimes described as the 'genius for organization'" (p. 91). Also, "It is not necessary to have meetings to establish good feeling between individuals or departments. It is not necessary for people to love each other in order to work together" (p. 92).

Despite Ford's considerable insight into the new mass economy, he typified a 19th-century owner-manager in his approach to organization and management. He insisted on making the decisions that affected every aspect of the business from production planning to product design, marketing, and distribution. The last thing he wanted around him was a group of managers, because he was convinced that they would turn his business into a mere backdrop for their own career ambitions. Ford boasted of the lack of formal organization, managerial titles, and orderly career paths in his company. All that, he reckoned, was nothing more than a platform for individuals to compete over power and influence. He believed that such competitive career dynamics would shift everyone's attention from the real work at hand—production:

> This habit of making the work secondary and the recognition primary is unfair to the work. It makes recognition and credit the real job. . . . It produces the kind of man who imagines that by "standing in with the boss" he will get ahead. (Ford, 1922, p. 96)

Business historians have argued that this lack of attention to organization and management led to the disastrous results that Ford Motor experienced by 1927, when its market share collapsed to under 10% (Tedlow, 1990, p. 163). The company saturated its markets with one kind of car that sold at extremely low margins. Already in 1924, the profit per car had dropped to only two dollars;

most of the company's revenue derived instead from sales of parts and from other sources. Ford had lost sight of the growing complexities of consumer demand. This new environment was one that Ford had a major role in fashioning, but it now required more from a company than simply a product. Marketing, new product development, and more complex pricing, sales, and distribution strategies—in addition to the focus on products and their production—would be the new ingredients necessary to sustain a firm's growth and financial success. As historian Richard Tedlow (1990) explains it:

> The consumer had to be given a reason to purchase a new vehicle, and price could no longer be the sole appeal. . . . To meet the challenges of the "New Era," organization was essential. The company needed a structure that would act as an avenue toward rather than a barrier to the formulation and implementation of well-conceived strategy. And it needed to attract the best executive talent possible to make the organization work. (pp. 159–160)

The firm that made the greatest single contribution to developing and refining this new management organization was General Motors. As historian Alfred Chandler (1977) notes, "Because the executives at General Motors described their achievements in the new management journals, theirs became the standard model on which other enterprises later shaped their organization structures" (p. 459). In the early 1920s, General Motors, led by Pierre du Pont and later Alfred Sloan, created the *multidivisional structure:*

> In this type of structure, autonomous divisions continued to integrate production and distribution by coordinating flows from suppliers to consumers in different, clearly defined markets. The divisions, headed by middle managers, administered their functional activities through departments organized along the lines of those at General Electric and Du Pont. A general office of top managers, assisted by large financial and administrative staffs, supervised these multifunctional divisions. The general office monitored the divisions to be sure that their flows were tuned to fluctuations in demand and that they had comparable policies in personnel, research, purchasing, and other functional activities. The top managers also evaluated the financial and market performance of the divisions. Most important of all, they concentrated on planning and allocating resources. (Chandler, 1977, p. 457)

With the creation of these new structures, Chandler concludes, "the basic organizational structure and administrative procedures of the modern industrial enterprise were virtually completed" (p. 463).

During the first two decades of the 20th century, the combined pressures of mass production, vertical integration, and expanding markets blasted the owner-manager's role into a hundred fragments, each of which materialized in a new tier of management or a new set of specialized staff functions. These new structures gradually came to dominate the economic landscape, led by a still nascent but fast-growing cadre of professional managers whose authority derived from the property rights of the shareholders whose interests they represented. "A managerial hierarchy had to be created to supervise several operating units and to coordinate and monitor their activities" (Chandler,

1977, p. 486). During that 20-year period, the shift toward managerial capitalism was decisive, and by midcentury, professionally oriented, salaried career managers were the men who had taken charge of the large multiunit enterprises that dominated the American economy (Chandler, 1977).

The rapid growth of this new professional hierarchy has been one of the truly dramatic developments in the labor markets of the 20th century. In 1900, managers accounted for less than 1% of the labor force. By 1930, that figure had risen to 7.5%, 10.5% by 1970, and by 1990 it was approaching 14% (Osterman, 1996). This occupational growth needs to be understood in relation to other occupations. For example, between 1900 and 1940, the population of the United States increased by 73%, the labor force by 81%, the ranks of direct labor by 87%, and the numbers of administrative personnel in business enterprises—those engaged in managerial decision making, coordination, supervision, planning, record keeping, buying, and selling—by 244%! From 1897 to 1947, the ratio of administrative personnel to direct labor changed from 9.99% to 22.2% (Zuboff, 1996).

In a landmark study of this phenomenon published in 1951, Seymour Melman of Columbia University concluded that this trend in the growth of administrative overhead appeared to be consistent across businesses and industries. Moreover, it was not a function of size, mechanization, technical complexity, or of any one of a host of other variables that many had assumed were responsible. Instead, he hypothesized, it was due to the perpetual addition of new functions and activities, a process propelled by managers' attempts to control more of the factors that bore on the performance of the firm. This meant both more staff engaged in record keeping and data analysis and more executive management to address an increasing proliferation of activities related to marketing, strategic planning, finance, and the like. Others have noted that "a central aspect of managerial employment systems was the strong bias toward continually increasing managerial employment" (Osterman, 1996, p. 5). The United States leads the world in managerial intensity, with Canada, Britain, and Australia not far behind. Some scholars have argued that this pattern can be attributed to patterns of executive compensation that tend to link salary increases to increases in the size of the unit that a manager oversees (Milgrom & Roberts, 1992).

Melman's (1951) analysis has withstood the test of time. Between 1960 and 1980, the ratio of managers, including line and staff, to establishments increased by 280%, whereas the ratio of production employees decreased by about 50%. During the 15 years between 1975 and 1990, the numbers of managers in the manufacturing sector alone more than doubled, from approximately 1.2 to more than 2.5 million, in spite of well-publicized attempts to eliminate excessive layers of hierarchy in these industries (Attewell, 1992). In 2000, the absolute number of blue-collar workers was roughly the same as it was in 1972, whereas the number of managers and administrators had risen by about 41%.

In a review of several studies of managerial employment, economist Paul Osterman concluded in 1996 that, despite the recessions of the 1980s and early 1990s, managerial employment slightly increased during this period, and managers continued to experience healthy income growth. However, middle managers in the early years of their careers did become more vulnerable to displacement than in any other decade; they experienced more "churning" in their careers than had previously been associated with managerial work. He concluded that, despite some "fraying around the edges of the previously secure managerial world . . . the data do not suggest the kind of revolutionary change implied by most of the popular literature. Managerial employment has not fallen, indeed it has risen slightly" (Osterman, 1996, p. 11).

The Bureau of Labor Statistics, in its projections of occupational employment to the year 2006, predicts that:

> Professional specialty occupations; marketing and sales occupations; executive, administrative, and managerial occupations; and technicians and related support occupations are projected to increase their share of total employment over the 1996–2006 period, as they did between 1986 and 1996 . . . clerical; operators, fabricators, and laborers; precision production, craft, and repair occupations; and agriculture, forestry, fishing, and related occupations will continue their decline as a proportion of total employment. (U.S. Department of Labor, 1998, p. 58)

Specifically, between 1996 and 2006, the managerial group is expected to grow by some 17%, though that is slower than the 28% growth rate of the prior decade. However, the predictions of slower growth are based on the questionable assumption that "restructured" organizations will require fewer middle managers (U.S. Department of Labor, 1998, p. 59).

Anecdotal evidence has already surfaced that raises more doubts about the assumption of slower growth in the numbers of managers. The Association of Executive Search Consultants reported that between 1997 and 1998, searches for general managers below the division-head level increased by 58% (Lancaster, 1998). The *Wall Street Journal* reports:

> After years of downsizing and "delayering" the management hierarchy, [people] are hot again. Companies that once bragged about their reengineered work processes and new quality measurements now are extolling the importance of human beings . . . many companies are spotlighting managers in an effort to rebuild cultures disrupted by mergers and cost cutting. (Lancaster, 1998, p. 81)

In a 1998 *Fortune* magazine article, the president of a large executive search firm, Management Recruiters International, writes: "There is higher demand for middle managers today than I have seen in my 33 years in this business. There are more middle-management job openings than there are people to fill them—and this has never happened before" (Colvin, 1998, p. 223).

As the number of managers grew, so did their means of acquiring credentials and professional identity. Though their authority was founded on property rights, it was bolstered by their claims to unique expertise and specialist knowledge that enabled them to oversee the increasing complexities of the industrial enterprise. In 1900, there was barely a trace of professional management, whereas by 1920 there was what Chandler has called a "flourishing" presence of societies, journals, university training, and specialized consultants. In the emerging rationale for managerial authority, "college-bred men" and scientific experts would impose technical standards on production for the good of all (Haber, 1964). One well-known academic who wrote an influential 1920 business text argued that success in business depended on formal training and a scientific attitude (DeHaas, 1920). The entrepreneurial tradition was no longer a match for the challenges of business administration: "Every lack of knowledge means lessened efficiency, high cost, smaller profits, and possible failure" (DeHaas, 1920, p. 6).

In 1875, only about one third of the most prominent businessmen had any education beyond high school. By 1920, two thirds of all top managers had attended college (Bendix, 1974, pp. 230–231). In 1952, a study of 8,300 "big businessmen" showed that 76% had attended college, 57% had graduated, and 19% had advanced degrees (Warner & Abegglen, 1959, p. 105). Every sociological analysis since reveals the same pattern. Education allocates people to high-status jobs, particularly in management and the professions. Gradually, the MBA degree was used to further differentiate educated candidates and allocate them appropriately in the corporate hierarchy. In 1920, 100 of the then-new MBA degrees were granted; by 1950 that number had risen to 4,335; in 1970 it was 21,561; and by 1996 it was 93,982 (Hugstad, 1983; U.S. Department of Education, 1999). That's nearly a 1,000% increase in 76 years! In 1958, there were 120 graduate business programs in the United States, and now there are 750 (Hugstad, 1983; Miller, 1998).

The growth of the managerial hierarchy was motivated by the technical requirements of mass production and mass distribution, but it never was the realm of pure rationality on which its credentials rested. From the start, it was enmeshed in the intrigues of any social hierarchy, fully burdened with the thrills and terrors of the hunt. Managers developed a common outlook and code of conduct together with behavioral norms, language, values, and even collective standards of dress and personal grooming. In short, the growth and diffusion of the professional managerial hierarchy gave rise to managerial culture as well as to managerial capitalism. La Bruyere (1922), an observer of court society in 17th-century France, wrote:

> Life at court is a serious, melancholy game, which requires of us that we arrange our pieces and our batteries, have a plan, follow it, foil that of our adversary, sometimes take risks and play on impulse. . . . A man who knows the court is master of his gestures, of his eyes and his expression; he is deep, impenetrable. He dissimulates the bad turns he does, smiles at his enemies, suppresses his ill-temper, disguises his passions, disavows his heart, acts against his feelings. (pp. 101–102)

And like the nobles drawn to the court by the promise of titles and land, those drawn to the corporate hierarchy tend to have a natural ardor for the rewards of status, power, and wealth that it can bestow. The climb through the hierarchy, motivated by these incentives, is what came to be known as a *career*, and the most successful careers were those that carried men toward the top of the organizational pyramid. Career advancement, much as Ford had feared, became an intensely political game with rules that demanded exquisite levels of interpersonal skill; studious observation of behavioral subtleties, particularly among superiors; and unflinching attention to group norms, values, and standards of conduct. To play this game well requires relentless concentration on the unique political dynamics that unfold within organizational space; in other words, an intense inward focus.

These demands of personal politics were evident from the earliest days of professional management. In 1902, a "how-to" book written for young aspirants to business success warned "Be manly, and look it" (Fowler, 1902, pp. 101–102). The fact that there were few objective criteria for judging the future potential of managers contributed to the political charge of everyday behavior. When success was equated with the ownership of a large enterprise, many books outlined the qualities of character associated with that single-minded achievement. But as success came to be equated with status in the managerial elite, the criteria were no longer clear. The message began to shift from an earlier emphasis on character to a new concern with "personality." To get ahead one had to "get along with others, conquer self-created fear, and develop personal efficiency" (Weiss, 1981, p. 415). These themes were popularized by Dale Carnegie (1936): "We are evaluated and classified by four things: by what we do, by how we look, by what we say, and how we say it" (p. 4); and further legitimated by Chester Barnard (1938): "Learning the organizational ropes" was a matter of learning the "who's who, what's what, why's why, of its informal society. . . . The most important single contribution required of the executive . . . is loyalty, domination by the organization personality" (p. 121).

As professional managerial hierarchies grew in size and proliferated across industrial sectors and geographic boundaries, this new political universe developed a life all its own. Meetings, socializing, and paperwork dominated the lives of executives and managers. By the 1950s sociologists had turned their attention to unraveling the cultural mysteries of this new and powerful group. Books like C. Wright Mills's *White Collar* (1951), William H. Whyte's *The Organization Man* (1956), and Melville Dalton's *Men Who Manage* (1959) were classic studies of the executive manager at midcentury. An executive observed to Whyte (1956):

> You're always selling, everything I do is subject to review by all sorts of people, so I have to spend as much time getting allies as I do on the project. You have to keep pace with people on all levels. Sometimes I get worn to a frazzle over this. (p. 152)

Whyte concluded that this intense involvement with others according to a prescribed set of norms and values was at the heart of the manager's work—getting things done through other people. The further up the pyramid one climbed, the more demanding the role. Success put a premium on the theatrics of conformity, managing the impressions of subordinates, peers, and superiors at the expense of one's own tastes and opinions. Executives worked long hours and submerged themselves in the business of the corporation to the exclusion of family or leisure pursuits.

Today it is chic to say that the "organization man" is dead, but nothing could be further from the truth. Indeed, the facts suggest just the opposite. Organizational life has consumed most people. Physical labor has receded so far into the recesses of our economy and our culture that it is no longer the standard by which other, "newer" forms of work are judged. Most people take for granted that "work" is meetings, work is talk, work is interpersonal influence, communication, and implementing ideas through the efforts of other people (Zuboff, 1988). And though more people today may bridle at the conformity of organizational life, most of that rebellion is expressed through superficial adaptations such as casual dress or more flexible work hours. Every ethnography of corporate life, every book extolling the virtues of leadership, every "how-to" primer on change management written in the last quarter of the 20th century echoes the themes, not just of Whyte, Dalton, Barnard, and Carnegie, but of La Bruyere himself (e.g., Argyris, 1970; Kanter, 1977; Kotter, 1982; Mintzberg, 1973). The most recent literature on organizational change fails to offer a way out. Highly intelligent efforts such as Ghoshal, Bartlett, and Moran's "A Manifesto for Management" (1999) or David Nadler's *Champions of Change* (1998) repeat the inward focus.

A Legacy of Contempt

The inward focus on the product and its production, together with the growing size of industrial organizations and their swirling dramas of power and influence known as "career advancement," dramatically widened the distance between producers and consumers. But that distance was never merely neutral; it was never just a question of producers being simply too busy, too disciplined, and too efficient to look up from their demanding work and connect more directly with their end consumers. That distance was all too frequently charged with a contempt for end consumers (Marchand, 1985). Once the basic organizational structure and administrative procedures of the modern industrial enterprise were completed with the consolidation of the managerial hierarchy (Chandler, 1977, pp. 6–12), the new distance between producers and consumers presented itself, not as something to be overcome, but as something to be managed. The new discipline created for this project came to be called *marketing,* together with its subsidiary functions of advertising and public relations. Its principal responsibilities were persuasion and logistics. If persuasion worked, then the distance between producers and consumers, and especially the contempt that helped to maintain that distance, would be adequately camouflaged. If logistics worked, then consumers would be so awash in plentiful well-priced products that they would not be motivated to complain. Why combine to exert change on a system that produced a cornucopia of affordable goods such as the world had never seen?

During the first half of the 20th century, it was only the large corporations that even established marketing departments (Marchand, 1985). In those firms, marketing was relegated to specialists, while management maintained its inward focus on production. This was the one group whose formal responsibility was to look beyond the organization, toward end consumers. But their responsibility was not to bridge the distance or to invert the system. It was, rather, to both stimulate and manipulate consumer demand in the service of the firm's already established production strategy. They conducted market research and analysis, hired and managed relations with advertising firms, designed public communications, and led the way in forecasting and budgeting sales.

By the mid-1920s, some businesses had publicly begun to worry about overproduction. There was an increasing recognition that high-velocity consumption was critical to the well-being of their firms, and ad creators came to be seen as the experts at facilitating that process (Marchand, 1985). During the late 1920s, professional marketers began to delegate most of the responsibility for communicating with the public to these "ad men." Total advertising volume in the United States increased from $682 million in 1914, to nearly a billion and a half dollars in 1919, to $3 billion in 1929 (Marchand, 1985). The ratio of advertising to total distribution costs nearly doubled in the 10 years between 1919 and 1929, rising from 8% to 14% (Marchand, 1985). National magazine advertising increased 600% between 1916 and 1926 (Marchand, 1985). Business leaders, including the Secretary of Labor, claimed that advertising would bring an end to business downturns and prevent future depressions (Marchand, 1985). The ultimate evidence of advertising's new economic power came in 1927, when a surly and recalcitrant Henry Ford, who a year earlier had eliminated all advertising from his budget, announced a massive advertising campaign in support of the new Model A (Marchand, 1985).

In the 1920s, advertising shifted from the fact-based "factory viewpoint," with its emphasis on communicating product characteristics, to a more evocative psychological approach meant to stimulate a desire for consumption (Marchand, 1985). Yet for all of the success of this new profession, the "ad men" looked on their role with ambivalence. In social class, education, and values orientation, they identified with their clients and the "production ethic" of the business world. But they had been hired to do the "dirty work" that their clients wished to avoid. In their role it was necessary to pay attention to consumers, their psychology, and their habits. They were required to proselytize the very hedonism and impulse toward self-gratification they despised (Marchand, 1985).

Advertisers felt debased by having to communicate with an "irresponsible public" whose "tabloid minds" demanded a diet of frivolity and emotional appeals. The president of the American Association of Advertising Agencies wrote in 1927, "Average intelligence is surprisingly low. It is so much more effectively guided by its subconscious impulses and instincts than by its reason" (quoted in Marchand, 1985, p. 85). Throughout the trade literature of the period, in the articles that advertisers wrote for one another, they emphasized the average mental age of the consumer to be between 9 and 16 years old. Their colleagues in the popular press reinforced this image of an unintelligent public. *Time* magazine, in describing to a trade audience its own editorial approach, proclaimed its unwillingness to dilute its news content with a "multitude of features dedicated to 'Mr. and Mrs. Moron and the Little Morons'" (Marchand, 1985, p. 67). Closely related to the notion of limited intelligence was the assumption of public lethargy. One prolific advertising writer in his book about the profession noted that "man in the mass," except when caught up in emotion, "won't exert himself beyond the line of least resistance" (Marchand, 1985, p. 63).

The more despised its audience, the more the modern enterprise relied on advertisers' specialist skills to undertake the role of communicator and mediator. Advertisers were the ones expected to shout across the distance, even though they lived their own professional and private lives within a narrow circle, socially, intellectually, and culturally separate from the mass of consumers. In other words, advertisers suffered from the same inward focus that they were paid to compensate for, as the sermons within their own trade journals on the subject "Know Thy Audience" attest. Copy writers were constantly urged to go out and sell something, mingle, and "slum." But as Marchand (1985) observes, these rebukes tell us more about the agencies' anxieties than they do about their actual practices, much as today's managers are urged toward greater customer responsiveness.

The Sex of Contempt

The contempt that producers felt toward consumers generated much of the psychological energy that sustained the distance between production and consumption created by mass production and the politics of the new managerial hierarchy. It oriented managers toward their counterparts inside the organization. That was the group with whom they identified and from which they acquired their frames of reference. But producers' contempt also had a strong sexual charge. Some aspects of this story are well known to historians, but there has been relatively little recognition of the role this sexualized contempt played in defining and maintaining the distance between producers and consumers. Sexual acrimony infused the age-old mistrust between buyers and sellers and profoundly alienated producers from end consumers and their experiences. This story begins with some well-documented history on the "separate spheres" that men and women began to inhabit in the 19th and especially 20th centuries. Because there is so much excellent historical work on this subject, I highlight just a few of the most relevant themes.

The problem of sexual contempt between producers and consumers begins at home. In the 18th century, the home was the seat of power; it was the center of commercial and political life as well as the sphere of domestic life. "Command of the house signified command of all its power functions, and understandably men retained control of these places where significant business occurred" (Bushman, 1992, p. 424). During the 19th century, the role of the home changed as business moved out to newly constructed state capitols, factories, and offices. As men left home to go to work, they took power with them (Bushman, 1992). Urbanization, mass consumption, and the subsequent emergence of mass production in the early 20th century meant that the separation and gender identification of the spheres of home and work became all the more definitive (Baron, 1991; Gamber, 1998; Horowitz & Mohun, 1998; Kwolek-Folland, 1998; Peiss,

1998; Scott, 1998). Men were required to enter the world of production to provide for their families with wages and salaries, while women ran the household and managed most of the work associated with consumption (Leach, 1993). By the 1920s and 1930s, ample statistics showed that women did the bulk of the nation's retail buying. Women were referred to by the ad agencies as the "purchasing agents" for their families. Advertisers understood their task to be that of communicating to masses of women (Coontz, 1988; Frederick, 1929; Marchand, 1985). The salience of women's role in consumption spread across the lines of nation and class (Benson, 1996; Coffin, 1995; McKendrick, 1974; Scott & Tilly, 1987). Working-class women in the United States, the United Kingdom, France, and other industrializing countries were expected to be good household managers (Benson, 1996, p. 220; Scott & Tilly, 1987).

This sexual division of labor appears benign enough. Men produced to earn a livelihood for their families, and women invested those wages in consumption to meet their families' needs for sustenance, comfort, and improvement. In fact, this division was anything but benign. From the start, the tradition of contempt that charged producers' attitudes toward consumers had a fiercely misogynist bent. Men looked back with derision from the newly constructed world of production. Once they traded homes for offices and factories, they belittled the importance of what they left behind (Bushman, 1992). Consumption had become feminized and so it no longer merited the time or attention of the men who had set out to make a new world. Women were viewed as fickle and debased consumers who were naturally inferior and cursed with poor taste, lethargy, and ignorance (Marchand, 1985). George Gallup, as a young man employed by the Young and Rubicam agency, wrote that he could not account for the amazingly low level of taste displayed by the typical female newspaper reader and noted that his interviews found "stupid women" in city after city (Marchand, 1985, p. 70).

When Henry Ford capitulated to the need to style and market his automobiles, he complained sourly to the press that he was now in "the millinery business." Nearly 20 years later, Henry Dreyfuss, who designed appliances for General Electric, spoke to the Canadian Manufacturers Association at a meeting in Toronto in May 1952. He announced that it was a good thing industrial design had entered the home "through the back door" into the kitchen, where "wear and tear were faster" and the housewife, "a gadget-conscious mammal," could be persuaded to have her house brightened up with handsome machinery (Horowitz & Mohun, 1998, p. 17). Resentment of and resistance to the need to modify and style products to meet women's tastes and needs had endured. The pattern has been documented for products and services as diverse as electric ranges and telephone service (Fischer, 1992, pp. 234–236; Marchand, 1998a, p. 72; Parr, 1998, pp. 165–187).

More than any other commercial invention of the early 20th century, the department store was designed to cater to women. These stores were fabulous worlds unto themselves, offering a lavish and elegant atmosphere of light and color, fantasy, luxury, and abundance, where women could appear in public without embarrassment (Benson, 1986; Leach, 1993). The same managers who invented this sumptuous atmosphere deeply resented their own customers (Benson, 1986). Department store managers longed for male customers, even though it was well known that they bought less: "They found a male style of making a discrete purchase personally more appealing and less disruptive of store operations" (Benson, 1986, p. 99). Across the world, the same story could be told. According to a study of Australian sales literature between 1900 and 1930 (Reekie, 1991), a variety of profiles were constructed to describe their (mostly female) customers, and few of them were flattering—sanguine, nervous, phlegmatic, calmly indifferent, prejudiced, logical, emotional, overcareful, grumpy, overbearing, argumentative, frigid, procrastinating, vacillating, hesitating, quiet, quick tempered, doubting, the customer who cannot say yes, and the customer who is just having a look around. Psychologists and anthropologists were brought in to advise retailers. They emphasized women's primitive instincts; one classical scholar advised that women's predilection for hats and jewelry was evidence of their affinity with savages (Reekie, 1991, pp. 364, 370).

The evidence suggests that men not only left the world of consumption, but felt an urgent need to denigrate it, in large part because it was now identified as only and merely female. Their ambivalence toward the customers they were required to serve shaded into contempt, not only because of the typical suspicions that have always reigned in the marketplace, but because men felt acutely uncomfortable having to serve the very women they dominated on the streets and in their homes. For many men in new occupational roles such as "department store manager" or "insurance executive," their masculinity was threatened by the new more abstract and service-oriented nature of their work (Kwolek-Folland, 1998; Lubar, 1998; Marchand, 1998a). They were not producers, in any traditional sense. Worse still, they had to pander to a fickle public and "to adopt a dependent, almost servile attitude toward customers who were 'always right.' And those customers, more to the mass retailer's humiliation, were overwhelmingly women" (Marchand, 1998a, p. 14). The better known among them assiduously cultivated their reputations for seriousness and hard work. Rowland H. Macy "worked indefatigably" and was known as a "hard-bitten economizer." Marshall Field "maintained a penchant for austerity, a contempt for frivolity, and a 'steely cold' disdain for any decision not based on fundamental business principles" (Marchand, 1998a, p. 14). They also adopted a tactic well known to their counterparts in insurance—the people who worked at the "lowest" levels were also women. It was they who would be assigned the unpleasant tasks of encountering the feminine public.

This strategy of hiring women to mediate between producers and their (largely female) end consumers caught on in many businesses. Home economists were hired to oversee customer service training or advise on sales techniques. In many cases, they advised manufacturers on technical design, based on their knowledge of how women used specific products (Kwolek-Folland, 1998). In showrooms, in advertisements, and in power company offices, women instructed other women in the use of electric ranges, irons, lamps, and other "power tools" (Williams, 1998). Mass-consumer businesses hired women to represent them, even going so far as to have them impersonate the company owner, an industry expert, or even the role model for a brand name. In some cases, fictitious female identities were created to more effectively sell products into a female market (Peiss, 1998).

The story of sex segregation in the workplace is not new, nor is the fact that men and women were even more broadly segregated in the worlds that came to be known as production and consumption. As we have seen, some historians have already begun to explore the derisive attitudes of businessmen toward the women who consumed their goods and services (Baron, 1991; Benson, 1986; Fisher, 1992; Horowitz & Mohun, 1998). It was generally known that men retreated to their dens, that they retreated to their clubs, and now it is known that they also retreated to their workplaces, there to find themselves "at home" in a new way, in a new male culture. But here is what's new: In distancing themselves from women, they also distanced themselves from consumption. In deriding women, they turned their backs on the true nature of their markets. In this way, a once legitimate inward focus succumbed to the pathology of organizational narcissism.

Consequences of Organizational Narcissism

Organizational narcissism, then, arises from mass production and the necessities of managing it. It is not confined to manufacturing; the same managerial approaches long ago migrated to the service industries, bringing with them the same inward focus. The distance that arose between producers and end consumers was created on practical grounds, but has persisted for less savory and more intractable reasons. Contempt animated that distance. It was part of the age-old mistrust between sellers and buyers in every marketplace the world has known. But it was also a uniquely 20th-century expression of a newly problematic, anxious, and uncertain masculinity defining itself through opposition to what it most feared. That anxiety resulted not only in sexual domination within the organization, but also in the sexual dominion of producers over consumers. The consequences of this second form of domination for lost wealth and retarded economic growth are even more far reaching. This domination cemented the notion that the worlds of producers and consumers were not only separate but unequal. It created an opposition between organization space and consumption that eventually became reified. And by defining commercial activity as something that occurs in organization space, it cost the modern enterprise a foothold in the changing structure of consumption, allowing the organization to become formally indifferent to the human beings it means to serve (White, 1981).

References

Argyris, C. (1970). *Intervention theory and method*. Reading, MA: Addison-Wesley.
Attewell, P. (1992). Skill and occupational changes in manufacturing. In P. Adler (Ed.), *Technology and the future of work* (pp. 46–88). New York: Oxford University Press.
Barnard, C. (1938). *The functions of the executive*. Cambridge, MA: Harvard University Press.

Baron, A. (1991). *Work engendered: Toward a new history of American labor.* Ithaca, NY: Cornell University Press.

Bendix, R. (1974). *Work and authority in industry.* Berkeley: University of California Press.

Benson, S. P. (1986). *Counter cultures: Saleswomen, managers, and customers in American department stores, 1890–1940.* Urbana: University of Illinois Press.

Benson, S. P. (1996). Living on the margin. In V. de Grazia & E. Furlough (Eds.), *The sex of things* (pp. 212–243). Berkeley: University of California Press.

Bushman, R. L. (1992). *The refinement of America: Persons, houses, cities.* New York: Knopf.

Carnegie, D. (1936). *How to win friends and influence people.* New York: Simon & Schuster.

Chandler, A. D. (1977). *The visible hand: The managerial revolution in American business.* Cambridge, MA: Harvard University Press.

Coffin, J. G. (1995). Consumption, production, and gender: The sewing machine in France. In L. Frader & S. Rose (Eds.), *Gender and the reconstruction of European working-class history* (pp. 111–141). Ithaca, NY: Cornell University Press.

Colvin, G. (1998, March 2). Revenge of the nerds. *Fortune,* pp. 223–225.

Coontz, S. (1988). *The social origins of private life: A history of American families, 1600–1900.* London: Verso.

Couzens, J. (1921). What I learned about business from Ford. *System, 40,* 261–361.

Dalton, M. (1959). *Men who manage.* New York: Wiley.

DeHaas, J. A. (1920). *Business organization and administration.* New York: Gregg Publishing.

Fischer, C. (1992). *America calling: A social history of the telephone to 1940.* Berkeley: University of California Press.

Ford, H. (1922). *My life and work.* New York: Doubleday.

Ford, H. (1926). Mass production. In *Encyclopedia Britannica supplement* (13th ed., Vol. 2, pp. 821–823). Chicago: Encyclopedia Britannica Press.

Fornell, C., Johnson, M., Anderson, E., Cha, J., & Bryant, B. E. (1996). The American customer satisfaction index: Nature, purpose, and findings. *Journal of Marketing, 60*(4), 7–18.

Fowler, N. C. (1902). *The boy: How to help him succeed.* Boston: Oakwood.

Frederick, C. (1929). *Selling Mrs. Consumer.* New York: The Business Bourse.

Gamber, W. (1998). A gendered enterprise: Placing nineteenth-century businesswomen in history. *Business History Review, 72,* 188–217.

Ghoshal, S., Bartlett, C. A., & Moran, P. (1999). A manifesto for management. *Sloan Management Review, 40,* 9–20.

Haber, S. (1964). *Efficiency and uplift: Scientific management in the progressive era 1890–1920.* Chicago: University of Chicago Press.

Horowitz, R., & Mohun, A. (1998). *His and hers: Gender, consumption, and technology.* Charlottesville: University Press of Virginia.

Hugstad, P. S. (1983). *The business school in the 1980s.* New York: Praeger Publishers.

Kanter, R. M. (1977). *Men and women of the corporation.* New York: Basic Books.

Kelman, H. C. (1961). Processes of opinion change. *Public Opinion Quarterly, 25,* 57–78.

Kelman, H. C. (1997). Group processes in the resolution of international conflicts: Experiences from the Israeli–Palestinian case. *American Psychologist, 52,* 212–220.

Kelman, H. C., & Hamilton, V. L. (1989). *Crimes of obedience: Toward a social psychology of authority and responsibility.* New Haven, CT: Yale University Press.

Kimberly, J. (1975). Environmental constraints and organizational structure. *Administrative Science Quarterly, 20,* 1–9.

Kotter, J. (1982). *The general managers.* New York: Free Press.

Kwolek-Folland, A. (1998). *Incorporating women: A history of women and business in the United States.* New York: Simon & Schuster.

La Bruyere, J. (1922). Cararcters: 'De la cow.' In *Oeuvres* (Vol. 2, pp. 101–102). Paris: Hachette.

Lancaster, H. (1998, April 14). Middle managers are back (but now they're high impact players). *Wall Street Journal,* p. 81.

Leach, W. (1993). *Land of desire.* New York: Random House.

Lubar, S. (1998). Men/women/production/consumption. In R. Horowitz & A. Mohun (Eds.), *His and hers: Gender, consumption, and technology* (pp. 7–38). Charlottesville: University Press of Virginia.

Marchand, R. (1985). *Advertising the American dream: Making way for modernity 1920–1940.* Berkeley: University of California Press.

Marchand, R. (1998a). *Creating the corporate soul: The rise of public relations and corporate imagery in American big business.* Berkeley: University of California Press.

Marchand, R. (1998b). Customer research as public relations: General Motors in the 1930s. In S. Strasser, C. McGovern, & M. Judt (Eds.), *Getting and spending: European and American consumer societies in the twentieth century* (pp. 85–109). Cambridge, England: Cambridge University Press.

McKendrick, N. (1974). Home demand and economic growth. In N. McKendrick (Ed.), *Historical perspectives: Studies in English thought and society in honour of J. H. Plumb* (pp. 152–210). London: Europa.

Melman, S. (1951). The rise of administrative overhead in the manufacturing industries of the United States (1899–1947). *Oxford Economic Papers, n. s. 3,* 62–112.

Milgrom, P., & Roberts, J. (1992). *Economics, organizations, and management.* Englewood Cliffs, NJ: Prentice Hall.

Miller, E. (1998). *Barron's guide to graduate business schools* (6th ed.). Hauppauge, NY: Barron's Educational Series.

Mills, C. W. (1951). *White collar.* New York: Oxford University Press.

Mintzberg, H. (1973). *The nature of managerial work.* New York: Harper & Row.

Nadler, D. (1998). *Champions of change.* San Francisco: Jossey-Bass.

Osterman, P. (1996). *Broken ladders: Managerial careers in the new economy.* New York: Oxford University Press.

Parr, J. (1998). Shopping for a good stove. In R. Horowitz & A. Mohun (Eds.), *His and hers: Gender, consumption, and technology* (pp. 165–187). Charlottesville: University Press of Virginia.

Peiss, K. (1998). Vital industry and women's ventures: Conceptualizing gender in twentieth century business history. *Business History Review, 2,* 219–241.

Pfleeger, J. (1996). U.S. consumers: Which jobs are they creating? *Monthly Labor Review, 6,* 7–17.

Reekie, G. (1991). Impulsive women, predictable men: Psychological constructions of sexual difference in sales literature to 1930. *Australian Historical Studies, 97,* 364–370.

Sabel, C., & Zeitlin, J. (Eds.). (1977). *World of possibilities: Flexibility and mass production in Western industrialization.* New York: Cambridge University Press.

Scott, J. W. (1998). Comment: Conceptualizing gender in American business history. *Business History Review, 72,* 242–249.

Scott, J. W., & Tilly, L. A. (1987). *Women, work, and family.* New York: Methuen.

Scranton, P. (1997). *Endless novelty: Specialty production and American industrialization, 1865–1925.* Princeton, NJ: Princeton University Press.

Stinchcombe, A. (1965). Social structure and organization. In J. March (Ed.), *Handbook of organizations* (pp. 142–193). Chicago: Rand McNally.

Tedlow, R. (1990). *New and improved: The story of mass marketing in America.* New York: Basic Books.

Urwick, L. (1943). *Elements of administration.* London: Pitman.

U.S. Department of Education, National Center for Education Statistics. (1999). *Digest of education statistics 1998.* Washington, DC: Author.

U.S. Department of Labor, Bureau of Labor Statistics. (1998). *Employment outlook, 1996–2006: A summary of BLS projections* (Bulletin 2502). Washington, DC: Author.

U.S. Department of Labor, Bureau of Labor Statistics. (2002). *Employment and earnings.* Washington, DC: Author.

Warner, W. L., & Abegglen, J. C. (1959). The social origins and acquired characteristics of business leaders. In W. L. Warner & N. Martin (Eds.), *Industrial man* (pp. 1–105). New York: Harper.

Weiss, J. (1981). Educating for clerical work: The nineteenth century private commercial school. *Journal of Social History, 14,* 407–423.

White, H. (1981). Where do markets come from? *American Journal of Sociology, 87,* 517–547.

Whyte, W. H. (1956). *The organization man.* New York: Simon & Schuster.

Williams, J. (1998). Getting housewives the electric message: Gender and energy marketing in the early twentieth century. In R. Horowitz & A. Mohun (Eds.), *His and hers: Gender, consumption, and technology* (pp. 95–114). Charlottesville: University Press of Virginia.

Zuboff, S. (1988). *In the age of the smart machine.* New York: Basic Books.

Zuboff, S. (1996). Work. In *Encyclopedia of the United States in the twentieth century* (Vol. 3, pp. 1091–1126). New York: Scribner.

8

Peace Architecture: The Prevention of Violence

Luc Reychler

This chapter is a plea for research on peace architecture. The writing was motivated by a mixture of frustration and inspiration. The frustration has to do with the high number of violent conflicts in the world and the slow pace of peace building. The Conflict and Human Rights Map of 2001 identified 178 places with violent political conflicts, 78 places with low-intensity conflicts, and 26 places with high-intensity conflicts (Jongman, 2001). The inspiration for writing this chapter is Professor Herbert Kelman, whose work has significantly contributed to the development of today's peace architecture in several ways. He developed, tested, and refined one of the most important prenegotiation tools: the interactive problem-solving workshops. These workshops consist of nonbinding micro processes, which can contribute to macro-level negotiations but in no way are a substitute for them (Kelman, 1992). Kelman also drew attention to the crucial role of unofficial diplomats or of scholar/practitioners in the peace-building process. His pioneering work furthered the democratization of the peace-making process. Kelman focused on the less visible and often overlooked deeper layers of conflicts: the perceptions, attitudes, and feelings of the antagonists. Sustainable peace building requires not only structures, but also the appropriate psychological requisites or software (Kelman, 1965). He researched how to motivate and mobilize people to prevent violence and to participate in peace building. Of crucial value is his study of the rules, roles, and values that lead to different views of the citizen's responsibility in the face of questionable policies of destructive orders (Kelman & Hamilton, 1989). Professor Kelman is a careful peace architect who distrusts grand plans and believes that sustainable peace building results from the efforts of many minds and hearts. And finally, when confronted with painful setbacks, as in Middle East peace process, Herbert Kelman does not give up.

Mainstreaming Peace Research

Since the middle of the 1990s, the international community has moved into the peace-building business. Consequentially, there is a growing demand for mainstreaming peace research into the decision-making process. This recent development contrasts sharply with the period before, when peace research was a sideshow. Since the 1960s both the Peace Movement and the Green Movement have alerted the international community to the deterioration of the environment and the danger of nuclear conflict. The Green Movement quickly transformed itself into political parties, departments, jobs, environmental impact assessments, and several international organizations. The first publication of the Club of Rome, *The Limits to Growth* (Meadows, Meadows, Randers, & Behrens, 1972), acted as a catalyst. The book raised life-and-death questions that confront humanity and claimed that the most important business on earth is planning for the future of the planet.

In contrast to the Green Movement, the Peace Movement evolved differently. There were some peak moments such as the peace marches in the 1980s, but the impact of these events seemed to be weaker and less decisive. One explanation for this lesser influence is that the Peace Movement had to cope with the powerful bureaucracies of foreign offices and defense departments, which claimed greater expertise. Another explanation is that the Peace Movement has not been unanimous in defining peace as a collective good. Conflicts that were distant were not seen as threatening the vital interests of the organizers. The cruise missiles that could hit the gardens of the organizers inspired huge peace marches, whereas the snipers in Sarajevo did not. Yet another reason for the limited influence of the Peace Movement is that the costs of violence continued to be underestimated through inadequate accounting of the costs of failed conflict prevention (Reychler, 1999b).

A last explanation for the minimal influence of the Peace Movement implicates the state of peace research. Despite a great deal of progress and creativity (Reychler, 1992), this field of research remains hampered by three weaknesses. The first weakness is the "inadequate field experience" of many peace researchers and the concomitant near absence of close cooperation between peace and development professionals working in the field ("field diplomats") and peace researchers. A synergy between the "speculari and operari" (thinkers and doers) would enhance the peace-building business considerably. A second weakness is the fact that a great many of the conflict prevention efforts are compilations of well-intentioned, one-dimensional measures. Not enough attention is being paid to the possible negative side effects (Anderson, 1999; Uvin, 1998).[1] A third weakness is the toolbox approach that is characteristic of peace-building initiatives. This approach involves identifying and classifying measures that are generally considered to address causes of violent conflict. An example is a catalog compiled by the Conflict Prevention Network of the European Union (Lund & Mehler, 1999). This catalog clusters 131 measures into 16 types of interventions, such as awareness training, strengthening the role of political and public institutions, and access to basic needs. The problem is that decision makers tend to select a number of interventions (monitoring elections, development, cooperation, mediation, etc.), without spending sufficient time to reflect on the synergetic or cross impact of these measures. The result is that too many countries in conflict end up with piles of peace-building stones but no sustainable peace building.

---

[1]Since the publication of Mary Anderson's (1999) book, many studies have highlighted the negative impact on the peace-building process of one-dimensional but well-intentioned efforts (e.g., humanitarian and structural aid, peace keeping, democratization). Peter Uvin's (1998) work on this subject has been remarkable.

Despite these problems, peace research is quickly reducing the gap by which the Green Movement has been more effective than the Peace Movement. The prevention of violent conflicts has become a major item on the agendas of the foreign offices in the United States and Europe and also of major international organizations such as the United Nations, the Organization of Security and Cooperation in Europe, the North Atlantic Treaty Organization, the European Union (see Conflict Prevention Network, 1999), and the Organization of African Unity. The driving forces were not so much moral or legal, but consisted mainly of cost–benefit considerations. Once a conflict crosses the threshold of violence, it becomes much more difficult and costly to manage. Violence causes not only humanitarian suffering and economic destruction but also political, social, cultural, ecological, psychological, and spiritual costs (Reychler, 1999c). The costs of failed conflict prevention are very high. Countries with troubled political and economic transitions, such as those in Central Asia, pose a serious threat to human security (United Nations Development Programme, 1999a, 1999b). Human insecurity implies a condition that entails a decline in life expectancy; a high level of morbidity, poverty, and income and wealth inequality; rising gender inequality; educational decline; unemployment; and many less tangible costs. It has become clear that proactive conflict prevention is more cost effective than reactive conflict prevention and that efforts before a conflict has escalated are more cost effective than efforts to contain and reduce the intensity, duration, and geographic spillover of a conflict after it has become violent (Brown & Rosecrance, 1999). There are limits to the level of violence that the world can afford. Sustainable development is not possible without sustainable peace building.

Peace Architecture

One of the challenges faced by the international community in this decade will be to create a more effective system to prevent violence. An essential part of this challenge will be the development of a better peace architecture or more cost-effective ways of creating sustainable peace-building processes. As an initial step toward this goal, I researched the catalog of the Library of Congress in Washington, D.C., for books and articles about peace architecture. I found only one title, *The Moral Architecture of World Peace,* which was published in the summer of 2000 (Cobban, 2000). This book contains inspiring contributions by nine winners of the Nobel Peace Prize from five different continents. Their personal journeys have taken them toward a greatly increased awareness of both the interconnectedness of all humankind and the negative consequences of the use of violence. Their deliberations indicated that these interconnections need to be further explored if a sturdy architecture is to be envisioned for the future world at peace. Despite this precious find, I was somewhat disappointed by the small yield of my research about peace architecture. I continued my inquiry by trying other terms, such as *strategy, design,* and *plan.* Strategists, designers, and planners are also concerned with the practice of building habitable human environments effectively and efficiently. This time I had more luck. I found, for example, nearly 100 peace plans that had been drafted before the Second World War.

Although there is a great deal of flexibility and overlap in the meaning of the terms *strategy, design, planning,* and *architecture,* I favor the term *architecture.* The term *strategy* continues to be strongly associated with nations, security, enemies, and threats and with military forces and commands. The term *peace plan* suffers from reductionism. Most peace plans, I found, were legal blueprints for the creation of world peace and are overly abstract and devoid of context. The term *design* has more appeal but is associated with business; the development of products, tools, components, or processes; and the construction of conflict management systems (e.g., Constantino & Merchant, 1996; Magolin & Buchanan, 1998; Slaikeu & Hasson, 1998; Ury, Breet, & Goldberg, 1988). Personally, I prefer to use the metaphor *peace architecture* because it draws attention to the architectural principles that have to be addressed in sustainable peace-building processes as well as to the need to identify the necessary preconditions or building blocks for different types of violence or peace. The term *peace architecture* also fosters comparative research on successful and less effective peace-building efforts and on good and bad peace architects or architectural teams. Peace architecture is the science, the art, and the practice of peace building. It is action oriented and transdisciplinary in nature. Imagination and creativity are essential parts of the building process.

Architectural Considerations and Principles

One of the first tasks of research is to identify the principles of good architecture. Preliminary research on successful peace-building experiences suggests the following principles of good peace architecture:

1. *A clear and compelling definition of the peace one wants to build.* This implies imagining a more attractive future, estimating costs and benefits, and reconciling the concerns of the stakeholders and the competing values and needs of the owners[2] who will have to live in the "peace building."
2. *A valid conceptual framework indicating the conditions enhancing or inhibiting the realization of the kind of peace one wants to build.*
3. *A contextual and comprehensive assessment—that is, an appreciative inquiry—of the available peace-building capacity and of the needs that must be met to maintain a peace-building process.*
4. *The development of a coherent peace plan.* A coherent plan refers to the achievement of synergy between peace-building efforts that occur in different domains and on different system levels and layers of the conflict. Also of crucial importance is good time management. The details of the differing domains, levels, layers, and time factors appear in Figure 8.1. Whereas the term *levels of conflict* refers to the system levels

---

[2]The term *owners of the conflict* refers to the people who are directly involved in the conflict. The term *stakeholders* encompasses not only the owners, but all external parties whose interests are at stake. These could be neighboring countries, external conflict entrepreneurs, and third parties who try to facilitate peace building.

Levels/Actors
Internet:
 Global
 Regional
 Subregional
National:
 Elite
 Middle
 Local

Domains/Measures
Diplomatic
Political
Economic
Humanitarian
Education/information
Military

Time Factors
Timing of entry/exit
Lead time:
 Long
 Middle
 Short
Synchronic or sequential
Duration

Layers
Public layers:
 Public behavior/opinion
Deeper layers:
 Private opinion
 Perceptions
 Wishes, expectations
 Feelings, emotions
 Historical memory

Figure 8.1.   Coherence among domains, levels, time factors, and layers of a conflict.

for which interventions are planned (e.g., intrapersonal, interpersonal, international), the term *layer* indicates the depth of the impact of the intervention, starting with the outer layer of public behavior and opinion, and extending to the deeper layer of perceptions, attitudes, feelings, and the unconsciousness.

5. *An effective implementation of the peace plan.* This principle involves not only the commitment of sufficient time and means to build the sustainable peace process, but also coordination and effective leadership.

6. *Recognition and inclusion of the owners and stakeholders in the conflict transformation process.* Four groups of stakeholders can be distinguished: (a) the owners of the conflict or those who are directly involved in the conflict (at elite, middle, and local levels), (b) the neighboring actors whose national or private interests are influenced by the conflict, (c) other foreign actors whose interests are at stake, and (d) third parties whose peace-building initiatives or lack of them could significantly influence the conflict dynamic.

7. *An identification and dismantling of the* senti-mental walls *that inhibit the peace-building process.* The term *senti-mental wall* refers to concepts, theories, dogmas, attitudes, habits, emotions, and inclinations that inhibit a constructive transformation of conflicts. The existence of senti-mental walls increases the chances of misperceiving the situation, misevaluating the interests at stake, lowering the motivation to act on an opportunity, and failing to develop the necessary skills and know-how. The hyphenation of *sentiment* and *mental* to *senti-mental* is intended to make people aware of the fact that mental walls tend to be linked to emotions and that efforts to dismantle them tend to be confronted with emotional resistance. Senti-mental walls can have a long history but are basically man-made obstacles. They can be created, restored, reinforced, and dismantled.

Building Blocks of Violence and Peace

Another challenge of architectural analysis is the classification of different types of violence and peace and the identification of their causal antecedents or necessary building blocks. There are several types of violence, such as political conflicts with some violence, low-intensity and high-intensity wars, deep-rooted conflicts, political terrorism, and genocidal violence. Each type of conflict has a different etiology and remedy. The development of peace architectures also demands a classification of different types of peace. The Pax Romana, Pax Germanica, and Pax Sovietica are very different from the peace built within the European Union after the Second World War. The latter type of peace has all the characteristics of sustainable peace building. From a comparative study of the architecture of the genocides in Bosnia, Rwanda, and Burundi, seven necessary ingredients or building blocks of genocide were distilled (Reychler, Calmeyn, & de la Haye, in press). These ingredients are the following:

1. a country in transition with a high level of political, economic, and cultural insecurity and frustration
2. an authoritarian government that attributes the responsibility for the problems to a particular group
3. a small group of fanatical leadership and a pliable majority
4. a systematic dehumanization of the victimized group(s)
5. a plan for extermination or ethnic cleansing
6. a relatively powerless victimized group
7. an international community that morally disapproves of the genocidal behavior but does not take effective measures to prevent or stop the massacres.

At the other end of the spectrum of war and peace, there is sustainable peace. Sustainable peace could be defined as a situation characterized by the absence of physical violence;[3] the elimination of unacceptable political, economic,

---

[3]This could also be positively defined as a situation characterized by objective and subjective security (i.e., people are and feel secure).

and cultural forms of discrimination; self-sustainability; a high level of internal and external legitimacy or approval; and the propensity to transform conflicts constructively. Research on the architecture of sustainable peace building indicates that this transformation requires the installation of six building blocks (Reychler, 1999b):

1. an effective system of communication, consultation, and negotiation at different levels
2. political and economic peace-enhancing structures (consolidated democracy and social free market system)
3. an objective and subjective security system
4. an integrative moral political climate, characterized by the expectation of an attractive future resulting from cooperation, a replacement of exclusive nationalism with multiple loyalties, reconciliation, and a dismantlement of senti-mental walls
5. political, economic, and security cooperation at a multilateral level
6. a critical mass of internal and external peace-building leadership.

Comparative Analysis and Evaluation of Peace Architectures

Another challenge of architectural research is the development of ways to improve sustainable peace-building processes. A comparative analysis and evaluation of successful and less successful peace-building efforts could make successful peace building easier to learn. In such a comparative study, three phases can be distinguished. In the first phase an analysis is made of the conflict to be transformed. This analysis will give an indication of the problems to be solved and the degree of difficulty to be expected. In the second phase an evaluation is made of the effectiveness, efficiency, and satisfaction of the peace-building efforts. Finally, in the third phase a synthesis is made of the lessons learned.

Phase 1: Analysis of the Conflict

In this phase a diagnosis is made of the conflict and of the ongoing peace-building efforts. First, a good diagnosis of the conflict indicates the type of conflict one is confronted with and allows an estimate of the costs and difficulty of the efforts to transform the conflict. Conflicts between two ethnic groups with a history of violence, for example in Rwanda and Burundi, are very difficult to transform. Such conflicts can be asymmetric in the sense that there are significant differences in power, population, and interests between the contending parties. Second, an analysis needs to be made of several parts of the peace-building effort: the process leading to the peace agreement, the peace agreement, and the implementation of the agreement itself. The process can be peaceful or violent, inclusive or exclusive, and prescribed from above or elicited from the owners of the conflict. The peace agreement can address the necessary requirements for achieving a sustainable peace comprehensively or partially; the peace plan can be coherent or incoherent. The implementation could be hampered by inadequate resources, coordination, and leadership.

Phase 2: Assessment of the Effectiveness, Efficiency, and Satisfaction of the Peace-Building Efforts

First, an assessment is made of the effectiveness of the efforts involved in the prevention of violence and the peace-building process. The effectiveness of the efforts is assessed in terms of the nature of the outcome and its durability. The nature of the outcome is assessed by checking how and to what extent the above-mentioned criteria for sustainable peace are satisfied. The durability is assessed by studying the installation and consolidation of the necessary preconditions of sustainable peace. Then the efficiency and satisfaction of the peace-building efforts are reviewed. This is the most difficult part of the comparative study because it requires a thorough understanding of what is needed to create an efficient and satisfactory peace-building process. For assessing efficiency, two sets of measures could be used: direct and indirect ones. The direct measures assess (a) the tangible and intangible costs of the transition, such as the human, economic, social, psychological, cultural, ecological, political, and spiritual costs; (b) the amount of time wasted and missed opportunities; and (c) the impact of the transition on the relations between the conflicting parties.

The indirect measures examine a series of factors that tend to enhance or inhibit transition processes, such as the following:

1. *The involvement or lack of involvement of the people who view themselves as deeply affected by the peace-building process.* The inclusion or exclusion of the owners and stakeholders makes the difference between failure and success. At the heart of the decision-making process should be the people who perceive their interests as being deeply affected. Others who should be included, consulted, or informed are those who could block implementation, those whose advice or assistance is needed, and those whose approval will be required to enable the project to proceed (Kraybill, 1997).
2. *The effectiveness or ineffectiveness of the communication, consultation, negotiation, and mediation.* Effectiveness tends to be enhanced by an elicitive[4] rather than a prescriptive approach and an acquaintance with effective methods of negotiation and mediation that tend to enhance win–win agreements, low transaction costs, good relations, and durable outcomes.
3. *The quality of the contextual and comprehensive analysis of the problems responsible for the conflict.* Special attention needs to be given to the components of sustainable peace that are absent or inadequately installed and consolidated.
4. *The conflict management style.* In contrast to the problem-oriented approach, which focuses on the past, the problems, and the weaknesses, an appreciative inquiry turns the attention to the future and the

---

[4]The term *elicitive* was coined by Jean Paul Lederach (1997). He distinguished between approaches that impose (prescribe) a conflict-building process and approaches that draw on the commonsense knowledge of the disputants to facilitate the creation of culturally appropriate models.

strengths on which one could build; it focuses on the strengths and the peace potential in the conflict-ridden zone.

5. *The clarity and attractiveness of the definition of the peace.* The conflict behavior of the parties is strongly influenced by their respective expectations about the future. Therefore, the projection of a clear and attractive future could significantly catalyze the conflict transition process.

6. *The appropriate or inappropriate use of tools for conflict transformation and peace building.* Different types of tools can be selected: official diplomacy, unofficial conflict management methods, military measures, economic and social measures, political development and governance measures, judicial and legal measures, and communication and education measures (Lund, 1997; Lund & Mehler, 1999). The selection of the tools should be based on a comprehensive needs assessment.

7. *The coherence or incoherence of the peace-building plan.* This consideration involves the synergy or the interaction of actions so that the total effect is greater than the sum of the individual effects. Attention is paid to the interactive impact of the efforts in different domains (political, diplomatic, military, humanitarian, and economic), at different levels (internal, i.e., elite, middle, local; and external), on different layers (public behavior, opinions, perceptions, and feelings), and on different time factors. The purpose of this examination is to enhance the positive and synergetic impact of the peace-building efforts and to prevent or reduce the negative effects (Reychler, 1999a).

8. *The presence or absence of an effective conflict impact assessment system.* The aims of a conflict impact assessment systems are (a) to assess the positive and/or negative impact of different kinds of intervention (or the lack thereof) on the dynamics of the conflict; (b) to contribute to the development of a more coherent conflict prevention and peace-building policy; (c) to serve as a sensitizing tool for policy-shapers and policymakers, helping them to identify weaknesses in their approach (such as blind spots, incoherence, bad timing, and inadequate priority setting); and (d) to further the economy of peace building.

9. *The use or misuse of time.* As a vital and nonrenewable resource, time should not be wasted. Because time can make the difference between life and death, many violent conflicts are histories of missed opportunities. Therefore, more research should be undertaken about the role of time and timing in conflict transformation. This research concerns attitudes toward time; proactive versus reactive mind-sets; the relative importance paid to the past, present, and future in the design of a reconciliation process; the lead time of projects; the preference for short-, middle-, or long-term programs; and the duration of the intervention. Other important timing issues include when to enter as a mediator in the conflict and when to get out, whether to schedule the interventions consequentially or simultaneously, whether elections can be organized if there is no agreement about power-sharing, whether there is an economic threshold below which efforts for democratization would be useless, and how political democratization and economic privatization should be linked.

10. *The availability or lack of an intelligent early-warning system.* An intelligent early-warning system not only anticipates threats and the risk of violent escalation, but it also pays attention to the opportunities to intervene proactively, the costs of different conflict transformation policies, and the impact of planned policies, programs, or projects on conflict dynamics. The development and installation of an effective conflict impact assessment system would considerably increase the chances of establishing a system for preventing conflict.

11. *The effectiveness of the implementation of peace-building plan.* This factor implies the commitment of sufficient time and means, the coordination of the peace-building activities of the parties involved, and leadership.

12. *Unlearning or the identification and dismantling of senti-mental walls.* Peace building is not only about construction but also about deconstruction. To analyze and transform conflicts, more attention needs to be paid to political-psychological variables. Peace builders need to identify and dismantle senti-mental walls. In a comparative study of genocide, it became clear that the behavior of all actors was distorted by senti-mental walls (Reychler et al., in press). The victims were paralyzed by despair, pluralistic ignorance, and political inefficacy. The offenders justified the heinous behavior by historical falsification, stereotyping, dehumanization, distrust, indifference, overly optimistic or pessimistic assessment of the consequences of decisions, and ideological beliefs. The ineffective response of third parties was influenced by the principles of neutrality or nonintervention in domestic affairs, cultural arrogance, a moral-legal approach, and an attitude of waiting until the conflict is ripe. Finally, the analyses made by the experts were inadequate because of their one-dimensional quality; the use of invalid theories, pseudoscientific doctrines, myths, or taboos; elitist analysis; and incorrect assessment of future developments.

13. *A critical mass (or a lack) of peace-building leaders.* Without a critical mass of leaders, within and beyond the conflict region, who can motivate, guide, and commit people to the peace-building process, the chances for successful peace building are very poor.

Phase 3: Lessons Learned

A systematic comparative study of successful and unsuccessful peace-building efforts in the past and in the present could flatten the learning curve. Such a study would contribute to development of a better peace architecture. It could also further the design of more adequate conflict impact assessment systems and thereby raise the accountability of decision makers for their conflict management.

A Critical Mass of Peace-Building Leadership

Could a leader make a difference in bringing people together? Do unfortunate countries lack leadership, or is the level of conflict too powerful for any leader to overcome (Davis, 1996; Gardner, 1993, 1996)? My premise is that an essential ingredient of sustainable peace building is a critical mass of peace-building leaders who can raise hopes, generate ways and means, build peace, and commit people to the peace-building process. Appropriate leadership necessitates not only peace-building skills, but also the will to take some risks to achieve certain ends.

The leadership that is required depends on the specific context of the conflict. Some conflicts can be transformed successfully by the internal leadership; others necessitate external leadership to support the process. The internal leadership to be involved in peace building could be situated at different levels. The top level comprises the key political and military leaders in the conflict (Lederach, 1997). These people are the highest representative leaders of the government and opposition movements—or they present themselves as such. The middle-range leaders are not necessarily connected to or controlled by the authority or structures of the major opposition movements. They could be highly respected individuals or people who occupy formal positions of leadership in sectors such as education, business, religion, agriculture, health, or humanitarian organizations. The grassroots leaders include people who are involved in local communities, members of indigenous nongovernmental organizations carrying out relief projects for local populations, health officials, and refugee camp leaders.

Also high on the agenda of architectural research should be research to identify the characteristics of successful peace-building leaders, such as Nelson Mandela, F. W. de Klerk, Mohandas Gandhi, Mikhail Gorbachev, Vclav Havel, Jean Monnet, Helmut Kohl, George Marshall, Martin Luther King, Jr., and Jacques Delors. This research involves differentiating successful and unsuccessful peace builders and identifying the similarities and differences between successful and unsuccessful peace builders and between peace builders and peace destroyers. A preliminary review of successful peace builders, especially of Jean Monnet, suggests the following characteristics (Kohnstamm, 1981):

1. The overall aim of successful peace builders is to create a win–win situation or a mutually beneficial sense of interdependence between all the parties involved and to embed the peace building into institutions that reinforce and sustain the process. Jean Monnet (1976) repeatedly stressed the importance of helping the Europeans to understand their common interests (*leur intérêt commun*). Monnet also pleaded for the creation of "supranational" institutions (such as the European Commission) that could facilitate cooperation.

2. Peace is seen as the as the result of a reconciliation of competing values, interests, and needs, such as freedom, justice, affluence, security, truth, mercy, and dignity. It also flourishes best in a democratic environment. Jean Monnet (1976) succeeded in convincing the Europeans that cooperation would bring them not only security but also freedom and affluence.

3. A great deal of effort is expended on the development of a good process (Kraybill, 1995). First, Monnet (1976) tried to create an inclusive process.

He insisted on talking to all participants (government, business, and unions). He tried to engage all stakeholders in the peace-building process. The assumption is that people have a stake in a future if they participated in its creation; then they will work much harder and with more dedication to achieve success (Bennis & Nanus, 1985, p. 244). Second, Monnet believed that nothing positive could be expected from a peace plan built on ground rules that imply unequal parties. He insisted on negotiating on the basis of equality and did not accept the idea of *primus inter pares* [first among equals]. Third, to build confidence, he tried to make the process transparent. All plans that Monnet proposed were clear and simple. He believed that the creation of confidence is easier than most people think. It is precisely by simplicity that it can be attained. When initially some negotiators were suspicious, slowly they saw that he had nothing to hide.

4. Peace builders' problem-solving approach is enriched by an appreciative inquiry (Global Excellence Management, 1999). Appreciative inquiry is a far more complex process than the simple positive-thinking approach with which it is sometimes confused. The appreciative mode of inquiry involves challenging the status quo by envisioning a preferred future and identifying the existing peace-building potential. The articulation of a realistic and attractive future, a condition that is in some important ways better than what now exists, and the identification of strengths can accelerate the conflict transformation considerably.

5. Another characteristic of peace builders is their proactive mind-set. Monnet was a mover, not a caretaker. A caretaker manages as well as possible with what exists. A mover not only finds the turning point on the historical road, he helps to create it (Stoessinger, 1979). Monnet not only envisioned the European Union but also tried to assess proactively the impact of policy alternatives.

6. Also typical of peace builders is their open-minded search for alternative ways to build peace in an effective and efficient way. Peace builders are not ideologues who dogmatically assert how to attain peace. Peace builders make a distinction between interests and positions (Fisher & Ury, 1992; Lederach, 1997). Whatever the demands or the positions may be, successful peace builders strive toward an outcome that meets the underlying interests—the things they care about. They search actively for formulas that mutually satisfy the conflicting parties. In some cases, this approach could produce integrative solutions, such as the creation of the European Union, the new South Africa, or the unification of East and West Germany. In other cases, this approach could produce disintegrative solutions, such as the relatively peaceful dissolution of the empire of the Soviet Union or the smooth divorce of the Slovak and Czech people. A great deal of time is devoted to searching for and developing alternative solutions.

7. Peace builders prefer decisions to be made not on the basis of pressures or emotions, but on their merits. Essential is the use of fair and objective standards and procedures for evaluating alternative policy options.

To convey the costs and benefits of alternative futures, Monnet (1976) made ample use of balance sheets that listed the advantages and disadvantages, "the costs and benefits" of alternative options.

8. Important also is peace builders' networking and their engagement of leaders in different domains and at different levels in the process. Monnet did not perform as a prima donna, but preferred to give the limelight to the politicians. "Since they take the risks, they should have the laurels" (Monnet, 1976, p. 273).

More systematic research on the characteristics of peace architects such as Jean Monnet and other successful peace architects would significantly contribute to more effective peace building. Such research would help not only to identify and strengthen the potential for building peace but also to track and weaken the spoilers of the peace-building process. Appropriate research would also help to eliminate some of the stereotypic images of peace builders, such as the portrayal of them as pacifists. These individuals are not pacifists, but practical peace builders. They not only construct but also deconstruct. They cut through dogmas, taboos, doctrines, etiquette, cynicism, and other senti-mental obstacles on the way to progress. Monnet thus challenged the ideas of political prestige and economic protectionism; he pleaded for supranationalism and he questioned the belief in "archenemies" (erfvijanden) and the existence of a politically independent economic sphere (Reychler & Stellamans, 2003). He was a professional with a cause.

References

Anderson, M. (1999). *Do no harm: How aid can support peace—or war.* Boulder, CO: Lynne Reinner.

Bennis, W., & Nanus, B. (1985). *Leaders: The strategies for taking charge*. New York: Harper & Row.

Brown, M., & Rosecrance, R. (1999). Comparing costs of prevention and costs of conflict: Toward a new methodology. In M. Brown & R. Rosecrance (Eds.), *The costs of conflict: Prevention and cure in global arena* (pp. 1–22). Lanham, MD: Rowman & Littlefield.

Cobban, H. (2000). *The moral architecture of peace: Nobel laureates discuss our global future*. Charlottesville: University Press of Virginia.

Conflict Prevention Network. (1999). *Peace-building and conflict prevention in developing countries: A practical guide*. Ebenhausen, Germany: Stiftung Wissenschaft und Politik.

Constantino, C. A., & Merchant, C. S. (1996). *Designing conflict management systems*. San Francisco: Jossey-Bass.

Davis, S. (1996). *Leadership in conflict: The lessons of history*. New York: St. Martin's Press.

Fisher, R., & Ury, W. (1992). *Getting to yes: Negotiating without giving in*. Middlesex, England: Penguin Books.

Gardner, H. (1993). *Creating minds: An anatomy of creativity*. New York: Basic Books.

Gardner, H. (1996). *Leading minds: An anatomy of leadership*. New York: Basic Books.

Global Excellence Management. (1999). *Appreciative inquiry: Practitioner's handbook*. Washington, DC: Weatherhead School of Management.

Jongman, A. J. (2001). *World conflict and human rights map 2001*. Leiden: Interdisciplinary Research Programme on Causes of Human Rights Violations (PIOOM).

Kelman, H. C. (1965). *International behavior: A social psychological analysis*. New York: Holt, Rinehart & Winston.

Kelman, H. C. (1992). Informal mediation by the scholar/practitioner. In J. Bercovitch & J. Rubin (Eds.), *Mediation in international relations* (pp. 64–96). London: Macmillan.

Kelman, H. C., & Hamilton, V. L. (1989). *Crimes of obedience*. New Haven, CT: Yale University Press.

Kohnstamm, M. (1981). *Jean Monnet: The power of imagination*. Florence, Italy: European University Institute.

Kraybill, R. (1995). *Development, conflict and the RDP: A handbook on process-centered development*. Cape Town, South Africa: Cape Town University, Center for Conflict Resolution.

Kraybill, R. (1997). *Process design*. Unpublished manuscript, Eastern Mennonite University, Harrisonburg, VA.

Lederach, J. P. (1997). *Building peace: Sustainable reconciliation in divided societies*. Washington, DC: United States Institute of Peace Press.

Lund, M. (1997). *Preventing and mitigating conflicts: A revised guide for practitioners*. Washington, DC: Creative Associates International.

Lund, M., & Mehler, A. (1999). *Peace-building and conflict prevention in developing countries: A practical guide*. Ebenhausen, Germany: Stiftung Wissenschaft und Politik.

Magolin, V., & Buchanan, R. (Eds.). (1998). *The idea of design*. Cambridge, MA: MIT Press.

Meadows, D., Meadows, D., Randers, J., & Behrens, W. (1972). *The limits of growth: A report for the Club of Rome's project on the predicament of mankind*. New York: Universe Books.

Monnet, J. (1976). *Mémoires*. Paris: Librairie Arthme Fayard.

Reychler, L. (1992). Peace research II. In J. Nobel (Ed.), *The coming of age of peace research* (pp. 89–96). Groningen, The Netherlands: Styx.

Reychler, L. (1999a). The conflict impact assessment system (CIAS). In P. Cross & G. Rasamoelina (Eds.), *Conflict prevention policy in the European Union, Yearbook 1998/99, Stiftung Wissenschaft und Politik-Conflict Prevention Network* (pp. 144–162). Baden-Baden, Germany: Nomos Verlagsgesellschaft.

Reychler, L. (1999b). *Democratic peace building: The devil is in the transition*. Leuven, Belgium: Leuven University Press.

Reychler, L. (1999c, December). *Vrede is geld waard* [Peace pays off]. Paper presented at the University of Amsterdam.

Reychler, L., Calmeyn, S., & de la Haye, J. (in press). *A blueprint for genocide*. Leuven, Belgium: Leuven University Press.

Reychler, L. & Stellamans, A. (2003). Peace building leaders and spoilers. *Cahiers Internationale Betrekkingen en Vredesonderzoek, 66*, 1–27.

Slaikeu, K., & Hasson, R. H. (1998). *Controlling the costs of conflict: How to design a system for your organization*. San Francisco: Jossey-Bass.

Stoessinger, J. (1979). *Crusaders and pragmatists*. New York: Norton.

United Nations Development Programme. (1999a). *Human security in Southeast Europe*. New York: Author.

United Nations Development Programme. (1999b). *Transition 1999: Human development report for Central and Eastern Europe*. New York: Author.

Ury, W. L., Breet, J. M., & Goldberg, S. (1988). *Getting disputes resolved: Designing systems to cut the costs of conflict*. San Francisco: Jossey-Bass.

Uvin, P. (1998). *Aiding violence: The development enterprise in Rwanda*. West Hartford, CT: Kumarian Press.

Comments on Chapters 7 and 8

Jeffrey R. Seul

Herbert Kelman delights in the fact that his former students are engaged in very different types of work, both inside and outside the academy. The contributions to this book provide strong evidence of the varied professional pursuits of those students he has mentored or otherwise influenced, and chapters 7 and 8 wonderfully display that variety. Both of the contributors are social psychologists, but neither teaches in a psychology department. One of them, Shoshana Zuboff, teaches at a prominent business school in the United States; the other, Luc Reychler, is a member of the international relations faculty of a European university. I write from the perspective of a corporate lawyer and former law teacher. It probably is safe to say that the three of us have little in common professionally, apart from the influence that Herbert Kelman and his work have had on each of us.

As we would expect, Zuboff's and Reychler's disparate topics reflect their very different professional commitments. Zuboff (chap. 7, this volume) explores the phenomenon she calls *organizational narcissism*. She argues that corporate managers are obsessively concerned with the *re*-production of existing goods and services, as well as the maintenance of institutional hierarchies and the betterment of their respective places within them. Rather than directing their attention and energy externally by attempting to discern, and then responding to, consumers' true and constantly changing needs and preferences, their focus is excessively internal. Despite a succession of management fads that purport to put clients and customers first, corporate managers ultimately view "business" as something that happens from the inside out, rather than from the outside in.

Reychler (chap. 8, this volume) hopes to contribute to the development of a *peace architecture:* design principles that can be utilized to construct sustainable peace in the aftermath of international or intercommunal conflict. He offers a taxonomy of the conditions that produce genocide, on the one hand, and peace, on the other. He outlines a method for comparative study of peace-building processes intended to reveal what makes them succeed or fail. Finally, Reychler identifies the qualities he believes leaders must exhibit, the objectives they must share, and some of the tasks they must accomplish if there is to be a successful transition from conflict to peace.

Although Zuboff's and Reychler's respective topics are very different, their contributions to this section arguably share at least two significant features. First, each piece reflects its author's sense of moral purpose. Zuboff envisions a world in which corporate managers are not fixated on maintaining or advancing their status within unjust corporate cultures, but are genuinely concerned with and consistently responsive to the needs of those their organizations purport to serve (as well as the legitimate needs of their coworkers). Reychler envisions a world in which violent conflict does not beget further violent conflict. Both contributors write in service of their convictions.

Second, each contributor attributes the status quo, at least partially, to mental habits and organizational or cultural assumptions that individuals tacitly conspire to insulate from examination, criticism, and potential revision—if they are perceived at all. Organizational narcissism, as Zuboff explains, is a constellation of such habits and assumptions. Reychler argues that *sentimental walls*—"concepts, theories, dogmas, attitudes, habits, emotions, and inclinations that inhibit constructive transformation of conflicts"—often must be razed before peace can be built. Each scholar no doubt sees reflective inquiry—practices and processes that help individuals and groups probe and challenge their own limited perspectives—as a potential contributor to fulfillment of his or her moral vision.

These common features do more than demonstrate the affinity between Zuboff's and Reychler's work. They also demonstrate the affinity between the work of these scholars and that of their teacher, Herbert Kelman. Whether he is investigating and developing theories regarding attitude change, the dynamics of social influence, or group processes designed to contribute to the resolution of seemingly intractable conflict, Kelman's work always has been more than a mere descriptive exercise: It has been a visible manifestation of his moral convictions. He has investigated the social psychological roots of prejudice, morally reprehensible conduct in obedience to authority, and intergroup violence, among other unjust and destructive behaviors, not merely to describe their causes and effects, but to contribute to their eradication.

This approach is perhaps nowhere more evident than in Herbert Kelman's foundational contributions to the emerging field of conflict resolution. He has done a great deal to help other scholars understand the social psychological dynamics that produce violent conflict, but he also has done much more than that. Building on the early work of John Burton (1987), he has developed—and, through decades of application, refined—a method for helping adversaries resolve their conflicts. Interactive problem solving might be best described as a process that creates optimal conditions for collective reflection on the root causes of a conflict, the obstacles to its resolution, and possible approaches to overcoming those obstacles. Participants in "Kelman workshops" often are surprised by their changed views about the conflict, their adversaries, their own group, and even themselves.

It is tempting to suggest that we can hear Herbert Kelman speaking through Shoshana Zuboff's and Luc Reychler's work. At a minimum, their contributions to this section seem to reflect his influence. Based on my own experience as Kelman's former student, and as his colleague and friend, I am certain that his influence on Zuboff's and Reychler's lives and life work has been both profound and lasting.

Reference

Burton, W. J. (1987). *Resolving deep-rooted conflict: A handbook.* Lanham, MD: University Press of America.

Part III

Social Psychological Approaches to the Practice of Conflict Resolution

9

Extending the Interactive Problem-Solving Method: Addressing Multiple Levels of Conflict, Unacknowledged Trauma, and Responsibility

Donna Hicks and William Weisberg

Much of Herbert Kelman's work has been dedicated to peacemaking. It has also been characterized by an unusual combination of persistence and flexibility. Although persistent in his dogged pursuit of a safer and more equitable world, he has displayed great flexibility as he fine-tunes his methods, attempting to find just the right approach to working with extremely complex human behavior. His important work developing the interactive problem-solving (IPS) method of addressing intergroup conflict has been a model of reflective practice. We are proud to have this opportunity to honor our friend and mentor by contributing a chapter that walks in step with his persistent, flexible pursuit of peace and justice.

The interactive problem-solving method of intergroup conflict resolution was originally designed by John Burton (1969, 1990) and has been refined during the past three decades by Herbert Kelman (1972, 1998) and others (Fisher, 1997; Hicks et al., 1994). The IPS method, which addresses the intersocietal dimension of protracted intergroup conflict by gathering influential members of the communities in conflict for needs assessment and joint problem solving, has been applied to conflicts in Northern Ireland, the Middle East, Cyprus, the Balkans, and other places. As an applied social scientific technique, the method seeks to prove useful in real-world conflicts. To be effective, it must be adapted to suit each conflict and particular conflict stages. This chapter is an examination of the method as it has been applied in Sri Lanka by the authors and raises questions about three areas in which the method might be extended:

1. *Levels of conflict.* Can interactive problem solving be successfully applied within parties in conflict, as well as between them? How can it address the influence of parties who are not of the communities in conflict but outside them?
2. *Unaddressed injury and injustice.* Does the interactive problem-solving method allow for a discussion of the injuries, both physical and

psychological, that people have endured as a consequence of the conflict as well as the sense that these injuries were unjustly perpetrated?

3. *Role of acknowledgment and responsibility.* As facilitators, we are fully aware of the importance of having one's experiences acknowledged, particularly when parties perceive that they have been the victims of politically motivated violence and injustice. As much as we are aware of the importance of acknowledgment as a tool for healing and reconciliation, methods for soliciting and fostering it have not always been systematically integrated into the IPS process. In this chapter, we argue that a different orientation to the process might produce the kind of acknowledgment and responsibility taking necessary, in our view, to address the deeply rooted injuries and injustices endured by the parties.

Burton, Kelman, and others have grappled with aspects of the three areas we identify here (Burton, 1990; Kelman, 1993; Weisberg & Hicks, 1999). Our purpose is to examine these issues and ponder further how they might be applied using the problem-solving method.

We proceed by providing a brief history of the Sri Lanka problem-solving project and the IPS method, followed by discussions of the preceding questions and recommendations for addressing them.

Sri Lanka: Decades of Violent Intercommunal Conflict

The armed conflict in Sri Lanka between the Sinhalese government and the Liberation Tigers of Tamil Eelam (LTTE) has endured in spite of a number of attempts to find a negotiated solution. Recent efforts have been made by the parties themselves as well as ongoing attempts by the Norwegian government, resulting in little movement toward a negotiated solution as of the year 2000.[1]

Sri Lanka is a small island in the Indian Ocean, off the southeast coast of India. The armed conflict in Sri Lanka is between the LTTE and Sri Lanka's government armed forces. Sri Lanka's population of approximately 18 million is 74% Sinhalese and 18% Tamil (Rotberg, 1999, p. 4). The majority and principal minority groups are separated primarily by language (Sinhalese and Tamil). Although there is no agreement on exactly what role religion plays in the conflict, some have argued that religion is at the center of the division between the groups (Little, 1994). Sinhala Buddhism represents the overwhelming religious identification of the majority group, and Hindu the principal religious identification of the Tamils. Islam and Christianity are small but significant minority religious groups within both the Sinhalese and Tamil communities. Documents dating back to the 2nd century B.C. describe Buddhist views of the important role that Sri Lanka has in the survival of Sinhala Buddhism and the expectation that the

---

[1]The reader should note that since this paper was presented in 2000 there has been dramatic progress toward the resolution of this conflict. As of October 2003, a cease-fire has held for 20 months and several rounds of talks have been held between the government of Sri Lanka and the LTTE, with Norwegian facilitation. This progress has resulted from a confluence of factors, including pressure on the government from the business community to end the war, pressure on the LTTE from the U.S.-led international effort against terrorism, Norwegian facilitation, and courage on the part of leaders on both sides of the conflict.

island will be a bastion of Buddhism and protected from other groups that might pose a threat (Little, 1999, p. 44). Sinhala nationalism was revived in the postcolonial period as the Sinhalese sought to assert their own prominence to recover dignity deprived under colonial rule. The British left in 1948.

In 1956, President Bandaranaike, the father of the current president, was elected on a platform that favored the Sinhala Buddhist over the Tamil. He pressed a "Sinhala-only" language law that made Sinhalese the official language of business and many institutions of higher education, an action that put the Tamils at a disadvantage. Many Tamils spoke English, the prior official language.

In 1973, the LTTE was formed by its leader, Vellupillai Prabhakaran, as one of several armed groups fighting for Eelam, or a separate homeland for Tamils in the north and east of the island. (The LTTE has since become the only Tamil group fighting the government; it wiped out or marginalized some groups, and other groups have joined the government as political parties in parliament.) The killing of 13 government soldiers in the North of the island (Jaffna) in 1983 precipitated horrible ethnic violence in the South (Colombo), mostly by bands of Sinhalese against Tamil civilians, who before the incident in Jaffna lived peacefully together as neighbors. Perhaps as many as 600 people were killed, and 79,000 were left homeless (Smith, 1999, p. 18). The civil war took hold, and since that time, the armed struggle between the LTTE and Sri Lankan armed forces has claimed tens of thousands of lives, and more than 1,000,000 Sri Lankans have become refugees.

At three points during the Sinhala–Tamil conflict, one of them before the LTTE–government war, the parties came together for talks. The first two resulted in pacts that the government quickly abandoned in the face of challenges from the opposition party, Buddhists, and nationalists. The second agreement came after the Indian peacekeeping forces attempted unsuccessfully to enforce a cease-fire in the north, where the fighting has been centered, and then brokered an agreement. The third set of talks, in 1995, failed when the LTTE issued an ultimatum to the government for movement on particular issues under negotiation and bombed a government naval vessel when the date of the ultimatum arrived without the movement demanded.

Throughout her term, the current president of Sri Lanka, Chandrika Bandaranaike Kumaratunga, has pursued a two-track approach to the ethnic divide. On one track, she has alternated between calling for negotiations and pursuing war with the LTTE. On the other, she has promoted a set of constitutional reforms to devolve expanded powers to the provinces, a step intended to give greater autonomy to Tamil-populated parts of the country, specifically the Northern Jaffna area and parts of the Eastern province. The troubled "devolution package" was finally brought to the parliament in late August and early September 2000, but had to be withdrawn in the face of opposition from the United National Party and the Buddhist clergy, who conducted a hunger strike.

The Sri Lanka Problem-Solving Project

In our work with the Program on International Conflict Analysis and Resolution (PICAR), we have been working since 1993 to foster problem-solving dialogue in unofficial efforts to support movement toward a just and lasting negotiated settlement to the conflict between the government of Sri Lanka and the Liberation Tigers of Tamil Eelam. We have conducted three sets of problem-solving workshops.

The interactive problem-solving approach convenes confidential meetings with members of conflict communities for an intensive three- or four-day period to engage in "joint thinking" about solutions to the problems that divide them. Such joint thinking is promoted by the careful choice of participants, by a well-developed set of ground rules, and by bringing the basic human needs of identity, security, recognition, and belonging into the foreground of the political discussions. A team of trained facilitators acts as a third party, representing a repository of trust for the parties in combat and guiding the process by structuring the analysis and keeping the discussion on track; the third party's intervention is facilitative, leaving the substantive input to the parties themselves (Kelman, 1998).

The PICAR Sri Lanka project began in 1993 with problem-solving workshops for expatriate Tamils, Sinhalese, and Muslims living in the United States, under the auspices of the American Friends Service Committee. The workshops were designed to bring together influential members of the three communities for a discussion of their needs, fears, and concerns, and to jointly develop actions responsive to the concerns of all sides that would support a peace process back home. The U.S. expatriate workshops were also intended to reduce the tensions in the expatriate community that mirrored the conflict back home. The workshops were successful in producing a very thoughtful, sophisticated analysis of the needs and fears of the three major Sri Lankan communities—the Sinhalese, Tamils, and Muslims—and demonstrated the universality of many of the strivings of each group for security, identity, belonging, and a movement away from displacement of populations and bombing of civilians toward normalization of daily life. Among the striking features of the dialogue were the concerns of the Muslim community, which had been chased out of the North by the LTTE. One of the expatriate Muslims verbalized his vivid, concrete physical fear of even coming to a U.S. dialogue with supporters of the LTTE. Another such feature was a moment during which one of the Tamils, a health care provider formerly of Jaffna, described her worry that the innocent infants she helped bring into the world 16 years ago were those most likely to be dying now in the war. The participants from all three communities were moved to tears by this discussion—yet the only party who acknowledged the pain or trauma of the loss of children's lives was a member of the third party of facilitators.

One of the positive outcomes of the expatriate workshops was the desire of some participants to bring this type of facilitated problem-solving work to high-level associates of the government and the LTTE; despite the enthusiasm generated for some participants, other participants told us that these workshops served to harden their positions. All three communities had very thoroughly described their needs. None had taken any responsibility for the injuries to the other or for working to improve bilateral relations. Tamil participants have noted that the discussion of the Sinhala participants made it clear to them that they were being invited to be second-class citizens of Sri Lanka. Suggestions that Tamil needs for security could be met through individual human rights left the Tamils with the fear that the group rights of their community as a minority would never be understood by the majority. The Sinhalese would always be dominant. The Tamils would, consequently, be better off with their own state. Some of the Sinhalese took on hardened positions following the workshops, perhaps because the Tamils expressed the opinion that only independence could protect them from the majority, leaving the Sinhalese with the fear that these "extreme" Tamils could not be worked with.

The first set of workshops left us with questions about what role the traumas suffered by Tamils or Muslims, which were not directly addressed or acknowledged, might play in the process of interactive problem solving. It also raised the question for us of responsibility, because taking of responsibility by one group might have addressed the trauma suffered by the other in a constructive way and avoided the hardening of positions that occurred for some members of the group.

In 1996, we held another joint meeting with Tamil and Sinhalese participants from Sri Lanka and the United States. This meeting focused on joint action to bring the combatants together for talks. The meeting was successful in bringing consensus on a plan to solicit the support of international donor countries, such as Japan or Norway, to support a negotiated settlement of the conflict. As outreach was conducted to the larger U.S. Sinhalese community, however, significant resistance was encountered. There was concern at the time that any invitation for greater involvement of the international community would be perceived as undermining their own government, which had labeled the war an internal problem. Coming from a bilateral group of Tamils and Sinhalese, appeals to the international community would be seen as counter to the partisan interests of the majority group.

Although participants in these first two series of meetings encouraged us to gather a high-level group affiliated with the government and the LTTE, the attempts that we made, together with participants, were not successful. The first attempt was rejected by the LTTE because they were calling for official negotiations with the government through an official international mediator and did not want this approach potentially undermined by unofficial contacts. Under other circumstances, if we had thought it beneficial, it might have been possible to gather a group of influential people from the Tamil and Sinhala communities without LTTE cooperation, but not in the context of this conflict. Tamils supportive of the LTTE would not participate without LTTE approval, anti-Tiger Tamils tend to be closer to the government than the liberation movement, and Tamils who are not affiliated would be reluctant to participate for fear of raising the ire of the Tigers.

The second attempt was frustrated by an escalation of the war and by the government's attendant suppression of any travel by representatives of nongovernmental organizations to the North to meet with the LTTE. Being unable to travel to meet with the LTTE leadership made it impossible for us to consummate this second attempt. Our travel to Sri Lanka and meetings with government and LTTE officials, advisers, academics, other parties, and religious leaders, under the sponsorship of the United States Institute of Peace, did enrich our understanding of the conflict, though, and did lead to the third set of workshops to build intraparty consensus.

People affiliated with the government recommended a series of interactive problem-solving meetings on the intraparty level on the Sinhalese side to build greater national consensus in an effort to move toward bilateral negotiations with the LTTE. Intraparty work would be beneficial not only in light of the obstacles to interparty work at this time, but also because the intraparty tensions were presenting an obstacle to successful negotiations. In the Sinhalese community, partisan squabbles over negotiating strategy or possible concessions between the governing and opposition coalitions, coupled with the fears and nationalist leanings within the Buddhist clergy, made it difficult to locate consensus for a negotiated settlement. In the Tamil community, the differences between the LTTE and other Tamil voices, such as representatives of the Tamil United Liberation Front (TULF), which participates in the parliament as part of the governing coalition, have been so severe that a spokesman for the TULF, Neelan Tiruchelvam, was assassinated in 1999 by a suspected LTTE bomber. The government negotiates its constitutional reform package with the TULF and other Tamil parliamentary parties rather than the LTTE. According to LTTE supporters, the LTTE considers the other parties traitorous because they feel that the other parties do not live in the North and do not have firsthand knowledge of the needs of the Tamils in that region. Intraparty work on the Tamil side, though it might advance the peace process, is not a practical approach, because the Tigers contend that they are the only legitimate representatives of the Tamil liberation struggle and have made clear that they would sit down with other Tamil groups only after a settlement is reached.

Following the advice of advisers and people sympathetic to the People's Alliance (PA), the political coalition supporting the president, and the opposition United National Party (UNP), in December 1999, we convened a group of leading Sinhalese clergy, academics, and political advisers from both parties to meet for three days in the Maldives to conduct an analysis of the opportunities for and obstacles to a negotiated settlement. At the time of the meeting, prior to the recent elections, the group conducted this analysis with an eye toward recommended actions intended to assist in the formation of a national consensus. The confidentiality agreement from this meeting prevents us from detailing its analyses and recommended actions here, but the general proposal for action was for an intensive meeting between UNP and PA representatives at the highest level on a specific topic that the participants thought would be beneficial for future bipartisan consensus building.

This next step was delayed in 2000 by official developments. Shortly after the meeting in the Maldives, the official PA and UNP leadership commenced a series of weekly meetings intended to create consensus on a package of constitutional reforms. The reforms devolve power to the provinces in a move that seeks to maintain a unified country while increasing local autonomy, presumably addressing the need of Tamils in the North and the part of the East that is predominantly Tamil for greater control over their lives. This development toward consensus on the official front delayed the proposal for unofficial consensus-building work as hope for movement focused on the official discussions. Although some consensus was reached, mostly consisting of the UNP giving an unenthusiastic go-ahead to the PA to submit its devolution proposal, the consensus broke down just before the reform package went to parliament in contentious, partisan electoral maneuvering.

The Challenges and Recommendations

Any progress generated by the three sets of interactive problem-solving workshops through greater consensus reached and disseminated was accompanied by several challenges and setbacks posed by destructive elements of conflict. There are many obstacles and challenges, including military and economic factors, but here we choose to focus on a few we think have implications for the interactive problem-solving process. As indicated earlier, we have suggested that the IPS methodology, as we have practiced it in the past, is not designed to address some of the complex dynamics being played out in the current stage of the conflict in Sri Lanka. First, this methodology does not traditionally focus on the hostile intraparty rivalries, as well as outside influences such as the role of regional actors. The intense hostility between the Tigers and other Tamil groups, and between the PA and UNP in the government, constantly threatens to undermine any possible movement toward a negotiated settlement. Traditional interparty problem-solving groups might not be the best forum to address these tensions. This was one reason an intraparty group was convened for the third series of problem-solving meetings. As was found after our second series of meetings, interparty problem-solving groups also might not have been the best method of engaging important international countries with power to influence the conflict, because the majority group considered outreach to the international community counter to the majority interests.

Second, the IPS method does not directly elicit a discussion of what appears to be a critical source of intractability in the conflict: the collective traumas endured by the communities as well as the sense of injustice felt as a consequence of being "wronged" as a people. As Tamils spoke of the slaughter of children or the anti-Tamil violence of 1983, or Muslims spoke of ethnic cleansing in the North, their concerns were not sufficiently addressed by their expression of security needs for the future. Discussion of future security is not directly responsive to the pain that one feels because one has lost relatives or friends in seemingly senseless violence.

Finally, the orientation of the IPS method is such that the direction of the dialogue is toward addressing the unfulfilled needs (security, identity, belonging, recognition) of both sides. This orientation focuses on the articulation of what the parties "require" before the conflict could be resolved. Our interpretation is that some of the hardening of views that followed our first set of problem-solving meetings was the result of the exclusive focus on needs and avoidance of responsibility. It is our view that, in addition to the discussion of what each party's needs are, there should be a discussion of each party's responsibilities to bring an end to the conflict.

This section examines each of the above and makes recommendations for elaborations in the theory and process of IPS that could accommodate these concerns. New wrinkles have been added over the decades by John Burton, Herbert Kelman, and their students. In the recommendations, we describe new approaches, some of which have been attempted and some have not, that could be incorporated into the IPS method.

The First Challenge: Reaching Beyond the Interparty Level of Conflict to the Intraparty and International Relationships

The IPS method is primarily aimed at improvements in the interparty relation-ship—the tension between the combatants. There are several other conflict relationships that influence whether a protracted conflict will improve or worsen. Here, we examine some of those other relationships in the Sri Lanka conflict.

In 2000, following the hopeful sign of weekly high-level meetings between the PA and UNP to establish consensus on constitutional reforms, the two par-ties recommenced bickering. The president accused the opposition leader of having prior knowledge of the assassination attempt against her. The leader of the UNP, Ranil Wickremesinghe, withdrew his support for the president's con-stitutional reforms just before she sent them to parliament. Then, in October 2000, after the parliamentary elections, the parties embarked on a new round of cooperation. These cycles, vacillating from outright feuding between enemy political parties to tenuous strategic cooperation devoid of substantive agree-ment, have persisted for decades.

As noted in the prior section, each time the party in power moves toward a negotiated settlement, the party in opposition at the time works to undermine the negotiations. Two agreements have been reached to end the conflict, but both have been scuttled in the ensuing battle with the opposition and nationalist elements.

The IPS method is designed to address the intersocietal dimensions of con-flict by bringing together groups from two communities in conflict for needs analysis and joint problem solving. Its focus is primarily on the interparty ten-sion. At the same time, a cross section of points of view from each community is invited to the table to unofficially represent different key factions within each body politic (Kelman, 1993). In this way, there is also an attempt to create dia-logue and build consensus within each party, or at the intraparty level. This intraparty consensus building would benefit from more attention.

We have observed that progress must be made at three levels of the conflict for it to move toward resolution: (a) the intraparty level, or among the constitu-encies within each of the communities in conflict; (b) interparty, or between the combatants; and, (c) international, or between the parties in conflict and the external actors with influence over the conflict and its resolution (see Figure 9.1) (Weisberg & Hicks, 1999).

In Sri Lanka, within each party (intraparty level), there is the Sinhala body politic on one side and the Tamil body politic on the other. On the Sinhala side, there are the constituent groups (e.g., Buddhist clergy, business interests, Christians, Muslims) and the political factions (the PA, UNP, JVP, Muslim coali-tion, and Tamil parties). In the Tamil community, there is the working coalition that must function among various factions within the community, primarily between the LTTE and other Tamil voices. It is somewhat difficult to place the Tamil political parties within one side or the other, because the relationship between the LTTE and other Tamil parties, as noted in the prior section, can be characterized as internecine warfare. The Tamil parties often cooperate with the Sinhala ruling government coalition. Because they do represent a Tamil interest group, we have included them within both groups.

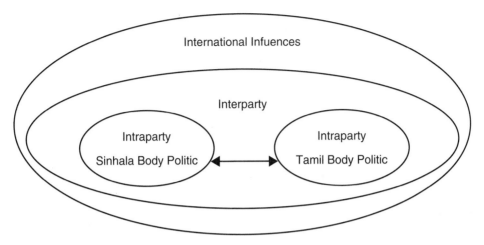

Figure 9.1.   Three levels of conflict in Sri Lanka.

At the international level, there is the working relationship that the com-
batant parties, the government and LTTE, have with the regional power,
India, and with other relevant international actors, such as Norway, the desig-
nated official facilitator; Japan, the major donor state; the United States; and
the United Kingdom. India has been identified as critical to any settlement of
the conflict. India considers Sri Lanka its "backyard," had quietly allowed the
armed Tamil factions to train in southern India at the beginning of the war in
its Tamil state of Tamil Nadu, had sent a peacekeeping force to Sri Lanka from
1987 to 1990, and had brokered one of the two prior agreements that faltered.
The LTTE is suspected of carrying out the assassination of former Indian Pre-
mier Rajiv Gandhi. The LTTE leader, V. Prabhakaran, is wanted for extradi-
tion by India for this case. India has straddled an internal political tension in
reference to the war in Sri Lanka. The Indian governments have neither
wished to alienate the 50 million Tamils in India's southern province, nor to
support too many concessions to the Tamils of Sri Lanka for fear of the ramifi-
cations for India's own violent ethnic separatist conflicts. Analysts recognize
the importance of India's support for a negotiated settlement, and Norway has
been careful to consult India at key intervals throughout its facilitation
efforts. It appears unlikely that the conflict can be resolved without cooperation from India.

The interactive problem-solving method, while addressing the interparty
dynamic directly and the intraparty relations indirectly in the relatively brief
preworkshop session, does not typically devote separate, explicit attention to
the intraparty level and does not bring in external or international actors at all.
An argument can be made that this is for the best, because there is room to
address some intraparty and international issues with a group of influential
people from the two sides in the conflict. They can arrive at joint strategies
aimed at the intraparty or international level. In addition, of concern is that
attempts to address too many dimensions of the conflict would complicate the
process to the point of paralysis.

On the other hand, the focus on the interparty dimension of the conflict tends to exclude some important intraparty constituencies and relevant international actors. Interparty meetings that include the LTTE or its supporters would cause the Buddhist nationalist voices on the Sinhalese side to self-select out of the process because they would not want to be at the same table. Although this makes interparty dialogue possible, it impedes intraparty consensus building. India, Japan, and the United States, international actors that could influence the combatants toward a negotiated settlement, have not been included in the interactive problem-solving sessions to date.

The challenge we are identifying is this: Can the interactive problem-solving process be expanded to better influence conflict resolution at the important intraparty and international levels?

The First Recommendation: Extended Intraparty Sessions

The third set of interactive problem-solving sessions that we conducted with the Sinhalese were, by necessity, limited to factions within the government side of this conflict. Nevertheless, some degree of consensus building within parties will be needed to avoid undermining future negotiated settlement.

The IPS method typically includes brief meetings with each community separately prior to the joint interparty sessions. The purposes of these sessions are to allow each community to voice some concerns prior to the joint meetings and to allow them to see how far others from their community will let them go "out on a limb" in attempting to locate creative, integrative strategies. These intraparty sessions could be extended, with good effect, to whole problem-solving meetings that intensively address the intraparty relations and consensus building.

The intraparty problem-solving workshop could be composed of the same basic sequence of work as in the traditional interparty problem-solving workshop—starting with recommendations for constructive discourse and moving on to needs analysis and joint problem solving. The needs analysis examines the needs of each faction within the community. The joint thinking sessions are devoted to strategies to build greater consensus within the broader community for a negotiated just and lasting peace.

This argument was the experiment of our third IPS workshop, with a cross-section of people supportive of the governing and opposition parties. The format worked, with participants remarking that, although they see each other frequently, the facilitated, structured discussion led them to much more constructive dialogue and work plans than they had experienced before. Although the meetings were constructive and led to a plausible plan for building greater national consensus, as yet unimplemented, one concern arising from intraparty meetings in a bloody conflict is that, without the voice of the other ethnic group present, the resulting consensus could tend toward a more hardened, hawk-like stance. This outcome did not occur in the Maldives meeting, but could potentially occur. We describe later in this section a new session to be introduced in the interactive problem-solving method, which could be applied in intraparty discussion and could also serve to avoid movement toward a harder line.

How to include the international level in IPS is more challenging. In certain types of analyses—such as a Sri Lankan analysis of what went wrong in past negotiations and what could be done better the next time—there might be an appropriate time to include Norwegian or Indian nonofficials. It is also possible to include important international constituencies by inviting them to join the third party of the IPS team. The individuals would have to be chosen carefully so they would have something to contribute as a third party and would not intimidate the participants or have a chilling effect on the dialogue. Outside influences could also be included in conflict resolution initiatives by funding problem-solving and other efforts. An underlying theory of the IPS approach is that participants will learn and disseminate important perspectives on the conflict back to the constituent groups with whom they are affiliated. This should be no less true of the international constituencies involved in problem-solving groups in some fashion.

In summary, important intraparty tensions can be addressed in intraparty IPS. The international level can also be brought in to the process.

The Second Challenge: Unacknowledged Trauma and Injustice

Unacknowledged traumas and the accompanying feeling of being unjustly wronged characterized the history of the Sri Lankan communities far earlier than the outbreak of violence between the Tamils and Sinhalese in 1983. Under British colonial rule, the majority Sinhalese were marginalized by the British, giving the Tamil minority the advantage by teaching them English and favoring them for civil service jobs and university education. Moreover, Christian missionaries came to Sri Lanka and attacked and marginalized Buddhism in an attempt to convert the Sinhalese people. In the pre-British colonial period, the Buddhist clergy were highly esteemed by the Sinhalese people and considered to be the most respected leaders of the community. According to David Little (1994), British colonial policy provoked what might be called a revenge cycle by the Buddhist clergy, in an effort to regain their dignity in the eyes of the Sinhalese community:

> The British, who occupied Sri Lanka in the late eighteenth century, introduced a number of aggressive political, educational, and religious policies that eventually provoked a counter-reaction by the Buddhist clergy, leading to what has been called Buddhist revivalism. (p. 45)

The unacknowledged humiliation suffered by the loss of identity and status for the Buddhist clergy, we would argue, is still alive today in the form of extreme Buddhist chauvinism. The Buddhist clergy has, in modern times, been a loud voice for Buddhist dominance in Sri Lanka. They have pressed for Sri Lanka to be officially named a Buddhist state in the new constitution. (It is our view that this desire to ensure that Sri Lanka remain a Buddhist state, in spite of the religious diversity on the island, is directly rooted in the historical trauma endured by the Buddhist clergy when they were marginalized by the British.) In September 2000, when the President sent the devolution proposal to the parliament, she did so with Buddhist clergy holding a hunger strike in the streets to oppose what they saw as a package that gives away Buddhist identity. This pressure appears to be one of the elements that has delayed political progress toward a settlement.

As a consequence of British colonial "divide and rule" policy, the relationship between the Tamil and Sinhalese communities deteriorated. Before British colonization, the relations between the two communities were never violent and could be described as amicable (Little, 1994). The communities, although maintaining separate ethnic identities and territorial homelands, in the sense that their languages and religions were different and they clustered into geographically separate "kingdoms," did intermarry and peacefully coexist. During colonial rule, the Sinhalese resented the fact that the Tamil community was favored by the British, leaving them in the humiliating position of being "second-class citizens," notwithstanding their majority status on the island. One could argue that the intercommunal resentment provoked by the discriminatory British policy is one of the causal factors in the breakdown of the relationship between the two peoples.

After independence, in reaction to being subjugated by the British, a strong nationalist current ran through the Sinhalese body politic (Rotberg, 1999, p. 6). In 1956, President Bandaranaike was elected on a platform that favored the Sinhala Buddhist over the Tamil. As noted earlier, he pressed a "Sinhala-only" language law that made Sinhalese the official language of business and many institutions of higher education, a policy that disadvantaged the Tamils, many of whom spoke English, the prior official language. One could argue that this was a retaliatory step toward the Tamil community, who failed to come to the aid of the Sinhalese people during colonial rule, enjoying the privilege and advantage bestowed on them by the British. The communities reversed roles, and the Tamils became the subjugated people.

Hostilities escalated between the two communities. Attempts were made to redress the discriminatory policies put in place by the Bandaranaike government. Unfortunately, these attempts were thwarted by the extreme Buddhist factions, as well as the opposition party. The postcolonial history of discrimination and subjugation of the Tamils, and the failed attempts at reforms that promoted equality between the two communities, created the conditions for the development of the LTTE and its more extreme and violent approach to achieving the liberation of the Tamil people. For example, when the 13 soldiers were killed in Jaffna (in the North) by the LTTE and their bodies brought back to Colombo (in the South), this incident provoked some of the most heinous acts of violence that the 20-year war has produced. During these "Colombo riots," thousands of Tamils were displaced from their homes, and many were brutally murdered by their Sinhalese neighbors. Those who were lucky enough to survive the attack were left with the scars and related terror that inevitably lingers with such traumatic experiences (Herman, 1992). To make matters worse, the Sinhalese government did not come out and condemn the violence, adding to the fear and rage that was and is still felt by the Tamil people. These retaliatory acts have characterized the interactions between the two communities since 1983.

On the Sinhalese side, hundreds of innocent civilians were the victims of the LTTE suicide bombings. These random bombings have instilled deep fear into the Sinhalese community. Living with the unpredictability of the occurrence of such attacks has created a real existential threat for all Sinhalese people country-wide.

Some scholars have argued that the aftereffects of traumatic injuries that communities endure, particularly (but not exclusively) by the group who is being dominated by another by use of force, coercion, and other destructive forms of influence and power, not only linger until addressed, but also are transmitted to future generations (Volkan, 1988). The injury persists and remains alive within the individual and community until it is appropriately responded to. On numerous occasions in individual meetings and in our dialogue groups with members of the Sinhalese and Tamil communities, we have witnessed emotional and passionate accounts of traumas that people have endured, many of which happened decades ago. Buddhist Monks reference the indignities visited on Sinhalese by foreigners hundreds of years ago; Tamils speak of chauvinist acts against them 40 years ago. In an individual interview, one of the more vocal and well-known political operatives opposed to Sinhalese concessions to Tamils was still able to tearfully recount hiding Tamil neighbors in his house in Colombo so they would not be burned to death by Sinhalese mobs in 1983. He can recount the trauma, even as a member of the majority group, without making any connection to the need for the Sinhalese to take responsibility for these acts or to the need for greater Tamil autonomy. It might require facilitated dialogue to work through a process that allows for these connections to be made.

It appears that traumatic memories are often as vivid and alive in the present as when they first occurred (Herman, 1992). The traumas are transmitted from generation to generation, preserving and maintaining the deep emotional scars. The pleas of traumatized people for recognition of both the injustice and the suffering that they have endured have not lost any of their urgency. Add to the historical memory of the traumatic events more recent traumas, and one can see how the cycle of revenge maintains its strength and vitality, feeding the deep mistrust and justification for the dehumanization of the other.

The consequences of threatening or acting on the impulse to annihilate the other, justified by one's own feeling of being wronged, have a profound effect on sustaining the conflict. It is not simply a matter of battling over positions and interests and resources. It is our view that the effect of engaging in destructive behaviors toward the other, in itself, can escalate and maintain the conflict. Using power destructively to achieve one's desired outcome to the conflict has its consequences. Destructive patterns of interactions have a profoundly negative effect on the parties' ability to resolve the conflict. Direct assaults to one's integrity, either psychological or physical, not only rob individuals of their basic human needs, but also create injuries that trigger a revenge reaction, which can give rise to a violent retaliatory cycle of interaction.

These cycles lock the parties in a destructive relationship characterized by deep mistrust and suspicion, which provides the rationalization to dehumanize the other, the motivation to stay away from the negotiating table, and the ability to seemingly ignore the obvious solutions available to end the conflict.

Unaddressed traumatic experiences that communities have endured, in combination with the belief that the trauma was unfairly perpetrated on them, contribute to the inability to resolve long-standing intercommunal conflict. The unaddressed traumas are not only sources of intractability in keeping a conflict alive but also sources of threat to the sustainability of a peace agreement, should one be found.

In summary, the failure to address what people have endured in times of war—either by ignoring it or diminishing its importance—has serious implications for a sustainable peace between the communities. Even if the parties find ways to adequately address their needs and interests in a political settlement— that is to say, even if both sides have agreed to a particular constitutional arrangement where power is shared, thereby putting an end to inequality and discrimination—there is still a need to come to terms with the brutality people endured, the way communities have treated one another, and the victim's need to have that brutality acknowledged in some form. Parties cannot simply sign a political settlement and expect that they will be able to live together in the future. There is a need for the development of a process in which victims and perpetrators come to terms with their relationship during the time of conflict and face up to the consequences of violating the integrity of the other.

Does the IPS approach address these critical issues of trauma and injustice? To date, our practice has been influenced by the concern that discussions of injustice might undermine the nonadversarial interchange we attempt to create if the ensuing discussion leads to competing claims of injustice. Some practitioners have also voiced the concern to us that a discussion of trauma could create a more "therapeutic" rather than strictly "political" feel to the dialogue, which might undermine the method's objective of facilitating resolution at the political level. The ground rules of the IPS workshop state that the issues of history and justice are not appropriate to the kind of non-adversarial discussion encouraged by the workshop. The purpose of this ground rule is to avoid a blaming approach and legalistic arguments. Although not explicitly forbidden, the telling of personal stories of the traumas and suffering that participants have experienced is not encouraged. The emphasis in the problem-solving workshop is on the development of creative political ideas (based on an understanding of the basic human needs that would have to be fulfilled before the conflict could be resolved) that could be injected into the public and political debate as well as the decision-making process. Discussion of injury or trauma leaves some third-party practitioners concerned that, if not handled correctly, this will lead to an adversarial debate about rights and wrongs and will prevent joint problem solving. The important point to be made here is both theoretical and practical. We are suggesting that an articulation of the basic human needs, such as the need for identity, belonging, recognition, and security that Burton originally claimed as the core issues that needed to be addressed before an enduring end of the conflict could be found, is not enough to make a breakthrough in the conflict relationship. We are arguing that it is important to find a way to introduce into the dialogue the felt experience of having those needs violated (the traumas and suffering people have endured) as well as the belief that a great injustice has been perpetrated by the denial of those needs. The challenge, then, is to find an approach that allows trauma and injustice to be addressed without escalating the adversarial conflict dynamic. In the Sri Lanka conflict, if one were not familiar with the colonial history of the asymmetrical treatment of the Sinhalese and Tamil peoples by the British, one would entirely miss the experience of humiliation and loss of dignity felt by Buddhist clergy. One's understanding of the cycles of retaliation and revenge that have characterized the relationship between the two communities would be distorted. The injustice felt by the Buddhist clergy that has fueled their chauvinism to the present would not be factored into the causal chain of events that are at the core of the conflict. More importantly, perhaps, the injustices experienced by both the Sinhala and Tamil communities would not be responded to in a fashion that would allow them to forge a peaceful, just future.

The Second Recommendation: Addressing Trauma and Injustice in Interactive Problem Solving

Although it is common wisdom that acknowledgment of the traumatic experiences communities have endured is a necessary step in the conflict resolution process, the IPS methodology is not designed to address it directly. There is no systematic attempt to build into the process a way in which people can recount their experiences and have them acknowledged and validated by either the other side or the third party. Although discussion of traumatic experiences frequently occurs in IPS workshops, we have not yet formulated an approach to process these discussions as a constructive element of the problem-solving endeavor. What the IPS approach does is allow both sides to articulate the needs, fears, and concerns that would have to be addressed before a sustainable resolution to the conflict could be found. The articulation of one's needs is one step removed from describing the actual events that created a violation of those needs. Herman (1992) has argued that victims of violence and trauma need an opportunity to discuss what happened to them and to recount the story of their experiences in a setting that feels secure for them so that they can put the traumatic experiences to rest. Articulating a need for identity is very different from telling the story of being persecuted or marginalized that gave rise to the violation of one's identity; or telling what it was like to experience the terror of a suicide bomb is perhaps more than just a step removed from saying one has a need for security. People who have been traumatized need to be able to talk about what happened to them and to express their beliefs that what they endured was unjustly perpetrated on them.

It is our view that not only do victims benefit from telling their story, but perpetrators also benefit by being exposed to the suffering of the other, which could break the cycle of dehumanization that justified their aggressive acts. McClellan (2000, p. 82) argued that one of the essential conditions for treating another with civility is the belief that one is dealing with someone who is fully human. Denying others their humanity is the first step in justifying one's violent actions toward the other. In his description of "humanity," McClellan pointed out that we tend to think of it in strictly positive terms, particularly by emphasizing the need to respect the dignity and worth of all peoples. He added that it is equally important to integrate the "negative" aspects of humanity, that part of us that is imperfect and, because of our imperfections, capable of destructive and antisocial behaviors such as selfishness, greed, revenge, and any number of violent acts. The acceptance of both aspects of humanity is fundamental to embracing the totality of what it means to be human. The implications of this more integrated view of "accepting one's humanity" is profound for the work of conflict resolution, a discussion to which we will return when we address the importance of taking responsibility in the next section.

In summary, the IPS approach, by emphasizing the articulation of needs, fears, and concerns, does not invite participants to discuss the traumatic experiences they have endured as well as the feeling that what they have been through was unjust. The literature on recovery from traumatic events consistently describes the need to retell the story of what happened to the victim in a way that is not challenged and does not require the victims to defend their experiences (Chambers, 2000). What we recommend is that the participants have the opportunity, as part of the methodology, to express their personal stories that illustrate how their needs have been deprived. This elaboration of the process could take place before the articulation of the needs, which is traditionally the first major session of the IPS approach. This kind of session could only strengthen the needs analysis, by adding a human dimension to what is currently a more analytic approach to understanding each other's experiences. Telling one's personal stories of what one has experienced as a result of the conflict closes the gap between the human suffering and the consequences of the suffering (the deprived needs).

When parties have introduced a discussion of injustice in our recent work, it has been possible to proceed through the tension that arises for the other party during this discussion to a dialogue that is not more adversarial in the end. Once an environment is created in which each party can describe injustices suffered and perpetrated, a more complex, multilayered picture is painted. The resulting dialogue is less adversarial. Likewise, when traumas have been described by parties in our recent work, it did not take away from discussion of political issues and toward a "therapy" session addressing individual psychological needs. As we view it, it led to a deeper understanding of the experience of conflict on the social and political level and was a vivid reminder of why the conflict must be resolved. In addition, it is our experience that directly addressing the traumas during the sessions has a positive effect on the quality of the ideas that are produced in the joint thinking session. When the participants feel that their experiences have been validated and acknowledged, they feel more capable of "giving" to the other side, producing more enduring ideas to be fed into the political process.

The Third Challenge: Acknowledgment and Responsibility-Taking

Due to the ongoing history of both psychological and physical injuries and unresolved and unacknowledged injustices experienced by communities in conflict, both sides feel like the victim and neither thinks that it is responsible for the solution to the conflict (Kelman, 1997). In Sri Lanka, the long history and recent experiences of trauma endured by both parties, the perception of injustice, and the failure to implement past agreements have contributed to the mutual suspicion and dehumanization felt by both sides. Given this historical and recent context, the orientation that the parties have taken toward ending the conflict is one in which both sides are waiting for the other to take the first step. This is not uncommon in conflict relationships in which both sides feel like the victim and believe that their experience of being wronged justifies their position that the other side is responsible for the solution. Our observations as practitioners lead us to the conclusion that the mutual belief that the other is "responsible" for one's suffering and perceived injustice and, therefore, is responsible for the solution locks parties into the mind-set that they are the most wronged party and therefore hold no responsibility for their actions. They appear to justify their aggressive actions as a reaction to being threatened. They let the other's aggressive behavior justify their own aggressive acts.

Given the mutually held victim orientation (both sides have endured traumas and feel a sense of injustice that has not been acknowledged or redressed), both parties feel that it is their "right" to be heard, acknowledged, and even apologized to. We have seen this dynamic countless times in our dialogues, not only with Tamils and Sinhalese, but in discussions with Israelis and Palestinians. The more one side cries out for recognition of their suffering, the more the other side comes back with "yes, but we have suffered, too." There appears to be an inability to "de-link" their experiences of suffering from those of the other. This inability to differentiate creates a competition for who suffered the most. As a result, neither side is able to see the other side's suffering separate from its own. The acknowledgment and recognition that each side is demanding only anger the other side more because it, too, feels the need for acknowledgment. It appears virtually impossible for either side to acknowledge the experiences of the other without compromising its own suffering. Both sides are entering into the dialogue with the same expectations of each other: for the other to take responsibility for causing the suffering of their people.

This distortion in one's perception of responsibility (placing it all on the other) is common in conflict relationships. We have observed it in several identity-based conflicts. Under nonthreatening circumstances, parties to a relationship normally create a balance between "rights and responsibilities." It is easy for one to take responsibility for one's actions when one's identity does not feel threatened in doing so. However, when an existential threat undermines these implicit "rules for relationship," normal civility is jettisoned, replaced by a cycle of attack and revenge (McClellan, 2000). We must bear in mind that this breakdown in civility is a reaction to threat and trauma. Parties feel justified in behaving aggressively when someone is attacking them. Equally important to this analysis, not only do parties feel justified in acting aggressively, they are also unwilling to take responsibility for it.

In a workshop we conducted for students from the Balkans, the Middle East, and Greece and Turkey, the participants were asked if there were any stereotypes of their national group that they would like to dispel. Interestingly, they went beyond asking that others not think of them as militaristic, terrorists, or authoritarian to complete denial of any prior national wrongdoing. A Turkish student said she did not want others to think of Turks as perpetrators of a "so-called" massacre of Armenians. An Israeli said he did not want others to think of Israeli soldiers in the West Bank as subjugators of Palestinians, and a Croatian student did not want others to think that Croats had ever been Nazi sympathizers. This uniform urge to deny any wrongdoing, rather than simply acknowledging that only some members of one's group committed the injustice, is representative of the desire to be seen as purely good rather than to embrace complexity and take some responsibility. Expressing the need for a positive self-identity through denial of any wrongdoing damages bilateral relations when the members of the other group shudder at hearing their traumas disavowed.

What are the obstacles we face in fostering responsibility-taking? A return to McClellan's definition of "humanity" with both its negative and positive components may shed some light on the issue. He argues that to restore humanity to a relationship that is not mutually destructive, accepting each other's worth and dignity is a necessary but not sufficient step. Parties to the relationship must also accept each other's human limitations and imperfections. He points out that an essential part of being human is the capacity to cognitively understand and seek an "ideal" or ideal behavior, without necessarily being able to achieve that ideal state. It appears that in conflict relationships, the first thing that is lost is the capacity to embrace this complexity of the human condition. Expectations of the other fall into the realm of the "ideal" without any reflection on the limits of the other's capacity, especially under circumstances of threat. This sterilized view of what the other should do is devoid of the human vulnerabilities and obstacles that stand in the way of behaving in this ideal fashion. On the other hand, it could be argued that the moral exclusivity assigned to the self is an indication that one's own human vulnerability has been denied as well in the service of deflecting blame and responsibility (Opotow, 1990). It appears that the inability to see and take responsibility for one's own violent behavior and the consequences of one's actions is directly linked to denying the other the same human limits and imperfections.

It is our view that to "normalize" a conflict relationship, the distortions and the lack of self-imposed accountability that are part and parcel of the conflict dynamics have to be addressed. Emphasizing only what parties "need" to feel satisfied with the outcome of the conflict inadvertently contributes to the distortion. We would like to redress this imbalance by encouraging greater responsibility-taking.

The emphasis we are placing on the need for responsibility-taking is a departure from and supplements the common wisdom that parties need to engage in "taking the perspective of the other" if they are to better understand the others' needs, fears, and concerns. It goes without saying that perspective-taking is a critical exercise in understanding the experiences of the other side. The assumption is that if one better understands the reality of the other, it will be easier to soften one's enemy images of the other and to begin to "humanize" the other. In so doing, a shift in the destructive dynamics that characterize the conflict relationship is possible. However, we are arguing that taking the perspective of the other is important, but should be balanced by exercises that promote self-reflection and the need to examine the consequences of one's own behavior. Taking responsibility for one's actions is as critical as taking the perspective of the other. Without opportunities to reflect on the behavior of one's own community, both sides will perpetuate the distorted belief that the other is solely responsible for bringing an end to the conflict.

Even though both parties feel like victims in intercommunal conflict, it is often the case that one side holds more power than the other, which can be used to violate the fundamental human rights of the other party. Domination, subjugation, and discrimination of one group over the other is an unacceptable solution to the conflict. Although it is our view that the restoration of responsibility is necessary for both sides, we are in no way suggesting that the allocation of responsibility is symmetrical, or even qualitatively similar, given the asymmetrical power relationship that characterizes most protracted intercommunal conflicts (Rouhana & Korper, 1996).

As mentioned earlier, the orientation that IPS methodology takes in promoting dialogue between communities in conflict is one in which both parties express the needs, fears, and concerns that have to be addressed before an enduring end to the conflict can be found. According to the underlying assumptions of the process, basic developmental human needs are the focus of the analysis because (a) protracted ethnic conflicts are rooted in the deprivation or threat to these needs, and (b) the examination of the two parties' needs moves them from a destructively confrontational posture to an opportunity for joint work because the needs are much less threatening to the other than are the demands. (It is easier to help the adversary obtain autonomy than to entertain the zero-sum claims over the same piece of land.)

In our work in Sri Lanka, a primary need expressed by the Tamils is for sufficient autonomy to feel protected from persecution. A primary fear expressed by the Sinhalese is that Tamil independence will spread from the almost exclusively Tamil North, to the heterogeneous East, to the midplantation area that includes Tamil workers, to an eventual link with 50 million Tamils in southern India, resulting in the decimation of the Sinhala Buddhist island of Sri Lanka. This emphasis on what parties need for security and identity creates a "deficit" dynamic that can only be addressed by the other. Preserving Sinhala identity in Sri Lanka and creating sufficient Tamil autonomy to protect Tamils from persecution require that both sides look to the other for fulfillment of their needs. Although this focus on needs moves the parties from attack to nonthreatening analysis of items that can be mutually satisfied, it nonetheless results in a stalemate because each is awaiting the other rather than thinking about what it can do to take action to bring an end to the conflict.

The Third Recommendation: Introducing Responsibility Into Interactive Problem Solving

Our third recommendation is the introduction of a mechanism into the IPS approach that directly addresses the issue of responsibility-taking. In an Israeli–Palestinian workshop held in 2000, a discussion of the issue of responsibility for the plight of the Palestinian refugees in 1948 created a dynamic between the two communities that locked them into an impasse. The Palestinians demanded that

Israel take responsibility for the plight of the refugees, and the Israelis refused. No matter what we attempted, neither side was willing to back down from its position. The impasse was not only difficult for the first and second parties, but for the third party as well. We were unsure about how to proceed, when one of the junior members of the facilitation team suggested that we attempt to shift the dynamic from what each party needed from the other, to what steps each side could take to address the mistrust between the two communities. Just by changing the question from "What does your side need to bring an end to the conflict?" to "What can your side do to bring an end to the conflict?" instantly shifted the dynamics and broke the impasse. An Israeli participant, who had previously taken a relatively hard line on many of the issues, began by offering several things that Israelis could do to change the dynamics of the conflict. The other Israeli participants followed with more suggestions, after which the Palestinian participants followed suit, listing several things that their community could do to ameliorate the current situation.

Our recommendation is that the addition of responsibility-taking could take place at two different times: in the extended intraparty session (described earlier in the first recommendation section) and after the needs analysis during the interparty discussions. In the intraparty sessions, in addition to a full discussion of the needs, fears, and concerns of all factions within each community to reduce the tension and build consensus among them, we would also recommend adding a discussion of responsibility. Participants would ask themselves what their community has done to contribute to the conflict and what their community could do to put an end to the conflict. It is our view that a discussion of responsibility should first take place without the other side present, as an elaboration of the preworkshop sessions, so that each party can engage in an open discussion without defensiveness.

The second phase of the responsibility discussion could take place during the interparty workshop, after the needs analysis and before the problem-solving phase of "joint thinking." The responsibility-taking session could create the conditions that would enable the perpetrators of the suffering to take responsibility for their actions. Following from this point, it not only provides the acknowledgment that seems necessary but also paves the way for a more productive discussion of ways in which the needs of both sides could be achieved in a solution to the conflict (joint thinking). Finally, the addition of a responsibility-taking session could redress the "deficit" dynamic in the process in which each side is looking for the other to fulfill its needs without doing so for the other. This addition could create what appears to us to be the necessary balance between needs and responsibility.

Conclusion

Our work as scholar-practitioners in the Sri Lanka conflict has given us the experience and opportunity to think carefully and consider several aspects of the IPS approach to intercommunal conflict. The obstacles we have encountered—intraparty divisions, unaddressed trauma and the perception of injustice, and the need for responsibility-taking—forced us to push the boundaries of the approach to address the issues theoretically and practically. In doing so, we are fully aware of the inescapable trade-offs one encounters in any intervention: No one methodology can address all aspects of what needs to be attended to in these complex intercommunal conflicts. The IPS approach has focused on producing creative political ideas that can be fed into the political discourse in the communities in conflict. It is our hope that these elaborations can serve to strengthen the methodology and the ultimate outcome of unofficial interventions.

One of the principles that has guided our work is our commitment to self-reflective practice and an action research approach to theory building. It has always been the case that the insights gained from our practice inform the new development of theory, and, in turn, theory development gives us the opportunity to explore new types of interventions that could expand our understanding of intergroup conflict and ways to resolve it. It is in this spirit that we offer recommended additions to the IPS approach, with the hope that they can contribute in some small way to a process that has already revolutionized thinking about conflict and its resolution. Indeed, without the guidance, wisdom, and insight of John Burton and Herbert Kelman, we would not even be raising these issues. We submit this chapter in honor of Herbert Kelman's contribution to peace achieved, as it was, through a career of reflective practice and collaboration. We are proud to have worked with him and learned from him.

References

Burton, J. (1969). *Conflict and communication: The use of controlled communication in international relations.* London: Macmillan.

Burton, J. (1990). *Conflict: Human needs theory.* London: Macmillan.

Chambers, L. (2000). *Strategic choices in the design of truth commissions: Promoting victim healing.* Unpublished master's thesis, Harvard University, Cambridge, MA.

Fisher, R. (1997). *Interactive conflict resolution.* Syracuse, NY: Syracuse University Press.

Herman, J. (1992). *Trauma and recovery.* Boulder, CO: Basic Books.

Hicks, D., O'Doherty, H., Steiner, P., Taylor, W., Trigeorgis, M., & Weisberg, W. (1994). Addressing intergroup conflict by integrating and realigning identity: An Arab–Israeli workshop. In M. Ettin (Ed.), *Group process and political dynamics* (pp. 279–302). Madison, CT: International University Press.

Kelman, H. C. (1972). The problem solving workshop in conflict resolution. In R. L. Merritt (Ed.), *Communication in international politics* (pp. 168–204). Urbana: University of Illinois Press.

Kelman, H. C. (1993). Coalitions across conflict lines: The interplay of conflicts within and between the Israeli and Palestinian communities. In S. Worchel and J. A. Simpson (Eds.), *Conflicts between people and groups* (pp. 236–258). Chicago: Nelson-Hall.

Kelman, H. (1997). Social-psychological dimensions of international conflict. In I. W. Zartman & J. L. Rasmussen (Eds.), *Peacemaking in international conflict* (pp. 191–237). Washington, DC: United States Institute of Peace Press.

Kelman, H. C. (1998). Informal mediation by the scholar/practitioner. In E. Weiner (Ed.), *The handbook of interethnic coexistence* (pp. 310–331). New York: Continuum.

Little, D. (1994). *Sri Lanka: The invention of enmity.* Washington, DC: United States Institute of Peace Press.

Little, D. (1999). Religion and ethnicity in the Sri Lankan civil war. In R. I. Rotberg, (Ed.), *Creating peace in Sri Lanka: Civil war and reconciliation* (pp. 41–56). Washington, DC: Brookings Institution Press.

McClellan, A. (2000). Beyond courtesy. In L. S. Rouner (Ed.), *Civility* (pp. 78–93). Notre Dame, IN: Notre Dame Press.

Opotow, S. (1990). Deterring moral exclusion. *Journal of Social Issues, 46*(1), 173–182.

Rotberg, R. I. (1999). Sri Lanka civil war: From mayhem toward diplomatic resolution. In R. I. Rotberg (Ed.), *Creating peace in Sri Lanka: Civil war and reconciliation* (pp. 4–16). Washington, DC: Brookings Institution Press.

Rouhana, N. N., & Korper S. (1996). Dealing with the dilemmas posed by power asymmetry in intergroup conflict. *Negotiation Journal, 12,* 353–366.

Smith, C. (1999). South Asia's enduring war. In R. I. Rotberg (Ed.), *Creating peace in Sri Lanka: Civil war and reconciliation* (pp. 17–40). Washington, DC: Brookings Institution Press.

Volkan, V. (1988). *The need to have enemies and allies: From clinical practice to international relationships.* Northvale, NJ: Jason Aronson.

Weisberg, W., & Hicks, D. (1999). Overcoming obstacles to peace in Sri Lanka: An examination of third-party processes. In R. Rotberg (Ed.), *Creating peace in Sri Lanka: Civil war and reconciliation* (pp. 143–156). Washington, DC: Brookings Institution Press.

10

Identity and Power in the Reconciliation of National Conflict

Nadim N. Rouhana

There is an increasingly acceptable distinction in the conflict resolution literature between conflict settlement and reconciliation as two qualitatively different processes that lead to different endpoints in the negotiation between ethnonational parties in conflict. In this literature, reconciliation is a relatively new term that is being widely used in the political discourse and is becoming a subject of scholarly interest. This widespread currency of the term is due, in large part, to major international developments that brought issues of justice and reckoning with history to the core of social agendas in many countries and increased international awareness of the importance of the issues for resolving ethnic conflict. This has been the case, for example, in countries that witnessed transitions from authoritarian regimes involved in gross human rights violations against their own citizens to fledgling democratic regimes in which issues of what was termed "transitional justice" (Crocker, 1999) became central (e.g., El Salvador, Argentina, Chile, Guatemala, the Philippines, and countries in the Eastern European bloc). Similarly, some democratic countries began examining past evils such as genocide of native populations, slavery, and war crimes (e.g., United States, Australia, and Japan), and other countries began examining why and how segments of their population collaborated with oppressive occupiers or why they failed to protest genocidal policies. For example, after the fall of the Berlin wall, leaders of many East European states offered apologies to the Jewish people for either collaboration or failure to prevent the Nazi extermination project; some settler society states have offered apologies to their indigenous populations. Seeking apology, which is linked by many to reconciliation, became an accepted part of discourse between nations and groups that experienced conflict and violations of human rights (Barkan, 2001). And, finally, the dramatic change in South Africa from an apartheid system to a democratic regime, and the role that the South African Truth and Reconciliation Commission played in that transition, emerged as a case of its own magnitude in increasing international awareness of the role of reconciliation in transforming ethnic conflict. Although more than 20 commissions were established around the world (Hayner, 2001), the South African case stands out in the international consciousness as one in which reckoning with past injustice played a central role in the peaceful transition from undisguised oppression to exhilarating liberation and in the transformation of the relationship between the groups in conflict.

The widespread use of the term reconciliation, its novelty in academic and political discourse, and its link to other concepts such as apology and forgiveness overload the term with multiple meanings and at the same time contribute to ambiguity about its precise meaning. Reconciliation, which was a central goal of truth and reconciliation commissions created mainly in non-Western societies, is in danger of being reconstructed in the West with religious overtones and cultural loadings. For example, under the influence of Christian theology, forgiveness, with a strong religious implication, became strongly linked to reconciliation. Forgiveness according to traditional Christian theological view is a first step in reconciliation (Wink, 1998). Similarly, the imposition of a therapeutic model, at the center of which stand concepts of healing and trauma, threatens to reduce a powerful intergroup process with clear implications for social restructuring to an intrapsychic process. This process overlooks the centrality of group identities formed over generations of conflict by power relations, dominance, oppression, and group exploitation. Such a model not only misplaces the focus of analysis from intergroup patterns of behavior that are the outcome of power structures to their interpersonal manifestation, but also obscures the chain of causality with grave theoretical and moral implications. Furthermore, once the concept of reconciliation is given its Western, mainly American framing, it is pressed on people who are victims and perpetrators of severe human rights violations—often for generations (Dwyer, 1999).

Conflict Settlement, Conflict Resolution, and Reconciliation

One way to contribute to clarifying the concept of reconciliation, both as a process and as an end state, is first to distinguish it from two often-used terms: *conflict settlement* and *conflict resolution* as defined by Burton (1990). The three processes are qualitatively different and, therefore, are not designed to achieve the same endpoint. As summarized in Table 10.1, conflict settlement, conflict resolution, and reconciliation differ in terms of goals of agreement, parties to the agreement, nature of the desired relationship, importance of mutual acceptance, and importance of future relations between the parties. Conflict settlement seeks a formal termination of conflict based on mutual interests and is represented by an agreement between the conflicting parties that reflects the power relations on the ground; a settlement does not necessarily reflect equitably the needs of the parties and often does not represent the weaker party's long-term interests. In conflict settlement, the agreement is reached by governments without necessary involvement of elites. The settlement does not necessarily concern itself with relations between societies or with genuine mutual recognition between the parties; accordingly, the peace between the conflicting parties could be either cold or warm as long as the two parties' interests are met and as long as they enjoy a tolerable coexistence. The agreement between Iran and Iraq in 1975 that settled their border dispute represents an example of conflict settlement. The agreement reflected the power relations at the time in favor of Iran, but it was violated, triggering one of the most devastating wars in the region.

Table 10.1. Conflict Settlement, Conflict Resolution, and Reconciliation: Similarities and Differences

	Conflict settlement	Conflict resolution	Reconciliation
Goals	Formal agreement	Principled compromise	Historical reconciliation
Parties	Governments	Elites	Societies
Nature of peace	Irrelevant	Sustainable peace	Genuine, no further claims
Future relations desired	Abiding by agreements	Working relations	Good relations
Importance of mutual acceptance	Not important	Important	Essential
Terms of reference	Power relations	Basic human needs	Justice
Truth about wrongdoing	Ignored	Not central	Should be commonly acknowledged
Historical responsibility	Ignored	Not central	Should be acknowledged and faced
Social and political restructuring	Not required	Substantial restructuring	Major restructuring

In conflict resolution, on the other hand, an understanding seeks to address the causes of conflict and accordingly to reach an historic compromise. The agreement is designed to address the basic human needs of both sides, regardless of the power relations between them; the political needs of both parties are equally addressed, not in accordance with power relations between them, but in the framework of a new relationship that promotes equality and reciprocity. The agreement, although reached by elites, aims to achieve peaceful relations between societies and represents mutual acceptance between the parties. It seeks not only coexistence, but also cooperation that reflects a warm and sustainable peace in which the parties should not make any further claims against each other. The agreement between Israel and Jordan in 1995 was perceived by Israel as a case of conflict resolution, although the subsequent failure of the peace process with the Palestinians weakened popular support for the agreement, at least on the Jordanian side.

Reconciliation, as conceived in this chapter, is a qualitatively different process and seeks to achieve a kind of relationship between the parties that is founded on mutual legitimacy. The open, public, and socially based granting of legitimacy—the culmination of the process—becomes the defining feature of the relationship and the cornerstone of mutual recognition and genuine security. As such, reconciliation, although it does not prevent strains in the relationship and future disputes between the parties, does guard against reversal of the relationship to a stage in which the very legitimacy of each side is questioned again. In this sense, reconciliation is defined as a process that brings about a genuine end to the existential conflict between the parties, and it transforms the nature of the relationship between the societies through a course of action that is intertwined with psychological, social, and political changes. The towering example of a successful reconciliation process remains the South African case. This definition is consistent with existing conceptions of reconciliation in the literature such as those by Kriesberg (1999) and Ross (2001). Yet, this conception of reconciliation differs from these other definitions of reconciliation and departs from conflict resolution in that it requires the parties to address specific central issues in their conflict. Although the analysis that follows applies most directly to cases in which the conflict involves a higher and a lower power party, and in which the former has engaged in systematic violations of human rights of the latter, it should not be limited to such cases. It is not always the case that only one side in conflict is the perpetrator; often both sides are involved in mutual atrocities against each other.

Key Requirements for Reconciliation

I maintain that for genuine reconciliation to take root, four key issues must be addressed: justice, truth, historical responsibility, and restructuring of the social and political relationship between the parties. Thus, the parties will need to agree not only on redistribution of power and resources, but also on each side's historical responsibility during the conflict, the truth about past injustice, and a framework of justice that can maintain the new relations. In this section, I discuss the four issues required for reconciliation.

Justice

First, the term of reference for reconciliation is justice, not the existing power relations between the parties as is the case in conflict settlement or even the basic human needs of the parties as advocated by conflict resolution (see Burton, 1987, 1990). Justice, which is central to reconciliation, is not a central part of the applied or theoretical conflict resolution discourse. Although those involved in official international conflict resolution often invoke the language of just agreements, in fact, power relations—not justice—generally determine the outcome of agreements. Even the unofficial conflict resolution literature is thin on the issue of justice. With a few exceptions (e.g., Deutsch, 1974, 1985; Grillo, 1991; Kelman, 1996; Opotow, 1990), justice has most often been overlooked. One notable exception can be found in Kelman's repeated attempts to incorporate the requirements of justice in his work on interactive problem solving (Kelman, 1981, 1996). He operationalized the quest for justice as "the search for a solution that addresses the fundamental needs and fears of both parties" (Kelman, 1996, p. 106), thus anchoring the search for justice in the subjective reality of each party. But justice was not taken as a frame of reference for the conflict resolution approach, perhaps because such a framework was assumed to compromise the conflict resolution effort.

The absence of justice from the analysis of conflict and conflict resolution is striking in light of injustices that take place in conflicts and their importance to parties in conflict. Injustice becomes part of any protracted conflict, which often goes through stages of open violence and destructive dynamics. Both sides get involved in unjust acts of violence and atrocities. However, one should bear in mind a fundamental distinction between injustices that lie in the root of some conflicts, such as ethnic cleansing or colonization, which are committed by the high-power group, and injustices committed as a consequence of and in reaction to these acts by the low-power group. Equating the two types of injustice is morally questionable and theoretically problematic. If these two kinds of injustice are equivalent, it should be equally challenging for both parties to face them as part of the reconciliation process. This is not the case; the injustice committed by the low-power group, which starts as self-defense and as a result of and in reaction to the historical injustice committed by the high-power group, is constructed in its collective identity as part of its resistance, which the group openly admits and of which it is usually proud. Yet the low-power group will have to face the unjustifiable means of violence if it resorts to such means. It is easier for the low-power group to face such injustice, to apologize for its excesses and for the suffering it caused the other. This is not so for the high-power group, because facing the consequences of historical injustice gives rise to the realities of oppression and domination that become intertwined—consciously or unconsciously—with the group's self-image and identity, and because taking responsibility for the injustice can carry steep moral, legal, and economic costs. The high-power group has no incentive to face historical injustice or to agree to introduce a discourse of justice to international conflict resolution. The absence of justice from the official and unofficial international conflict resolution theory and practice (notwithstanding the exceptions mentioned earlier) is not unrelated to the high-power group's interest in excluding it altogether from such practice.

A main argument for the exclusion of justice is that justice is a subjective construct, and allowing it to become a subject of negotiation would open the door for additional conflict. As articulated by Bar-Siman-Tov (2001):

> Since fairness and justice are not self-defining and objective terms, it may be difficult for the parties to agree what is fair and just. The assessments of what is fair and just are often biased by self-interest. The resulting conflict in perceptions of what constitutes fair and just agreement may create barriers to peace implementation and relations. (p. 8)

Asserting that justice should be avoided because it is socially constructed is an easy way to avoid introducing the issue of justice in conflict resolution and often into the public political discourse on the conflict. The fact that justice is socially constructed should not exclude the possibility of broad agreements between the parties on what is unjust and on some basic principles of justice. Even if the parties accept a conception of justice that is independent of realistic external moral guidelines, there is still space within this contextual subjectivity for agreement on some components of justice, for without such minimum agreement it will be impossible for individuals and communities to interact as actors in the same human society and international system. For example, parties can agree that ethnic cleansing, occupation, and legal discrimination are unjust or that equality between individuals and groups is a virtue.

If justice becomes central to the peace efforts in a conflict, the questions of subjectivity and the social construction of justice return in full force in the most direct ways: What is just? Who defines justice? And what kind of justice is required? These questions are difficult but are not unanswerable in a reconciliation framework based on acknowledgment of history and responsibility.

In contrast to various approaches to conflict resolution, my conception of reconciliation takes justice as the framework for the new relationship between the parties. Although well taken, the contention that justice is hard to define, not attainable, or only achievable at the expense of further injustice does not excuse avoiding the issue. On the contrary, the literature on reconciliation examines where justice fits in the new relationship (Crocker, 1998), how and whether it can be achieved (Dwyer, 1999), whether justice is retributive versus restorative (Lyons, 1984), whether it is absolute versus attainable (Khalidi, 1998), and whether a "different kind of justice" could be conceptualized (Little, 1999, p. 67). Achieving some kind of justice, based not solely or necessarily on the subjective realities of the parties, is thus central to the process of reconciliation and to the end state of reconciliation between groups in conflict.

Truth

Reconciliation should place special importance on historical truth, particularly truth about wrongdoing. Many conflict resolution practitioners, emphasizing a nonadversarial problem-solving approach, do not encourage debates about historical truth, and others sidestep issues of historical truth as being too controversial and therefore to be avoided (see, for example, Bar-Siman-Tov, 2001). This argument is predicated on the assumption that each party has its own narrative, its own version of history, and usually a strong sense of victimization (Rouhana & Bar-Tal, 1998). Thus, each party incorporates the historical facts within its own cognitive schema of the conflict, and discussions of these facts will lead only to irresoluble clashes of narratives that will highlight the differences and leave the parties frustrated.

There is much to this argument. The facts that each of the two sides to a conflict has its own narrative and that each side often develops a strong sense of victimization are not sufficient to justify maintaining that both narratives are equally valid or equally legitimate or that the parties' subjective reality should determine the historical truth. The narratives themselves, and the sense of victimization, should be subjected to examination in the context of unequal power relations that affect both the political interaction between the parties and the way these interactions are presented and experienced. For example, White South Africans had their own narrative and they too felt victimized while perpetrating and justifying one of the most heinous political systems in modern history. Similarly, Protestant settlers in Northern Ireland, who perpetrated gross human rights violations, felt threatened and victimized and they constructed narratives to justify their behavior (Akenson, 1992). It is true that a narrative is experienced as valid, but the narratives of the perpetrator and the victim cannot be granted equal moral weight. A narrative, in principle, can be based on distortions, denials, and myths (White, 1987). These are all legitimate subjects of study and examination that should be deconstructed in the appropriate context of power relations between the parties, particularly in the cases of occupation, domination, and exploitation

For reconciliation, I maintain that truth is central and has to be commonly acknowledged by the two parties for the process to proceed (Crocker, 1999; Dwyer, 1999; Little, 1999; Minow, 1999; Popkin & Bhuta, 1999; Tutu, 1999). Indeed, the word *truth* appears in the official names of most commissions that have dealt with reconciliation. The argument here is that truth should be established and publicly disseminated and that there are many reasonable ways of arriving at the truth. In this context, the assertion that different groups have different "truths" does not hold well. Crocker (1999) differentiated among three levels of truth: "forensic truth," which refers to hard facts about human rights violations; "emotional truth," which refers to psychological and physical impact on victims; and "general truth," which refers to plausible interpretations. There are many ways for achieving these truths even when groups have diverging views such as in the pioneering effort of a Bosnia and Herzegovina Truth and Reconciliation Commission (Little, 1999). In this case the central goal of the commission was "the establishment of a historical accounting" of wrongdoings by starting one truth commission that included members of all ethnic groups in order to "establish consensus history" (Little, 1999, p. 80).

Historical Responsibility

It is essential for reconciliation to have the parties agree on the historical responsibility for human rights abuses. The parties involved in mass physical and cultural violence such as colonization, occupation, genocide, ethnic cleansing, and state-sanctioned oppression or discrimination are expected to unambiguously face their historical responsibility and their role in human rights violations. Past abuses have to be faced and responsibility assigned. In many cases the task of the truth commission is to prevent willful forgetting (such as the conflicts in El Salvador and Guatemala; see Hayner, 2001). The Historical Clarification Commission in Guatemala, for example, focused on the institutional responsibility, including that of the state, the army, and the United States (Popkin & Bhuta, 1999); the South African Truth and Reconciliation Commission placed responsibility on the apartheid system (Wilson, 2001). Thus, although assessing individual responsibility of perpetrators and dealing with it in a way that will not disrupt societies in transition has differed from case to case, facing and taking historical responsibility has seemed to be at the center of the process in all cases.

Truth and historical responsibility are of utmost importance not only because they validate the experience of the victims, but because this validation is essential for the victims' transcendence of a history of domination and abuse. These processes are also critical to reassuring the victims that past wrongdoing will not reoccur and to determining future steps needed to rectify the past and plan the future.

Political Restructuring

Reconciliation entails political and structural change guided by some sort of justice once historical responsibility is clearly assigned. The structural changes can be dramatic and are determined by universal standards of equality, human rights, and human dignity regardless of the implication for the acquired privileges and dominant identity of the perpetrators, who will inevitably have to lose some of the privileges they unjustly gained. Restructuring takes the past wrongs and their inequitable consequences into consideration when establishing new political and social institutions. It is the political behavior, the institutionalizing, and the restructuring that become the focus of a future relationship between the parties based on equality and human dignity. This restructuring creates the conditions that are conducive to fulfilling human needs and to respectful coexistence and cooperation between the various conflicting parties.

In this analysis, forgiveness and healing are not essential to reconciliation. If justice, truth, taking historical responsibility for past wrongs, and political restructuring are the essence of a reconciliation process, then offering apology by the perpetrators becomes a natural part of the process that can expedite and deepen reconciliation. However, this is not the case for forgiveness. The perpetrator does not have to seek it, nor does the victim have to offer it. Forgiveness is seen here as a personal component of the process that different individual members are entitled to deal with in a manner of their own choosing without the imposition of religious imperatives or cultural paradigms. Similarly, healing becomes both a social and personal process that is the outcome of structural and political change, not a substitute for it; healing acquires its very meaning in intergroup relations from such political changes. The social context of healing is achieved by having the collective truth validated and responsibility assigned to perpetrators, while the individual part of healing—work with victims who underwent traumatic experiences—is facilitated by trained professionals working within that social context. Placing the emphasis on individual healing without attending to the larger social and political context simply misses the target and becomes the dubious privilege of those who can afford to deny, avoid, or overlook the need for political change and its social implications.

All four components of reconciliation—justice, historical truth, facing historical responsibility, and social and political restructuring—lead the parties into the type of relationship that the conflict resolution pioneers, who developed their work in an international cold war context dominated by interstate conflicts (Azar, 1990; Burton, 1990; Kelman, 1986), have aimed to achieve. This relationship is characterized by genuine mutual recognition, trust, mutual granting of legitimacy, and achieving existential security based on the conviction that one's own and the other's collective existence are not in question.

In the context of intrastate conflict in which one territory becomes the focus of both parties' identity, and in which parties are involved in historical injustices, genuine reconciliation between the parties cannot be achieved without first going through the processes described in the prior paragraphs. This conceptualization of reconciliation, therefore, takes into consideration some elements of conflict resolution theory and practice, primarily those developed within the framework of basic human needs theory, in particular, the work on interactive problem solving, which aimed at reaching the kind of relationship described earlier (Burton, 1990; Kelman, 1986).

It is not the case that parties in every conflict will need to reach the type of relationship described earlier as reconciliation. Depending on the type of conflict and the desired type of relations, parties can seek conflict settlement, conflict resolution, or reconciliation. Conflict settlement can lead to working relations between states whose conflict is not a social one, but one rooted in a defined set of differences such as disputes over borders, natural resources, or the appropriate terms of a commercial treaty. International mediation literature gives numerous examples of such settlements (Bercovitch, 1986; Touval, 1992; Touval & Zartman, 1985). Conflict resolution is more appropriate for conflicts in which the societies themselves are embroiled, such as in protracted social conflict in which the identity, recognition, and security needs of parties have to be addressed in order for resolution to occur (Azar, 1991; Burton, 1987, 1990; Fisher, 1990; Kelman, 1992; Mitchell, 1990). Conflicts in which parties have engaged in past evils and historical injustice can reach a point of "end of conflict" between their societies only through a reconciliation process that involves the elements that I have described.

Factors That Influence Parties' Willingness to Engage in Reconciliation

Willingness to embark on a mutual process of reconciliation depends on a number of factors that determine the extent of each party's interest in seeking reconciliation. Perhaps the most important factors are the power relations between the parties and the extent of power asymmetry. For each party, depending on its position in the power-relations matrix, reconciliation entails differing risks in terms of threats to national identity and national narrative, political restructuring, and permanent political loss. The risks and costs for the high-power group are generally greater, because by definition, rectification of the injustice involves upsetting a status quo and ending the perpetrators' dominance. Thus, the costs of such a process are also asymmetrical in reverse: The cost for the high-power group is greater than the cost for the low-power group. Therefore, the more powerful party seeks to avoid such a process and the weaker party, even when interested in the process, has no means to impose reconciliation.

Another major factor in considering reconciliation is whether the injustice can be undone and what the precise implications of undoing the injustice are for the dominant party. Thus, killing a person cannot be undone, but stealing a person's house or destroying it can largely be undone by returning the stolen house or rebuilding the destroyed one. On the collective level, eliminating an ethnic group cannot be undone, but expulsion and ethnic cleansing, at least insofar as the physical displacement goes, can be, to a large extent. It might be harder to accept responsibility in cases where injustice can be partly undone, such as expulsion of an ethnic group that demands to return, than in cases where the injustice cannot be undone, such as in cases where the ethnic group has been eliminated or almost eliminated. Reconciliation might be harder in the first case because of the implications that facing the responsibility has for the perpetrators. These implications can be both political (in the broad sense, including legal) and psychological. In cases of ethnic cleansing such as in the former Yugoslavia, the political implications can involve such steps as power sharing, political transformation, and return of refugees; these consequences are usually framed in terms of existential threat to identity and to national security. However, in cases where the ethnic group has been eliminated or reduced such as the Native Americans, facing responsibility does not involve a similar price.

The psychological implications for an injustice that can be undone are also serious. If the perpetrators do not intend to correct an injustice that can be corrected, recognizing the injustice has clear psychological implications for national identity, national narratives, historical myths, and self-image. Even when an injustice, such as genocide, cannot be undone, the perpetrators, if not forced, do not recognize the crime nor do they take moral responsibility for it. To this day, more than 85 years after it had been committed, the Armenian genocide is still denied by Turkey—by both its government and its people (Hovannisian, 1999).

Another factor is the clarity of the injustice and the moral issues involved in the conflict. The importance of the moral component, even if underestimated in international relations, cannot be overemphasized for the party on the receiving side of injustice. For a reconciliation process to be urged on the perpetrator, the moral case should be clear not only to the victim but to the international community as well. The more powerful party usually develops a system of defense mechanisms against moral arguments, and its members can become immune to the moral case of their victims. Without the support of the international community for the moral case of the low-power party, that party loses one of its few means of rectifying the power imbalance. Low power usually comes with less access to international media and fewer material and human resources to invest in public relations, so the powerful party is free to put out its version of the conflict story and its interpretation of developments as "fact." The low-power group sometimes resorts to terrorism, the tool of the powerless, to protest the injustice to the international community, but contrary to its purpose, this means contaminates the clarity of their moral case. Compare, for example, the simplicity and salience to the international community of the African National Congress's moral case in the South African apartheid system with the ambiguity of the Tamils' case in Sri Lanka or the case of the Palestinians in their struggle against the Israeli occupation in the West Bank and Gaza (not to mention the original colonial project in pre-1948 Palestine). The international moral attitude against injustice can provide substantial pressure on the high-power group to engage in reconciliation.

The emergence of a new generation within the dominant group who did not commit the original wrongdoing but is only its benefactors can also increase the willingness of the high-power group to pay the cost of reconciliation. For one thing, the descendants of the perpetrators do not carry the same psychological burden as their forefathers. Not that the psychological burden disappears, but it is lighter than that of those who actually committed the injustice. The longer the time that has elapsed, other things being equal, the easier it becomes for new generations to face historical responsibility—unless the injustice is ongoing, in which case new generations become heavily invested in it, even if only indirectly, such as happens with ongoing colonization.

In summary, the likelihood that a more powerful party will engage in a reconciliation process and willingly shoulder its political and psychological cost increases as the psychological and political implications of undoing an injustice become less onerous, the clarity of the moral case of the victims becomes stronger, international support for their cause grows, and the length of time since the injustice increases.

Patterns of Historical Reconciliation

One can find four major patterns in the historical reconciliation experience in which perpetrators are motivated or compelled to face responsibility for historical injustices. None of these patterns, briefly mentioned in the next paragraphs, applies to a case in which there is a gross power asymmetry in favor of the perpetrator.

First, reconciliation becomes possible when external or internal forces defeat the perpetrating system and a democratic order is installed (e.g., the defeat of Germany in the Second World War or the collapse of the regime in Romania in the post-Communist era). Notice that defeat without replacing the existing regime is not sufficient (as in the case of defeated Yugoslavia under Milosevic or defeated Iraq under Saddam Hussein). Similarly, the collapse of the regime and its replacement by an undemocratic regime is not sufficient. The system should be defeated on grounds that include its own injustice.

Second, reconciliation becomes possible when the existing (oppressive) system faces an imminent defeat that can be avoided only by accepting profound political and social transformation, as occurred in, for example, South Africa. In this case, the perpetrating system concluded that without transformation, the system might collapse and the interests of the powerful group could be irreparably damaged (Tutu, 1999). The transformation itself came out of negotiations that preserved some of the interests of the powerful group.

Third, reconciliation becomes possible when the weaker party is either eliminated or reduced to a status that cannot significantly threaten the existing social and political order (such as the Native population in the United States, Canada, and Australia). In this case reconciliation is much less costly for the high-power group, because the changes of narratives do not necessarily require significant political restructuring. The elites in the high-power group who lead the revision of narratives are not required to give up any of the gains they acquired at the expense of those who were eliminated or reduced. The new generations—those who did not perpetrate the injustice—adopt a new narrative in return for psychological self-cleansing at very low cost.

Fourth, the conditions for historical reconciliation gradually develop in a democratic regime that committed injustice against racial or ethnic groups within its own sovereign jurisdiction. These conditions are usually created by the victims' struggle for equal inclusion within the system itself. The historical injustice of slavery in the midst of the largest Western democracy has not been completely reconciled, at least not by the slaves' descendants. Although the conditions for reconciliation have been gradually created in a long process that has transformed the face of American society and the place of the African American community within it, the debate over apology to the African American community and the proper compensation for material and psychological losses they endured has just started, almost 150 years after the formal, "political" end of slavery.

Reconciliation in the Context of Power Relations and Group Identity

My analysis so far refers to reconciliation as both a process and an end state. As a process, reconciliation entails that both sides of a conflict that involved grave human rights violations, such as genocide, massacres, kidnapping, assassinations, ethnic cleansing, property confiscation, and occupation, commonly acknowledge historical truths about these violations and agree on the perpetrators' responsibility. The process entails social restructuring that leads to a political arrangement guided by a new framework that seeks to rectify past injustice and guarantee equality and human rights to all groups and individuals. As an end state, reconciliation requires that the parties reach mutual recognition and consider the peace agreement as reasonably just, the sources of the conflict adequately addressed, and the conflict between them terminated. Accordingly, the parties agree to work toward a peaceful future based on social cooperation.

A serious obstacle arises when applying this analysis to ongoing conflicts with vast power asymmetries. The difficulty stems from a major difference between cases in which truth and reconciliation have been sought and ongoing conflicts in which the high-power party sees a negative incentive for engaging in such a process and the low-power party cannot impose a reconciliation framework on the practice of conflict resolution or even on the conflict analysis discourse. When a Truth and Reconciliation Commission is established to investigate the past actions of primarily one party, or when a party to the conflict offers an apology, such acts by themselves clearly mean that the side that has been involved in human rights violations is identified and that it has been locally and internationally recognized as responsible for the violations. Assigning clear responsibility and/or apologizing happen when the identities of the oppressor and oppressed and the perpetrator and victim are clear.

In contrast, in many ongoing conflicts, the high-power party denies its involvement in historical injustices and its role as a perpetrator of human rights violations. Such parties often deny the very imbalance of power relations or even perceptually reverse it. Thus, the settler societies in South Africa and Northern Ireland felt threatened, respectively, by the Blacks in South Africa and the Republicans in Northern Ireland despite the vast power asymmetry. Similarly, many Israelis feel that Palestinians threaten Israel's very existence despite the strict systems of military and political control that Israel has imposed on Palestinians in the occupied territories. In such conflicts, an examination of reconciliation that does not consider the power relations or that erroneously assumes symmetrical power relations between the parties can lead to flawed conclusions. Either in the name of neutrality or simply by overlooking the role of power asymmetries, conflicts are often analyzed regardless of the power relations or the parties' group identity whose formation is largely affected by power, dominance, resistance, and force.

The existing power relations should be a departure point for any analysis of reconciliation, because within them is embedded the reality of dominant/dominated, oppressor/oppressed, and ethnic cleanser/ethnically cleansed. It is such realities, generated by the power asymmetry, that determine the human experience of the group members in conflict, the psychological underpinnings of their experience, the context of the mutual violence and its moral foundations, the salience of justice for each party, the meaning of reconciliation, and, most importantly, the requirement for real reconciliation between the parties. Even the most fundamental processes that are believed to be symmetrical in conflict, such as denial of the other's legitimacy or negative images of the enemy, can take different forms in asymmetric conflicts. Needs for recognition, security, and identity have different meanings for parties who have unequal power, because they emanate from drastically different collective experiences and from a different relationship to the other group. Symmetrical analysis of the case defeats the main elements of reconciliation: achieving justice, truth, historical responsibility, and political change.

Conclusion

This chapter presents a conceptualization of reconciliation in national conflict, particularly in conflicts in which past injustices have been committed. The conceptual framework argues that in such conflicts, to bring about new relationships that "end the conflict," end mutual claims, and cause mutual legitimacy to emerge, parties should face historical truths and historical responsibility for past injustices. In addition, political and social restructuring should be guided by a framework of some sort of justice or attainable justice rather than by the power relations or the subjectively defined human fears and threats of the parties. In this regard, this conceptual framework, although it considers some elements of conflict resolution, goes beyond the existing conflict resolution approaches and theories. In particular, this conceptual framework of reconciliation places emphasis on truth and historical responsibility as deconstructed in the context of asymmetrical power relations and not the symmetrical subjectivity of needs and fears of parties in conflict regardless of the power relations. It also considers the identity and narratives of both sides in the context of power and accordingly advises against symmetrical treatment of narratives and their validity.

Unlike applied conflict resolution frameworks, such as the problem-solving approach, this conceptualization of reconciliation does not lend itself easily to direct derivation of an applied model. One major difficulty is getting the high-power party in conflict to get involved in reconciliation efforts on the basis of a framework that emphasizes justice, truth, and historical responsibility, such as the one presented earlier. However, it is usually possible to find partners from the high-power party who will engage with partners from the low-power group in conflict resolution efforts that aim to discuss political changes based on such a framework. Although such efforts might produce less "practical" ideas as measured by the yardstick of real politik, they can contribute to reconciliation by emphasizing a political vision defined by moral clarity and a political discourse that delineates the requirements of true mutual legitimacy between parties in conflict.

References

Akenson, D. H. (1992). *God's peoples: Covenant and land in South Africa, Israel, and Ulster.* Ithaca, NY: Cornell University Press.

Azar, E. E. (1990). *The management of protracted conflict.* Hampshire, England: Dartmouth Publishing Company.

Azar, E. E. (1991). The analysis and management of protracted conflict. In V. D. Volkan, J. V. Montville, & D. A. Julius (Eds.), *The psychodynamics of international relationships* (Vol. 2, pp. 93–120). Lexington, MA: Lexington Books.

Barkan, E. (2001). *The guilt of nations: Restitution and negotiating historical injustices.* Baltimore: Johns Hopkins University Press.

Bar-Siman-Tov, Y. (2001, February). *Dialectics between stable peace and reconciliation.* Paper presented at the Leonard Davis Institute, Hebrew University, Jerusalem.

Bercovitch, J. (1986). International mediation: A study of the incidence, strategies and conditions of successful outcomes. *Cooperation and Conflict, 21,* 155–168.

Burton, J. W. (1987). *Resolving deep-rooted conflict: A handbook.* Lanham, MD: University Press of America.

Burton, J. W. (1990). *Conflict: Resolution and provention.* New York: St. Martin's Press.

Crocker, D. A. (1998). Transitional justice and international civil society: Toward a normative framework. *Constellations, 5,* 492–517.

Crocker, D. A. (1999). Reckoning with past wrongs: A normative framework. *Ethics & International Affairs, 13,* 43–64.

Deutsch, M. (1974). Awakening the sense of injustice. In M. Ross & M. J. Lerner (Eds.), *The quest for justice: Myth, reality, ideal (proceedings of a conference held at the University of Waterloo, May 1972)* (pp. 19–42). Toronto, Canada: Holt, Rinehart & Winston.

Deutsch, M. (1985). *Distributive justice: A social-psychological perspective.* New Haven, CT: Yale University Press.

Dwyer, S. (1999). Reconciliation for realists. *Ethics & International Affairs, 13,* 81–98.

Fisher, R. (1990). Needs theory, social identity and an eclectic model of conflict. In J. Burton (Ed.), *Conflict: Human needs theory* (pp. 89–112). New York: St. Martin's Press.

Grillo, T. (1991). The mediation alternative: Process dangers for women. *Yale Law Journal, 100,* 1545–1610.

Hayner, P. B. (2001). *Unspeakable truths: Confronting state terror and atrocities.* New York: Routledge.

Hovannisian, R. G. (1999). Denial of the Armenian genocide in comparison with Holocaust denial. In R. G. Hovannisian (Ed.), *Remembrance and denial: The case of the Armenian genocide* (pp. 201–236). Detroit, MI: Wayne State University Press.

Kelman, H. C. (1981). Reflections on the history and status of peace research. *Conflict Management and Peace Science, 5,* 99–123.

Kelman, H. C. (1986). Interactive problem-solving: A social-psychological approach to conflict reso-lution. In W. Klassen (Ed.), *Dialogue toward interfaith understanding* (pp. 293–314). Jerusa-lem: Tantur Ecumenical Institute for Theological Research.

Kelman, H. C. (1992). Informal mediation by the scholar/practitioner. In J. Bercovitch & J. Z. Rubin (Eds.), *Mediation in international relations* (pp. 64–96). New York: St. Martin's Press.

Kelman, H. C. (1996). Negotiation as interactive problem-solving. *International Negotiation: A Journal of Theory and Practice, 1,* 99–123.

Khalidi, R. (1998). Attainable justice: Elements of solution to the Palestinian refugee issue. *Inter-national Journal, 53,* 233–252.

Kriesberg, L. (1999). Paths to varieties of intercommunal reconciliation. In H. Jeong (Ed.), *Conflict resolution: Dynamics, process and structure* (pp. 105–130). Aldershot, United Kingdom: Ash-gate Publishing.

Little, D. (1999). A different kind of justice: Dealing with human rights violations in transitional societies. *Ethics & International Affairs, 13,* 65–80.

Lyons, D. (1984). *Ethics and the law of law.* New York: Cambridge University Press.

Minow, M. (1999). *Between vengeance and forgiveness: Facing history after genocide and mass vio-lence.* Boston: Beacon Press.

Mitchell, C. (1990). Necessitous man and conflict resolution: More basic questions about basic human needs theory. In J. Burton (Ed.), *Conflict: Human needs theory* (pp. 149–176). New York: St. Martin's Press.

Opotow, S. (1990). Moral exclusion and injustice. *Journal of Social Issues, 46*(1), 1–20.

Popkin, M., & Bhuta, N. (1999). Latin America amnesties in comparative perspective: Can the past be buried? *Ethics & International Affairs, 13,* 99–122.

Ross, M. (2001). *Ritual and the politics of reconciliation.* Paper presented at the Leonard Davis Institute, Hebrew University, Jerusalem.

Rouhana, N. N., & Bar-Tal, D. (1998). Psychological dynamics of ethnonational conflict: The Israeli–Palestinian case. *American Psychologist, 53,* 761–770.

Touval, S. (1992). The superpowers as mediators. In J. Bercovitch & J. Z. Rubin (Eds.), *Mediation in international relations* (pp. 232–248). New York: St. Martin's Press.

Touval, S., & Zartman, I., W. (Eds.). (1985). *International mediation in theory and practice.* Boulder, CO: Westview Press.

Tutu, D. (1999). *No future without forgiveness.* New York: Doubleday.

White, H. (1987). *The content of the form: Narrative discourse and historical representation.* Balti-more: Johns Hopkins University Press.

Wilson, R. A. (2001). *The politics of truth and reconciliation in South Africa.* Cambridge, England: Cambridge University Press.

Wink, W. (1998). *When the powers fall: Reconciliation in the healing of nations.* Minneapolis, MN: Fortress Press.

Comments on Chapters 9 and 10

Rebecca Dale

The chapters by Donna Hicks and William Weisberg (chap. 9, this volume) and Nadim N. Rouhana (chap. 10, this volume) treat interactive problem solving (IPS) in an expanded fashion, including components of acknowledging responsibility, addressing injustice, and facing trauma. Both chapters suggest that those areas traditionally not focused on in IPS are the ones that need to be included to shift the conflict dynamics further toward dialogue and transformation. As Hicks and Weisberg note: "Taking responsibility for one's actions is as critical as taking the perspective of the other." These approaches also expand what is required from third parties to support and contain such processes. Yet what are the responsibilities of third parties in these more complex processes? What may be lost? And how will these processes affect the facilitators?

Rouhana notes that there is a bias among conflict analysts, third parties, and high-power groups that leads them to focus on the symmetries of the conflict, often in the pursuit of neutrality or the interests of settlement. This tendency obfuscates the central element of asymmetrical conflict, which is that the identity and experience of the parties is constructed differently given their relative high- or low-power position. Rouhana asks those interested in reconciliation to focus on the asymmetry of the existing power relations. Each party, depending on its role in the asymmetry, will have to go through different processes as part of reconciliation.[1]

On a practical level, what does it mean for people to take responsibility for grievous acts in front of the other side? When people are face to face, the various escalatory psychosocial dynamics quickly manifest themselves. Dialogue becomes difficult because polarization, defensiveness, and dehumanization can dominate on both sides. It can be difficult for participants to acknowledge responsibility, particularly when others are blaming them. Rather, the parties attempt to match the other side's suffering with their own, and a competition of suffering can ensue. Such responses are typical when there is a traumatic history and people are being asked to increase their own ambivalence and to embrace the complexity of a conflict.

---

[1]As a third-party facilitator, I face the dilemma of reconciling my own identity with my role as a third party. I am British and therefore from a traditionally high-power group in many conflicts, including, historically, the Middle Eastern and Sri Lankan conflicts. I am also a woman and therefore from a traditionally low-power group in many conflicts. This situation leads me to consider what third parties can and should do in dealing with conflicts when they themselves come from a high-power group, a low-power group, or both.

In chapter 9, Hicks and Weisberg suggest extending the IPS process to include intraparty work. Intraparty meetings can allow for difficult questions, such as acknowledging responsibility, to be faced rather than avoided. Interspersing interparty and intraparty meetings could be beneficial to the overall process. In the workshops that the School for Peace at Neve Shalom/Wahat al-Salam in Israel held among Palestinians, Arab Israelis, and Jewish Israelis, the facilitated intraparty meetings that occurred throughout the process enabled a different kind of dialogue. Mixing intraparty and interparty meetings may prevent some of the hardening of positions that Hicks and Weisberg mention as a danger in both kinds of encounter. Having an intraparty environment in the workshop could be the start of a new pattern of internal dialogue and could help prepare people for reentry into their communities. The intraparty environment provides an arena in which the dissonance aroused by the interparty experience can begin to be integrated into participants' understanding of the conflict and their own identity.

Both chapters emphasize responsibility-taking as essential to breaking some impasses to reconciliation. Third-party facilitators need to consider the processes that might allow the parties to a conflict to take responsibility. Perhaps some form of healing is necessary. In chapter 10, Rouhana points out that it is important to avoid seeing healing only as individual treatment for people who are sick or traumatized. Here the concern is that a focus on "curing individuals" in effect ignores structural problems, and the underlying issues and power relations remain unchanged. There is the danger of medicalizing the problem through sending psychologists to treat the "traumatized" in crises such as those in Bosnia and Rwanda. This step may actually further disempower people because they are seen as victims who need taking care of rather than as active agents whose grievances need to be addressed. This danger does not mean that the therapeutic model and its processes of healing should be abandoned. Instead, a major challenge for the field of social psychology is to begin to understand trauma and healing as an interactive group process. It is necessary to situate work such as IPS within the healing process (see Herman, 1997). Thus, practitioners can begin to understand why processes such as IPS become blocked at certain stages and how they might move forward.

Denial is a critical part of power. An important weapon in conflict is the maintenance and control of people's ignorance. It is the privilege of the higher power group to choose not to know and to control that ignorance, particularly within its own group (chap. 10, this volume). This issue was vividly illustrated for me in the summer of 2000 in my facilitation work for Arab and Israeli youth, carried out with the Seeds of Peace Center for Coexistence. At one point, discussions focused on the Israeli settlements in Gaza and the West Bank, and the Israeli participants insisted that they did not know anything about the settlements and therefore could not be blamed for them. One of the Palestinian youths said, "That is what is really upsetting. That you don't know." The Israeli youth were relying on their own ignorance to relieve them of blame, when it was that very ignorance that was most devastating for the Palestinians. This denial is a highly developed coping mechanism for people in conflict and traumatic situations. The new directions suggested in both chapters directly confront this denial and therefore could encounter resistance both within and outside the workshop.

One question I am struck by is the following: What would third-party facilitators be asking parties to a conflict to give up in the processes outlined in the two chapters? It is not just a question of what barriers have to be overcome to move away from conflict, but rather what needs, perhaps even basic needs, the conflict relationship and the lack of shared understanding fulfill. According to the two chapters, much of the identity of a party in conflict is constructed by the group's historical and current experience of the conflict and its traumas. The zero-sum construction of identity in the Israeli-Palestinian conflict is the psychological core of the conflict according to Kelman (1987). What happens to identity if relationships are formed between parties and the conflict begins to be resolved? For instance, if Israelis or Palestinians accept responsibility for what they have done to the other, are they still Israeli or Palestinian? How does their national identity have to be transformed to include these factors? Certainly, as the other side is humanized, people lose the ability to project all negative images of their own side onto the other side.

The aftermath of workshops is also a concern in terms of both the safety of the participants and the transfer of learning from the workshop. Kelman has long been concerned with addressing this reentry issue (Kelman, 1972, 1993). Participants enter a workshop, increase their ambivalence, begin to reevaluate the roles of their side and the other side, and then have to return home to the conflict. Participants also have to navigate their existing roles in their community and live with great psychological risk and sometimes physical risk. It is possible that during the next week they may be in a battle with the other side and have to kill someone. By exposing participants to the workshop experience, are IPS practitioners taking away their coping mechanisms? Is there a danger that progress inside the workshop may stifle progress on the outside if it becomes a substitute for, rather than a catalyst for, change?

As the role of the third party becomes more complex, how do workshop facilitators police themselves? Third parties go through processes similar to those of their participants, mirroring the dynamics of the workshops (Hicks et al., 1994). When properly managed, this transference can be very valuable, providing additional data on the workshop dynamics. However, if denied and mismanaged, it can be destructive to the workshop process and to the facilitators themselves. If workshops begin to include more recounting of trauma and to tackle issues such as justice and responsibility, the level of transference will be very high. Like the two parties in the workshops, the third parties need intraparty meetings of their own to process their experiences. Third parties should take responsibility for themselves and avoid falling into patterns of denial and polarization so that they can respond as effectively as possible to their participants.

The escalating situation in the Middle East makes this time one of great ambivalence and disillusionment among conflict resolution practitioners. These individuals are questioning the validity of the processes in which they have been involved. As the external situation implodes and fragments, there is a potential for the field of conflict resolution to do the same. Will it contain this ambivalence effectively so that the field can transform? Herbert Kelman throughout his work during the past 30 turbulent years has engaged in and inspired rigorous reflection on the IPS process and its impact. In these two chapters this tradition continues. It is a great honor for me, as a student of Herb Kelman, to be a part of this process of reflection and transformation.

References

Herman, J. (1997). *Trauma and recovery* (2nd ed.). New York: Basic Books.

Hicks, D., O'Doherty, H., Steiner, P., Taylor, W., Trigeorgis, M., & Weisberg, W. (1994). Addressing intergroup conflict by integrating and realigning identity: An Arab-Israeli workshop. In M. Ettin (Ed.), *Group process and political dynamics* (pp. 279–302). Madison, CT: International University Press.

Kelman, H. C. (1972). The problem solving workshop in conflict resolution. In R. L. Merritt (Ed.), *Communication in international politics* (pp. 168–204). Urbana: University of Illinois Press.

Kelman, H. C. (1987) The political psychology of the Israeli-Palestinian conflict: How can we overcome the barriers to a negotiated solution? *Political Psychology, 8,* 347–363.

Kelman, H. C. (1993). Coalitions across conflict lines: The interplay of conflicts within and between the Israeli and Palestinian communities. In S. Worchel & J. A. Simpson (Eds.), *Conflicts between people and groups* (pp. 236–258). Chicago: Nelson-Hall.

11

The Contribution of Bicommunal Contacts in Building a Civil Society in Cyprus

Maria Hadjipavlou

This chapter focuses on Cyprus and illustrates the process involved in conflict resolution workshops and their importance for the development of a civil society. The work in Cyprus has been greatly influenced by the contributions made at both theoretical and applied levels over the years by Herbert Kelman, and specifically by the insights we gained from his work of many years on the Israeli–Palestinian conflict (e.g., Kelman, 1979, 1993). One of the main differences shown in this chapter, however, is that the work in Cyprus has focused primarily on community building and civil society development across ethnic lines rather than on the development of specific political options as such to be fed directly to the macrolevel so as to move the official negotiations ahead as in the Israeli–Palestinian case. Of course, one similarity is that in both cases what happened in the workshop format did contribute to the more general public debate. One other more general distinction we can make is that the Cyprus work contributed more to peace building (discussed later), whereas Kelman's work has contributed to peacemaking—but both have aimed at transforming the adversarial relationships and paving the way for reconciliation.

In this chapter I first review the history of the Cyprus conflict. Second, I outline the conflict resolution framework and the goals of the conflict resolution training workshops in Cyprus. Third, I assess the ideas developed during interethnic encounters that were held either in Cyprus or abroad. Fourth, I look at specific current projects aimed at creating a civil society and, fifth, I describe suggestions for implementing a shared vision. I conclude with lessons learned from the case of Cyprus.

Cyprus: History of the Conflict

The geographically strategic location of Cyprus in the easternmost part of the Mediterranean, which is 40 miles from the south coast of Turkey, 60 miles from Syria, 100 miles from Lebanon, 250 miles north of Egypt, and 600 miles southeast of Greece, has made it vulnerable to outside conquests and interference. Whichever power dominated the region also controlled Cyprus. The Mycenaean Greeks settled on the island in the second millennium B.C., formed city-kingdoms on the Minoan model, and introduced the Greek language and culture. To this day, the Greek Cypriots (GCs) refer to this period as a way to stress their Hellenic heritage and its continuity to the present. The Turkish Cypriots (TCs) stress the three centuries of the Ottoman presence (1571–1878), which determined the interethnic character of the island. After the Ottoman rule, the Moslems who stayed on the island formed what later became the TC community.

By 1960 the TCs comprised 18% of the population and Greeks 80%, with 2% Armenians, Maronites, and Latins (Koumoulides, 1974; Papadopoulos, 1965). In 1878 the British took control of the island, and Cyprus officially became a British colony in 1925. During the anticolonial struggle from 1955 to 1959, the Greeks of Cyprus fought the British for *enosis* (union) with "motherland" Greece and the Turks of Cyprus for *taxim,* partition and union of part of the island with "motherland" Turkey.

The 1950s were also a period of intense interethnic mistrust and fear. For instance, according to TC writers, the TC leadership expected that sooner or later the Greek fighters would terrorize and subjugate the TC community (Necatigil, 1989), and so by 1957 the Turkish Resistance Organization (TMT) was formed in an effort to counteract the EOKA (National Organization of Cypriot Fighters). Meanwhile, the British politicized communal differences to serve their colonial interests in the Middle East (Pollis, 1973). This reinforced the rise of the two antagonistic nationalisms and competing visions for Cyprus, based on each group's attachment to its respective motherland. A compromise settlement was worked out by outside parties (Greece, Turkey, and Britain). Referred to as the London and Zurich agreement, it led to the creation in 1960 of the "reluctant" Cyprus Republic (Xydis, 1973).

Cyprus is a clear case of an imposed settlement that ignored local realities and microlevel concerns (Kitromilides, 1977). The imposed accommodation remained fragile, and interethnic violence broke out in December 1963 and later in 1967. This change resulted in the creation of a "Green Line," a dividing line in the capital of Nicosia to keep the two warring factions apart. This line was drawn by the British commander and was later patrolled by United Nations peacekeeping forces. Turkish Cypriot enclaves were set up in the major cities of the island where TCs were moved for security reasons. In 1967 the first concrete move for division and segregation of the two communities was witnessed. The Cyprus Republic was ineffective in dealing with all of its citizens' fears and needs. Since then the government of the Cyprus Republic has come under GC control, only in principle representing the TCs (Bahcheli, 1990). The problem was then internationalized: The United Nations sent a peacekeeping force on March 15, 1964, which has been on the island ever since, preserving the cease-fire.

The period from 1963 to 1974 was a time of unequal social and economic development, a factor that drew the two communities further apart. GCs experienced economic prosperity and modernization, whereas TCs entered a period of economic and cultural dependency on Turkey, which they regarded as their protector from GC domination (Necatigil, 1989). A "Provisional Turkish Administration" had been established with its own laws, police, and economic policies. This meant the pursuance of Ankara's policy in Cyprus, which was not necessarily in the interests of the majority of the Turkish Cypriots. [This incompatibility of interests holds true today in that the majority of the TC community desires to join the European Union (EU), but Turkey threatens to annex the northern part in case the Cyprus Republic joins the EU prior to a solution being found.] Thus, the creation of a Cypriot consciousness was continually being trapped from both sides. The sociopsychological gap drew the two communities apart despite isolated efforts at economic collaboration:

> The Cyprus government failed to find ways of overcoming the exclusive control of the leadership in order to bring the mass of the Turkish Cypriots into fuller integration with the Cypriot economy. But in conditions where their leaders had disrupted their links with the Cyprus Trade Union movement and its protection, had isolated them from freedom of movement and contact with Greek Cypriot businessmen and government officials . . . [t]his task would have been difficult for the Cyprus government. But making the effort would have meant a major transformation of the Cypriot society. (Attalides, 1976, p. 66)

The military dictatorship that took power in Greece in 1967 directly affected political life in the Greek Cypriot community. The period between 1967 and 1974 is characterized by high intracommunity tensions and divisions. A nationalist rhetoric for the revival of the "Hellenic-Christian ideals" was promoted by a group of anti-Makarios extremists by the name of EOKAB (Ethniki organosis kyprion agonoiston B or National Organization of Cypriot Fighters the Second), an underground organization led by General George Grivas. This group, under the orders of the Athens junta and aided by Greek officers and members of the national guard, staged a coup d'etat to topple the democratically elected government of President Makarios on July 15, 1974. Their aim according to Stern (1984) was twofold: to get rid of Makarios, whose unaligned policies were not to the liking of either the Greek junta or the U.S. State Department and, once this was achieved, to facilitate a NATO-inspired solution that would be acceptable to both Greece and Turkey. (The likely solution would have been the partitioning of the island.) Makarios was not killed, but the island was de facto partitioned as a result of the Turkish invasions that followed on July 20 and August 14, 1974.

This event was experienced by the Turkish Cypriots as a "peace operation" to liberate them from the domination of the Greek majority, and many came out in the streets welcoming their Turkish brethren (Volkan, 1979). For the GCs this meant massive forced displacement of nearly one third of the GC population. Forty percent of the island's territory came under Turkish military control. About 3,000 people were killed; to this day the fate of 1,619 people is still unknown and they have been declared missing. More than 70% of the economic resources were lost and fear for the future was very high (Attalides, 1979). Recently, in the new round of intercommunal talks both Cypriot leaders have brought up the question of the missing people and have acknowledged it as being a joint humanitarian problem.

This de facto geographical partition was followed by the transfer of all TCs still living in the south (about 60,000) to the northern part according to the Vienna agreement of 1975. The segregation that began in the mid-1960s was completed in 1975. In 1983 the TC leadership declared the "Turkish Republic of Northern Cyprus" (TRNC) but failed to gain recognition by any other state but Turkey. This led to international isolation of the TC community and increased dependency on Turkey.

A long series of intercommunal, high-level negotiations have been conducted on and off since 1975 under the United Nations auspices, but no agreement has been reached. The latest series of negotiations began in December 2001 and continue to this day. It is the first time that a serious momentum is being created in view of the accession of the Cyprus Republic to the EU. Each side still projects a different vision of what kind of Cyprus it wants, and conflicting interpretations of the terms *bizonality, bicommunality,* and *federation* are being discussed. These are political concepts used in the agreements of 1977 and 1979, which were accepted by the leaders of both communities and in a series of UN resolutions on Cyprus. The GCs favor a unified federal state with a strong central federal government and thus one international personality, but the TC official view supports two separate states linked together very loosely.

In the meantime, new generations are growing up on each side of the dividing line knowing nothing about the other, and stereotyping, psychological distancing, and feelings of mistrust grow deeper. Selective histories and memories are used as "text" to dehumanize the other and thus justify the division. It is within this context that groups and individuals from both sides are trying to challenge the status quo. They hope to articulate alternative discourses to the official adversarial ones and build a new political culture based on mutual understanding, respect, cooperation, and inclusion.

The majority of people from both communities support accession to the European Union as a way to help change the status quo. One of the questions that is part of the public discourse is whether Cyprus will enter the EU before or after a political solution. The most preferred outcome would be for the new federal Cyprus to enter so that both GCs and TCs would enjoy all benefits as EU citizens. As of now, the accession negotiations are being carried out with the Republic of Cyprus represented only by the GCs. The TC leadership has resisted participation in the talks, putting the "recognition" of the self-proclaimed state in the north, currently recognized only by Turkey, as a precondition. The EU Commission has repeatedly called on the TC leadership to join the negotiation teams, but TCs have often felt that the GCs, being the dominant group, patronized them, and that choices and decisions were being made on their behalf. What the TCs want, as is often expressed in joint conflict resolution workshops, is to work on the EU possibility in partnership with the GCs and the EU Commission. This need constitutes, in part, what TCs call "political equality" (Alemdar, 1993; Joseph, 1999).

One important effort at breaking through the historical enmity involves conflict resolution workshops in which members from each side are brought together. I contend that the Cypriot bicommunal citizens' efforts at peace building challenge the omnipotence of the state and the dominant narratives of nationalists in the GC and TC communities; the latter are based on the superiority and absolute righteousness of one's own side. The bicommunal peace builders stress *citizenship* as a shared value and a unifying point of reference rather than the traditional ethnic identities historically exploited by the official discourses on both sides and turned into points of contest and separation. The dualisms, bipolarity, and perceived homogeneity in each community are challenged as oversimplifications of a much more complex social landscape. My general thesis is that unless Cypriots have a well-developed, self-critical civil society committed to the peace-building processes, the best political agreement signed at the official diplomatic level will be very difficult to "sell" and will fail to crystallize in the long term. In the case of Cyprus, the top-down agreement of 1960 did not work for long due to lack of loyalty and commitment by the people (Hadjipavlou-Trigeorgis, 1987).

Conflict Resolution: New Frameworks

Before assessing new frameworks, it is important to set the stage by understanding the consequences of the old frameworks in greater depth. I turn first to these consequences, after which I discuss peacemaking via conflict resolution workshops and interethnic encounters.

Consequences: Need for Recognition

Recognition is important to both sides. Neither recognizes the other. The official GC agenda has operated on two levels: On the one hand, it tries to preserve the international recognition of the Republic of Cyprus; on the other hand, it strives to prevent at all levels (international, regional, and national) any recognition of the illegal state in the northern part of the island. In contrast, the TCs try hard to gain state recognition and make every effort to gain legitimacy; they blame the international community for exclusion and for denying them their separate voice. However, they avoid making any reference to the presence of more than 35,000 Turkish troops in the northern part of Cyprus since 1974, which the international community regards as occupation forces. Often citizens' joint meetings and contacts are prohibited on the grounds that meeting the "other," or the "enemy," might entail "recognition" of what each side considers illegal. Using this as a pretext, authorities in the north do not grant permission to TC peace builders to cross to the buffer zone where the joint workshops are being held. In this way, contacts become political instruments manipulated by authorities across the divide for fear of recognition, as if it were the citizens' contacts and cooperation that may grant recognition to states (Papadakis & Constantinou, 2001).

Consequences: Competing Identities

Geography and history have contributed to the identity debate of the island. Some of the old nationalist claims include these: The "island has always been Greek (for 9,000 years) and will so remain" (Greco-centric); or "Cyprus belongs to Turkey (300 years of Ottoman rule) and will go back to Turkey" (Turco-centric view); or "Cyprus belongs to the Cypriots" (Cyprio-centric).

More recently, the "European identity" of the island has been promoted by various groups in each community and the EU Commission. Specifically, in

1997 commissioner Van den Broek (1997) delivered a speech to groups from both communities stressing the "deep-lying bonds which, for two thousand years, have located the island at the very fount of European culture and civilization" (p. 3). He noted that the European influence is apparent in the values shared by the people of Cyprus and in the conduct of the cultural, political, economic, and social life. This shows "beyond all doubt, [Cyprus's] European identity and character and confirms its vocation to belong to the Community" (Van den Broek, 1997, p. 3). This is a good example of the contingency aspect of constructing identities (the instrumentalist school of thought) whereby identities wax and wane due to new situational needs, political goals, and a variety of other variables; this is contrary to the ethnocentric view of unchanging nature and eternal continuity of identity (i.e., the primordialist school of thought), which argues that identity is biologically based and passed on from generation to generation, as is, for instance, the argument for the unchanging, eternally Greek character of the island.

After the 1999 Helsinki EU Commission meeting, the concept of *Europeanization* of the Cyprus conflict has been used by many analysts. This concept implies that, because Cyprus is on the way to full EU membership, the political conflict should be of concern to the EU, which together with the international community should reinforce the official peace negotiations and also support and finance citizens' peace-building efforts and joint projects.

Peace Building and Conflict Resolution Workshops

In the last four decades or so, fundamental changes in our understanding of international conflicts have occurred. Cypriot citizens' peace-building efforts fall within the new approaches to resolve deep-rooted ethnonational conflicts. According to Burton (1990), "there have been changes in questioning traditionally held assumptions and in gathering together knowledge which has been scattered throughout different disciplines" (p. 59). Since the end of the bipolar world of the Cold War, Cypriots have been experiencing a period of transition. The old order reflecting bloc politics and ideological contests has come to an end. Various stresses in the global system have produced new types of conflicts (mainly intrastate) as well as new challenges. The international relations realist paradigms, which dealt mainly with interstate conflicts and employed traditional tools of diplomacy based on the concept of power and national interest and a win–lose mind-set, have been seriously challenged as inadequate to meet the complexity of conflicts in which different types of insecurity, such as human rights violations and traumas, are core issues (Rupensinghe, 1992).

The interdisciplinary field of conflict resolution (CR) informs us of the complexity and multilayered aspect of deep-rooted and protracted conflicts (Azar, 1990; Burton, 1987). It provides new analytical frameworks that both broaden and complement the old paradigm. Social psychology, for instance, informs us about the escalation, stalemate, and perpetuation of international conflicts. CR legitimizes the citizens' political participation and stresses the importance of reframing adversarial relationships between citizens and the state, and between citizens and the "other," in the context of continuous interactions on multiple levels.

Unofficial third-party-based interventions have grown in popularity during the last 20 years, as has the range of techniques and expertise employed. The citizens' unofficial efforts, coined *Track II diplomacy* (Montville, 1987) or *multitrack diplomacy* (Diamond & McDonald, 1991), all indicate a broad range of unofficial contacts between groups outside the governmental system. Furthermore, they open a new social space for citizens' needs and concerns to be articulated and promoted, with the aim of linking them to macrolevel processes. Thus, any agreement reached should be "owned" by both levels. As Harold Saunders (1991) noted:

> Some things only governments can do, such as negotiating to commit large groups. Some things citizens outside government can do better, such as probing the human dimensions of conflict and changing relationships among groups enough to permit formal mediation and negotiation or resolution of conflict by other means. (p. 234)

Research has also shown that the characteristics of intractable and deep-rooted conflicts increase resistance to resolution (Azar, 1985, 1990; Kelman, 1986; Rouhana & Bar-Tal, 1998). Such characteristics include existential fears, the "us and them" mentality; unaddressed historical grievances and traumas; economic asymmetries; and the frustration of unfulfilled human needs such as identity, security, recognition, dignity, participation, and justice.

International conflict is no longer an intergovernmental or interstate affair; it concerns societies, too:

> Thus, analysis of conflict requires attention, not only to its strategic, military, and diplomatic dimensions, but also to its economic, psychological, cultural, and social structural dimensions. Interactions along these dimensions, both within and between the conflicting societies, shape the political environment in which governments function. (Kelman, 1997, p. 199)

Protracted ethnonational struggles become an inescapable part of daily life for the members of the communities.

Perceptual and cognitive processes create barriers and resistance to redefining and resolving the conflict. Each party perceives the other as a carrier of hostile intentions. In the face of their own vulnerability, their interaction produces a self-fulfilling dynamic, making it difficult to discover shared interests. Assignment of blame is a key element in the parties' analysis and evaluation of the conflict (Volkan, 1979). Political leaders, for instance, invest energy in the need to persuade themselves, their own people, the rest of the world, and even historians that the blame rests totally with the enemy and that their own cause is just and good. CR workshop processes help participants see the spiraling effect that mirror images produce and depart from blaming the other in order to acquire the capacity to redefine the conflict as a shared problem to be solved cooperatively (Kelman, 1997, p. 225).

The Cyprus case bears most of the characteristics just mentioned. The existential fears of the GC community refer to the whole occupation of the island by Turkey given the appropriate conditions, whereas the TCs fear that the Greeks will throw them into the sea one day. Each group feels itself the victim of the other and of the other's motherland. The lack of response to each side's fundamental needs as well as institutional failure to satisfy them perpetuate the conflict. When the official level is caught in this escalatory dynamic, then citizens' active participation can increase awareness and capacities to break the cycle of mutual victimhood and thus help policymakers produce a more inclusive and flexible political agenda.

In Cyprus the conflict is now going through its third generation. Thus, at least two generations have never seen or interacted with the "other." They learn about each other through mediated information; they develop deep insecurities, animosities, and negative collective memories about the "other" whom they have never met. As a survival mechanism, people tend to adapt to the conflict and the status quo, especially when there is no daily interethnic violence. Everywhere in Cyprus the conflict and enemy images are visible in the barbed wires, the military posts, the blue berets, and the blue and green posters that read "Buffer UN Zone," "Beware Mine Fields," "No Entry—Occupied Zone," "Dead Zone," and "No Photographs—Security Zone." Flags of all kinds wave together or apart: the Greek flag, the flag of the Cyprus Republic, the red Turkish flag, the blue UN flag, and the TRNC flag. Often such societies view their differences as irreconcilable and are unable to craft a joint language for talking about the possibilities. CR unofficial third-party interventions help the conflicting parties explore opportunities for shared needs and interests, thus opening space for joint thinking.

Traditional international politics implies a process of mutual influence in which each party seeks to maximize its own interests and shape the behavior of the other using threats and coercion. Within such a framework, negotiations become a contest to be won. In contrast, CR broadens the repertoire of influence strategies with a variety of positive incentives that take the form of economic benefits, sharing resources, international approval, or integration in regional institutions (Kelman, 1997; Kriesberg, 1982). A CR perspective views the goal of negotiations as not merely a legalistic agreement, but also a long-term peace. The latter is achieved by introducing both structural and social changes in the form of confidence-building measures and even symbolic gestures. We may mention such examples as President Sadat's speech in the Israeli Knesset in 1977, or the efforts of TC peace builders to have photographs of atrocities removed from the Turkish checkpoint in 1999. Those photographs showed the killing of innocent TC citizens by GC extremists during the 1963–1964 and 1967 interethnic violence; their display was an effort to project the barbarity of GCs at that time, implying that nothing had changed ever since. This gesture, which was appreciated by many GC groups who are trying to convince officials in the government to reciprocate, would not have taken place had influential TCs not attended bicommunal CR workshops and realized the value of confidence-building measures.

Conflict Resolution Training Workshops in the Cyprus Context

In CR training workshops the Cypriot participants, many of whom have never met before, enter into a new type of interaction. They move past conflict norms (i.e., the us vs. them mentality, the blame and defend mind-set, mutual victimization, and exclusion) and are encouraged to engage in perspective-taking, which means understanding and legitimizing the other's grievances and rights as much as one's own. Learning to differentiate the enemy image and gaining insights into what perpetuates the conflict will eventually lead the participants to jointly develop new ideas and creative options for solutions. A new shared narrative often develops that includes both groups' fears, expectations, hopes, and needs.

Goals

Many of the goals associated with the work done in Cyprus are based on a social psychological understanding of international conflicts as outlined by Kelman and his associates (Kelman, 1965, 1997; Rouhana & Kelman, 1994) and also Allport's (1954) contact hypothesis, whereby people in conflict lack knowledge of the other and need opportunities to get to know each other. Once contact happens, individuals discover that underneath the group identity lies a deeper common identity as a human being. Contact, however, is likely to have positive effects on mutual attitudes only if it occurs under certain specified conditions such as equal status, interdependence, pursuit of common goals, and institutional support. After a workshop, for instance, participants often say: "So, not all Turks are bad. Mehmet and Gul are really nice," or "My 'enemy' has acquired a face and a name now, and is not so different from me," or "I never knew we had so many interests in common!" The stereotypic homogenization of the "other" gradually fades away across the divide that created an artificial cohesion and coalitions are then built across ethnic lines (Kelman, 1993). Kelman cautions, however, that these coalitions across conflict lines should not become too cohesive and it is important that the group membership of the participants remains salient in these contacts.

One of the challenges for the workshops is determining how to sustain and build on these positive experiences when the outside environment is filled with confrontation and multilayered asymmetries.

The CR training workshops also aim to provide skills in dialogue, conflict analysis, and cooperative problem solving. The process itself humanizes the "other," legitimizes both parties' historic pains and grievances, and develops a safe environment in which a new joint narrative can emerge based on direct face-to-face experiences rather than on mediated information received in each community. The process of individual learning and critical thinking challenges the official propaganda and national partisan media. In short, the broad aim of the CR training workshops is both educational and political (Kelman, 1986).

The Cyprus Fulbright Commission in 1999 produced a report from interviews with more than 200 people from both communities who had participated in CR workshops (Angelica, 1999). This report noted that the direct goals from the perspective of participants and local trainers included the following: to develop positive relationships between members of the GC and TC communities by (a) breaking down stereotypes and misconceptions of the other community, (b) increasing understanding of the perspectives of others, and (c) building trust between members of the two communities. The workshops do so through three processes:

1. They offer opportunities to develop communication and conflict resolution skills that participants can use in their work, community, and personal lives.
2. They build support for community reconciliation in conjunction with a political solution to the conflict by (a) enabling the development of friendships and professional relationships between members of the two communities; (b) encouraging a focus on the future; and (c) developing joint projects to address shared social, environmental, and economic concerns on the island.
3. Finally, they aim to have participants understand the Cyprus problem in new ways and generate creative ideas for a resolution to be used by policymakers or third parties.

The overall goal is to promote a new political culture of tolerance, respect for differences, bridging of power asymmetries, and long-term coexistence. This sophisticated view of the other community should make it easier to support ideas that move the parties toward a resolution.

Different models for intervention have been used in Cyprus, such as multitrack diplomacy (Diamond & McDonald, 1991), the interactive problem-solving workshop (Fisher, 1991, 1997; Kelman, 1986), interactive management (Broome, 1998), and humanistic transformative mediation. (For an overview of CR work in Cyprus, see Hadjipavlou-Trigeorgis, 1989, 1993, 1998). I provide here a short chronology of the CR training workshops and the main groups formed before and after 1997.

The Peace-Building Community: Strengthening Civil Society

By December 1997, thousands of citizens had made efforts at reconciliation and contact (Hadjipavlou-Trigeorgis, 1998). Such a desire challenges the official Turkish discourse that GCs and TCs cannot live together in a future settlement. As a consequence, the TC authorities often arbitrarily stopped granting permits to the TC participants to cross to the buffer zone for the meetings. The alternative venue to Nicosia became Pyla, a mixed village under UN supervision 50 miles away from Nicosia and not easily accessible to many people. Despite this "embargo," various public activities (peace and cultural festivals) were held in the Peace Park outside this village and were attended by thousands of citizens demonstrating their will to build bridges for future coexistence.

Between 1993 and 2001 more than 60 interethnic groups were formed and received formal training in conflict resolution skills, communication, mediation, negotiation, interactive management methodology, intercultural education, and dialogue (Hadjipavlou-Trigeorgis, 1998). The training was carried out initially (between 1993 and 1997) by American trainers and Fulbright scholars who were experts in the field of CR. In 1995 a "train-the-trainers" workshop produced a local team of Cypriot conflict resolution trainers, thus limiting dependency on foreign trainers. Despite the political obstacles, many of these bicommunal groups of professionals and people representing special interest groups continued to meet (e.g., women's groups, students, young environmentalists, businessmen, educators, academics, citizens' group, a bicommunal choir, artists, a management group, a federation study group, and a European Union study group). A coordinating body was set up to facilitate channels of communication and transfer of information among the members of the peace-building community. For this purpose, two nongovernmental organization (NGO) resource centers on each side of the divide were established by the United Nations Office for Project Services. The need for more peace structures still remains.

In the mid-1990s the legitimization of the Cypriot citizens' peace-building work was acknowledged by both the international community and outside peace research centers. For example, the International Conflict Resolution Program of Columbia University and the Oslo Peace Research Institute facilitated meetings between members of the Cyprus Business Forum with the support of then-U.S. presidential envoy Richard Holbrook.

Another significant conflict resolution intervention tool has been the Technology for Peace project, which includes Internet activity. It was set up in 1998 as a response to the permit embargo. According to a six-month report covering the period from January to June 2000, 12 bicommunal peace groups have used the system, sending more than 1,356 e-mail messages to one another (Laouris & Tziapouras, 2002). In addition, the Web site www.Peace-Cyprus.org has been set up on the initiative of two TCs and two GCs. This team believes that the Internet and computer technology can play a big role in peace building in Cyprus. Already this Web site has conducted political activities such as posting a petition on citizens' perceived basic needs and beliefs about a solution to the conflict, which was signed and sent to all the parties involved in the negotiations. A letter to the UN secretary-general signed by 41 different grassroots organizations was also sent urging a speedy solution. Another forum reported on the arrest in July 2000 of the TC editor of *Aruba*, who was accused of "spying for the Greeks" for publishing articles criticizing Turkish authorities and their lack of democratic procedures. A declaration signed by thousands of citizens generated support and solidarity across ethnic lines, and the TC authorities were forced to release all journalists for lack of evidence. Such citizens' activism points to the growth of civil society and their courage to stand up against the terror induced by the state.

This tool, which is in use extensively today, helps transcend the political and other barriers, resulting in new opportunities for interethnic communication. One such activity, which was prepared and organized through the Internet by five Youth Encounters for Peace (YEP) groups, was held in the village of Pyla on July 1, 2000. It represented an important shift in the public peace process because there was no foreign third-party facilitation. It was an indication that citizens' peace building was being "owned" by locals. This activity was inspired by two teachers, local facilitators of the YEP groups—one from each side. It brought together hundreds of Cypriots who lived in mixed villages or towns but had been forcibly separated after 1974 (some even since the mid-1960s):

> Like many people in Cyprus, Nicos and Ibrahim found their friendship cut
> short in 1974, when Turkish troops invaded and the island was split into two

mutually hostile zones. But Nicos, and others like him on both sides of the divide, are using the modern technology to reach out to people they haven't seen in more than a quarter of a century. They are part of the grass roots campaign that aims to break the political impasse and bring down the barriers between the two sides. (O'Malley, 2000, p. 22)

The event was widely publicized and was covered by local and international media. It also created a powerful grassroots dynamic that, when mobilized, can exert pressure on the leaderships. Civil society seems to be in the making, and Cypriot citizens are participating in the unofficial peace process in new, constructive ways.

Let us now examine other specific ideas and products of different groups.

Joint Products of Conflict Resolution Groups: Obstacles, Visions, and Values

In trying to understand the roots of the conflict, the participants in these CR groups used the interactive management methodology to develop a "map of obstacles" that reflected the many layers of the conflict. Below I give specific examples generated by these groups at different workshops between 1995 and 2000.

The *Bi-Communal Women's Group* (1995–1996) tried to understand what has contributed to pain and suffering in Cyprus. I was a participant-observer in that group. Insights about obstacles to conflict resolution can be classified into four broad categories: (a) psychological, (b) structural, (c) historical and political, and (d) philosophical considerations. These were, in turn, sometimes specific to GC women, sometimes to TC women, and sometimes shared.

Some of the most prominent concerns and obstacles experienced by GC women included the external interventions in the affairs of the island, specifically the Turkish invasion and expansionist plans. They also identified with their glorious Hellenic past, which they saw as a factor underplaying the Cypriot part of their identity. The GC women expressed their sadness that TC did not understand the tragedy of the 1974 events and the consequences on their lives. There was more philosophical reflection of the part of GC women than TC women on such issues as happiness, self-actualization, self-criticism, and militarism. This is not surprising in view of the fact that they belong to the community that enjoys international recognition and have resolved basic needs such as economic survival and can thus afford to move to other higher needs. The TC women expressed strong fears of being dominated by the GC majority and Turkey, and thus they felt that they were sandwiched between the two. They also feared losing their Cypriot identity due to the influx of Turks from Turkey and lack of recognition; they felt isolated and deprived of privileges the GCs enjoy. Both GCs and TCs, however, saw the patriarchal structure of the social organization as well as the absence of women from decision-making bodies and the peace process as major obstacles to gender equality and the proper functioning of democracy in Cyprus.

In addition, other shared concerns included social and constitutional anachronistic prejudices against mixed marriages, lack of institutions and structures to promote knowledge, and inadequate understanding of the other's culture. Increase in structural and domestic violence was a serious mutual concern, as was the fear of expressing their true feelings about the national issue, contrary to the official discourses and narrative. Their unhappiness and anger at having to live in only one part of the island while fantasizing about the other part was a major concern. It was not unrelated to their concern about being more aware both of their strengths as women and of the work that would be required to make a positive contribution to the history of the island. The obstacles as articulated by GC and TC women present a complex picture. Long-term work is needed within and across the communities, as well as prior to, during, and after a solution. The "conflict-habituated system" due to the deep-rootedness of the issues would take more than one generation to deconstruct the conflict and gradually consolidate a culture of mutual trust, cooperation, and long-term peace. Clearly, self awareness and group awareness of the other's needs are necessary to build a civil society alongside the appropriate institutional arrangements and structures. Let us consider some more examples.

The *Bi-Communal Conflict Resolution Trainers* (1996) worked for nine months in one community and, when possible, in both communities, and identified many of the same fears and concerns as obstacles to Cypriot peace building. Specifically, they pointed out concerns that can be organized into 12 categories: (a) education, (b) socialization into the conflict, (c) the many historical traumas between Greeks and Turks, (d) personal economic interests in maintaining the status quo, (e) the lack of a mentality supporting peace and inclusion, (f) massive influence of outside forces, (g) the concern TCs have of the perception among Greeks and GCs that Cyprus is a Hellenic island, (h) fear of losing and betraying one's own national group, (i) lack of information about what federation would mean to the people, (j) lack of a tradition of democracy in the TC community, (k) different understandings of the meaning of peace, and (l) GC frustration stemming from perceived Turkish inflexibility in the official negotiations. This list once again reinforces the view of the complexity of ethnonational conflicts and the hard work that needs to be undertaken at both the structural and institutional levels. The engagement of citizens from both ethnic groups is of paramount importance to build the necessary human infrastructure that will, in turn, facilitate the political agreement.

Another active bicommunal group is the *Bi-Communal Business Forum* (1997), which was formed in response to the Brussels theme "in economic cooperation lies mutual benefit." This theme implies that when groups in conflict share a superordinate goal, like mutual economic and security interests, then cooperation becomes easier to achieve despite historical enmities. This group originally met in Brussels, Belgium, and their main focus was economic development on the island of Cyprus, while identifying the large economic asymmetry that exists between the two sides. This group was particularly worried about the massive arms buildup in both parts of the island—Cyprus is considered to be one of the most heavily militarized areas in the world. The security issue and the need for greater stability for joint business ventures were stressed.

The *Bi-Communal Youth* (1997) voiced a need for social change. This group was critical of the political leadership and of the political culture that favors elites, patron-client politics, and deprivation of citizens' rights to decide on their country's future. At this time young TCs were forced to emigrate due to a bad economy, lack of confidence in the TRNC, compulsory military service, and international isolation. GC youth expressed concern about the increase of violence in their daily lives and stressed the need to learn CR skills to solve problems nonviolently. Thus, shortcomings in education and curriculum were pointed out as crucial factors in the absence of a nonviolent culture. Cypriot youth seemed as concerned about structural and institutional violence as about the political conflict.

The need to intensify efforts both at the official and unofficial diplomatic levels to change the status quo was articulated by a large bicommunal group of CR trainers and citizens at a joint meeting held for a week in the summer of 2000, in the village of Neve Shalom in Israel. The preferred option of accession to the EU for the whole of the island as well as the EU's mediation efforts still inspired the hope that individual and collective safeguards would result. The unofficial citizens' work represented in these examples challenges the often-stated GC position that once a political settlement is signed, there will once again be no problem in establishing people-to-people cooperation and coexistence. The bicommunal work has shown that such wish is a fantasy, and there is much serious work to be done to deconstruct the conflict mentality and structural norms that have sustained the conflict for generations.

Next I examine some projects aimed at creating peace in Cyprus.

Overcoming Obstacles: A Collective Vision Map

After the Bi-Communal Conflict Resolution Trainers (1995–1996) group, which had worked with one community and then jointly, identified the obstacles and gained a deeper shared understanding of the conflict, they turned to the question of the desired goals and joint ideas for peace building in Cyprus. The *Vision Map* they created provided direction and guidance to overcome the obstacles by producing and categorizing hundreds of ideas. The collective vision resembled the construction of a building with many levels.

The foundation, or the first level, on which the vision was built was *communication*. This meant dissemination of open and unbiased information, free flow of ideas, and the right of people to meet freely, so as to create shared meanings and opportunities for interaction. One element was the establishment of intercommunal institutions and centers to promote specific bicommunal activities such as commerce, health, education, sports, and culture. Contacts with decision makers were considered important in consolidating long-term social change. Such an environment would build the right climate in which ethnic identities would not be threatened and which would provide space for public support for the accession of Cyprus to the EU. The latter factor can help bridge the economic gap between the two communities (the gross national product of Greek Cypriots is currently four times that of Turkish Cypriots).

The collective vision also dealt at a second level with engaging the societies in the peace-building process through strengthening the peace movement and promoting the idea in the GC community that the existence of the TC community is vital for the whole of Cyprus. Such an inclusive mentality would do away with the effects of ethnonationalism and promote a multiethnic federal society in accordance with EU values.

The third level on the map dealt with two concerns: gaining a better understanding of basic needs, fears, and aspirations concerning the sensitive issue of property and also stimulating freedom of movement throughout the island. The latter step would both provide open space to work for an independent, bicommunal, bizonal, federally united Cyprus with full respect for human needs and rights and also develop the appropriate public mentality to support it. If successful, this third level would lead to an "upper level," where the security problem for both communities would be minimized through demilitarization and non-outside interference. Finally, it would be possible to create a Cyprus where everybody's needs would be everybody's concern. This Vision Map constitutes an important document created by the unofficial peace builders from both communities and can be a resource in appeals to those who have official roles.

Suggestions for the Implementation Phase

This same Bi-Communal Conflict Resolution Trainers group, which had been working for a whole year, next addressed the question of what would be needed to implement the above collective vision. An *Options Field Map* concretely guided the steps for constructing the human infrastructure that provided opportunities for communication and contacts. The group envisioned that this would be done through CR workshops, dialogue groups, and education seminars. Accomplishments included the installation of a telephone system and the Technology for Peace project, whereby hundreds of individuals communicate through e-mail. In addition, two weekly, call-in radio peace programs were started by members of the peace-building community. Many new groups, mainly of young people, joined in. Several youth peace camps have already been funded and are taking place annually abroad. In less than a decade rapprochement has become an accepted social policy and a peace tool.

The need for scientific data, the establishment of a research center, and joint publications were stressed in this final phase of the vision statement. Lobbying at the decision-making level needs to be thought out carefully. Exchange programs, curriculum development, and learning each other's language remain to be promoted. Many of these suggestions were submitted to UN Secretary-General Boutros Boutros-Ghali, in 1993; he included them in the package of confidence-building measures, which was given to both parties at that time. This event was an example of the successful transfer of citizens' workshop products to the macrolevel.

Conclusion and Lessons Learned

As was pointed out in this chapter, the case of Cyprus informs us of the many layers of ethnonational conflict. It helps to remind us that there are many points of entry into a conflict-habituated system for generating structural and social psychological change. At the same time, it is evident that traditional diplomacy is limited in scope and tools to address and deal with such complex issues of identity, historical traumas, and human security. The multidisciplinary field of conflict resolution provides us with a number of key theoretical approaches for conflict analysis and specific tools such as interactive problem-solving workshops, dialogue, community-building processes, and unofficial third-party facilitation. In situations in which the ontological needs (identity, security, and recognition) are frustrated, the conflict will continue, as in the Cyprus case. Both Burton (1993) and Kelman (1992) have provided academics with a major challenge:

> We must go back to fundamental assumptions and reexamine them. In particular, we must move from institutions to persons as units of analysis and deduce a political theory on this basis. From such a political theory we must then deduce policies, and then move to application. At this stage there is new material to be fed back into our consideration of hypothesis. (Burton, 1993, p. 59)

The analysis of the Cyprus conflict presented here has demonstrated the significance of employing microlevel processes in our understanding of conflict and its protractedness. Despite the fact that there is currently no interethnic violence in Cyprus, it has a history of mutual victimization, "double asymmetry" or "double minorities": Both parties see themselves as minorities depending on their point of reference. The Turkish Cypriots are the minority on the island, but Greek Cypriots are the minority in the region. (Similarly, Palestinians are the minority in Israel, but Israelis are the minority in the region.) Another striking theme is the ethnocentric tendency to attribute positive traits and values to one's own society and blame the protractedness of the conflict on the other. The CR microprocesses challenge belief systems and behaviors to move beyond conflict norms to foster modified perspective taking and modified values in support of dealing with otherness and difference. The impact the Cypriot citizens' efforts have exerted at the grassroots level and the influence at the macrolevel still need to be researched thoroughly. I note a lack of linkage between the groups' work toward a peace-building culture and structural realities in the communities at large as well as at the decision-making levels. How can this be explained? What are the lessons thereby learned about CR interventions?

We can address this question from the point of view of logistics, power dynamics, and psychological realities. Due to the de facto partition of Cyprus, bicommunal work has relied on outside third parties to carry messages to and from the line in order to grant permission to the TC participants to cross to the buffer zone for the workshops. Often bicommunal work is contingent on the stage of the conflict, the type of relationship that prevails between Greece and Turkey, and whether or not formal negotiations take place. There is not enough appropriate building space in which to hold the meetings, and financial and material resources are scarce as well. When the Cypriots organize workshops, it is up to the individuals to cover all the expenses, because no fund-raising mechanism has been set up; it was after a great deal of pressure that an international nongovernmental agency (UNOPS) took an interest in this local demand.

Lack of institutionalization of the Bi-Communal Peace Building Movement in Cyprus is connected to the recognition issue; for example, if such an NGO were set up, where would it be registered—in the TRNC or in the Republic of Cyprus?

Furthermore, third parties, mostly American trainers, introduced from the start a nonpolitical frame (the "we are not here to solve the Cyprus conflict" ground rule) and focused more on the skill-training and educational aspects rather than sensitizing participants to the political task and social change implications of their intervention. As a result, the perception often expressed from both the left wing and the nationalists is that CR psychologizes the conflict and inhibits participants from tackling the tough political issues. It must also be noted that the United Nations in Cyprus, which for 39 years has kept a strict peace-keeping agenda, has failed to broaden this agenda to include peace building and peacemaking. This is true despite the changing realities, the needs of the communities, and the numerous UN resolutions stressing the significance of building bridges of communication, trust, and confidence in working on joint projects between and across the two sides. It is high time the UN mandate in Cyprus became flexible and open to local demands and its local staff trained in peace-building processes. Participants have often brought up this issue with UN representative in Cyprus and the usual answer has been "It is beyond our mandate!"

In some leftist circles on the island the argument has been raised that these CR efforts are often elite oriented in that participants come from the educated class. The language restriction prevents many people who wish to from joining, because they do not know English. This barrier, however, has been overcome in the last three years by the Co-Villagers Project, which was initiated by the YEP groups and local facilitators. Cypriots who lived in mixed villages speak each other's language and do not need to know English.

Peace work is a sensitive issue in divided societies, so members of reconciliation groups are often vulnerable to societal and press criticism for "meeting with the enemy"; their patriotism and motives are often questioned. In addition, peace work is carried out on a voluntary basis, individuals who participate in this effort frequently burn out, and no support system exists to help them and provide empowerment. Courage and dedication are needed to continue the work. In the last few years the active involvement of the EU and the legitimization of the rapprochement ideology through financing of bicommunal projects and programs at various levels has opened opportunities for citizens' involvement across the ideological spectrum. A positive outcome has recently been the EU support at both the macro (leadership) and the micro (societal) levels of the peace-building effort. The participation of the TCs in the accession negotiating team would help all Cypriots build a consciousness for a healthy, participatory civil society, ensuring that top-down orchestrated solutions are a practice of the past.

References

Alemdar, S. (1993). International aspects of the Cyprus problem. In C. H. Dodd (Ed.), *The political, social, and economic development of Northern Cyprus* (pp. 123–139). London: Eothen Press.

Allport, G. W. (1954). *The nature of prejudice*. Reading, MA: Addison Wesley.

Angelica, P. M. (1999). *Evaluation of the conflict resolution training efforts sponsored by the Cyprus Fulbright Commission (1993–1998)*. Manuscript submitted for publication.

Attalides, M. (1976). Relations between Greek and Turkish Cypriots in perspective. Paper presented at the International Symposium of Political Geography, Nicosia, Cyprus.

Attalides, M. (1979). *Cyprus: Nationalism and international politics*. Edinburgh, Scotland: Q Press Ltd.

Azar, E. E. (1985). Protracted social conflict: Ten propositions. *International Interactions, 12,* 59–70.

Azar, E. E. (1990). *The management of protracted social conflict*. Aldershot, United Kingdom: Gower.

Bahcheli, T. (1990). *Greek–Turkish relations since 1955*. Boulder, CO: Westview Press.

Broome, J. B. (1998). Overview of conflict resolution activities in Cyprus: Their contribution to the peace process. *Cyprus Review, 10*(1), 47–67.

Burton, W. J. (1987). *Resolving deep-rooted conflict: A handbook*. Lanham, MD: University Press of America.

Burton, W. J. (1990). *Conflict: Human needs theory*. New York: St. Martin's Press.

Burton, W. J. (1993). Conflict resolution as a political system. In D. Sandole & H. van der Merwe (Eds.), *Conflict resolution theory and practice* (pp. 55–65). Manchester, England: Manchester University Press.

Diamond, L., & McDonald, J. (1991). *Multi-track diplomacy: A systems guide and analysis* (Iowa Peace Institute Occasional Paper 3). Grinnell, IA: Iowa Peace Institute.

Fisher, R. J. (1991). *Conflict analysis workshop on Cyprus: Final report*. Ottawa, Canada: Canadian Institute for International Peace and Security.

Fisher, R. J. (1997). *Interactive conflict resolution*. Syracuse, NY: Syracuse University Press.

Hadjipavlou-Trigeorgis, M. (1987). *Identity conflict in divided societies: The case of Cyprus*. Unpublished doctoral dissertation, Boston University, Boston.

Hadjipavlou-Trigeorgis, M. (1989). Conflict resolution mechanisms: A comparative study of four societies. *Cyprus Review, 1*(1), 67–92.

Hadjipavlou-Trigeorgis, M. (1993). Cyprus: An evolutionary approach. *Journal of Conflict Resolution, 37,* 340–360.

Hadjipavlou-Trigeorgis, M. (1998). Different relationships to the land: Personal narratives, political implications, and future possibilities. In V. Calotychos (Ed.), *Cyprus and its people, nation, identity, and experience in an unimaginable community, 1955–1997* (pp. 251–277). Boulder, CO: Westview Press.

Joseph, S. J. (1999). Cyprus and the EU: Searching for a settlement in the light of Accession. *Cyprus Review, 11*(1), 33–58.

Kelman, H. C. (1965). Social-psychological approaches to the study of international relation: Definition of scope. In H. C. Kelman (Ed.), *International behavior: A social-psychological analysis* (pp. 3–39). New York: Holt, Rinehart & Winston.

Kelman, H. C. (1979). An interactional approach to conflict resolution and its application to Israeli–Palestinian relations. *International Interactions, 6,* 99–122.

Kelman, H. C. (1986). Interactive problem-solving: A social-psychological approach in conflict resolution. In W. Klassen (Ed.), *Dialogue toward inter-faith understanding* (pp. 293–314). Jerusalem: Tantur Ecumenical Institute for Theological Research.

Kelman, H. C. (1992). Informal mediation by the scholar/practitioner. In J. Bercovitch & J. Z. Rubin (Eds.), *Mediation in international relations: Multiple approaches to conflict management* (pp. 64–96). New York: St. Martin's Press.

Kelman, H. C. (1993). Coalitions cross conflict lines: The interplay of conflicts within and between the Israeli and Palestinian communities. In J. Simpson & S. Worchel (Eds.), *Conflict between peoples and people* (pp. 236–258). Chicago: Nelson-Hall.

Kelman, H. C. (1997) . Social-psychological dimensions of international conflict. In I. W. Zartman & J. L. Rasmussen (Eds.), *Peacemaking in international conflict: Methods and techniques* (pp. 191–236). Washington, DC: United States Institute of Peace Press.

Kitromilides, M. P. (1977). From coexistence to confrontation: The dynamics of ethnic conflict in Cyprus. In M. Attalides (Ed.), *Cyprus reviewed* (pp. 143–186). Nicosia, Cyprus: Jus Cypris Association.

Koumoulides, J. (1974). *Cyprus and the War of Greek Independence, 1821–1829.* London: Guilford and Sons.

Kriesberg, L. (1982). Non-coercive inducements in international conflict. In C. M. Stephenson (Ed.), *Alternative methods for international security* (pp. 105–120). Washington, DC: University Press of America.

Laouris, Y., & Tziapouras, G. (2002). Technology used for peace in Cyprus. *Peacebuilding, 3*(3), 4–8.

Montville, V. J. (1987). The arrow and olive branch: A case of track two diplomacy. In J. McDonald & D. Bendahmane (Eds.), *Conflict resolution: Track II diplomacy* (pp. 112–127). Washington, DC: U.S. Government Printing Office.

Necatigil, M. Z. (1989). *The Cyprus question and the Turkish position in international law.* Oxford, England: Oxford University Press

O'Malley, J. (2000, July 28). Cyprus citizens' meeting. *London Times Supplement,* pp. 22–27.

Papadakis, Y., & Constantinou, M.C. (2001). The Cypriot state *in situ:* Cross ethnic contact and the discourse of recognition. *Global Society, 15,* 125–148.

Papadopoulos, T. (1965). *Social and historical data on the population (1570–1881).* Nicosia, Cyprus: Cyprus Research Center.

Pollis, A. (1973). Intergroup conflict and British colonial policy: The case of Cyprus. *Comparative Politics, 5,* 575–599.

Rouhana, N. N., & Bar-Tal, D. (1998). Psychological dynamics of intractable ethno-national conflicts: The Israeli–Palestinian case. *American Psychologist, 53,* 761–770.

Rouhana, N. N., & Kelman, H. C. (1994). Promoting joint thinking in international conflicts: An Israeli–Palestinian continuing workshop. *Journal of Social Issues, 50,* 157–178.

Rupensinghe, K. (1992). Democratization processes and their implications for international security. In *Peace and conflict issues after the Cold War* (UNESCO Studies on Peace and Conflict, pp. 72–98). Paris: UNESCO.

Saunders, H. H. (1991). Officials and citizens in international relations. In V. Volkan, J. Montville, & D. Julius (Eds.), *The psychodynamics of international relations: Unofficial diplomacy at work* (Vol. 2, pp. 41–71). Lexington, MA: Lexington Books.

Stern, L. (1984). Bitter lessons: How we failed in Cyprus. *Foreign Policy, 19,* 34–78.

Van den Broek, H. (1997, December 2). *Bicommunal cooperation: The path to mutual trust and reconciliation.* Speech delivered at the Ledra Palace, Nicosia, Cyprus.

Volkan, V. D. (1979). *Cyprus: War and adaptation: A psychoanalytic history of two ethnic groups in conflict.* Charlottesville: University Press of Virginia.

Xydis, S. G. (1973). *Cyprus: Reluctant republic.* The Hague, The Netherlands: Mouton.

12

Assessing the Social Psychological Support for Kelman's Interactive Problem-Solving Workshops

Cynthia Chataway

Interactive problem-solving workshops (IPSWs) are off-record unofficial dialogues in which analytical discussion and problem solving are facilitated between influential members of nations or groups in conflict (Fisher, 1997). IPSWs were designed primarily to create movement in protracted social conflicts—conflicts that are characterized by multiple hostile crises over generations, a breakdown of communication between societies, polarized negative stereotypes, and a deep sense of victimization on both sides (Azar, 1990; Burton, 1969).

The goals of this process have been modest, given the entrenched nature of protracted social conflicts. The primary goals have been to give influential members of the disputing societies an opportunity (a) to develop constructive working relationships through which their attitudes toward the other society and the conflict might be positively influenced, (b) to bring these new attitudes into their interactions outside of the workshop, and thus (c) to influence the public dialogue and policymaking process. Between 1971 and 1996, Herbert Kelman held 26 one-time Israeli–Palestinian workshops and five meetings of a continuing workshop (1990–1993) that involved most of the same participants throughout. Since the beginning of formal Middle East peace negotiations, the continuing workshop has evolved into a more task-oriented working group that has met more than 13 times since 1994 to produce public documents on particularly difficult issues (Kelman, Chataway, & Neufeldt, 1998).

Conflict resolution practices such as IPSWs have generally been criticized as atheoretical; and, if theoretical, they have been criticized for not engaging in sufficient research to test for their expected contributions. For instance, Lewicki, Weiss, and Lewin (1992) suggested that most conflict resolution models "have risen to their places in the literature on face validity and inherent appeal alone" (p. 219). However, this criticism overlooks both the extensive research that supports the logic of conflict resolution interventions and the research that has been carried out directly on these methods.

In this chapter, I outline four different social psychological ways in which the IPSW has been evaluated: (a) Experimental research in social psychology has informed and grounded the key design features of the IPSW, (b) several exploratory studies have been completed on attitudes and behaviors expressed in actual

IPSWs, (c) simulations of protracted social conflicts with an IPSW condition have tested the extent to which people can learn and apply the IPSW approach, and (d) IPSW products have been collectively judged and thus evaluated.

Workshop participants are chosen, not solely for their individual characteristics, but also because they themselves have important influence, credibility, and authority in their societies. Thus, if the relationship between the participants is changed in the microcosm of the workshop, and if workshop participants carry this experience and any new insights and frameworks for understanding the conflict into the broader political arena, it is plausible to expect some change in the political discourse and relationship between their societies. From relationship change at one level emerges the possibility for relationship change at another. The research that I describe in this chapter begins to illuminate the kinds of influence that may be occurring as a result of Kelman's IPSWs.

Basic Social Psychological Research

Many, perhaps most, of the established research findings in social psychology support the value of the key design features of an IPSW: (a) confidential dialogue, (b) facilitated discussion of underlying needs and fears, and (c) joint problem solving by the parties to the dispute. To the extent that support has been found for beneficial effects from each of these design features, we might expect that the IPSW as a whole will have positive effects.

I now illustrate this approach briefly. Confidential dialogue has been found to support the sharing of information and clarification of fears and aspirations that motivate aggressive behavior (Ross & Ward, 1995). Such dialogue also appears to generate more openness to new ideas and reevaluation of stereotypes than nonconfidential dialogue, particularly among politically accountable participants (Pruitt, 1995; Tetlock, 1992). A focus on the underlying needs and fears that motivate conflict behavior has been found to increase perspective-taking, self-understanding, and subsequent changes in thinking and behavior (Greenberg, Rice, & Elliott, 1993; Izard, 1993). Problem solving by the parties to a dispute, rather than by a party outside the dispute, has been found to result in greater commitment by disputants to any solutions they devise (Petty, Priester, & Wegener, 1994; Stephenson & Wicklund, 1983), the maintenance of the essential trust relationship with the facilitator (Hiltrop, 1989), and reduced in-group bias (Aronson, Blaney, Stephan, Sikes, & Snapp, 1978).

The criteria for selecting people as workshop participants have been very similar to the criteria for minority influence: people who (a) are generally respected within their societies, (b) have reputations as competent and contributing members, and (c) are articulate and have the ability and confidence to present new positive social norms. Social psychological research on minority influence suggests that such people have the greatest ability to be influential in the event that they choose to articulate alternative ideas (Bray, Johnston, & Chilstrom, 1982; Tindale, Davis, Vollrath, Nagao, & Hinsz, 1990).

However, research also suggests that attitudes are extremely difficult to change, and if changed as a result of an intervention, tend to erode over time toward the positions previously held (Cook & Flay, 1978). This research suggests that to counteract the tendency for attitudes to erode over time, a workshop should provide more emphasis on emotional and behavioral (in addition to analytical) interventions (Tesser & Shaffer, 1990). In addition, there should be follow-up after a workshop to maintain exposure to and support for the new attitudes (Petty, Haugtvedt, & Smith, 1995).

To truly solidify new attitudes, it seems necessary to engage the behavioral, emotional, and cognitive components of an attitude in complementary fashion. IPSWs, while not prohibiting behavioral and emotional work by participants, have focused on the cognitive domain. The focus on rational discussion and thus on the cognitive component of attitudes, while downplaying behavioral and emotional interventions, likely decreases the impact on potential participants, given the considerable social and psychological pathology that protracted social conflicts are understood to produce (Staub, 1990; Volkan, Montville, & Julius, 1990).

Research on minority influence also suggests that the influence of new ideas, and the likelihood that participants will articulate them outside of the workshop, would be enhanced if workshop participants worked together after a workshop to support one other (Tindale et al., 1990). As a minority voice of one, workshop participants are much less likely to speak up with new ideas once they return to the hostile conflict context than if this minority opinion is spoken by two or more people at once. This consideration suggests that IPSWs might be structured to involve participants who will be in regular contact after a workshop and to support follow-up contact between participants. In addition, facilitators might consider building in regular long-term contact with and between participants to discuss the ideas of the workshop, because repeated exposure to new ideas tends to solidify new attitudes (Cacioppo & Petty, 1985).

The social psychological experiments that lie behind these findings sacrifice the complexity of a protracted social conflict in the interest of testing the influence of isolated design variables on individuals' thoughts and behavior. The complex interaction of design variables, and their particular functioning within the context of high emotion and identification with the conflict, cannot be generated within the context of an experiment. However, social psychological experiments have provided invaluable direction for the design of the workshop, which has then been further adapted through reflective practice and action research (e.g., Cohen, Kelman, Miller, & Smith, 1977).

Research on Workshop Interaction

This chapter makes available for the first time the results of the small exploratory studies that have been carried out over the years on Kelman's IPSWs by students and associates. This research has focused primarily on interaction between participants in a workshop and on the participant's attitudes and political behavior after a workshop. The final step, by which these participants then influence the political relationship between the conflicting societies, is theorized but largely not researched (Chataway, 2002).

As facilitators of workshops, Kelman's associates and former students have always wanted to know the extent to which our perceptions of workshop interaction are supported by empirical research. We want to know if workshop participants engage in the kind of interaction expected during a workshop: sharing information, clarifying needs and fears, and becoming more open to new ideas. However, direct research has been limited by a desire not to interfere with the intervention process. For example, in a workshop with Israeli and Palestinian women, we tried to build in a research component by having participants write down their goals prior to the workshop (in separate groups), with the plan to revisit these goals two or three times during the workshop. Participants did write down their initial goals but then became so engaged in fruitful interaction that they did not want to separate or redirect their attention to revisit the original goals. We gave up our evaluation approach at their request and focused on facilitation. However, some studies have been completed, particularly within the context of Kelman's graduate seminar, International Conflict: A Social Psychological Approach. In this context, students participated in actual workshops with Jewish-Israeli and Palestinian participants, observing from behind a one-way mirror or from within the IPSW room and taking notes for use in producing an informal transcript of the workshop.

In 1982, one student (Horowitz, 1982) attempted to systematically assess the content and process aspects of a workshop using data on the frequency of interaction between participants in the workshop, levels of discussion (i.e., societal, personal, situational), and SYMLOG field diagrams (Bales & Cohen, 1979). SYMLOG is a method for coding the communication of groups according to who talks to whom in what way, the content of the discussion, positions and attitudes, participants' reactions, and the level of abstraction in the concerns raised. Over time Horowitz found role specialization within groups, a shift in the discussion to more personal references, and a more positive and future task orientation. These findings suggest that the workshop facilitated or allowed participants to consider future resolution efforts and to move beyond abstract, peripheral discussions about the workshop situation, society, or fantasy, to concrete discussions of self, other, and group. In addition, Israelis and Palestinians spoke mainly to each other rather than to the third party, indicating that the two sides were, in fact, interacting. Interaction between parties in protracted conflict can be, in itself, a rare event.

Ambady (1986) content-analyzed approximately two thirds of the informal notes taken by student observers of workshop dialogue for themes (analytical, historical, or procedural) and for 11 interaction process categories, similar to those of Bales (1950). Her analysis suggested that the workshop proceeded through three phases: search for formal structure, followed by analysis and expression, and, finally, task orientation. There was a marked decline in historical themes over the course of the workshop and a general increase in analytical content. In addition, there was evidence of the reentry effect (Walton, 1970), in that attitudes and interaction styles at the end of the workshop, as participants prepared to return to their communities and to the external conflict, regressed in the direction of attitudes and interaction styles observed at the beginning of the workshop. For example, distrust appeared to be highest during the first and final workshop sessions. Ambady concluded that the workshop was successful because participants exchanged concerns, perspectives, and ideas for solutions, and jointly drafted an invitation to Israeli Prime Minister Peres, PLO Chairman Arafat, and other Arab leaders to attend an international conference.

Gender differences have been noted informally by students and workshop facilitators over the years, with the usual observation being that female workshop participants seem to express more satisfaction with the workshop process, to take more advantage of the opportunities to talk and to build alliances with the other participants between sessions (in the lobby, etc.), and to follow up more with other participants after the workshop. Women also seem to be more prepared to draw analogies between their conflict and other conflicts in the world. Although these perceived differences, if they exist, may be related to power and status differences between the male and female participants in workshops, they do not seem to be related to the amount of experience that the participant has with dialogues with the other side. However, very little research has systematically compared the contributions of different types of participants during or after a workshop, with the exception of a study that I now describe.

D'Estree and Babbitt (1998) compared the transcript of an all-female workshop (involving Israelis and Palestinians) with a mixed male and female workshop that had taken place two weeks earlier in 1987, for which the outcomes were very similar. In the women's workshop, participants coded more expressions of personal experience, emotion, understanding, and acknowledgment; no reiteration of historical claims; and a greater sense of the conflict as a joint problem to solve (in contrast to telling the other side what they needed to do). In addition, although the mixed workshop scarcely discussed responsibilities that the two sides might have to each other, the women's workshop discussed responsibilities and rights in about equal proportion, as would be predicted by Gilligan's (1982) research. The perception of the five facilitators, who had all participated in several previous mixed-gender workshops, was that the women's workshop was characterized by a type of honesty and sharing of personal experience that is usually achieved only during the very best moments of most workshops. In follow-up interviews (with the women only), participants reported new understanding, respect, and acceptance of the other's perspective but said that they could not point to direct influences of the workshop experience on their political behavior. Some of the women noted that they would have appreciated repeated contact with the other side to maintain and support the gains made in the workshop.

Pearson (1990) studied an Israeli–Palestinian IPSW, a simulated Cyprus IPSW, and an ongoing dialogue group involving American Jews and American Arabs. The goal of her research was to explore the use of symbolic gestures in intercommunal dialogues. Symbolic gestures are words or actions that can signal, initiate, or catalyze a change in the relationship between conflicting parties. Pearson analyzed the form, content, and possible impact of important statements made during the dialogue, as well as the processes by which group members learned to construct effective gestures of reassurance. In interviews and questionnaires, Pearson (1990) asked participants about the statements and gestures that had had the greatest impact on them and compared their reports with the ratings of observers. Participants also watched videotapes of their discussions. Similar to findings from an earlier ethnography (Pearson, 1989), participant responses indicated that a statement by the other side had a positive impact on the viewer to the extent that it was perceived as risky to the speaker (e.g., admitting responsibility, losing face) and included some kind of acknowledgment of the humanity of the other side. In addition, the higher power participants (i.e., Jewish, Greek-Cypriot) seemed to be less accurate in assessing the impact of their statements on the lower power participants (i.e., Arab, Turkish-Cypriot) than vice versa. These findings were much clearer for the Cyprus simulation than the Arab–Jewish dialogue group, probably because of the small sample size in the latter.

From this research Pearson (1990) also concluded that viewing themselves on videotape induced considerable self-insight in participants, including an awareness of the possibilities for improving the intergroup interaction and of the patterns and omissions in their own behavior. By becoming observers of themselves, participants seemed to take more responsibility for their own influence on the interaction and hence for their own ability to improve the quality of the interaction. Use of video technology in this way might be a useful addition to workshop design in the future (Storms, 1973).

Overall, research on the interactions that take place between participants in a workshop suggests that workshops tend to proceed as expected. There is evidence of an increase in analytical discussion, positivity, mutual interaction, and future task orientation or problem solving. Statements that can have an impact are made, and participants may be more likely to take responsibility for their contributions to the conflict situation as a result of participating in a workshop. Ongoing questions pertain to the influence of particular kinds of participants (because women may be more effective within a workshop) and ways to reduce the reentry effect (perhaps through the use of technology such as video).

The reentry effect found by Ambady (1986) is particularly in need of deeper understanding. At present, the reentry effect should be considered both a challenge to and an indication of the effectiveness of problem-solving workshops. Evidence that trust level builds over the course of the workshop suggests that IPSW participants are engaged and absorbed in the workshop experience. The fact that they tend to back off as they prepare to take what they have learned from the workshop into the broader political context seems to indicate that they are thinking realistically rather than idealistically about the constraints that they will face on their attempts to bring about change. After all, the other workshop participants whom they have come to understand also have to return to the broader conflict context in which they maintain central positions within their societies. If workshop participants were to become overly identified with their counterparts on the other side, they would risk becoming alienated from their conationals and losing credibility, thereby forfeiting their political effectiveness and ability to promote a new consensus within their own communities (Kelman, 1993). It is important that workshop participants maintain a balance between understanding and trusting each other on the one hand, and a realistic focus on the conflict between their communities on the other. The reentry effect suggests that participants are engaged in the struggle to maintain this balance.

Simulated Workshops

Given that there is evidence of positive change in the interactions between parties in a workshop, what evidence do we have that the experience has a positive influence on the attitudes and behaviors of participants after a workshop, even in the short term? Tracking changes in participant attitudes would best be accomplished through pre- and postworkshop interviews or attitude questionnaires, which have been largely precluded by the sensitivities of the participants, whose frequent misgivings about participating in a workshop could have been deepened by requests to participate in research. Questionnaires have been disseminated in simulations rather than actual workshops.

Simulation participants are encouraged to adopt an alternative set of norms. In a simulated IPSW, participants take on the role of a character in a protracted conflict, are coached to take a typically polarized position regarding the conflict, and then are encouraged to move beyond these rigid positions to see the perspective of the other side and to attempt to collaboratively develop mutually acceptable solutions. Participants who are able to adapt to this different normative context and engage with the perspective of the other side provide evidence that more than one approach to the conflict is at least possible and that new information can be integrated. Although simulations have allowed us to test the impact of the process within a more complex environment, it has not been possible to generate the levels of commitment and intensity found in an actual multigenerational protracted conflict. Therefore, simulation studies are probably the least satisfying of the four approaches to evaluation discussed in this chapter.

Korper, Chataway, and Kelman (1988) simulated the Cyprus conflict with undergraduate participants and then compared the negotiations of those groups who had participated in a workshop with those who had participated in a more traditional form of negotiation preparation. In the more traditional condition, participants strategized within their own group, interacting with the other side only briefly to present a position statement before negotiations. The number of negotiated agreements reached by groups with the two types of negotiation preparation did not differ substantially, but the quality of the agreements reached by those negotiators following a workshop was higher. Workshop participants tended to reach agreements that were more detailed and more integrative as opposed to separatist. All workshop groups devised solutions in which the two sides would continue to interact on the island of Cyprus (although some only by sharing a United Nations post). On the other hand, in all of the groups with the more traditional preparation, all solutions involved a complete division of the island and the functions of the two societies. In addition, more responsibility for the interests and needs of people involved was taken by those who had participated in a workshop, such as the needs of refugees or the wishes of both sides to be represented at the international (United Nations) level. In a related study, Margolis (1988) found that student participants who were given information regarding the perspective of the other party were significantly more likely to cooperate in a simulated international conflict negotiation than those who did not receive this information.

In postnegotiation questionnaires, negotiations following workshops (compared to traditional preparation for negotiation) were judged more positively; participants were more satisfied with the solutions and believed the solutions had more potential long-term stability (Korper et al., 1988). Participants also reported the behavior of the negotiators following a workshop, especially the perceived behavior of the other side, to be markedly more productive and positive than the behavior of negotiators following the more traditional preparation. These results provide strong evidence that the participants were able to learn to use the skills and perceptions from the workshop experience in a remarkably short period of time and were able to apply the new knowledge in subsequent negotiations to devise cooperative, innovative, and responsible solutions to the conflict.

The most realistic example to date of a simulation of an IPSW was carried out by Cross and Rosenthal (1999). They brought Israeli and Jewish-American students together in pairs with Arab and Arab-American students to discuss the issue of Jerusalem. Participants were randomly assigned to one of three conditions, representing three different modes of conflict resolution: distributive bargaining, integrative bargaining, and interactive problem solving. Participants were instructed by facilitators trained in each particular model, and the instructions relevant to their condition were also written on a nearby blackboard. In the distributive bargaining condition, the instructions directed participants to clarify their positions and attempt to reach an agreement by negotiating the issues involved in Jerusalem. In the integrative bargaining condition, participants were instructed to develop a definition of the problem, clarify their interests, try to expand the alternatives, and negotiate an agreement that would meet the interests of both sides. In the interactive problem-solving condition, participants were instructed to develop a definition of the problem, clarify the needs and fears of both sides, and jointly generate ways to meet these needs and fears and to overcome the barriers to implementation.

Comparison of pre- and postnegotiation questionnaires indicated that interactive problem solving produced the most positive attitude change toward the other side; it was also most effective at decreasing divisive, pessimistic attitudes toward the conflict and beliefs that the positions, interests, and needs of the two sides were incompatible. The latter is important because resolution may be least likely when negotiating parties have doubts about success and accept the likelihood of failure (Rubin, Kim, & Peretz, 1990). Cross and Rosenthal (1999) concluded that instructions to participants to reach agreement (as in the distributive and integrative bargaining conditions) seem to have made it more difficult to attain other attitudinal outcomes such as recognition, empathy, and understanding and acknowledgment of the perspective of the other. This finding corroborates other research suggesting a sequencing of these different models in protracted social conflicts, beginning with a focus on the relationships between the disputing parties until attitudes and behavior are more cooperative, followed by integrative bargaining, and last by distributive bargaining as necessary (Keashly & Fisher, 1996; Walton & McKersie, 1965). The Cross and Rosenthal study, more than any other, combined the control of laboratory research with the realism of a complex protracted conflict, because it included participants who identified in some way with the conflict, in interaction with each other. Their results can therefore be interpreted with more confidence to suggest that in the early stages of contact between disputing sides in protracted conflict, a period of clarifying needs and fears without attempting to reach agreement can contribute to improved relations between the sides and improved attitudes regarding the possibilities for peace.

Overall, IPSW simulation research seems to indicate that the IPSW context allows for and encourages more positivity toward the other side and toward the possibilities of reaching a negotiated agreement, and more complex integrative (and therefore perhaps more long-lasting) agreements.

Evaluating Workshop Products as Interpretive Research

To recap the evaluation process so far: Basic research in social psychology has informed workshop design and allowed us to judge the likely effect of each design feature on participants' attitudes and behaviors; coding ongoing workshops has given us a better sense of the stages and kinds of dialogue that take place in a workshop; and simulations have helped us to consider how difficult it is for people to learn the workshop process and apply it intellectually to a protracted social conflict. Evidence of IPSW influence on the long-term attitudes and behaviors of participants, and on the intersocietal atmosphere and policymaking, has been much more difficult to document and to separate from changing events in the conflict itself.

Scholarship in political science suggests that the goals of unofficial diplomacy (such as IPSWs) should change considerably based on the stage and state of the conflict (Lund, 1996). For instance, when a conflict is very polarized, there is little official communication, and acts of hostility are frequent, several authors suggest it is counterproductive to focus participants on generating concrete suggestions for resolution. At this stage, building relationships across conflict lines is suggested as a more effective form of intervention that lays the foundation for official negotiations. Once official negotiations have commenced, greater task orientation becomes more relevant to unofficial diplomacy as well (Carnevale, Lim, & McLaughlin, 1989; Cross & Rosenthal, 1999; Keashly & Fisher, 1996; Lund, 1996).

Kelman's workshops have evolved considerably as a result of changes in the Middle East peace process. After many one-time workshops, Kelman was able to hold five meetings with a core group of influential Israelis and Palestinians between 1990 and 1993 (Rouhana & Kelman, 1994). The continuing workshop meetings, which I attended as an assistant, evolved from an atmosphere of guarded interchange in 1990, to considering disbanding in the context of a profound decline in mutual trust just after the Gulf War (June 1991), to open discussion and clarification of needs and fears and constructive efforts at joint thinking (August 1991).

This continuing workshop better provided the kind of support for attitude change that social psychological research and workshop participants have suggested is crucial to maintaining changes. For instance, the participants of the continuing workshop had contact with one another, and considerable contact with Kelman, outside of meetings. In addition, after official peace negotiations started, experience and relationships built in the workshops were carried into these negotiations, because four of the Palestinian participants were appointed to official negotiating teams. This provided a direct link between what might have been learned in the IPSWs and the formal policy process. With new members, the continuing workshop became the policy working group, drafting joint position papers on some of the most difficult negotiation issues (e.g., refugees, right of return, final status relationship). The relationships within this context thus progressed considerably from 1990 when several of the participants were reluctant even to sit down to talk with the other side (Rouhana & Kelman, 1994).

Products that can be evaluated from these processes are primarily Kelman's publications during the last three decades and more recently the working group's public policy documents (Alpher & Shikaki, 1998; Joint Working Group on Israeli–Palestinian Relations, 1998, 1999). Like interpretive research, a workshop is designed not to uncover some objective reality but to orient people toward an understanding that transforms their subjective reality and provides answers to the concerns that motivated the inquiry. Evolving interpretations can be evaluated by considering (a) the quality of the interpretation (Is it coherent? Does it correspond with external evidence?), (b) its impact on parties to the conflict (Do they reach consensus? Are they mobilized to action?), and (c) the reflexivity of the process by which the interpretation is derived (Do facilitators and participants actively reflect on the influence of the different resources and experiences each had to bring to interpretation?) (Burman, 2001; Packer & Addison, 1989).

With regard to quality and impact of interpretation, some of Kelman's writings seem to have been ahead of their time, at least predicting, if not influencing the future. For example, Kelman wrote about the importance of Arafat as Palestinian leader (Kelman, 1982) and the need for mutual reassurance and mutual recognition (Kelman, 1987). He also wrote that the peace process set into motion in 1993 would be undermined by violence, testing the personal commitment of the leaderships to reach a mutually beneficial agreement (Kelman, 1994). Each of these articles emerged from workshop analyses of the conflict over time, had a recognized coherence to publishing editors, and corresponded with the changing facts on the ground over time. It is too soon to judge the quality and impact of the working group's documents, except that their existence is evidence of a long process of consensus-building within the group.

Rouhana and Korper (1996) have questioned the extent to which IPSW facilitators are reflexive and whether the IPSW context allows sufficient support for discussion of the constraining influence of power relations on the dialogue and on resolution of the conflict in general. Engaging participants and each other in reflexive practice (e.g., Chataway, 1997) would seem to be one of the areas in which Kelman's students will further develop the IPSW process.

Conclusion

Contrary to charges that the IPSW is unevaluated, this chapter has reviewed four social psychological approaches through which IPSWs are evaluated. In its overall conception, there appears to be some empirical support for the design of the workshop and its intended influence. Experimental research in social psychology and our limited research on the workshops themselves suggest the efficacy of confidential discussion, a focus on needs and fears, and joint problem solving with a nonevaluative facilitator. In the short term, workshop participation seems to generate greater analytical interaction, more positivity and openness to new ideas and perceptions of the other side, the development of better relationships between participants, and the sharing of relevant new information that has a positive impact on the other participants. In the long term, Kelman's publications and those of the working group continue to contribute an evolving analysis of the Israeli–Palestinian conflict as it emerges from a consensus-building process and is recognized by scholars and others as relevant to resolution of the conflict. Kelman's students and associates are involved in improving the IPSW process by considering how to provide support for participants and facilitators to reflect on the influence of power within a dialogue, and to resist the reentry effect by supporting attitude change in both the short and long term.

References

Alpher, J., & Shikaki, K. (1998). *The Palestinian refugee problem and the right of return* (Weatherhead Center for International Affairs Working Paper No. 98-7). Cambridge, MA: Harvard University. [Reprinted in *Middle East Policy*, February 1999, *6*(3), 167–189]

Ambady, N. (1986). *A content analysis of a conflict resolution workshop*. Unpublished manuscript, Harvard University, Cambridge, MA.

Aronson, E., Blaney, N., Stephan, C., Sikes, J., & Snapp, M. (1978). *The jigsaw classroom*. Beverly Hills, CA: Sage.

Azar, E. (1990). *The management of protracted social conflict*. Hampshire, England: Dartmouth Publishing.

Bales, R. (1950). A set of categories for the analysis of small group interaction. *American Sociological Review, 15*, 257–263.

Bales, R., & Cohen, S. (1979). *SYMLOG*. New York: Free Press.

Bray, R. M., Johnston, D., & Chilstrom, J. T. (1982). Social influence by group members with minority opinions: A comparison of Hollander and Moscovici. *Journal of Personality and Social Psychology, 43*, 78–88.

Burman, E. (2001). Minding the gap: Positivism, psychology, and the politics of qualitative methods. In D. L. Tolman & M. Brydon-Miller (Eds.), *From subjects to subjectivities* (pp. 259–275). New York: New York University Press.

Burton, J. (1969). *Conflict and communication: The use of controlled communication in international relations*. London: Macmillan.

Cacioppo, J. T., & Petty, R. E. (1985). Central and peripheral routes to persuasion: The role of message repetition. In L. F. Alwitt & A. A. Mitchell (Eds.), *Psychological processes and advertising effects* (pp. 91–111). Hillsdale, NJ: Erlbaum.

Carnevale, P., Lim, R., & McLaughlin, M. (1989). Contingent mediator behavior and effectiveness. In K. Kressel & D. Pruitt (Eds.), *Mediation research: The process and effectiveness of third party intervention* (pp. 213–240). San Francisco: Jossey-Bass.

Chataway, C. (1997). An examination of the constraints on mutual inquiry in a participatory action research project. *Journal of Social Issues, 53,* 749–767.

Chataway, C. (2002). The problem of transfer from confidential interactive problem-solving: What is the role of the facilitator? *Political Psychology, 23,* 165–191.

Cohen, S., Kelman, H., Miller, F., & Smith, B. (1977). Evolving intergroup techniques for conflict resolution: An Israeli–Palestinian pilot workshop. *Journal of Social Issues, 33*(1), 165–188.

Cook, T. D., & Flay, B. R. (1978). The persistence of experimentally induced attitude change. In L. Berkowitz (Ed.), *Advances in experimental social psychology* (Vol. 11, pp. 1–57). San Diego, CA: Academic Press.

Cross, S., & Rosenthal, R. (1999). Three models of conflict resolution: Effects on intergroup expectancies and attitudes. *Journal of Social Issues, 55,* 561–580.

d'Estree, T. P., & Babbitt, E. (1998). Women and the art of peacemaking: Data from Israeli–Palestinian interactive problem-solving workshops. *Political Psychology, 19,* 185–209.

Fisher, R. J. (1997). *Interactive conflict resolution.* Syracuse, NY: Syracuse University Press.

Gilligan, C. (1982). *In a different voice.* Cambridge, MA: Harvard University Press.

Greenberg, L. S., Rice, L. N., & Elliott, R. (1993). *Facilitating emotional change: The moment-by-moment process.* New York: Guilford Press.

Hiltrop, J. (1989). Factors associated with successful labor mediation. In K. Kressel & D. Pruitt (Eds.), *Mediation research: The process and effectiveness of third party intervention* (pp. 241–262). San Francisco: Jossey-Bass.

Horowitz, B. (1982). *Meetings between Israelis and Palestinians: Phases of communication in conflict resolution workshops.* Unpublished manuscript, Harvard University, Cambridge, MA.

Izard, C. (1993). Four systems for emotion activation: Cognitive and noncognitive processes. *Psychological Review, 100,* 68–90.

Joint Working Group on Israeli–Palestinian Relations. (1998). General principles for the final Israeli–Palestinian agreement. *Middle East Journal, 53,* 170–175.

Joint Working Group on Israeli–Palestinian Relations. (1999). *The future Israeli–Palestinian relationship* (Weatherhead Center for International Affairs Working Paper No. 99-12). Cambridge, MA: Harvard University. [Also published in *Middle East Policy,* February 2000, 7(2), 90–112]

Keashly, L., & Fisher, R. (1996). A contingency perspective on conflict interventions: Theoretical and practical considerations. In J. Bercovitch (Ed.), *Resolving international conflicts* (pp. 235–262). London: Lynne Reinner.

Kelman, H. C. (1982). Talk with Arafat. *Foreign Policy, 49,* 119–139.

Kelman, H. C. (1987). The political psychology of the Israeli–Palestinian conflict: How can we overcome the barriers to a negotiated solution? *Political Psychology, 8,* 347–363.

Kelman, H. C. (1993). Coalitions across conflict lines. In S. Worchel & J. Simpson (Eds.), *Conflict between people and groups* (pp. 236–258). Chicago: Nelson-Hall.

Kelman, H. C. (1994, March 8). Three steps to advance Israeli–Arab peace. *Boston Globe,* op-ed page.

Kelman, H., Chataway, C., & Neufeldt, R. (1998). *An oral history of Israeli–Palestinian workshops between 1966–1998.* Cambridge, MA: Program on International Conflict Analysis and Resolution, Harvard University.

Korper, S., Chataway, C., & Kelman, H. (1989). *Investigation of the effect of a problem-solving workshop on a simulated intercommunal conflict.* Unpublished manuscript, Harvard University, Cambridge, MA.

Lewicki, R. J., Weiss, S. E., & Lewin, D. (1992). Models of conflict, negotiation and third party intervention: A review and synthesis. *Journal of Organizational Behavior, 13,* 209–252.

Lund, M.S. (1996). *Preventing violent conflicts.* Washington, DC: United States Institute of Peace Press.

Margolis, J. (1988). *Effect of perceived interaction history on competitive and cooperative behavior.* Unpublished master's thesis, Harvard University, Cambridge, MA.

Packer, M., & Addison, R. (1989). Evaluating an interpretive account. In M. Packer & R. Addison (Eds.), *Entering the circle: Hermeneutic investigation in psychology* (pp. 275–321). Albany: State University of New York Press.

Pearson, T. (1989, July). *Striving for acknowledgment: The impact of a relational focus on communication in a conflict interaction*. Paper presented at the meeting of the International Society for Political Psychology, Tel Aviv, Israel.

Pearson, T. (1990). *The role of "symbolic gestures" in intergroup conflict resolution: Addressing group identity*. Unpublished doctoral dissertation, Harvard University, Cambridge, MA.

Petty, R. E., Haugtvedt, C. P., & Smith, S. M. (1995). Elaboration as a determinant of attitude strength. In R. E. Petty & J. A. Krosnick (Eds.), *Attitude strength: Antecedents and consequences* (pp. 93–130). Mahwah, NJ: Erlbaum.

Petty, R., Priester, J., & Wegener, D. (1994). Cognitive processes in attitude change. In R. Wyer & T. Srull (Eds.), *Handbook of social cognition* (Vol. 2, pp. 69–142). Mahwah, NJ: Erlbaum.

Pruitt, D. (1995). Process and outcome in community mediation. *Negotiation Journal, 11,* 365–77.

Ross, L., & Ward, A. (1995). Psychological barriers to dispute resolution. In M. Zanna (Ed.), *Advances in experimental social psychology* (Vol. 27, pp. 255–304). San Diego, CA: Academic Press.

Rouhana, N., & Kelman, H. C. (1994). Promoting joint thinking in international conflicts: An Israeli–Palestinian continuing workshop. *Journal of Social Issues, 50*(1), 157–178.

Rouhana, N., & Korper, S. (1996). Dealing with the dilemmas posed by power asymmetry in intergroup conflict. *Negotiation Journal, 12,* 353–366.

Rubin, J., Kim, S., & Peretz, N. (1990). Expectancy effects and negotiation. *Journal of Social Issues, 46*(2), 125–139.

Staub, E. (1990). *The roots of evil. The origins of genocide and other group violence.* Cambridge, England: Cambridge University Press.

Stephenson, B., & Wicklund, R. (1983). Self-directed attention and taking the other's perspective. *Journal of Experimental and Social Psychology, 19,* 58–77.

Storms, M. (1973). Videotape and the attribution process. Reversing the actor's and observer's point of view. *Journal of Personality and Social Psychology, 27,* 165–175.

Tesser, A., & Shaffer, D. (1990). Attitudes and attitude change. *Annual Review of Psychology, 41,* 479–523.

Tetlock, P. E. (1992). The impact of accountability on judgment and choice: Toward a social contingency model. In M. Zanna (Ed.), *Advances in experimental social psychology* (Vol. 25, pp. 331–376). San Diego, CA: Academic Press.

Tindale, R. S., Davis, J. H., Vollrath, D. A., Nagao, D. H., & Hinsz, V. B. (1990). Asymmetrical social influence in freely interacting groups: A test of three models. *Journal of Personality and Social Psychology, 58,* 438–449.

Volkan, V. D., Montville, J. V., & Julius, D. A. (Eds.). (1990). *The psychodynamics of international relationships* (Vols. 1 & 2). Lexington, MA: Lexington Books.

Walton, R. (1970). A problem-solving workshop on border conflicts in Eastern Africa. *Journal of Applied Behavioral Science, 6,* 453–489.

Walton, R., & McKersie, R. (1965). *A behavioral theory of labor negotiations.* New York: McGraw-Hill.

Comments on Chapters 11 and 12

Rhoda Margesson

Maria Hadjipavlou and Cynthia Chataway present chapters that highlight different aspects of the workshop approach to the practice of conflict resolution. In this commentary, I briefly discuss their case examples in light of the social psychological barriers and opportunities present during conflict and reflect on the challenges for future research.

Case Examples in Conflict Resolution Practice

Hadjipavlou examines the usefulness of workshops in reestablishing contact between communities in conflict and developing new forms of coexistence and tolerance. The Greek and Turkish Cypriot citizens' efforts at peace building and training in conflict resolution help reinforce a citizenship concept. Hadjipavlou (chap. 11, this volume) suggests that this concept becomes a "shared value and a unifying point of reference," which may not only help individuals to challenge chauvinistic attitudes that might be present, but also encourage societies to understand and demand political agreements that incorporate themes of tolerance and plurality. She emphasizes the important role of the European Union as both a tangible and a symbolic example of the citizenship concept that allows each society to shift its emphasis toward creating trust and developing cooperation between communities.

Chataway (chap. 12, this volume) examines some of the components of nonintrusive evaluation of interactive problem-solving (IPS) workshops. Contrary to the argument that the IPS workshop is unevaluated, she points to four social psychological approaches that do provide evaluations. Initial results provide empirical support for the IPS model design and short-term success of the workshops. Chataway thus cites experimental research in social psychology, limited research available on the workshops themselves including the attitudes and behaviors of the participants, and simulations. Products generated from continuing workshops between Israelis and Palestinians, including publications by Herbert Kelman and public policy documents from members of the workshop, have also been collectively evaluated.

Both authors emphasize the benefits of the scholar-practitioner approach. Chapter 11 provides an actual case and examines the conflict in Cyprus; chapter 12 is more theoretical in its analysis but uses material drawn from workshops and simulations pertaining to the conflict in the Middle East. Each chapter establishes its theoretical framework as a basis for analysis. Side by side, the chapters emphasize the necessary relationship between theory and practice for third parties. Differences in approach and context are also evident, perhaps partly because of the unique background, experience, and perspective of each author. The understanding gained from living and working in conflict settings and observing community contact firsthand is, of course, different from the understanding that comes from examining the conflict as a third party through workshops and simulations. Each approach has its value and provides third parties with an important framework from which to view conflict. Furthermore, Hadjipavlou and Chataway examine two protracted and complex cases—Cyprus and the Israeli–Palestinian situation in the Middle East, respectively—which are at differing stages in the process toward peace. For the sake of brevity, I do not explore the specific points of divergence and convergence or the complicated details and histories of each conflict. Rather, I argue that there are similarities in the social psychological domain as a result of conflict.

Shifting the Social Psychological Barriers

Both chapters suggest, in keeping with the social psychological point of view, that each group and individual within these conflicts seeks belonging, identity, and legitimate existence. Given that communities share little trust of one another, outside interveners seek to help address and reconcile these needs on an official level. However, they also want to find ways to build peace in unofficial ways, to begin to soften the boundaries of conflict and influence the social psychological framework using the direct and indirect means that are available. For example, from within a conflict, events taking place on the ground, decisions made during formal negotiations, expectations surrounding discussions, or a workshop experience like the Israeli–Palestinian continuing workshop may have an impact on governments, groups, or individuals. Outside influences may change the conflict and incentives for resolving it, as may be the case in Cyprus, where the possibility of membership in the European Union is one such influence.

These chapters make an important contribution to unofficial third-party efforts in their analysis of the influences that workshops have on the social psychological makeup of those affected during the conflict itself and in the transition to peace. Although these authors provide a serious assessment of what has been accomplished, they also examine the kinds of complicating factors that third parties face or may anticipate. One such factor is the reentry effect, which consists of participants' regression toward their preworkshop attitudes and interaction styles as they prepare to return to their communities.

In the case of Cyprus, Hadjipavlou refers to the human dimension of conflict and the need to satisfy human needs, particularly after generations have been socialized into conflict. Seeing different points of entry for third parties, she refers to a number of bicommunal workshops involving face-to-face contact, ranging from conflict resolution training, to peace building among citizens, to the Technology for Peace project using e-mail and other computer-based programs. The grassroots initiatives in Cyprus have been extensive and have attempted to build on the positive experiences. Still, in looking at the potential lessons to be learned from the Cypriot citizens' initiatives, Hadjipavlou asks why the impact of these activities has not been greater. Many of the reasons appear to be tied to what is happening on the official level. For example, lack of freedom of movement between communities means that help is required from third parties most of the time. Bicommunal work is contingent on the conflict itself and the status of formal negotiations at the state level; the bicommunal peace-building movement is not institutionalized, thereby affecting its agenda, selection of participants, and resources available.

Similarly, despite positive indicators for the short-term success of the workshops, Chataway finds that long-term attitudes are difficult to change, revealing once again the human dimension of these protracted conflicts. Ongoing questions, which are difficult to research because of their impact on the intervention process, include the influence of particular kinds of participants, ways to reduce the reentry effect, and erosion of attitudes over time. These issues are critical for participants, who must try to balance a relationship with each other and with their own communities, which remain in conflict. Chataway (chap. 12) finds, "The reentry effect suggests that participants are engaged in the struggle to maintain this balance."

A striking theme in both of these chapters is the question of what influences the social psychological framework, given the difficulties of promoting new forms of contact and sustaining trust in building relationships across conflict lines. Together these papers bring out several additional important factors. First, evaluation itself presents challenges that are evident not only in conducting such research, but also in drawing out implications for conflict resolution practice. Second, there is a need to examine underlying assumptions by third parties with regard to their expectations and definitions of outcomes and success. Third parties, on an official or unofficial level, face the challenge of making the correct diagnosis. Taking a step back to review and evaluate progress—what does and does not work and why—is critical, as is establishing a standard against which such evaluation is conducted. Through unofficial efforts like these, new ways to adjust methods and approaches can be demonstrated in a particular conflict. Ideally, these insights will have applications in future conflicts as well.

Reflections for Future Research

Evaluation of unofficial processes like the workshop raises other questions and potential areas for future research. First, what are ways to expand the usefulness and application of the workshop experience to sustain and extend its influence without sacrificing the principles on which it was founded? This question is central to the further development of the IPS approach. Second, in the broader context, if official diplomatic channels could move beyond what some see as a tolerance of unofficial activities, how and at what point in the conflict would the information and experience derived from workshops add greater value to policymaking? Third, might there be some benefit to research on timing: When should the workshop approach be introduced for the greatest benefit?

As third parties review and reflect on these chapters, they may think about strategic partnerships and approaches to conflict resolution practice through unofficial efforts; at the same time, third parties need also to be thinking about whether the conflict resolution field in general is keeping pace with emerging contexts and whether it is building coherent strategies for dealing with other forms of conflict. For example, with the emergence of complex humanitarian emergencies as a leading challenge in foreign policy, where might this kind of analysis add the most value and what prescriptive advice is there for third parties working in these kinds of time-sensitive crises?

Having mentioned a few thoughts on research questions for the future, I end by pausing to acknowledge the work of Herbert Kelman, to whom this volume is dedicated. He was behind the development and evolution of the workshop approach, particularly in its application to the many changes in the Middle East peace process. He has brought to the community of conflict resolution scholars and practitioners (and to many directly affected by conflict) his experience in conducting the workshops, teaching in the classroom, and writing in his articulate and insightful prose. His work has established a strong framework within which to include the social psychological dimension in the practice of conflict resolution and pursuit of peace. From this point onward, scholars and practitioners will continue to learn, always reminded of what an enormous contribution Herbert Kelman has made and continues to make to this field.

Part IV

Reflections by
Herbert C. Kelman

13

Continuity and Change: My Life as a Social Psychologist

Herbert C. Kelman

When you reach a certain age, you become increasingly interested in reflecting on your life and writing autobiographically about your career and your ideas, and others become increasingly interested in hearing "your stories" (to quote Mica Estrada-Hollenbeck, one of my students, to whom collectively these remarks are dedicated). We all know, of course, that the interest in telling these stories and in listening to them is bolstered by social norms that legitimize older people's reminiscences and mandate younger people's polite attention. I am quite happy, however, to take advantage of these norms and to indulge my autobiographical musings.

In a recent collection of essays by Holocaust refugees and survivors who subsequently became social scientists (Suedfeld, 2001), I had the opportunity to reflect on the impact of the Holocaust on four topics that have been central to my work over the years: conformity and obedience, nationalism and national identity, ethnic conflict and its resolution, and the ethics of social research (Kelman, 2001a). In an article that I am writing for *Political Psychology* (and which is characteristically late), I trace the different ways in which interactive problem solving—my approach to conflict resolution (Kelman, 1998a, 1998c; see also Kelman, 1972a), derived from the work of John Burton (1969, 1979)— reflects central themes of my earlier work. Recent papers reviewing my work on the Israeli–Palestinian conflict (Kelman, 1999) and on the concept of legitimacy (Kelman, 2001b) have a decidedly autobiographical flavor. Furthermore, several years ago, some of my students initiated an oral history project, in which I have had the opportunity to talk about and reflect on each of the problem-solving workshops and related programs—over 60 events by now, mostly (but not entirely) with Israeli and Palestinian participants—that I have been involved in over the years. The project is now being brought to completion by Cynthia Chataway and Reina Neufeldt, with the collaboration of Rebecca Edelson. Also, my colleague Michael Wessells has been conducting a series of interviews with me, which he will eventually write up, focusing on the origins and development of my work in peace research, conflict resolution, and the social psychology of international relations.

The present chapter gives me another and very special opportunity to reflect on my work during the past 55 years. The focus of these reflections is my particular way of doing social psychology over these years—my way of expressing the core of my professional identity as a social psychologist. The background of these reflections, very appropriately, is the work of my students as exemplified in the chapters and comments in the preceding pages.

On Being the Subject of a *Festschrift*

I have always felt that the greatest tribute that can be paid to a scholar is to issue a *Festschrift* in her or his honor. The present *Festschrift*, therefore, is a gift that has profound meaning for me and that I value immensely. It validates my work over the years and gives me the sense that what I have tried to do has had an impact on others, that it has reverberated in what they chose to study and how they chose to study it, and that it is a link in that endless chain of efforts to understand and improve our world. I am deeply grateful to all who played a role in this enterprise—in planning, arranging, speaking at, and participating in the *Festschrift* conference in August 2000, in editing this volume, and in writing, presenting, reviewing, and editing the chapters and comments.

When Alice Eagly first spoke to me about the people to be asked to present papers and prepare chapters for the *Festschrift*, and later about the list of people to be specifically invited to participate in the August 2000 conference, I was very clear about one principle: I wanted my students and their work to be the primary focus of the enterprise. There is no necessary reason for a *Festschrift* to focus on the subject's students. It would be quite appropriate for the contributors to be nonstudent collaborators or even colleagues who neither studied nor collaborated with the subject but were influenced by his or her work. Indeed, in the present case, the conference invitation list included not only my students, but also my closest colleagues and collaborators over the years.[1] Still, it was my students (many of whom, of course, have also been and continue to be my close collaborators) whom I wanted to be the contributors to the *Festschrift* itself.

My criteria for claiming people as "my students" may be a bit expansive (or should I say expansionist?), as can be judged from the three lists included in Appendix A. The first list is not controversial. It includes, in chronological order, the 33 doctoral candidates for whom I served as the primary thesis adviser (or *Doktorvater*, to use the German designation that I find appealing). I was pleased to note that both the first and the last person on this list, Peter Lenrow and Rebecca Wolfe, respectively, were at the conference. Further analysis of this data set reveals that the median position on this list is held by Lee

---

[1] I was delighted to welcome at the conference current collaborators, like Lenore Martin, and close colleagues from earlier periods, like Arthur Gladstone (going back to the late 1940s and 1950s), William and Zelda Gamson (going back to the 1960s), and Gordon Bermant (going back to the 1970s), as well as Ai-Li Chin, the widow of Robert Chin, a close friend and colleague over many years. I would have been equally delighted to welcome other close collaborators from different periods of my life—such as John Burton, Stephen Cohen, Ronald Fisher, Jerome Frank, Harry Lerner, Christopher Mitchell, Morris Parloff, Thomas Pettigrew, Harold Saunders, Charlotte Schwartz, Brewster Smith, Michael Wessells, and Ralph White—who, regrettably, were not able to make the event.

Hamilton, who (among numerous other achievements) coined the term *crimes of obedience,* which made both of us famous (Kelman & Hamilton, 1989). Of the 33 individuals on this list, 26 received their PhDs from Harvard University, having worked with me either during my first five-year term (1957–1962) as Lecturer on Social Psychology or during my return engagement (1968–1999) as Richard Clarke Cabot Professor of Social Ethics. Six individuals received their degrees from the University of Michigan between 1965 and 1969, during my tenure there (1962–1969). (For the benefit of careful readers, I should note that in the academic year of 1968–1969, I was a professor both at the University of Michigan and at Harvard, but teaching at neither—a coup that I attribute to my low-key negotiating style.) Nadim Rouhana received his PhD from Wayne State University, but had come to Harvard—with the blessings of his Wayne adviser, Kalman Kaplan (who himself can be found on the third list in Appendix A)—to work with me on his dissertation. I was appointed adjunct professor at Wayne (needless to say, without pay) to serve as Nadim's adviser.

The second list in Appendix A includes individuals for whom—at various points in their graduate training—I served as academic adviser, research/practice adviser, member of the thesis committee, and/or thesis reader. Most of the people on this list were graduate students in my department at Harvard or Michigan. However, the list also includes a dozen individuals who received their doctorates from schools other than my own[2] on whose doctoral committees I played an active role. Interestingly, all 12 of these people at some point took or audited my graduate seminar on International Conflict: Social Psychological Approaches. Also included on this list are people who have been actively associated with PICAR, my Program on International Conflict Analysis and Resolution at Harvard's Weatherhead Center for International Affairs. For many of these, the association began with their participation in my graduate seminar on international conflict—which was clearly a major recruiting ground as well as socialization experience for my graduate students in the 1980s and 1990s. List II is definitely not complete. I constructed it from memory, since I have not kept systematic track of all of my advising and thesis-reading assignments. Names appearing on this list belong to those advisees in whose training I played an active role and with many of whom I have maintained continuing contact.

The third list in Appendix A includes postdoctoral fellows, research associates, and visiting scholars who came to Harvard or the University of Michigan under my sponsorship. I do not include in this list names that already appear on lists I and II. Moreover, like list II, this list is not comprehensive; of the names included, some are individuals with whom I have collaborated closely on joint research projects, and all are individuals with whom I interacted closely on shared intellectual interests. Again, I have maintained continuing contact with many of the people on this list. Whether I have a right to claim them all as

---

[2]The Harvard Graduate School of Education (Ariela Bairey-Ben Ishay, Winnifred O'Toole, Sara Roy, Pamela Steiner), the Kennedy School of Government (Thomas Princen), the Fletcher School of Law and Diplomacy (Daniel Lieberfeld), MIT (Eileen Babbitt), Boston University (Maria Hadjipavlou), the City University of New York (Bethamie Horowitz, Lynn Ruggiero), the University of Maryland (Jay Rothman), and the University of Oslo (Daniel Heradstveit).

my students is open to debate. The designation is entirely appropriate for those who came specifically as postdoctoral fellows shortly after receiving their degrees. I felt it was also appropriate for those who came to work with me as research associates at Harvard and the University of Michigan early in their careers. Including on this list people who came as visiting scholars at a later stage in their careers may be an indicator of the expansionism I mentioned. I justify it by the fact that many of them have themselves described me as their "mentor," thus feeding my expansionist tendencies. The best case in point is the last name on list III, Jorje Zalles. Although we interacted intensively during his year as a visiting scholar at the Weatherhead Center, he had actually not come specifically under my sponsorship. But, when he took to calling me *maestro* (even in print), I felt justified in including him on my list.[3]

These three lists do not exhaust the categories of people whom I feel I could rightfully claim as my students. Omitted from these lists are the sizable number of undergraduates at Harvard whose honors theses I supervised, some of whom have gone on to become accomplished social psychologists. One of these undergraduates, as it happens, did make list I; I refer to none other than Alice Eagly, who produced a *summa cum laude* undergraduate thesis under my supervision. (Her thesis experiment, along with one of my experiments, was later published in a joint article; see Kelman & Eagly, 1965.) Alice went on to the University of Michigan, where I joined her a year later and eventually became her doctoral thesis adviser. One of my qualifications for that role, I am sure, was that I had learned early on that the best way to supervise Alice was not to interfere as she proceeded with great competence to do what needed to be done.

Also omitted from the three lists are my students in the various graduate seminars and undergraduate courses that I taught over the years, unless I played additional, active roles in their graduate education. It is always a special treat to meet or hear from former students in my classes—including some who

---

[3]I want to remember warmly and pay tribute to six people on these lists whom we lost to premature death. Margaret (Peggy) Hofeller was my student at Michigan and spent her career as a teacher and dean at Hofstra University; my frequent discussions with her about the concept of legitimacy, which was the focus of her doctoral thesis, greatly helped me in developing my own ideas on this topic. Stanley Milgram was already an advanced graduate student when I first came to Harvard, but I served on his thesis prospectus committee and as a careful reader of the final product; in later years, we interacted on various occasions around our shared interest in obedience to authority and the ethics of human experimentation. Donald Warwick was an advanced graduate student when I arrived at the University of Michigan, and I served on his doctoral committee; later he became one of my closest colleagues and best friends at Harvard, where we cotaught a course, coauthored several chapters, coedited a volume on *The Ethics of Social Intervention* with Gordon Bermant (Bermant, Kelman, & Warwick, 1978), and jointly participated in various projects relating to ethical issues in social science. I first met Earl Davis in Germany in 1960, and we interacted frequently around several shared interests until his death in Ireland, where he had spent a large part of his career; he was a Visiting Scholar at Harvard under my sponsorship in 1982–1983. Anita Mishler and I were both research assistants at the National Training Laboratory for Group Development in Bethel, Maine, in the summer of 1948; in the late 1950s and early 1960s she worked, along with Lotte Bailyn, as my research associate on a project dealing with the impact of a year in the United States on Scandinavian exchange students. Finally, I met Jeffrey Rubin shortly after he arrived at Tufts in the fall of 1969 and we became good friends and collaborated on a variety of projects until his tragic death in 1995; he also spent a year as a visiting scholar at Harvard under my sponsorship.

took one of my large undergraduate courses and whose names or faces I would not have recognized if they had not revealed themselves. I am delighted when these former students tell me about the special memory, insight, or standpoint that they took away from the course—particularly when they tell me how the course has changed their lives or their view of the world. (Needless to say, I assume that these reported changes have been of positive value to their lives and to the world at large.) Special mention should be made here of my seminar on international conflict, which I taught at Harvard 17 times (the first two times with Stephen Cohen and the last two times with Donna Hicks) between 1971 and 1999. For many of the students and active auditors in this course (a total of perhaps 400 over the years)—whether or not their names appear on my three lists—participation in this intensive seminar and its associated practicum did, in fact, have substantial impact on their subsequent professional careers.

Finally, I restrained myself from including on the lists some of my younger colleagues in different fields who—though they were never my students in the conventional sense of the term and never worked under my sponsorship—have described me as their mentor or role model. In according me this honor, these colleagues were often communicating not only that their own work was influenced by mine, but that their definition of their professional roles was encouraged and legitimized by my model: in stepping outside of traditional disciplinary boundaries, in combining research with practice, in addressing current social issues, in attending to the ethical implications of the professional enterprise. I happily claim these colleagues as my students, but I do not feel entitled to add their names to my "official" lists.

The contributors to this volume are a sample of my students over the years.[4] Most of the chapter authors are drawn from list I, although lists II and III are represented by two authors each. The six commentators (all of whom can be found on list II) were all, in one way or another, my current students at the time of the *Festschrift* conference. Since then, three of them (Jennifer Richeson, Erin Driver-Linn, and Rhoda Margesson) have completed their work and received their PhDs. When I describe the contributors as a sample of my students, I do not imply that they are a random sample. They were selected to represent different eras, different interests, different orientations, different spheres of activity, different disciplines, different nationalities. Differences aside, they are all individuals whose work and ideas I value and toward whom I feel great friendship and affection. Though they are not a random sample, they do represent the body of my students, in that many others could have been invited to contribute to the *Festschrift* and all, individually and collectively, are of great personal importance to me. Indeed, many others of my students participated in the *Festschrift* conference—in some cases, coming from long distances. (John Smetanka, whom we tried very hard to trace, and eventually located in Bangladesh, gets the prize for making the longest journey.) Some spoke from the floor, others made moving remarks at the dinner. Several told me how much they enjoyed meeting their "siblings" from earlier or later generations.

---

[4]The one exception is Ann Locke Davidson, collaborator and coauthor of Janet Schofield. I have not met her personally, but am happy to welcome her to the family.

The astute reader will have noticed by now that my students, in all their categories and varieties—those who are listed and those who are unlisted, those whose contributions appear in the preceding pages, those who participated in the *Festschrift* conference and those who were unable to come (in some cases sending much appreciated messages of regret)—have, individually and collectively, occupied a central place in my life. I can only hope that I have added some meaning to their lives; I can say with assurance that they have given meaning to mine. This is hardly surprising, in view of the fact that the role of teacher was a central part of my identity during my 42 years of active faculty service at Harvard and Michigan—and, indeed, remains a central part of my identity more than 4 years into retirement, even though I no longer teach classes or (officially) take on new advisees. Many teachers develop a feeling of closeness to their students, especially graduate students with whom they work on their doctoral dissertations; it is no coincidence that familial terminology is often used to characterize the relationship. This feeling is particularly marked, however, for me and my wife, Rose, because we do not have children of our own. My students provide the richness and continuity that add meaning to our lives.

The Formative Years

Although I have spent most of my career in the teaching role, I did not begin serious teaching until 1957—10 years after starting graduate school and 6 years after receiving my PhD. Thus, I had a significant period of time in which I was able to develop my identity as a social psychologist before I even began to develop my identity as a teacher.

When I began my undergraduate studies at Brooklyn College in 1943, at age 16, I had only the vaguest career plans. I was still a member of the religious Zionist youth group that I had first joined in Vienna in 1938, after the Anschluss. The trajectory for members of this organization was to make *aliyah*—move to Palestine—and live in a *kibbutz*. I believe that, by the time I started college, I had pretty much decided that I was not going to follow that path, although I am not sure exactly when and how I had made that decision and dropped out of the group. Nevertheless, my expectation was that I would pursue a career somewhere within the domain of Jewish life—perhaps as an educator, community worker, journalist, or some combination thereof. Writing was always part of that package and so, in the absence of more precise career goals, I opted to major in English literature.

After the war, I became increasingly involved in the peace and civil rights movements. On the train back to New York from a conference in Chicago, organized by politically engaged pacifists—probably in the summer of 1945—I had a long conversation with Charles Bloomstein, a conscientious objector and editor of a thoughtful political newsletter during the war, which helped to crystallize my thinking about where to go next. He said that, if he were in college now, with my interests, he would study psychology or sociology, because the best ideas for work on peace and social change are likely to come from these fields. I followed his advice and, in my junior year, opted to become a psychology major.

(In the end, I graduated with a double major in English and psychology.) I picked psychology over sociology, in part, because I had a running start in psychology, having already taken the introductory course. In part, I believe, I was more comfortable with a psychological level of analysis because its focus on the individual brings it closer to both the observable data and the ultimate criteria for social policy.

My introductory course in social psychology, using Katz and Schank (1938) as the text, confirmed my interest in the field. I was particularly intrigued by the Lewin, Lippitt, and White (1939) work on group atmospheres and autocratic versus democratic leadership (see also Lippitt, 1940, and Lewin, 1948, chap. 5). The course instructor, Janet Kane—noting my performance in the course—strongly urged me to take more social psychology, and I followed suit. The course in advanced social psychology, taught by Daniel Katz (who was also department chair at the time), left me with the strong sense that this was the field for me. In the first half of the course, we read and discussed Floyd Allport's (1933) *Institutional Behavior* and Franz Oppenheimer's (1914/1975) *The State*. The second half was devoted to the detailed study of survey methodology—including questionnaire construction and interviewing—and each student actually designed and carried out a small survey. I found the combination particularly exciting; it persuaded me that social psychology—at least as practiced by Dan Katz—combined a focus on larger social and political issues with scientifically grounded empirical research. My laboratory course in experimental psychology gave me my first introduction to the autokinetic phenomenon (Sherif, 1936), which I later used in my first-year research project at Yale (Kelman, 1950a). For my course on personality, I wrote a term paper, titled "Towards an Explanation of Nazi Aggression," which drew heavily on the frustration-aggression hypothesis (Dollard, Doob, Miller, Mowrer, & Sears, 1939) and also used the work of Cantril (1941) and Fromm (1941). This paper foreshadowed my Lewin Memorial Address (Kelman, 1973) and my work with Lee Hamilton on crimes of obedience.

The Lewin address—given in response to receipt of the Kurt Lewin Memorial Award from the Society for the Psychological Study of Social Issues (SPSSI)—harks back to the Brooklyn College days in other ways as well. After taking Dan Katz's course, I repeatedly turned to him for advice about my future plans. On one occasion, he gave me some literature about SPSSI (of which he was secretary-treasurer at the time) and mentioned that it was an organization I might be interested in. Clearly I was and have been ever since; SPSSI epitomizes my reason for turning to social psychology. I joined in 1946, when I was still an undergraduate, and eventually became very active in it. When I received SPSSI's Lewin Award in 1973, it was—very appropriately— Dan Katz who presented it to me. Modesty notwithstanding, I cannot resist quoting two of Dan's comments in his presentation of the award. In commenting on my relationship to SPSSI, he described me as one of those "members who in their personalities reflect the total pattern of the objectives and practices of the organization" (Katz, 1973, p. 22). In comparing me to Kurt Lewin, he said that "Herb Kelman is in the pattern of Kurt Lewin in that he integrates the two roles [of social psychological researcher/theoretician and social actionist]. He utilizes theoretical analysis and research methods in his social action approach. The result of his work is both a better social world and a better social psychology" (Katz, 1973, pp. 21–22). There was no way I could have even dreamed in 1946, as I sat in Dan Katz's office, that I would receive such an award 27 years later. But it was precisely the possibility of integrating social action with social science that attracted me to social psychology—more precisely, to the kind of social psychology represented by Daniel Katz, Kurt Lewin, and SPSSI.

One highlight of this period was the appearance of Kurt Lewin on campus, giving a lecture on his group decision experiments. I found the work fascinating and concluded that this was the kind of work I would like to do. At the same time, I was worried about the ethical implications of using group-dynamics procedures to manipulate human behavior—an issue to which Lewin himself was by no means oblivious (Marrow, 1969, p. 179). Not surprisingly, when I decided in my senior year to apply to graduate programs in social psychology, my first choice was the Research Center for Group Dynamics, which had recently been established by Kurt Lewin at MIT. Unfortunately, Lewin died (at age 56) in February 1947 and the center suspended new graduate admissions, pending its move to the University of Michigan. Although I was not destined to study with Lewin, he and his tradition played an important role in my graduate training and my subsequent career, as will become apparent here and there in the coming pages. I am rather pleased, therefore, that Reuben Baron (chap. 1, this volume) calls me a Lewinian or neo-Lewinian. I have been told that before and have suspected it myself. But when Reuben tells it to me, I pay attention. Back in the early 1960s, when we worked together at the University of Michigan, he informed me that I was a functionalist (in the context of social psychological theory). He was right, of course, and I should have known it, particularly in view of Dan Katz's association with the functional approach (e.g., Katz, 1960). But my tendency has always been to draw ideas from wherever I found them without signing on to a theoretical school. Still, I was happy to declare myself a functionalist (e.g., Kelman & Baron, 1968, 1974) and to be so classified by chroniclers of the field (e.g., Himmelfarb & Eagly, 1974). To be called a Lewinian by Reuben Baron certainly feels right to me, as well as complimentary. He also calls me a "protodynamical systems theorist," which also sounds great, but I still need to figure out the implications of that designation.

Back to 1946: In my senior year in college, I had to decide what to do next. One option was to enter the Jewish Theological Seminary (JTS) for rabbinical studies—not because I wanted to become a pulpit rabbi, but because this seemed like the most appropriate training for a career in Jewish education or community work. I was well prepared for this option. While attending Brooklyn College, I also attended the Seminary College of Jewish Studies (affiliated with JTS) and indeed received a BHL (Bachelor of Hebrew Literature) degree from the college in 1947, at the same time as my BA. I proceeded with an application. At more or less the same time, I applied to several graduate programs in social psychology, recommended by Dan Katz. As it happened, I was accepted both by JTS and by the three programs—each with an interdisciplinary flavor—that I was most interested in once MIT dropped out of the picture: Yale, Harvard, and the University of Michigan. When I could no longer delay my decision, I knew that graduate school in social psychology was the way I wanted to go. Of my remaining three options, I eliminated Michigan, which had recently established an interdepartmental (sociology and psychology) doctoral program in social psychology that Dan Katz was to join in the fall of 1947, because they wanted me to take additional course work (notably in biology or physiological psychology) during the summer before entering graduate school, and I had other plans for the summer. I eliminated Harvard, which had recently established the interdisciplinary Department of Social Relations, because they initially offered me no financial aid, which I needed; later, in the summer, I was offered a scholarship, but by then I had already accepted at Yale. Yale offered me a research assistantship with Irvin Child, who was collaborating with anthropologist John Whiting on a cross-cultural study of the relationship between child-rearing practices and adult personality (Whiting & Child, 1953). The study utilized the ethnographies indexed in the Cross-Cultural File at Yale's Institute of Human Relations (later renamed the Human Relations Area Files) as its source of data. The work, the pay, and the interdisciplinary Institute of Human Relations—which I had already encountered in the volume on *Frustration and Aggression* (Dollard et al., 1939)—seemed to meet my needs and I accepted.

The decision to pursue graduate studies in social psychology did not mean that I had decided to become a social psychologist, any more than opting for JTS would have meant that I had decided to become a rabbi. But it certainly set me on a path toward adopting, shaping, and personalizing my identity as a social psychologist. My arrival in New Haven in the fall of 1947 began what I describe as my 10 formative years, in which I gradually defined my identity, not only as a social psychologist, but as the kind of psychologist that I remained for the rest of my life (so far, at least; I refuse to dismiss the possibility of change, even if the probability is very low). I shall try to describe the four phases of this formative period briefly, aiming not to be comprehensive, but to highlight the experiences that helped define my way of doing social psychology.

Yale

The Social Relations Department at Harvard or the Joint Doctoral Program in Social Psychology at the University of Michigan, it seems, would have been more natural training grounds for someone starting out with the interests that brought me to social psychology and ending up with the uses to which I ultimately put my training. Yale at the time appeared to be a bit too psychological in its social psychology, too behavioristic in its theoretical orientation, too exclusively experimental in its methodological tastes, too "basic science" in its agenda for someone like me. In fact, I considered switching to the Harvard program after my first few months at Yale—largely because I felt there was not enough social psychology in the department—and I had the opportunity to do so. In December 1947, Bennet Murdock and I went to Cambridge to explore options in the Social Relations Department. We met with Gordon Allport who, it turned out, was particularly interested in us because he felt that—with our Yale background—we could bring some needed strength in experimental psychology to the social psychology program. Shortly after our visit, he invited us to join the program, but, in the end, both of us decided to stay at Yale. In my own case, one consideration, no doubt, was the fact that I had made friends in the department and become integrated in the group of mostly unattached graduate students who spent most of their time at "the Institute" (i.e., the Institute of Human Relations, located in the Yale medical complex) where psychology was housed—along with anthropology, psychiatry, and child development. Most important, however, was that the prospects for social psychology at Yale began to look much brighter to me. First, at the urging of some of my fellow students and myself, Leonard Doob and Irvin Child agreed to offer a year-long graduate seminar in social psychology and personality. Second, Carl Hovland—the chair and leading presence in the department—received a Rockefeller grant to establish the Yale Communication Research Program (generally referred to as the "attitude-change project") and offered me a research assistantship in it. The invitation from Harvard gave me the opportunity to recommit myself to Yale—a decision that I have never had any reason to regret. Eventually, of course, I ended up teaching in the Social Relations Department at Harvard and the Joint Doctoral Program at Michigan, but fortified with my Yale training.

On balance, I found my Yale training more liberating than restrictive. To be sure, we had to take the department's dominant theoretical approach—Yale learning theory, derived from the work of Clark Hull (e.g., Hull, 1943)—as our point of departure and to become conversant in its language. But there was ample room for adapting the model to one's own needs and applying it to a broad range of problems. Indeed, the environment of the Institute of Human Relations encouraged many ambitious (if at times, perhaps, a bit reductionist) efforts to apply learning-theory concepts to the analysis of such diverse and socially relevant topics as frustration and aggression (Dollard et al., 1939—to which I have already referred), social learning and imitation (Miller & Dollard, 1941), personality and psychotherapy (Dollard & Miller, 1950), social attitudes (Doob, 1947), and even war and peace (May, 1943). As already mentioned, I was personally involved as a research assistant in two such enterprises: the research on child training and personality (Whiting & Child, 1953) during my first year in graduate school, and the research on communication and persuasion (Hovland, Janis, & Kelley, 1953) during the remaining three years. In keeping with the interdisciplinary flavor of much of the work at the institute, I had considerable exposure to other disciplines during my graduate training—a great deal to anthropology and psychoanalysis, less to sociology (in part because it was housed at the other end of the campus).

Carl Hovland, my mentor as of 1948 and my thesis adviser, played a critical role in allowing me to develop my own approach to the field. He was a first-rate theorist and experimentalist, but—though one of Hull's leading students and steeped in Hullian theory—he was more interested in addressing concrete problems than in testing theoretical systems. He was eclectic in his choice of theoretical concepts, as evidenced by his successful collaboration with such theoretically diverse colleagues as Irving Janis, Harold Kelley, and Muzafer Sherif. He often started with practical questions, such as those that the designers of a persuasive communication might raise: Would it be more effective to present both sides of the issue or only the side we are advocating? Would it be more effective to start out with our best arguments or to end up with them? To answer such questions, he would draw on relevant theoretical concepts, wherever he could find them, to develop complex hypotheses about the conditions under which different relationships hold, and then proceed to test these hypotheses with sophisticated experimental designs. This systematic way of defining the problem and designing the research that can address it is perhaps the most important lesson I learned from my association with Carl Hovland. As for selection of the problem to be addressed and the theoretical approach to be adopted, he always encouraged me to follow my own inclinations—of course, within the substantive and methodological framework of the attitude-change project. On the other hand, he had his ways of letting me know when he was not satisfied with the direction I was taking. As a result, it took three extensive tries before I came up with a mutually acceptable thesis proposal. At the time, I complained about Hovland's nondirective approach, but it soon became clear to me that his mentoring style, while clearly communicating his high standards, encouraged me to develop independent ideas and emphases in line with my own interests and concerns.

The emphasis in my Yale training on rigorous theoretical thinking, elegant experimental design, and sophisticated analysis was not only useful, but also congruent with my personal style. I was particularly captivated by analysis of variance and determined to use a Latin square design in my thesis even before I knew what the thesis would be about (and I followed through—see Kelman, 1953). Perhaps this training encouraged my bent toward linear thinking about a world that I have always known to be circular but, ultimately, it has given me tools to think systematically about complex issues, including interactive and dialectical processes. Yale training—at least in my days—also helped to anchor graduate students in the discipline of psychology as a whole, not only their specialty. Psychology at Yale emerged as a fairly unified field, largely because of the presence of an overarching theoretical framework that served as the point of departure for most (or at least the most influential) faculty members across the spectrum. The conflict between "hard" and "soft" psychologists that divided some other departments (leading, for example, to the partition of the Harvard Department of Psychology and the establishment of the Department of Social Relations in 1946) did not arise at Yale, since it was the "hard" psychologists themselves who chose to work on the "soft" issues. In this atmosphere, it was quite natural that I—though always committed to social psychology—would take my minor area exam in learning (based on an extensive yearlong course with Neal Miller) and would acquire a heavy dosage of clinical training (including a yearlong seminar and supervised practice in projective testing with Seymour Sarason and in psychotherapy with John Dollard, as well as regular attendance at psychiatric rounds).

I emerged from this training as a fairly well-rounded psychologist, a well-trained social psychologist, and a competent experimenter (as confirmed—I am happy to say—by Reuben Baron, chap. 1, this volume). In addition to its intrinsic value, this training gave me the firm ground from which to strike out in new directions and the credibility to do so. At the same time, the modeling and mentorship of my teachers at Yale, and particularly of Carl Hovland, provided validation and encouragement for social psychological work that starts with applied problems, that addresses larger social issues, and that takes an interdisciplinary orientation.

In assessing the impact of the Yale experience on my evolving identity as a social psychologist, I must stress that my theoretical training at Yale was not all S-R learning theory, and my social psychological training in those years did not all happen at Yale. We had a great deal of sympathetic exposure to psychoanalytic theory, with emphasis on the need to translate its propositions into empirically testable hypotheses—as was indeed done by several of our professors. I was particularly interested in Freud's papers on technique (Freud, 1924/1950, pp. 285–402), which I studied carefully and have drawn on in my later teaching of psychotherapy and practice of conflict resolution. Kurt Lewin's theory of personality also received extensive coverage in our course readings and directly influenced some of the work of Irvin Child and Neal Miller. I immersed myself in the writings of Lewin and his associates, in both personality theory and social psychology, and did papers and reports drawing on that literature. I even published a polemical paper (Kelman, 1950b) that contained a review of the research literature on group dynamics as of that date. I developed a reputation as the resident Lewinian in the department.

But I also used my summers well, to broaden my training in social psychology in areas that were not represented at Yale—and incidentally to become acquainted with many birthright Lewinians and their work. In the summer of 1948, after my first year at Yale, I participated in the Training Laboratory for Group Development at Bethel, Maine (original home of the T-group), as a research assistant and trainee. It all started when Ronald Lippitt gave a colloquium on this emerging enterprise at Yale. I raised a question about the potential for manipulative use of such group processes. In his response Lippitt told me that it is typical of New Englanders to raise this kind of question—a response that, as a Jew from Vienna and Brooklyn who had lived in New Haven for about half a year, I found rather amusing. Whatever ethical questions I may have had, I asked Lippitt how I could get to Bethel and he helped to arrange the assistantship that brought me there. I continued to have ethical questions about training groups, as well as methodological ones (I had trouble, for example, with the concept of a group whose sole task was to study itself), but I learned a great deal at Bethel that I found useful in my later work (including how to ride a bicycle). I also had the opportunity to get to know the faculty members from the Research Center for Group Dynamics who were at Bethel that summer (in addition to Ronald Lippitt): Dorwin Cartwright, Jack French, and Alvin Zander.

I spent the second summer (1949) of my graduate years at the University of Michigan, where I was a student in the summer institute on survey methods and a research assistant at the Survey Research Center—all of it made possible by Daniel Katz. I did intensive course work in basic survey techniques, survey design, sampling, and scaling. For my assistantship, I had the responsibility of planning and carrying out the analysis of data from one of the studies in the SRC's program on human relations in industry (which was under Katz's general direction at the time; the study director for my project was Eugene Jacobson). I spent much of my spare time at the Research Center for Group Dynamics, interacting intensively with members of the final cohort of Lewin's students who were there at the time—teaching, working on research projects, and/or finishing up their dissertations: Harold Kelley, John Thibaut, Kurt Back, Stanley Schachter, Albert Pepitone, Murray Horwitz, and Ben Willerman (who was actually at the SRC). I also found time to draft my first thesis proposal (perhaps as a course paper), outlining an experimental test of the effects of group decision on attitudes, couched in Hullian terminology (replete with fractional anticipatory goal responses). I presented my ideas to Leon Festinger, who had conducted one of the earlier group decision experiments in Lewin's program and who was also at Michigan at the time, but he could see no reason why I would want to work on this topic. In the end, my professors at Yale were also insufficiently enthusiastic and I dropped the idea.

My summer in Ann Arbor was a turning point in my self-definition. Up to that point I thought of myself as a graduate student in (social) psychology. But, being away from an environment in which I was defined by my student role, and situated in an environment in which I was functioning as a full-fledged (albeit young) professional and treated as such, I began to think of myself as a social psychologist. It is not that I was unaware of my continuing status as a student; I was certainly reminded of it when my first two thesis proposals failed to elicit clear support from my advisers. But I had now made a commitment to social psychology as an identity and a career. Increasingly, I acted as a young professional—and as one with his own perspective on the field. After my return from Ann Arbor, I gave a colloquium on the innovative approach to scaling developed by Clyde Coombs, with whom I had taken a course at the summer institute. I also reported to Carl Hovland on the as yet unpublished work on social communication that Leon Festinger and his associates were engaged in; Hovland later told me that my recommendation contributed to the decision to bring Harold Kelley to the department the following year. In my last year at Yale, I collaborated with Arthur Gladstone (with whom I had also collaborated earlier in establishing Walden House, the student cooperative house that was my home between 1948 and 1951) in two efforts. Early in 1951, we gave a joint psychology colloquium on the social implications of psychological research, in which I spoke about manipulation of human behavior as an ethical dilemma confronting many areas of research and practice in the field (remarks that, more than a dozen years later, became the basis of a symposium paper and article—see Kelman, 1965b). Around the same time, we published a letter in the *American Psychologist* (Gladstone & Kelman, 1951), in which we proposed that some of the basic assumptions of pacifist thinkers were consistent with psychological theories and findings and that it would be important to subject them to systematic research—a proposal that led to the establishment, in the following year, of the Research Exchange on the Prevention of War. These activities were concrete expressions of my interest in integrating my ethical and activist concerns with my professional work—which had led me to social psychology in the first place—and they set the pattern for the kind of social psychologist I was to become for the rest of my career.

My dissertation experiment used a fixed, persuasive communication, following the paradigm of the Yale attitude-change project (see Kelman, 1953). In the write-up, I freely mixed (without apology) S-R and Lewinian terminology and sources. My central concern—the relationship between overt conformity to social norms or social pressures and internalized change in attitude—was the starting point of my theoretical and empirical work for years to come. I decided that I would explore the internalization of attitudes in a real-life context as well as in the laboratory and—in view of my evolving interest in psychotherapy—I concluded that group therapy would be an ideal setting to pursue this interest. I therefore applied, successfully, for a postdoctoral fellowship from the Social Science Research Council to study group therapy—not as a clinician, but as a social psychologist interested in it as an intensive influence situation, potentially conducive to important changes in attitude and personality. I felt enormously validated when Hovland (who had become Carl at the end of my orals), commenting on the direction I planned to take, told me that he believed internalization was the most important topic to which the field needed to turn.

Johns Hopkins

The SSRC gave me carte blanche in selecting the site for my postdoctoral fellowship. I explored a number of options and boiled them down to a choice between Baltimore and the Boston-Cambridge area. I found active group therapy projects in four Boston hospitals and interesting research on group process—especially the work of Freed Bales—in the Department of Social Relations at Harvard. Bales extended a warm invitation to house my fellowship in his laboratory; the Boston Psychopathic Hospital (now Massachusetts Mental Health Center) was also ready to house me. The Boston area clearly offered a rich, stimulating environment for my fellowship. My only worry was that I would be overwhelmed by all the options, try to do everything for the first few months, and eventually settle on one program—having lost precious time in the process. Baltimore created no such worries. There was only one thing going on there that was relevant to my interests, but it was clearly of high quality and very congenial to me: the group psychotherapy research project at the Phipps Psychiatric Clinic, Johns Hopkins Hospital, under the direction of Jerome Frank. It was one of the earliest systematic and methodologically rigorous research programs on the evaluation of psychotherapy. I had read some of Frank's papers on group therapy when I began exploring that topic. Most important, however, I was familiar with his earlier work. Before going to medical school, Frank received a PhD in psychology from Harvard and went on to do postdoctoral work at Cornell with Kurt Lewin (with whom he had also worked earlier in Berlin). One of the products of this period was a series of studies on social pressure and resistance thereto (Frank, 1944a, 1944b)—anticipating some of the findings of Milgram's obedience research—which influenced my own dissertation.

I chose to go to Baltimore, which turned out to be a wise decision. In the end, I stayed at Johns Hopkins for three years. After completing my year as an SSRC fellow, I wanted to extend my stay—primarily because I had started a psychoanalysis, which I did not want to terminate prematurely. I was fortunate to receive a postdoctoral fellowship from the National Institute of Mental Health (NIMH) for 1952–1953, which later was renewed for an additional year. For the first year and a half of my time in Baltimore I was housed at the Phipps

Clinic; after that, I moved to the Homewood Campus, so I would have more time to pursue my own work. I should mention that my plans during that period were complicated by my resistance to the military draft. We were in the middle of the Korean War and, having finished my studies, I was called up for induction shortly after I came to Baltimore. I had registered as a conscientious objector, but my New Haven draft board denied me CO status (on the basis of a narrow interpretation of the religious criteria for that status). I lost my appeals, and, having exhausted my legal options, I chose to refuse induction. I was prepared to go to jail—knowing that the customary sentence for draft refusal was a year and a day—and I was making plans for using my prison time most productively. Fortunately, however, the grand jury that considered my case, on the recommendation of the district attorney, ruled in my favor. The draft board finally gave up on me, granted me the CO classification, and even agreed to designate my NIMH fellowship as the alternative service required of COs in those days.

The three postdoctoral years that I spent in Baltimore played a critical role in my personal and professional development. The activities I pursued and the ideas I formulated during that period laid the foundations for most of my subsequent work. What helped to make this such a fruitful period, I believe, is the fact that I was by then a fully credentialed, independent professional, no longer constrained by my student status, yet at the same time not tied down by the duties of a regular job. I thus had maximal freedom to pursue my own interests and define my own identity.

At the personal level, the most important foundational experience of those years is that Baltimore is where I met, courted, and married my life partner, Rose. This is clearly a foundation the two of us have built on over the years, having reached, in August 2003, the 50th anniversary of our marriage. Also, as already mentioned, I was in analysis throughout my three years in Baltimore. It was a fairly classical, Freudian analysis. Needless to say, it contributed a great deal to my understanding of the therapeutic process and relationship. It did not produce dramatic personal changes—no overarching new insights and no recovered childhood memories. It did not even break my lifelong habit of coming late (after a while, my analyst gave up trying to interpret it). What it did accomplish, I believe, is to make me more reflective about my goals and relationships and more accepting of myself—more tolerant of my limitations.

At the professional and intellectual level, I continue to draw and build on the ideas that I developed during those years. In many ways, my activities in Baltimore set the direction of my future work. It was at Hopkins that I worked out the distinction between the three processes of social influence and at Morgan State College in 1954 that I carried out the first experiment testing that model (Kelman, 1958). I started out with the distinction between compliance and internalization, supported by my dissertation. As I explored the literature on various real-life influence situations, I concluded that this dichotomy did not adequately capture some of the most interesting instances of social influence—particularly brainwashing and religious or political conversion (the phenomenon of the true believer), as well as certain aspects of childhood and adult socialization. I think Lee Hamilton (chap. 4, this volume) is right when she suggests that the process of identification—which I introduced to capture these diverse manifestations of influence—is the most complex and interesting of the three processes (and, I might add, the most uniquely social psychological).

The group therapy project, which originally brought me to Hopkins, provided many experiences and learning opportunities on which I have drawn and built in many ways. Through regular and extensive observation of therapy groups, participation in staff meetings, frequent conversations with colleagues (especially Morris Parloff and Jerome Frank himself), and active involvement in evaluation research (Kelman & Parloff, 1957; Parloff, Kelman, & Frank, 1954)—along with my personal psychoanalysis—I acquired a wealth of "anthropological" knowledge about the field of psychotherapy. Frank's commonsense approach and emphasis on the role of the therapist and the patient–therapist relationship in determining therapeutic outcome (see Frank, 1961) was particularly helpful in my subsequent teaching and writing (e.g., Kelman, 1963) about psychotherapy from a social psychological perspective. The experience in evaluation research was also relevant to my later work in evaluating the impact of international exchange programs (e.g., Kelman & Ezekiel, 1970). Finally, while in Baltimore, I continued my interest in group process (following up on my Bethel experience) and, together with Harry Lerner, edited an issue of the *Journal of Social Issues*, comparing group methods in psychotherapy, social work, and adult education (Lerner & Kelman, 1952). My exploration of group process in these different settings directly influenced my subsequent work with problem-solving workshops in conflict resolution (see, for example, Kelman 1991a, 1997a).

My work in peace research and the social psychology of international relations also has strong roots in this period. The letter that Arthur Gladstone and I published in the *American Psychologist* stimulated correspondence and meetings that led to the formation in 1952 of the Research Exchange on the Prevention of War—which, as far as I know, represented the first organized effort to promote the field of peace research (Kelman, 1991b). The Research Exchange published a *Bulletin*, edited by Arthur Gladstone (with myself as book review editor), in which I published several articles on my evolving views on the study of war and peace and the psychological aspects thereof. The Research Exchange also organized symposia (two of which were published) and discussion meetings at various professional conventions, as well as two summer workshops. (Rose and I attended the workshop at Fellowship Farm, Pennsylvania, in the summer of 1953, in lieu of our honeymoon—setting a pattern for the rest of our lives.)

Although my teaching career did not begin until 1957, I did have my first teaching experience at the Baltimore College of Commerce, where I twice taught a course on business psychology. I needed to supplement my meager fellowship income to pay for my four weekly analytic sessions. In the course, we used a text on business psychology, but my lectures dealt with basic topics in social psychology and personality. The course contained the seeds of the main undergraduate course that I was to teach—under different titles and with gradually changing content—throughout my teaching years.

I cannot end my account of the Baltimore years without mentioning that I played an instrumental role in founding a chapter of the Congress of Racial Equality (CORE) shortly after arriving in Baltimore and was an active participant in its successful nonviolent direct-action campaign to open dime-store lunch counters and other facilities to the Black population. Rose and I spent many a date on a picket line or sit-in at Woolworth's or Grant's. I was active in CORE and other civil rights activities both before and after my Baltimore years (serving as national field representative of CORE between 1954 and 1960), but the Baltimore period stands out in a number of ways. When I arrived in Baltimore, it was a completely segregated city, but one ready for change. It took a lot of dedicated work, skill, and coordination to produce the change, but it was exciting to be able to see our efforts make a real difference. Another feature of Baltimore CORE was the active involvement of members of the city's very vital Black community, including its labor union, church, and university sectors. We were very much part of this community, engaged in a joint effort to create social change. The experience taught me a great deal about social change, particularly the role of nonviolent direct action (see Kelman, 1968b, chap. 9) and the importance of combining it with other strategies, as we did in our CORE work: public education, negotiation with local store managers, and campaigns directed to the national headquarters of chain stores.

As my third fellowship year drew to a close, I had to think about finding a job. My search for an academic position was unsuccessful and I began negotiations for a research position at the National Institute of Mental Health. In the meantime, I received an invitation to join the initial group of fellows at the Center for Advanced Study in the Behavioral Sciences, newly established by the Ford Foundation on the Stanford campus. (It is probably no coincidence that Carl Hovland was a member of the board.) Some older colleagues advised me that it was time to get a real job. Dissatisfied with that advice, I turned to David Riesman, who was a visiting professor at Hopkins that semester; I was sitting in on his seminar and had gotten to know him fairly well by that time. He told me what I wanted to hear: that I will have other opportunities to get a job, but that the invitation to the center represented a rare opportunity. It was one of many bits of good advice that I received from David Riesman over the coming years.

Center for Advanced Study in the Behavioral Sciences

In my final analytic session, my analyst became uncharacteristically directive (we were sitting face to face in that session) and told me that the only way to go to California was to drive across the country. When I pointed out that I had no car and did not know how to drive, he told me to buy a car and take driving lessons and assured me that by the end of the trip I would know how to drive. He even told me how to handle mountain roads. Rose and I did buy a car and had a great time driving across the country.

When I arrived at the center, I found a very interesting and diverse group of colleagues. The distribution of fellows in that initial year was bimodal, including a sizable number of very senior people (such as Franz Alexander, Kenneth Boulding, Clyde Kluckhohn, Harold Lasswell, Paul Lazarsfeld) and a sizable number of quite junior people of whom, at age 27, I was one of the youngest. In part, this was by design: One of the early ideas for constituting a center class was to invite a number of senior scholars along with a group of younger satellites for each. That concept never took hold in that first year—in fact, a strong egalitarian atmosphere evolved, in which each fellow, regardless of age, was treated as a fully independent scholar—and it was soon dropped. Another reason for the bimodal distribution, I believe, was that recruitment for the first class started very late, so that the people who were free to accept the invitation were either senior enough to obtain a year's leave on short notice, or junior enough to have no stable job (or, like myself, no job at all) to take leave from.

I probably should have devoted this year of complete freedom to writing up my three-process model and my experimental test of it. But it seems that I preferred to take advantage of the rich array of intellectual pursuits that were represented at the center and to learn about the concepts and methods that colleagues from several disciplines were advancing. I participated in a wide variety of activities—ranging from a research project on psychological correlates of different somatic disturbances (see Kelman, Alexander, & Stein, 1958) to a study group on social movements in which I presented my own analysis of the Sabbatian movement (an influential Jewish messianic movement of the 17th century).

The year at the center did generate some concrete products in the peace research domain. Encouraged by the collegial atmosphere at the center, I called together a number of the fellows—including Kenneth Boulding and Anatol Rapoport—to talk with them about the Research Exchange on the Prevention of War and get their advice on how to move forward more rapidly (I was impatient in those days) on the development of a professional base for the organization and how to attract international relations specialists to this enterprise. These discussions led to the proposal to establish a new journal, which would replace and expand on the *Bulletin of the Research Exchange.* We decided to name the new publication *Journal of Conflict Resolution: A Quarterly for Research Related to War and Peace,* and to base it at the University of Michigan, since Boulding was there, Rapoport was about to move there, and William Barth and Robert Hefner—both Michigan graduate students at the time—were already producing the *Bulletin of the Research Exchange* there. The *Journal of Conflict Resolution* is now in its 47th year of publication. During the year at the center, I also completed work on an issue of the *Journal of Social Issues,* addressed to research on war and peace, that I coedited with Barth and Hefner (Kelman, Barth, & Hefner, 1955), including my closing article, which clearly reflected the interdisciplinary setting in which it was produced (Kelman, 1955).

The most important impact of my stay at the center was that it helped me define myself, at this early stage in my career, as part of an interdisciplinary community of behavioral and social scientists. I was, of course, strongly predisposed in this direction, but the year at the center provided ideas, contacts, and validation for interdisciplinary work and, above all, rewarding experiences of interaction across disciplinary lines. Thus, it set the pattern of my career as a social psychologist—firmly anchored in my mother discipline—who has always operated in interdisciplinary settings and in relation to colleagues from other fields, whether clinicians, ethicists, political scientists, international relations scholars, or Middle East specialists.

By the end of the year, I had not yet succeeded in locating a suitable academic position, despite strong support of my candidacy for an opening in the Department of Social Relations at Harvard from Clyde Kluckhohn, and despite the efforts of Ralph Tyler—the center's first director—to find an opening for me in the Committee on Human Development at the University of Chicago. I decided to resume negotiations with the National Institute of Mental Health and accepted a position in the Laboratory of Psychology, part of the NIMH intramural program, based at its Clinical Center in Bethesda.

National Institute of Mental Health

A good part of my first year at NIMH was taken up with fighting to hold on to my job. I was terminated (as was Rose, who had taken a position as social worker at the National Institute of Neurological Diseases and Blindness) because the Department of Health, Education, and Welfare's (HEW's) security office—established at the height of the McCarthy period and still very much in place in 1955—questioned my past political activities and my associations (see Kelman, 1957). After six months of struggle, with excellent legal help from Richard Schifter (whom I knew from his Yale law student days in New Haven, where he lived in one of our sister co-op houses and was active—with support from me, among others—in establishing an ACLU chapter, and who was later to become assistant secretary of state for human rights), and with moral and financial support from SPSSI and APA, we achieved a complete reversal of the termination action, including an apology from the Secretary of HEW. This successful outcome would not have been possible without the unwavering support of my superiors and colleagues in the Laboratory of Psychology and elsewhere in the NIMH system.

Because of the friendships that I formed with colleagues at NIMH, deepened by their stand on my behalf in the face of the political pressures of the day, I view my experience there as a positive contribution to my formative years, despite the obstacles that I had to overcome. The relationships with three colleagues in the Laboratory of Psychology stand out in particular. David Shakow, chief of the laboratory, became a valued mentor, who was very supportive of my ethical and social concerns and my approach to the scholarly enterprise. Morris Parloff, with whom I had collaborated closely at Johns Hopkins, was chief of my section at NIMH and instrumental in bringing me there—and continues to be a valued and respected friend to this day, more than half a century after I first met him. Donald (Mike) Boomer shared his office with me, as well as his wisdom and humor; among other things, he agreed to supervise me in short-term therapy with a patient, thus doubling my experience as a therapist and adding a Sullivanian model to the Freudian/behaviorist model that John Dollard provided in his supervision of my one previous venture into therapeutic practice.[5]

---

[5] It should also be mentioned that my relationship to NIMH as an institution over the years—both before and after my position on the staff—was very positive. In addition to the two years of postdoctoral fellowships at Johns Hopkins (1952–1954), NIMH granted me a Special Research Fellowship to spend a year (1960–1961) at the Institute for Social Research at Oslo. (The latter—not coincidentally—was offered to me after I had been denied a Fulbright grant for entirely political reasons, apparently based on incomplete information about my case at NIMH.) NIMH also supported my research program on social influence and behavior change with a series of research grants, as well as the International Conference on Social-Psychological Research in Developing Countries that I organized at the University of Ibadan in December 1966 to January 1967. In turn, I served on NIMH's Psychology Training Review Committee for several years, as well as other NIMH committees.

New research plans in the psychiatric wards of the Clinical Center—including a study that Charlotte Schwartz and I were hoping to conduct on an experimental program for psychotic patients and their parents—did not materialize. I did manage, however, to analyze and write up some earlier data and to work on some theoretical papers. My major—and not insignificant—achievement during this two-year period, however, was completion of a nearly 200-page manuscript, presenting my three-process model of social influence and the experimental evidence in support of it (Kelman, 1956). I submitted this manuscript (anonymously, as required) in successful competition for the Socio-Psychological Prize of the American Association for the Advancement of Science. The biggest mistake I made in my professional life was my failure to publish this manuscript at the time. I signed a contract with John Wiley & Sons, who were prepared to publish the manuscript with just the addition of an introductory chapter and virtually no other changes. But I felt it was not ready, wanting to do some additional experiments and some theoretical elaboration. I did conduct some further experiments and revise and elaborate some of the text, but in the meantime the literature grew, the task became more daunting, and I was distracted by a variety of other interests. As a result, although the ideas and some of the research have been partially presented in articles and other books, I have never produced that promised full statement of the model and detailed presentation of the data—at least so far: I have not entirely given up yet, and Erin Driver-Linn is proactively working with me in putting the old manuscript (as already revised) into a form and context that might make it interesting to contemporary readers.

Returning to 1957, it was clear to me (as well as to my colleagues) that—despite the rewarding features of my NIMH experience that I have described—I really belonged in a university, rather than a psychological laboratory based in a governmental medical facility, even one that allowed researchers as much autonomy as I had at NIMH. A university was obviously a more appropriate environment in which to pursue my interest in international relations, to comment on public issues, and to explore the relationship between social research and social action. Thus, when I was offered a faculty position in the Harvard Department of Social Relations, starting in the fall of 1957, I was delighted to accept.

The Teaching Years

My formal teaching career began with my first Harvard appointment in 1957. I had no teaching experience as a graduate student; teaching was never even an available option. The teaching I did at the Baltimore College of Commerce was a valuable experience and I certainly took it seriously, but it was a job rather than a central element of my identity. It was only in 1957 that my identity as a teacher began to take shape, but it soon became central to my personal identity and has remained so throughout the years. During my 42 official teaching years, starting in 1957 and ending with my retirement from teaching in 1999, I have held only three jobs in two universities—not counting over a dozen appointments, of varying lengths of time, as visiting professor, fellow, or scholar in different institutions in the United States and abroad.

Because of my poor planning and self-indulgence, the preceding section used so much of the generous amount of space made available to me that there is not enough space left to give the kind of detailed account of the 42 years covered in this section that I gave to the 14 years covered in the preceding section. At best, I figure that I have about a third as much space to cover three times as many years. I maintain, however, that this imbalance is quite appropriate to the focus of this *Festschrift* on my students and their work, for two reasons. First, my teaching years require less elaboration because they are well represented by the samples of my students' research and thinking that are offered in the preceding chapters. This is not so much because of a correspondence in the content of their work and mine (which applies more in some cases than in others) but because their work picks up, in one or another way, the kind of social psychology that I have practiced, taught, and stood for. Second, in a book in which and through which my students pay tribute to me, it is important that I, in turn, pay tribute to my teachers and mentors. I hope this is part of what the detailed account of my formative years conveys, explicitly and implicitly—in its references especially to my primary mentors, Daniel Katz and Carl Hovland, but also to others who have played an important mentoring role, such as Irvin Child, Leonard Doob, Jerome Frank, David Riesman, and David Shakow. Their most important contribution has been to encourage me to be and become myself, and I hope that I have played a comparable role in my relationship to my own students. More generally, the emphasis on my own formative years reminds us of the flow of influence across generations in the development of scholarly traditions. For the reasons given, then, I am content to limit myself (particularly since I have no other choice) to just a few general observations about my 42 teaching years.

(1) By the time I entered the teaching role, I had pretty much developed my identity as the kind of social psychologist that I was to remain—with some variations on the basic themes—for the rest of my career. As a consequence, most of my teaching from the beginning has been in the areas of my special concern, and my teaching and advising were nicely integrated with my interests in research, theory, and practice. Of course, over the years, I did my share of the teaching that had to be covered, including coteaching the undergraduate introductory course (albeit the semester that covered social psychology, personality, and psychopathology) and the proseminar in social psychology, as well as running general research seminars. Many of the undergraduate theses I supervised were in areas outside of my special interest; a large proportion of students I advised were in special concentrations (such as conflict studies), in joint concentrations between psychology and other disciplines (sociology, government, Far Eastern studies), or in Harvard's interdisciplinary social studies program. At the graduate level, too, I often took on students who were working on independent projects, unrelated to the research programs of any of the faculty members, and more often than not using nonexperimental methods. (Roger Brown was also known to take on students with diverse interests, not necessarily related to his own work; both of us, in this regard, were following in the footsteps of Gordon Allport.) I also spent a lot of time in careful editing of my students' work, as many of my advisees will testify. In short, I did not just use

my teaching and supervision in the single-minded pursuit of my own agenda, but I did find great synergy between my teaching or advising and my research. Many of my best ideas developed or became crystallized in the course of interactions with my graduate students, discussions in my seminars, or preparation of lectures.

(2) It is interesting that, in each of my three academic appointments, one of my "outside" interests—my exercises in reaching out to other fields, beyond the confines of social psychology: whether psychotherapy, international relations, or ethics—was a key factor in my selection. To be sure, my credentials as a bona fide social psychologist, including my Yale degree, my experimental work, and my theoretical contributions, were by no means irrelevant and indeed gave me the requisite "idiosyncrasy credits"—to use Edwin Hollander's (1958) concept. I know, for example, that the AAAS Socio-Psychological Prize contributed significantly to my invitation to Harvard in 1957. But my primary credentials for the particular position for which I was recruited that year derived from my work in psychotherapy.

The appointment was specifically in the clinical program within the Department of Social Relations and the initiative for it came from David McClelland, head of the clinical program at the time, who was interested in my social psychological perspective on psychotherapy and my analysis of it within a general framework of social influence and behavior change. In line with this interest, I developed and taught a yearlong seminar, required of all third-year clinical students, alongside of their practicum training in psychotherapy (which was, of course, supervised by a clinician). The first semester—which virtually all of the graduate students in social psychology took as well—focused on processes of social influence and covered the theoretical and experimental literature in that field (including, of course, the three processes) and various real-life influence situations *other than psychotherapy* (such as childhood and adult socialization, political and religious conversion, and assimilation). The second semester focused on theory and research in psychotherapy, with emphasis on the patient–therapist relationship and the therapeutic interaction (comparing, in particular, Freud's, Sullivan's, and Rogers's views on these matters).

I was appointed for a five-year term as Lecturer on Social Psychology, a title I preferred, because it both expressed my professional identity and communicated clearly that—though teaching about psychotherapy—I was not claiming clinical credentials. While based in the clinical program, I taught a middle-level course on Attitudes and Their Change, and had extensive contacts with colleagues, graduate students, and undergraduates in social psychology.

In 1962, when my five-year term at Harvard came to an end, I moved to the University of Michigan as Professor of Psychology and Research Psychologist at the Center for Research on Conflict Resolution. At the University of Michigan, my tenure and my academic duties were in the Department of Psychology. It was understood from the beginning that I would be centrally involved in the Joint Doctoral Program in Social Psychology, a collaborative enterprise between the Sociology and Psychology Departments. For a short time, in fact, I was chair of the program. I took on the assignment at a time when the program was about to collapse because of differences between the two departments in their size and operating style. My colleagues and I believed that, in view of my strong commitment to an interdisciplinary view of social psychology, I might be able to keep the program alive. Unfortunately, however, my strong commitment was not matched by sufficiently strong political skills and so—to my profound regret—I ended up presiding over the dissolution of this experiment.

My outreach beyond the confines of my own discipline, once again, played a significant role in my appointment at the University of Michigan, which was—as noted—a joint appointment between the Psychology Department and the Center for Research on Conflict Resolution. The center was an outgrowth of the *Journal of Conflict Resolution,* which, as I mentioned earlier, was based at the University of Michigan. The community that developed at the university around the editorial work on the journal decided to push the work forward through the establishment of an interdisciplinary research center in the field, and the idea gained support from the university administration. The desire to expand the number of faculty members with an interest in the center's interdisciplinary work, my continuing involvement with the *Journal of Conflict Resolution* as a founding member of its editorial board, and Dan Katz's key role both in the center and the Psychology Department all contributed to my invitation to come to the University of Michigan.

Another one of my "outside" interests—my concern with ethical issues—played a significant role in my invitation, in 1968, to return to Harvard as Richard Clarke Cabot Professor of Social Ethics. This chair was established in 1966 to commemorate Richard Clarke Cabot and the Department of Social Ethics, which he chaired (along with his professorship in the Medical School) between 1920 and 1931, when it was absorbed in a new Department of Sociology. The chair is not intended for a professional ethicist, but for a scholar in any department of the Faculty of Arts and Sciences who focuses on ethical questions confronting individuals in modern society.

According to the endowment, the incumbent "should deal with problems of practical ethics, should help students face ethical questions frankly and openly, and should help them relate themselves thoughtfully to the social issues of the day, so that they might at least envisage the possibility of careers in either social or public service" (Bentinck-Smith & Stouffer, 1991, p. 109). The first incumbent of the chair, very appropriately, was Gordon Allport, who had started his Harvard teaching career as an instructor in social ethics under Cabot. Allport, unfortunately, died in 1967, at age 70, within a year after the appointment. The Department of Social Relations—as the historical successor (via Sociology) of the Department of Social Ethics—was given the opportunity to search for the next incumbent and it chose to nominate me.

Clearly, the department would not have offered me a professorship had I lacked strong credentials in my own discipline. But it was my focus on ethical issues that provided the additional qualifications stipulated in the description of the chair: my work on the ethics of social research, on the psychology of social issues, on war and peace, and on justice and social change. My book, *A Time to Speak: On Human Values and Social Research* (Kelman, 1968b), which was in press at the time of the appointment, was probably one of the most important items in my bibliography when my candidacy was being considered.

Rose and I were reluctant to leave the University of Michigan, but the invitation from Harvard was hard to resist. One of the special attractions was the nature of the chair, which turned my "extracurricular" activities into part of the job description. Another was, of course, the special meaning of being named as Gordon Allport's successor, particularly since I had gotten to know him quite well during my first appointment at Harvard and he had been a source of encouragement and inspiration.

(3) Over the course of the years, the center of gravity of my work shifted from social influence to international conflict and its resolution. This is evident from my own writings and from the research of the students I supervised. The shift can be noted, for example, as one moves across the chapters in the present volume. Perhaps the best indicator of the shift is the topic of my trademark graduate seminar, which traditionally met on Wednesday evenings. In the earlier years, the title of my trademark seminar was Processes of Social Influence or some variant thereof, and it followed the format of the seminar described earlier that I first introduced in 1957. Needless to say, students heard and read a lot about my three processes of social influence, but the seminar covered the experimental literature on social influence and examined a number of real-life influence situations. In the later years, my graduate seminar on International Conflict: Social Psychological Approaches became my trademark Wednesday evening event. The seminar dealt with social psychological dimensions of international relations and approaches to the resolution of international/intercommunal conflicts, with special emphasis on *interactive problem solving*—the term I came to use to designate my own approach. The seminar used the Middle East conflict as its special illustrative case and included an intensive Israeli–Palestinian problem-solving workshop in which the seminar students participated as apprentice members of the third party. (In 1979, the illustrative case, to which the workshop was also devoted, was the Cyprus conflict.)

Despite the shift I have noted in the center of gravity of my work, I believe that there has been a remarkable degree of continuity over the years. It is true that a major turning point in my work occurred in the late 1960s and early 1970s, when I became acquainted (in 1966) with John Burton's work in conflict analysis and resolution, began to build on it theoretically and methodologically (e.g., Kelman, 1972a), made my first efforts to apply the approach in the Middle East, and finally committed myself (in 1973) to putting conflict resolution in the Middle East at the center of my professional agenda. However, my interest in the social psychology of international relations and in conflict resolution goes back to the very beginnings of my career, as I pointed out in the preceding section. This interest played an important role in my original selection of social psychology as a field of study, and it was reflected in much of my work in the 1950s and 1960s, including participation in the founding of the Research Exchange on the Prevention of War and the *Journal of Conflict Resolution*, editing of *International Behavior* (Kelman, 1965a), research on the impact of international educational and cultural exchanges (e.g., Kelman & Bailyn, 1962; Kelman & Ezekiel, 1970), and research on nationalism and the relation of the individual to the national system (e.g., DeLamater, Katz, & Kelman, 1969; Katz, Kelman, & Flacks, 1964; Kelman, 1969).

By the same token, social influence has remained a continuing theme, even as the center of gravity of my work shifted toward international conflict. My work with Lee Hamilton, culminating in *Crimes of Obedience* (Kelman & Hamilton, 1989), explores influence processes in hierarchical relationships. Furthermore, my conflict resolution work itself centers on a model of mutual influence in a conflict relationship and has drawn on my early interest in group processes as a source of significant attitude changes (see Kelman, 1997a). More generally, conflict as a multifaceted process of mutual influence is one of the key propositions in my analysis of the nature of international conflict (Kelman, 1997c), and influencing the other side is one of the key components of the macroprocess of negotiation (Kelman, 1996). In fact, I have tried to link the analysis of influence in international relations to my three processes of influence, and I believe I have come closest to doing so in my recent formulations of reconciliation, to which I shall return in the next section.

Finally, the continuity in my work over the years is provided by certain central themes that have characterized my work on social influence as well as on international conflict. In both areas, I have been particularly concerned with the depth and durability of change—whether in response to persuasive communications or to conflict resolution efforts; the role of individual change as a vehicle for change in the larger social system; the role of legitimacy in the relationship of individuals to hierarchical organizations and to the nation, the state, or other collectivities and institutions; and the moral dimension in human relations, including the ethical issues generated by the process and outcome of social scientists' own research and practice.

(4) In addition to my trademark graduate seminar, I have offered a trademark undergraduate course throughout my teaching career. The course had different titles at different times and its contents changed and evolved over the years, reflecting developments in the field (and in the world), new emphases in my own work, and differences in the definition of the overall theme of the course. But, many topics and illustrations survived over the years—including some of the jokes I used in my lectures, which I was reluctant to drop as long as they seemed to produce the desired response. In my first term at Harvard, the course was called Attitudes and Their Change. At the University of Michigan it became Attitudes and Social Behavior, a title already in the catalog. When I returned to Harvard as Cabot Professor of Social Ethics, I introduced a general education course entitled Human Values and Social Psychological Research to reflect the mission of my chair. I later moved the course, with appropriate modifications, into my department with the title Individual and Social Change. I also, during that period, included a weekend exercise as part of the course, using SIMSOC, an instructive simulation of the formation and functioning of a society developed by my colleague William Gamson (1978). On one occasion, we did a simulation of the Israeli–Palestinian conflict. In the fall of 1985, as Sterling McMurrin Distinguished Visiting Professor of Liberal Education at the University of Utah, I taught a course on Stability and Change: Recurrent Themes in Social and Political Psychology. On returning to Harvard, I restructured my trademark course and taught it under the title Stability and Change in Attitudes and Social Relations.

The last version of my trademark undergraduate course, which I taught five times in the 1990s, was a large-enrollment core curriculum course entitled Individual and Social Responsibility: A Social Psychological Perspective. Harvard's core curriculum identifies several different ways of knowing, not necessarily corresponding to established disciplines, to each of which students are expected to have some exposure. My course, which was part of the area of social analysis, was developed and originally taught with the assistance of Susan Korper, who has a superb level of knowledge and understanding of all strands of my work—including my work on attitudes, social influence, authority, ethics, conflict resolution, and the Middle East. She helped to devise an outline that somehow covered and integrated all of those domains, put together an appropriate reading list, and selected and edited a series of films illustrating central themes of the course. The course, using my own version of a rule-consequentialist approach to moral decision making, covered a wide range of topics in social psychology and related fields bearing on the question of how individuals—through personal and collective effort—determine and assume responsibility for their own actions and for public policies and practices. At various points throughout the course, I introduced "reflexive exercises," designed to turn our analysis of individual and social responsibility back on the behavior of social scientists themselves. This course gave me the opportunity to pull together virtually all of the themes that I had addressed over the years and to relate them to each other in a meaningful way. I found it particularly rewarding to present these ideas to a broad spectrum of students, most of whom concentrated in the natural sciences or humanities, and—in keeping with the terms of the Cabot chair—to offer them some of the tools for dealing with the ethical questions they would face in life and relating themselves to the social issues of the day.

A Social Psychological Perspective

The subtitle of my core curriculum course raises a question to which I address the remainder of this chapter. What do I mean by "a social psychological perspective"? Or, to reverse the question: What is my perspective on social psychology? I believe that the best answer to this question is provided by the preceding chapters in this volume. Despite their diversity—or, perhaps, in keeping with their diversity—they all illustrate, in one way or another, the particular perspective on social psychology that my work represents. Perhaps the best way I can even come close to integrating this rich set of papers is to offer a few observations about my particular perspective on the field that, I propose, they all share.

Definition of Social Psychology

Inside my copy of the classic text in social psychology by Krech and Crutchfield (1948), I found some pieces of paper with reactions to their introductory chapter that, from all indications, I had written close to the time the book was published—in other words, early in my graduate student years. I had some misgivings about their definition of social psychology as "the science of the behavior of the individual in society" (p. 7), especially their argument that person objects are similar to other objects, except for possessing certain special properties. In my notes, I argue that our reaction to other human beings cannot be compared, for example, with our reactions to wind or water, even though these share some of the properties of human beings, such as mobility and capriciousness. The notes grapple with the question of what precisely makes human objects unique for us.

I ultimately found my answer in the concept of social interaction, as developed primarily by sociologically based social psychologists. I remember feeling a sense of recognition in the summer of 1949, when I first heard Freed Bales (in a lecture at the University of Michigan, where he was teaching summer school) define social psychology as the study of social interaction. This definition goes beyond Krech and Crutchfield's in focusing on the behavior in society of *individuals in relation to one another*. Moreover, social interaction is more than behavioral interaction—more than action and reaction of individuals in one another's presence. It refers to the interaction between "minded" individuals, each of whom assumes that the other—just like the self—brings a set of expectations, intentions, and goals to the situation. Thus, participants in social interaction, in pursuit of their own needs and interests, engage in a continuing process of taking the other's role in order to assess and address the other's expectations, intentions, and goals. Social interaction is informed and guided by its societal and organizational context, which defines the nature of the situation in which the interaction takes place and the norms and rules that govern the interaction.

As my own conception of social psychology evolved, I brought the societal and organizational context of interaction explicitly into my definition of the field, while maintaining the focus on social interaction. This formulation corresponds to Shoshana Zuboff's (chap. 7, this volume) idea of social psychology's "middle kingdom" and to José Ramón Torregrosa's (chap. 2, this volume) call to give the sociological dimension the place it is due in our conception of social psychology. Thus, in a statement also cited by Torregrosa, I offer the following definition of the field:

> Social psychology—which is a sub-field of psychology as well as sociology—is concerned with the intersection between individual behavior and societal-institutional processes. It follows from this concern that the primary focus for social-psychological analysis is social interaction, which is, par excellence, the area in which individual and institutional processes intersect. Social interaction is thus the level of analysis that is most purely and most distinctly social-psychological. (Kelman, 1965a, p. 22)

A full analysis of social interaction requires simultaneous attention to variables at the level of the individual and of the social system as both inputs and outcomes of the interaction: How is the interaction shaped by what the individual participants bring to it and the societal/organizational context in which it occurs, and how does it, in turn, impact the subsequent functioning of the participants and of the larger social system (the group, organization, society, or collectivity) within which their interaction is an episode?

According to this definition, the subject matter of social psychology clearly includes the study of social interaction processes themselves, such as verbal and nonverbal communication, interpersonal relations, or small group dynamics. It also includes the functioning of individuals, as shaped by their direct or indirect interactions with other individuals, media, and institutions in negotiating their social environment, and as expressed in social attitudes, social roles, or collective identities; as well as the microprocesses of societal and organizational functioning, such as the social interactions through which leadership is exercised, decisions are made, or conflicts are managed. Most distinctively social psychological topics are those topics that explore relationships across the individual and social-system levels of analysis—i.e., the effects of societal/ organizational inputs on the behavior of individuals, or the effects of individual inputs on the functioning of societies or organizations—with social interaction, explicitly or implicitly, as the mediating process. A good example of the former relationship is the process of socialization into a society, profession, or movement, whereby the rules, roles, and values of the particular social system are transmitted (through various socializing agents) to individual members and expressed in their attitudes, beliefs, and actions. A good example of the latter relationship is the process of social protest, whereby the motives and perceptions of members of a society are translated (through various forms of collective action) into changes in societal policies and practices.

Social psychology, as I define it, is particularly well suited to exploring the relationship between individual change and social change. Changes at these two levels can best be conceived as linked to each other in a continuous, circular fashion. Structural changes, by way of various processes of social interaction, produce changes at the level of individuals, which in turn, by way of another set of interaction processes, produce new changes at the system level, and so on. Thus, for example, the U.S. civil rights movement in the 1950s and 1960s was spurred on by structural changes in the United States and elsewhere—such as the rise of a Black urban middle class and the establishment of independent states in sub-Saharan Africa; the resulting group mobilization and mass action promoted psychological changes in the form of development of group consciousness and of a sense of entitlement and efficacy, which in turn encouraged the organized use of political influence conducive to civil rights legislation and to changes in occupational, educational, and political structures. My interest in the relationship between individual change and social change was a major factor in my initial choice of social psychology as my field of endeavor and it became increasingly central to the way I conceptualized my work. Thus, as I came to look at social influence in terms of the linkage between the individual and the social system—and at the three processes as representing different types and avenues of linkage (cf. Kelman, 1974; Kelman & Hamilton, 1989; Kelman & Warwick, 1973)—it became clear that changes in individuals' attitudes and behavior in response to social influence may have consequences for the social system within which the influence relationship takes place. In my later work, I have stressed that my approach to conflict resolution—interactive problem solving—and its operationalization in problem-solving workshops are quintessentially social psychological in that they seek to induce changes in individuals, through interaction in small-group settings, as vehicles for change in the larger system: in the official policies and the political cultures of the conflicting parties.

The definition of social psychology that I have outlined here seems to cover the work presented in all of the preceding chapters. I am not suggesting that all of the authors would necessarily subscribe to my definition, but what all of the chapters have in common—despite the breadth and diversity of the topics they address—is embeddedness in a social psychology that explicitly assigns a central role to the societal and organizational context of the behavior and interaction of individuals. This view of the field, corresponding to Thomas Pettigrew's (1991) concept of *contextual social psychology,* distinguishes the work presented in this volume from much of the work that characterizes mainstream American social psychology today.

Features of Social Psychology

My perspective on social psychology has certain distinct features that are well represented in the various chapters in this volume.

(1) A direct implication of my definition of social psychology is a view of the field as an *interdisciplinary* enterprise. I am not merely referring to the fact that social psychological work often requires forays into other disciplines—which in my case have included, over the years, anthropology, clinical psychology/psychiatry, ethics, political science, international relations, and Middle East studies. I view social psychology itself as an interdisciplinary field, anchored in both psychology and sociology and bridging the levels of analysis peculiar to each of these fields. A symbolic indicator of the coparentage of social psychology is the fact that the first two texts in social psychology, published in the same year, were written by a psychologist and a sociologist, respectively (McDougall, 1908; Ross, 1908). Personally, the fact that I served as both president of the APA's Division of Personality and Social Psychology (1970–1971) and chair of the ASA's Section on Social Psychology (1977–1978) attests to my commitment to social psychology as an interdiscipline. My students have gone in a variety of directions. Of the chapter authors in this book, four have made their careers in psychology departments, three in sociology departments, three in political science or international relations, and one each in a medical school, a business school, and a social service organization.

(2) Social psychology, in my view, must of necessity rely on a *multiplicity of methods.* I was trained as an experimental social psychologist and conducted an active experimental program in the 1950s and 1960s. The work included a number of experimental tests of my three-process model of social influence (see Kelman, 1974, 1980). In the 1960s, during my period at the University of Michigan, I collaborated with Reuben Baron and our associates in a series of experiments designed to test a functional analysis of the effects of attitude-discrepant behavior on attitude change (Kelman, 1980; Kelman & Baron, 1974; Kelman et al., 1969). I have never abandoned my commitment to experimental research as an important and uniquely valuable component of the social psychologist's

methodological repertoire—even though I have not personally pursued an experimental program for many years. Experiments make a unique contribution by constructing a working model of a phenomenon, which allows us to vary its dimensions systematically and to establish causal relations. But I do not believe that social psychology can be a *purely* experimental science, with the goal of establishing general laws of social behavior. The relations observed in the laboratory are limited by their historical and cultural context, as well as by the structure of the experimental situation itself (Kelman, 1967b). Experimental research becomes useful when it is put together with findings yielded by a variety of other methods, which identify the phenomena to be explored in a laboratory setting and which help establish the generality and external validity of laboratory findings—methods that include opinion surveys, intensive interviewing, systematic observation, participant observation, participatory action research, discourse analysis, and content analysis of documents. The research of my students—as exemplified by the chapters in this volume—has been carried out both in the laboratory and in the field, has used experimental as well as the entire range of nonexperimental methods, and has applied systematic approaches to both quantitative and qualitative data analysis. Some of the research programs described in the preceding chapters—as well as some of the doctoral theses I have supervised, including those of Tamra Pearson d'Estrée (Pearson, 1990) and Rebecca Wolfe (2002)—use a triangulation approach, exploring the same phenomenon in different contexts and with different methods, which significantly enhances the generalizability of the findings.

(3) Another aspect of my view of social psychology is its character as a *cross-cultural, international* enterprise. Cross-cultural research does not refer only to research in which cultures, or types of cultures, serve as the independent variable. Clearly, such research is instructive, in correcting for cultural biases in our conceptions of human nature and in sensitizing us to cultural differences in normative expectations and in modes of satisfying basic human needs. A challenge to this genre of research is to avoid the temptation of essentializing cultural differences, by recognizing that such differences arise from particular historical, structural, and situational circumstances and can change as these circumstances change, and that intracultural variations on psychosocial dimensions are often as great as or greater than intercultural variations. But cross-cultural research also refers to studies in which general propositions are tested with cross-cultural data, as in the Whiting and Child (1953) study, on which I held my first assistantship; in which related phenomena are explored in a variety of cultural settings, as exemplified in Lee Hamilton's multifaceted research program (chap. 4, this volume); or in which new research programs are shaped within a different cultural context than the one in which social psychology has so far evolved, well exemplified by the work of Ignacio Martín-Baró and Maritza Montero as discussed by José R. Torregrosa (chap. 2, this volume). Such cross-cultural work is essential to the scientific development of the field, in producing a body of propositions and findings with increasingly general validity and universal applicability. To this end, it is necessary not only to test hypotheses with cross-cultural data, but to assure wide participation of investigators throughout the world (including, of course, the Third World) in the definition of research problems, the formulation of hypotheses, and the interpretation of findings. Sci-

entific requirements thus coincide with the ethical requirements of avoiding exploitation of developing societies and assuring that research carried out in these societies addresses their own problems and serves their own interests (Kelman, 1967a, 1982a). More broadly, my view of social psychology calls for the development of a transnational community committed to enhancing the capacities and opportunities of scholars around the world to participate in building the field. This concept was the underlying purpose of the International Conference on Social-Psychological Research in Developing Countries at the University of Ibadan that I organized and chaired (Kelman, 1968a).

(4) *Applied research and practice* based on social psychological principles are as central to my view of the agenda of our discipline as basic and theory-driven research. Paraphrasing Lewin's (1951) famous dictum, I believe that there is nothing so conducive to theoretical insight as reflective application and practice, and nothing so practical as a good theory.[6] I do not maintain that all social psychologists must engage in applied work or that all social psychological research must have obvious relevance to applied problems. But I do maintain that applied research and practice are not only legitimate foci for social-psychological work, but important avenues for enriching the discipline. The relationship between theory and application can take a variety of forms, ranging from Carl Hovland's research on attitude change—which generally started out with applied questions that he sought to answer with sophisticated theoretical analyses and experimental designs—to action research (of which my work on conflict resolution is one variant), in which theory and practice are fully integrated. Lewin's belief that the "attempt to bring about change in a process is the most fruitful way to investigate it" (Deutsch, 1968, p. 478) suggests that application and practice are particularly capable of contributing to theoretical understanding insofar as they are geared to producing change. The relationship between theory, application, and practice as a central feature of social psychology is clearly proclaimed in the subtitle and the tripartite division of the present book and is reflected in every one of its chapters.

(5) The applications of social psychology that are of particular interest to me are those directed to addressing urgent *social issues* and to the betterment of the human condition. The issues with which I have been especially concerned over the years, from a social psychological perspective, are war and peace, social justice, conflict resolution, civil rights and civil liberties, intergroup relations, social protest, and responsible citizenship. I identify with a social psychology

---

[6]The exact wording of Lewin's statement is as follows: "Many psychologists working today in an applied field are keenly aware of the need for close cooperation between theoretical and applied psychology. This can be accomplished in psychology, as it has been accomplished in physics, if the theorist does not look toward applied problems with highbrow aversion or with a fear of social problems, and if the applied psychologist realizes that there is nothing so practical as a good theory" (Lewin, 1951, p. 169). Generally, only the last phrase of this statement is cited. In part, no doubt, this reflects the particular interest of those who cite Lewin on this point. In part, however, I believe it is simply due to the fact that the first half of the aphorism is not stated as succinctly and forcefully as the second half. The second half clearly asserts the value of theory to application, whereas the first half merely admonishes theorists not to scorn applied work, without asserting that applied work is actually of value to theory building. I believe—perhaps presumptuously—that my paraphrasing is a more sharply drawn and balanced statement of the point Lewin wanted to make.

that is engaged with the problems of our society at the domestic and global levels, that encourages the systematic analysis of social problems and the integration of research with social action, and that recognizes and takes into account the inevitable involvement of our social and political values in social research (Kelman, 1968b). In line with this orientation, I have been an active member of the Society for the Psychological Study of Social Issues, which—as already mentioned—I joined in 1946, when I was still an undergraduate. In later years, my social-issues orientation to the field has also been expressed through groups like Psychologists for Social Responsibility, the Society for the Study of Peace, Conflict, and Violence (the APA's Peace Psychology Division), and the ASA's Section on Peace, War, and Conflict.

(6) Finally, the *ethical dimension* occupies an important place in my view of social psychology. Many of the traditional topics for social psychological research can be seen as a continuation of moral philosophy in a different guise. Good examples are studies that point to the shortcomings in moral behavior resulting from social pressures and cognitive biases, such as social conformity, groupthink, unquestioning obedience to authority, bystander apathy, prejudice, stereotyping, resistance to new information, and legitimization of oppressive practices. Social psychological research has also focused on conditions that strengthen the moral foundations of social life, including studies of social justice, helping behavior, cooperation, empathy, personal responsibility, forgiveness, moral reasoning, integrity in living up to one's values, and legitimacy in the exercise of power. Social psychology can thus contribute to our understanding of the empirical conditions for moral decision making and behavior, as well as our formulation of the assumptions about human nature and social order that underlie our approach to moral justification. Apart from the ethical dimension in the content of social psychology, I also consider it imperative for social psychologists (and other social scientists) to give systematic attention—as an integral part of their professional role—to the ethical implications of the processes and products of their research (Kelman, 1968b, 1972b).

Social Psychology in Practice

To round out this discussion of my perspective on social psychology, let me offer a few comments on how this perspective has shaped my thinking on the two topics that have been central foci of my work over many years: social influence and international conflict—and the relationship between them.

(1) As Lee Hamilton (chap. 4, this volume) points out, my three-process model is a model of *social influence*, as is clear from the title of my original essay (Kelman, 1956) and from most of my writings—although I may have muddied the waters by referring to "processes of attitude change" (Kelman, 1958) and "opinion change" (Kelman, 1961) in the titles of two early articles. As a social psychological model, it starts out with the structure of the influence situation and looks at influence within the context of the relationship between the influencing agent (O) and the person being influenced (P). The three processes distinguish between three types of relationship, best captured by the source of O's relative power over P (i.e., O's ability to affect the achievement of

P's goals relative to P's own power and the power of competing influencing agents): O's means control in the case of compliance, attractiveness in the case of identification, and credibility in the case of internalization (Kelman, 1958).[7] In view of the nature of the relationship that characterizes each process, compliance-based behavior tends to be manifested and sustained only under conditions of surveillance by O, and identification-based behavior only as long as P's relationship to O remains salient and satisfying, whereas internalized behavior—though rooted in P's relationship to O—becomes part of P's own value system and independent of the original source.

From the beginning, I viewed the three-process model as relevant to the entire range of influence situations, well beyond the persuasive communication setting in which I originally tested it. Thus, I applied it to analysis of changes in psychotherapy (Kelman, 1963), effects of international exchange experiences (Bailyn & Kelman, 1962), and the development of individuals' ethnic identity (Kelman, 1998b). In the 1960s, with my work (in collaboration with Daniel Katz) on nationalism and personal involvement in the national system, and with my increasing fascination with the concept of legitimacy, I began to extend the model to the analysis of the relationship of individuals to the state or other social systems, and to the nation or other collective entities (e.g., Kelman, 1969, 1997b). These efforts eventually led me to reconceptualize social influence, generically, in terms of linkage between the individual and the social system, and the three processes as three ways in which individuals may be linked to the system—three ways in which they meet demands from the state, nation, society, organization, or group and in which they maintain their personal integration in it (Kelman, 1974).

Each process, in this view, refers to a distinct component of the social system that generates standards for the behavior of individual members and provides a vehicle for their integration in the system: system *rules* in the case of compliance, system *roles* in the case of identification, and system *values* in the case of internalization. Rules, roles, and values are social psychological concepts par excellence, in that they bridge the individual and the societal/organizational levels of analysis. Rules, roles, and values are properties of the social system (the society or organization) that define the relationship of its members to the system and that are adopted—to different degrees and in different ways—by individual members. (Individuals, of course, each have their own constellation of rules, roles, and values, corresponding to the array of groups with which they are affiliated.) Conceptualizing social influence in terms of linkages between the individual and the social system places the three-process model squarely within my definition of social psychology as the field concerned with the intersection between individual behavior and societal-institutional processes. Social interaction, it will be recalled, is the point at which individual and organizational processes intersect.

---

[7]The three-process model—in which the source of O's power is one of three distinct antecedent conditions postulated for each process, and the one that was manipulated in the first experimental test of the model—shows many points of contact with French and Raven's (1959) model, distinguishing five bases of social power, which they developed independently at the same time. The overlaps are not surprising in view of the fact that both models draw heavily on Lewin's discussion of own versus induced forces (see, e.g., Deutsch, 1968, pp. 457–460).

Accordingly, the microprocess of social influence—the relationship between P and O postulated for each of the three processes—can be seen as an episode within the larger social system that provides the context for their interaction and for which that interaction has consequences.

The rule–role–value distinction served as a basis for identifying different emotional reactions experienced by individuals when they find themselves deviating from societal standards of responsibility or propriety (Kelman, 1974, 1980). These distinctions generated a model that predicts the kinds of concerns that are likely to be aroused and the way individuals are likely to deal with them, depending on whether the standards they have violated are compliance based (rules), identification based (role expectations), or internalized (social values). When the violated standards are in the domain of responsibility, the concerns take the form of social fear, guilt, and regret, respectively; when they are in the domain of propriety, the concerns take the form of embarrassment, shame, and self-disappointment, respectively. Nancy Adler (1974) tested this model in her doctoral dissertation with women who had undergone abortion. As she reminds us (especially me) in her contribution to this *Festschrift* (chap. 5, this volume), the edited volume on varieties of discrepant action, to which I invited her to contribute a chapter, never saw the light of day. I am very grateful to her for using her chapter in this volume to present a summary of the model and of her findings. I have never undertaken any empirical tests of this model myself, but I have used it extensively in my undergraduate teaching; my lecture on embarrassment, in particular, was always the highlight of my course.

I have used the concepts of rules, roles, and values most extensively in the distinction between three types of political orientation that characterize the way in which individuals relate themselves to political authority and define the citizen role. Lee Hamilton and I, in collaboration with Frederick Miller and later also John Winkler, developed scales of rule orientation, role orientation, and value orientation (as well as scales of sentimental and instrumental attachment) to the political system. Discussion of the three political orientations and findings based on the use of the three orientation scales are central components of our analysis in *Crimes of Obedience* (Kelman & Hamilton, 1989). Rule, role, and value orientations also formed the core of an analysis of civic responsibility that I presented at the inauguration of Alfred Bloom (another one of my doctoral students) as president of Swarthmore College (Kelman, 1993b). Finally, in my analysis of movements of social protest (e.g., Kelman, 1970, 1984), I eventually distinguished between rule-oriented, role-oriented, and value-oriented protest movements, based on the extent to which a movement focuses primarily on struggle over resources, status, or policy, respectively.

(2) As my work came to focus increasingly on international conflict, I did not abandon my interest in social influence, as I have already pointed out in the earlier comments on the continuities in my work. The microprocess of interactive problem solving, to which I shall return later, is in essence a process of mutual influence. At the macrolevel, as well, influence is a central component of my analysis of international conflict (Kelman, 1997c) and negotiation (Kelman, 1996). As Reuben Baron (chap. 1, this volume) notes, I have even applied the distinction between my three processes of influence to international and

intercommunal conflict resolution—a natural extension, since in both lines of work I have been concerned with the *quality* of change: its depth, durability, sustainability, and integration in the belief systems of individuals and societies. What has eluded me for some time, however, has been a precise match of influence processes at the international/intergroup level to the three processes of social influence that I distinguished in my earlier work. I am indebted to Nadim Rouhana for providing that match with his treatment of conflict settlement, conflict resolution, and reconciliation as three distinct processes (chap. 10, this volume). Although my view of reconciliation—both in general and, specifically, in the Israeli–Palestinian case—differs from Nadim's in a number of important respects, I am persuaded of the value of the qualitative three-way distinction and I feel that it offers the link to the three processes of influence that I have been looking for.

Establishing this link is, of course, esthetically pleasing to me, but the ultimate question is whether it is analytically useful. Does the link of conflict settlement to compliance, conflict resolution to identification, and reconciliation to internalization provide conceptual handles for distinguishing qualitatively different types of peacemaking with distinct antecedent and consequent conditions? I argue that it does in a recent paper (Kelman, in press), which focuses in particular on the correspondence of reconciliation at the intergroup level to internalization at the level of the individual. I conceptualize reconciliation as a change in each side's group identity—at least to the extent of removing negation of the other as part of one's own identity—in a way that strengthens the *core* of the identity, just as internalization represents a change in specific attitudes and beliefs as a way of maintaining the integrity of the person's value system as a whole. In short, conflict settlement in this scheme involves a mutual accommodation of the parties' *interests*, conflict resolution an accommodation in their *relationship*, and reconciliation an accommodation of their *identities*. This distinction points to three broad tasks that all social entities—individuals, groups, organizations, societies—must address as they negotiate their social environment and seek to balance the requirements of self-maintenance and social order: protecting and promoting their interests, establishing and maintaining their relationships, and affirming and expressing their identities.[8]

Interests, relationship, and identity are social psychological concepts, in the sense that they refer to the relationship between individuals and the social system, and also in the sense that they refer to properties of both individuals and social systems. Individuals have interests, relationships, and identities, which they pursue and express through the various groups and organizations with which they are affiliated. The groups and organizations—formed, essentially, to serve their members—in turn develop their own interests, relationships, and identities, which become personally important to the members and

---

[8]This distinction was foreshadowed in an earlier paper on ethical issues in social science research (Kelman, 1982b), in which I distinguished three types of ethically germane impacts of research, conceptually linked to the three processes of influence and the three types of system orientation: impact on the concrete interests of research participants, on the quality of interpersonal relationships, and on wider social values.

which the members are expected to support. These three concepts broaden the three-process model to capture the interaction of individuals or groups with each other and with larger social systems in a variety of social contexts and their integration in these social systems. The microprocesses of social influence can be subsumed under this broader framework by distinguishing three foci for the interaction between P and O: The interaction may center on participants' *interests,* whose coordination is governed by a system of enforceable *rules,* with which individuals are expected to *comply;* on the participants' *relationship,* which is managed through a system of shared *roles,* with which individuals *identify;* or on participants' *identities,* expressing a *value* system that individuals *internalize.*

(3) In enumerating my mentors, I did not include John Burton, because I did not meet him until 1966, when I was 39 years old—well beyond what I described as my "formative years" earlier in this chapter. But Burton's work (e.g., 1969, 1979) on the analysis and resolution of international conflict and his model of unofficial diplomacy have had a profound impact on my subsequent work (see, e.g., Kelman, 1972a, 1999). What particularly excited me about his approach—when I first heard about it in 1966 and then had the opportunity later that year to participate in an exercise on the Cyprus conflict that he organized at the University of London—was that I saw it as a distinctly social psychological form of practice. Burton's method, in my parochial view, was a way of putting into practice the theoretical ideas about social psychological dimensions of international conflict that I had been thinking and writing about.

My particular variant of conflict resolution—which I have come to call *interactive problem solving*—has evolved out of the problem-solving workshops that my colleagues and I have conducted over the years, particularly on the Israeli–Palestinian conflict (Cohen, Kelman, Miller, & Smith, 1977; Kelman, 1986; Rouhana & Kelman, 1994). The basic principles and procedures of our approach are derived from Burton's work, although the precise form it has taken has been influenced by our particular disciplinary background and intervention style and by the nature and history of the particular conflict on which our efforts have focused. The work has remained exciting to me over the decades because it continues to evolve as historical circumstances change and we are faced with new challenges. What has made it personally rewarding as well is the extent to which it draws on virtually everything I have done as a social scientist and social activist over the years, including my work on international conflict, social influence, individual and social change, group process, nationalism and national identity, and international contact and exchange, and my experiences in nonviolent direct action and my personal involvement in the Middle East.

In my earlier discussion of the definition of social psychology, I repeated my frequent observation that interactive problem solving and its operationalization in problem-solving workshops are quintessentially social psychological in that they seek to induce changes in individuals, through interaction in small groups, as vehicles for change in the larger social system—in the policies and the political cultures of the conflicting societies. I like to tell people that I "think small," which is true in the sense that I organize small-scale events, on a modest budget, with individuals who are generally not political decision makers, and I make no claims to resolving the conflict and bringing peace by these means. My only claim is that we make a small *contribution* to the larger peace process by using our academic base to work with individuals and small groups from the conflicting societies. But, however small the contribution may be, our microprocess is designed systematically to promote change at the macrolevel. The problem of transfer of changes from the workshop to the political process is a central theoretical issue that I have addressed in my writings from the beginning (e.g., Kelman, 1972a, 1993a); more recently, Cynthia Chataway (2002; see also chap. 12, this volume) has written about the issue. Many of the features of the workshop are specifically designed to balance the requirements for maximizing change within the workshop against the requirements for maximizing transfer to the larger process. Most notably, we prefer to work with participants who are not officials, but who are politically influential in their own communities. They are thus less constrained in their workshop interactions, but they occupy positions that enable them to transfer what they have learned to decision makers, political elites, and the wider public.

My conception of the problem-solving workshop reflects my earlier experience with two other social constructions: the social psychological experiment and the nonviolent direct-action project, as illustrated by the lunch-counter sit-ins organized by Baltimore CORE in the early 1950s. As a form of action research, the workshop combines elements traceable to both of these models.

Like an experiment, the workshop creates a microcosm in a relatively isolated, self-contained, and controlled laboratory setting, in which some of the forces that operate in the larger system (or the real world) can be activated, observed, and analyzed.[9] Good conflict resolution practitioners, like good experimenters, know that the microcosm they have constructed is not the real world, and that the contribution of their work to understanding and changing the real world ultimately depends on systematic attention to how the products of the laboratory interaction are generalized and transferred to the larger system.

Like nonviolent direct action, interactive problem solving is based on a model of social change that envisages complementary efforts at many system levels. Microlevel activities, such as bringing together individual members of conflicting parties in a workshop or organizing a sit-in at a neighborhood department store, can contribute to the larger process by challenging assumptions, raising consciousness, and introducing new ideas, which gradually change the political culture and increase the likelihood of change at the level of political leadership, institutional bodies, and official policy. Microlevel projects are more likely to make such contributions insofar as they have built-in multiplier effects, achieved, for example, by strategic selection of the participants in a workshop or of the target of a direct-action campaign.

All three of these models rely on the cumulative effect of small efforts. Each workshop, each experiment, each direct-action project makes its contribution as

---

[9]It should be noted that workshops differ from experiments in that they are not simulations of the real world. They involve real members of the conflicting parties engaged in a very real and often consequential interaction around the issues that divide their societies.

one element in a larger program, which in turn is one program among many related undertakings that build on each other and together provide some of the insights and tools for gradually improving the world. To produce a cumulative effect, however, requires more than accumulating workshops, experiments, or campaigns. It requires integrating work at this level with work at other levels that it is meant to complement and reinforce. Thus, interactive problem solving needs to be integrated with official negotiations, grassroots efforts, and public education to promote conflict resolution at the macrolevel, just as experimental research needs to be integrated with survey, observational, and historical research to produce valid knowledge of the social world, and nonviolent direct action needs to be integrated with negotiation, political action, and economic pressure to promote change in social policies and practices.

Conclusion

The observation about the cumulative effect of small efforts seems like an appropriate point on which to conclude this chapter, whose underlying theme has been the cumulative effect of our enterprise across generations.

In the spirit of a *Festschrift*, the contributors to this volume have all commented on the influence that I have had on their work. This influence is not necessarily reflected in the content of the work, but may manifest itself in the kinds of problems they have chosen to work on, the way in which they have approached them, and the professional roles they have carved out for themselves. I like to believe that—apart from exposing them to a few useful ideas—I have contributed to the professional development of my students by encouraging, modeling, and legitimizing ways of doing social psychology that are congruent with their own interests and orientations, even if they do not always correspond to traditional patterns.

Contemplating the influence that I may have had on my students led me quite naturally to focus, in this chapter, on those who significantly influenced my own thinking and shaped the kind of social psychology that I practice—ranging from Kurt Lewin, who almost became my mentor; through Daniel Katz and Carl Hovland and my other mentors and teachers during my formative years; to John Burton and Gordon Allport, in whose footsteps I have had the privilege of following. I believe that influences from these diverse sources can be found, not only in my own work, but also in the work of my students. It is probably difficult, if not impossible, to trace specific influences, but the cumulative effect of the flow of influence across generations seems evident in the contributions to this volume.

I am not able to summarize or integrate this diverse set of contributions, but I can, in conclusion, sketch three elements of the perspective on social psychology that the contributions (and the contributors) seem to share:

- The contributions to this volume are all examples of contextual social psychology (Pettigrew, 1991), which systematically looks at the behavior and interaction of individuals in their societal and organizational context. Daniel Katz, incidentally, was a leading exponent of this view of psychology (see, e.g., Katz & Kahn, 1966). Of necessity, such an approach tends to be interdisciplinary, as illustrated by many of the contributions. In fact, perhaps a third of the contributors are not card-carrying social psychologists; they practice social psychology from a different disciplinary base.

- The work discussed in this volume is problem-driven, rather than method-driven or even theory-driven. Though many of the chapters feature theoretical analysis, they tend to direct this analysis to problems of application or practice, in the spirit of Carl Hovland and Kurt Lewin.

- All of the contributors focus on the study of social issues and the solution of social problems, in the spirit of SPSSI (in which Gordon Allport, Kurt Lewin, and Daniel Katz were all leading figures) and of John Burton and the scholar-practitioner model. In keeping with this orientation, they display sensitivity to the ethical dimension of the work of the social psychologist and other social scientists. They embrace a social science that seeks to find ways of enhancing one group's identity without denying the identity of other groups, of resolving social conflicts by peaceful and constructive means, and of otherwise contributing to the betterment of the human condition.

References

Adler, N. (1974). *Reactions of women to therapeutic abortion: A social-psychological analysis.* Unpublished doctoral dissertation, Harvard University, Cambridge, MA.

Allport, F. H. (1933). *Institutional behavior: Essays toward a re-interpretation of contemporary social organization.* Chapel Hill: University of North Carolina Press.

Bailyn, L., & Kelman, H. C. (1962). The effects of a year's experience in America on the self-image of Scandinavians: A preliminary analysis of reactions to a new environment. *Journal of Social Issues, 18*(1), 30–40.

Bentinck-Smith, W., & Stouffer, E. (1991). *Harvard University: History of named chairs.* Cambridge, MA: Harvard University.

Bermant, G., Kelman, H. C., & Warwick, D. P. (Eds.). (1978). *The ethics of social intervention.* Washington, DC: Hemisphere Publishing Corporation.

Burton, J. W. (1969). *Conflict and communication: The use of controlled communication in international relations.* London: Macmillan.

Burton, J. W. (1979). *Deviance, terrorism and war: The process of solving unsolved social and political problems.* New York: St. Martin's Press.

Cantril, H. (1941). *The psychology of social movements.* New York: Wiley.

Chataway, C. J. (2002). The problem of transfer from confidential interactive problem-solving: What is the role of the facilitator? *Political Psychology, 23,* 165–191.

Cohen, S. P., Kelman, H. C., Miller, F. D., & Smith, B. L. (1977). Evolving intergroup techniques for conflict resolution: An Israeli–Palestinian pilot workshop. *Journal of Social Issues, 33*(1), 165–189.

DeLamater, J., Katz, D., & Kelman, H. C. (1969). On the nature of national involvement: A preliminary study. *Journal of Conflict Resolution, 13,* 320–357.

Deutsch, M. (1968). Field theory in social psychology. In G. Lindzey & E. Aronson (Eds.), *The handbook of social psychology* (2nd ed., Vol. 1, pp. 412–487). Reading, MA: Addison-Wesley.

Dollard, J. L., Doob, L. W., Miller, N. E., Mowrer, O. H., & Sears, R. R. (1939). *Frustration and aggression.* New Haven, CT: Yale University Press.

Dollard, J., & Miller, N. E. (1950). *Personality and psychotherapy: An analysis in terms of learning, thinking, and culture.* New York: McGraw-Hill.

Doob, L. W. (1947). The behavior of attitudes. *Psychological Review, 54,* 135–156.

Frank, J. D. (1944a). Experimental studies of personal pressure and resistance: I. Experimental production of resistance. *Journal of General Psychology, 30,* 23–41.

Frank, J. D. (1944b). Experimental studies of personal pressure and resistance: II. Methods of overcoming resistance. *Journal of General Psychology, 30,* 43–56.

Frank, J. D. (1961). *Persuasion and healing: A comparative study of psychotherapy.* Baltimore: Johns Hopkins Press.

French, J. R. P., Jr., & Raven, B. (1959). The bases of social power. In D. Cartwright (Ed.), *Studies in social power* (pp. 150–167). Ann Arbor, MI: Institute for Social Research.

Freud, S. (1950). *Collected papers* (Vol. II). London: Hogarth Press. (Original work published 1924)

Fromm, E. (1941). *Escape from freedom.* New York: Rinehart.

Gamson, W. A. (1978). *SIMSOC: Simulated Society* (3rd ed.). New York: Free Press.

Gladstone, A. I., & Kelman, H. C. (1951). Pacifists vs. psychologists. *American Psychologist, 6,* 127–128.

Himmelfarb, S., & Eagly, A. H. (1974). Orientations to the study of attitudes and their change. In S. Himmelfarb & A. H. Eagly (Eds.), *Readings in attitude change* (pp. 2–49). New York: Wiley.

Hollander, E. P. (1958). Conformity, status, and idiosyncrasy credit. *Psychological Review, 65,* 117–127.

Hovland, C. I., Janis, I. L., & Kelley, H. H. (1953). *Communication and persuasion.* New Haven, CT: Yale University Press.

Hull, C. L. (1943). *Principles of behavior.* New York: Appleton-Century-Crofts.

Katz, D. (1960). The functional approach to the study of attitudes. *Public Opinion Quarterly, 24,* 163–204.

Katz, D. (1973). The Kurt Lewin Memorial Award presentation by the Society for the Psychological Study of Social Issues to Herbert C. Kelman. *Journal of Social Issues, 29*(4), 21–22.

Katz, D., & Kahn, R. L. (1966). *The social psychology of organizations.* New York: Wiley.

Katz, D., Kelman, H. C., & Flacks, R. (1964). The national role: Some hypotheses about the relation of individuals to nation in America today. *Peace Research Society (International) Papers, 1,* 113–127.

Katz, D., & Schank, R. L. (1938). *Social psychology.* New York: Wiley.

Kelman, H. C. (1950a). Effects of success and failure on "suggestibility" in the autokinetic situation. *Journal of Abnormal and Social Psychology, 45,* 267–285.

Kelman, H. C. (1950b). Group dynamics—neither hope nor hoax. *Quarterly Journal of Speech, 36*(3), 2–8.

Kelman, H. C. (1953). Attitude change as a function of response restriction. *Human Relations, 6,* 185–214.

Kelman, H. C. (1955). Societal, attitudinal and structural factors in international relations. *Journal of Social Issues, 11*(1), 42–56.

Kelman, H. C. (1956). *Compliance, identification, and internalization: A theoretical and experimental approach to the study of social influence.* Unpublished manuscript, submitted to the American Association for the Advancement of Science and awarded the AAAS Socio-Psychological Prize.

Kelman, H. C (1957, February). Security and federal employment: A recent case study. *SPSSI Newsletter,* pp. 1–4.

Kelman, H. C. (1958). Compliance, identification, and internalization: Three processes of attitude change. *Journal of Conflict Resolution, 2,* 51–60.

Kelman, H. C. (1961). Processes of opinion change. *Public Opinion Quarterly, 25,* 57–78.

Kelman, H. C. (1963). The role of the group in the induction of therapeutic change. *International Journal of Group Psychotherapy, 13,* 399–432.

Kelman, H. C. (Ed.). (1965a). *International behavior: A social-psychological analysis.* New York: Holt, Rinehart & Winston.

Kelman, H. C. (1965b). Manipulation of human behavior: An ethical dilemma for the social scientist. *Journal of Social Issues, 21*(2), 31–46.

Kelman, H. C. (1967a). Psychological research on social change: Some scientific and ethical issues. *International Journal of Psychology, 2,* 301–313.

Kelman, H. C. (1967b). Rigor vs. vigor: Some dubious issues in the debate on research philosophy. *Revista Interamericana de Psicología, 1,* 205–222. (See also chap. 6 in Kelman, 1968b.)

Kelman, H. C. (1968a). Social psychology and national development: Background of the Ibadan conference. *Journal of Social Issues*, *24*(2), 9–20.

Kelman, H. C. (1968b). *A time to speak: On human values and social research*. San Francisco: Jossey-Bass.

Kelman, H. C. (1969). Patterns of personal involvement in the national system: A social-psychological analysis of political legitimacy. In J. N. Rosenau (Ed.), *International politics and foreign policy* (rev. ed., pp. 276–288). New York: Free Press.

Kelman, H. C. (1970). A social-psychological model of political legitimacy and its relevance to black and white student protest movements. *Psychiatry, 33*, 224–246.

Kelman, H. C. (1972a). The problem-solving workshop in conflict resolution. In R. L. Merritt (Ed.), *Communication in international politics* (pp. 168–204). Urbana: University of Illinois Press.

Kelman, H. C. (1972b). The rights of the subject in social research: An analysis in terms of relative power and legitimacy. *American Psychologist, 27*, 989–1016.

Kelman, H. C. (1973). Violence without moral restraint: Reflections on the dehumanization of victims and victimizers. *Journal of Social Issues, 29*(4), 25–61.

Kelman, H. C. (1974). Social influence and linkages between the individual and the social system: Further thoughts on the processes of compliance, identification, and internalization. In J. Tedeschi (Ed.), *Perspectives on social power* (pp. 125–171). Chicago: Aldine.

Kelman, H. C. (1980). The role of action in attitude change. In H. E. Howe, Jr., & M. M. Page (Eds.), *Nebraska symposium on motivation, 1979: Attitudes, values, and beliefs* (pp. 117–194). Lincoln: University of Nebraska Press.

Kelman, H. C. (1982a). A changing social science for a changing world: A social psychologist's perspective. In H. Fahim (Ed.), *Indigenous anthropology in non-Western countries* (pp. 269–283). Durham, NC: Carolina Academic Press.

Kelman, H. C. (1982b). Ethical issues in different social science methods. In T. L. Beauchamp, R. R. Faden, R. J. Wallace, Jr., & L. Walters (Eds.), *Ethical issues in social science research* (pp. 40–98). Baltimore: Johns Hopkins University Press.

Kelman, H. C. (1984). Protest movements. In *The phenomenon of change* (p. 20). New York: Cooper-Hewitt Museum.

Kelman, H. C. (1986). Interactive problem solving: A social-psychological approach to conflict resolution. In W. Klassen (Ed.), *Dialogue toward interfaith understanding* (pp. 293–314). Tantur/Jerusalem: Ecumenical Institute for Theological Research.

Kelman, H. C. (1991a). Interactive problem solving: The uses and limits of a therapeutic model for the resolution of international conflicts. In V. D. Volkan, J. V. Montville, & D. A. Julius (Eds.), *The psychodynamics of international relationships, Volume II: Unofficial diplomacy at work* (pp. 145–160). Lexington, MA: Lexington Books.

Kelman, H. C. (1991b). On the history and development of peace research: Personal reflections. In J. Nobel (Ed.), *The coming of age of peace research: Studies in the development of a discipline* (pp. 25–37). Groningen, The Netherlands: STYX Publications.

Kelman, H. C. (1993a). Coalitions across conflict lines: The interplay of conflicts within and between the Israeli and Palestinian communities. In S. Worchel & J. A. Simpson (Eds.), *Conflict between people and groups* (pp. 236–258). Chicago: Nelson-Hall.

Kelman, H. C. (1993b). Conceptions of civic responsibility and the role of education in a multicultural world. In B. Schwartz (Ed.), *The Swarthmore papers, Vol. 1: Educating for civic responsibility in a multicultural world* (pp. 33–49). Swarthmore, PA: Swarthmore College.

Kelman, H. C. (1996). Negotiation as interactive problem solving. *International Negotiation: A Journal of Theory and Practice, 1*, 99–123.

Kelman, H. C. (1997a). Group processes in the resolution of international conflicts: Experiences from the Israeli–Palestinian case. *American Psychologist, 52*, 212–220.

Kelman, H. C. (1997b). Nationalism, patriotism, and national identity: Social-psychological dimensions. In D. Bar-Tal & E. Staub (Eds.), *Patriotism in the lives of individuals and groups* (pp. 165–189). Chicago: Nelson-Hall.

Kelman, H. C. (1997c). Social-psychological dimensions of international conflict. In I. W. Zartman & J. L. Rasmussen (Eds.), *Peacemaking in international conflict: Methods and techniques* (pp. 191–237). Washington, DC: United States Institute of Peace Press.

Kelman, H. C. (1998a). Interactive problem solving: An approach to conflict resolution and its application in the Middle East. *PS: Political Science and Politics, 31*, 190–198.

Kelman, H. C. (1998b). The place of ethnic identity in the development of personal identity: A challenge for the Jewish family. In P. Y. Medding (Ed.), *Coping with life and death: Jewish families in the twentieth century* (Studies in Contemporary Jewry: An Annual, Vol. XIV, pp. 3–26). New York: Oxford University Press.

Kelman, H. C. (1998c). Social-psychological contributions to peacemaking and peacebuilding in the Middle East. *Applied Psychology: An International Review, 47,* 5–28.

Kelman, H. C. (1999). Experiences from 30 years of action research on the Israeli–Palestinian conflict. In K. R. Spillmann & A. Wenger (Eds.), *Zeitgeschichtliche Hintergründe aktueller Konflikte VII: Zürcher Beiträge zur Sicherheitspolitik und Konfliktforschung,* Nr. 54, 173–197.

Kelman, H. C. (2001a). Dignity and dehumanization: The impact of the Holocaust on central themes of my work. In P. Suedfeld (Ed.), *Light from the ashes: Social science careers of young Holocaust refugees and survivors* (pp. 197–220). Ann Arbor: University of Michigan Press.

Kelman, H. C. (2001b). Reflections on the social and psychological processes of legitimization and delegitimization. In J. T. Jost & B. Major (Eds.), *The psychology of legitimacy: Emerging perspectives on ideology, justice, and intergroup relations* (pp. 54–76). Cambridge, England: Cambridge University Press.

Kelman, H. C. (in press). Reconciliation as identity change: A social-psychological perspective. In Y. Bar-Siman-Tov (Ed.), *From conflict resolution to reconciliation*. Oxford, England: Oxford University Press.

Kelman, H. C., Alexander, F., & Stein, M. I. (1958, September). *Some psychological correlates of six somatic disturbances*. Paper presented at the meeting of the American Psychological Association, Washington, DC.

Kelman, H. C., & Bailyn, L. (1962). Effects of cross-cultural experience on national images: A study of Scandinavian students in America. *Journal of Conflict Resolution, 6,* 319–334.

Kelman, H. C., & Baron, R. M. (1968). Determinants of modes of resolving inconsistency dilemmas: A functional analysis. In R. P. Abelson et al. (Eds.), *Theories of cognitive consistency: A sourcebook* (pp. 670–683). Chicago: Rand McNally.

Kelman, H. C., & Baron, R. M. (1974). Moral and hedonic dissonance: A functional analysis of the relationship between discrepant action and attitude change. In S. Himmelfarb & A. H. Eagly (Eds.), *Readings in attitude change* (pp. 558–575). New York: Wiley.

Kelman, H. C., Baron, R. M., Sheposh, J. P., Lubalin, J. S., Dabbs, J. M., & Johnson, E. (1969). *Studies in attitude-discrepant behavior*. Unpublished manuscript, University of Michigan, Ann Arbor.

Kelman, H. C., Barth, W., & Hefner, R. (Eds.) (1955). Research approaches to the study of war and peace. *Journal of Social Issues, 11*(1), 1–57.

Kelman, H. C., & Eagly, A. H. (1965). Attitude toward the communicator, perception of communication content, and attitude change. *Journal of Personality and Social Psychology, 1,* 63–78.

Kelman, H. C., & Ezekiel, R. S., with the collaboration of Kelman, R. B. (1970). *Cross-national encounters: The personal impact of an exchange program for broadcasters*. San Francisco: Jossey-Bass.

Kelman, H. C., & Hamilton, V. L. (1989). *Crimes of obedience: Toward a social psychology of authority and responsibility*. New Haven, CT: Yale University Press.

Kelman, H. C., & Parloff, M. B. (1957). Interrelations among three criteria of improvement in group therapy: Comfort, effectiveness, and self-awareness. *Journal of Abnormal and Social Psychology, 54,* 281–288.

Kelman, H. C., & Warwick, D. P. (1973). Bridging micro and macro approaches to social change: A social-psychological perspective. In G. Zaltman (Ed.), *Processes and phenomena of social change* (pp. 13–59). New York: Wiley.

Krech, D., & Crutchfield, R. S. (1948). *Theory and problems of social psychology*. New York: McGraw-Hill.

Lerner, H. H., & Kelman, H. C. (Eds.). (1952). Group methods in psychotherapy, social work and adult education. *Journal of Social Issues, 8*(2), 1–90.

Lewin, K. (1948). *Resolving social conflicts*. New York: Harper.

Lewin, K. (1951). *Field theory in social science: Selected theoretical papers*. New York: Harper.

Lewin, K., Lippitt, R., & White, R. K. (1939). Patterns of aggressive behavior in experimentally created social climates. *Journal of Social Psychology, 10,* 271–301.

Lippitt, R. (1940). An experimental study of the effect of democratic and authoritarian group atmospheres. *University of Iowa Studies*, *16*(3), 43–198.

Marrow, A. J. (1969). *The practical theorist: The life and work of Kurt Lewin*. New York: Basic Books.

May, M. A. (1943). *A social psychology of war and peace*. New Haven, CT: Yale University Press.

McDougall, W. (1908). *An introduction to social psychology*. London: Methuen.

Miller, N. E., & Dollard, J. (1941). *Social learning and imitation*. New Haven, CT: Yale University Press.

Oppenheimer, F. (1975). *The state*. New York: Free Life Editions. (Original work published 1914)

Parloff, M. B., Kelman, H. C., & Frank, J. D. (1954). Comfort, effectiveness, and self-awareness as criteria of improvement in psychotherapy. *American Journal of Psychiatry*, *111,* 343–351.

Pearson, T. (1990). *The role of "symbolic gestures" in intergroup conflict resolution: Addressing group identity*. Unpublished doctoral dissertation, Harvard University, Cambridge, MA.

Pettigrew, T. F. (1991). Toward unity and bold theory: Popperian suggestions for two persistent problems of social psychology. In C. W. Stephan, W. G. Stephan, & T. F. Pettigrew (Eds.), *The future of social psychology* (pp. 13–27). New York: Springer-Verlag.

Ross, E. A. (1908). *Social psychology*. New York: Macmillan.

Rouhana, N. N., & Kelman, H. C. (1994). Promoting joint thinking in international conflict: An Israeli–Palestinian continuing workshop. *Journal of Social Issues*, *50*(1), 157–178.

Sherif, M. (1936). *The psychology of social norms*. New York: Harper.

Suedfeld, P. (Ed.). (2001). *Light from the ashes: Social science careers of young Holocaust refugees and survivors*. Ann Arbor: University of Michigan Press.

Whiting, J. W. M., & Child, I. L. (1953). *Child training and personality: A cross-cultural study*. New Haven, CT: Yale University Press.

Wolfe, R. (2002). *Perceptions of equality: How power asymmetries affect joint problem solving*. Unpublished doctoral dissertation, Harvard University, Cambridge, MA.

Appendix A _____

Herbert C. Kelman's Graduate and Postgraduate Advisees

List I: Doctoral Candidates for Whom H. C. Kelman Served as Primary Thesis Adviser (*Doktorvater*)

Peter Lenrow (1960)
C. Keith Conners (1960)
John B. P. Shaffer (1961)
Jonas R. Cohler (1962)
Marjorie H. Klein (1964)
Alice H. Eagly (1965)
Margaret Hofeller (1966)
Anneliese Bowlby (1968)
Alan Guskin (1968)
John D. DeLamater (1969)
James Lubalin (1969)
Sumru Erkut (1972)
John C. Gibbs (1972)
Janet Ward Schofield (1972)
Nancy Adler (1973)
Alfred Bloom (1974)
V. Lee Hamilton (1974)

Frederick D. Miller (1975)
Kelin Gersick (1976)
Luc Reychler (1976)
John A. Smetanka (1977)
Michael Sam-Vargas (1980)
Shoshana Zuboff (1980)
Ruth Tebbetts (1981)
Neil Kressel (1983)
Kathleen A. Karpilow (1984)
Nadim N. Rouhana (1984)
Tamra Pearson d'Estrée (1990)
Jonathan A. Margolis (1991)
Cynthia Chataway (1994)
William Weisberg (1996)
Mica Estrada-Hollenbeck (1997)
Rebecca Wolfe (2002)

List II: Graduate Students for Whom H. C. Kelman Served as Academic Adviser, Research/Practice Adviser, Member of Thesis Committee, and/or Thesis Reader

Rosita Albert
Nalini Ambady
Eileen Babbitt
Wallace Bachman
Ariela Bairey-Ben-Ishay
Halim Barakat
Susan Cross
Rebecca Dale
Erin Driver-Linn
Jennifer Eberhardt

Rebecca Edelson
Ronald A. Feldman
Floyd Jackson Fowler
Neil Friedman
Maria Hadjipavlou
Ivan G. Harvey
Debra Heffernan
Daniel Heradstveit
Marvin Hoffman
Bethamie Horowitz

Glenn Jones
Laura Keane
Paul Kimmel
Susan Korper
Sebastian (Nic) Kraus
Hillel Levine
Daniel Lieberfeld
Sharon Lobel
Judy Long
Neil Lutzky
Rhoda Margesson
Stanley Milgram
Andre Modigliani
Reina Neufeldt
Hugh O'Doherty
Winnifred O'Toole
Morris B. Parloff
Thomas Princen

William Reynolds
Jennifer Richeson
Jay Rothman
Sara Roy
Lynn Ruggiero
Jeffrey Seul
Nicole Sigrist
Margaret Smith
Pamela P. Steiner
Victoria Steinitz
Sandra Tangri
Nancy Thalhofer
José Ramón Torregrosa
Paula Van der Werff
Donald Warwick
John D. Winkler
Robert J. Wolosin
Martine Latil Zucker

List III: Postdoctoral Fellows, Research Associates, and Visiting Scholars Sponsored by H. C. Kelman

Sufian Abu Nejeilah
Stuart Albert
Carlos Alvarez
Yehudit Auerbach
Lotte Bailyn
Dan Bar-On
Reuben M. Baron
Herbert Blumberg
Donald Charpentier
Rosalind Cohen
Earl Davis
Sebastian Eschenbach
Raphael Ezekiel
Uri Farago
Roseli Fischmann
Martin Greenberg
Donna Hicks
Kalman Kaplan
Vivian Khamis

Harriet Lutzky
Brian Mandell
Moshe Ma'oz
John Marks
Jane McHan
Anita Mishler
Linda Pelzmann
Paula Rhodes
Jeffrey Z. Rubin
Afif Safieh
Jack Sawyer
Annedore Schulze
John Sheposh
Judith Shuval
Robert Suchner
Bassam Tibi
Lloyd Vogelman
Jorge Zalles

Appendix B _____

Herbert C. Kelman's Publications, 1945–2003

1945

Kelman, H. C. Lehaganat ha-le'umiut (In defense of nationalism). *Nir* (Hebrew periodical of the Teacher's Institute of the Rabbi Isaac Elchanan Theological Seminary, Yeshiva University, New York), 32–34.

Kelman, H. C. Lishe'elat hishtatfut yehudit–aravit (On the question of Jewish–Arab cooperation). *Niv* (Bimonthly of Hanoar Haivri, New York), 7(4), 12–14.

1950

Kelman, H. C. Effects of success and failure on "suggestibility" in the auto-kinetic situation. *Journal of Abnormal and Social Psychology, 45,* 267–285.

Kelman, H. C. Group dynamics—Neither hope nor hoax. *Quarterly Journal of Speech, 36,* 371–377. (Excerpted) In W. G. Bennis, K. D. Benne, & R. Chin (Eds.), *The planning of change* (pp. 259–264). New York: Holt, 1961.

1951

Gladstone, A. I., & Kelman, H. C. Pacifists vs. psychologists. *American Psychologist, 6,* 127–128.

1952

Kelman, H. C. Two phases of behavior change. *Journal of Social Issues, 8*(2), 81–88.

Kelman, H. C., & Gladstone, A. I. Pacifism and psychology: Further comments. *American Psychologist, 7,* 159.

Kelman, H. C., & Lerner, H. H. Group therapy, group work and adult education: The need for clarification. *Journal of Social Issues, 8*(2), 3–10.

Lerner, H. H., & Kelman, H. C. (Eds.). Group methods in psychotherapy, social work and adult education. *Journal of Social Issues, 8*(2), 1–90.

1953

Kelman, H. C. Attitude change as a function of response restriction. *Human Relations, 6,* 185–214. (Excerpted) In A. C. Elms (Ed.), *Role playing, reward, and attitude change* (pp. 14–17). New York: Van Nostrand Reinhold, 1969.

Kelman, H. C. Comments on the logic of psychological research on war prevention. *Bulletin of the Research Exchange on the Prevention of War, 1*(3), 1–5.

Kelman, H. C., & Hovland, C. I. "Reinstatement" of the communicator in delayed measurement of opinion change. *Journal of Abnormal and Social Psychology, 48,* 327–335.
  (Reprinted) In S. Himmelfarb & A. H. Eagly (Eds.), *Readings in attitude change* (pp. 138–149). New York: Wiley, 1974.

1954

Kelman, H. C. Public opinion and foreign policy decisions. *Bulletin of the Research Exchange on the Prevention of War, 2*(4), 2–8.
Kelman, H. C. A proposed framework for the study of war and peace. *Bulletin of the Research Exchange on the Prevention of War, 2*(6), 3–13.
Kelman, H. C. (Ed.). Relevance of social research for war prevention—A symposium. *Journal of Human Relations, 2,* 7–22.
Parloff, M. B., Kelman, H. C., & Frank, J. D. Comfort, effectiveness, and self-awareness as criteria of improvement in psychotherapy. *American Journal of Psychiatry, 111,* 343–351.

1955

Kelman, H. C. Societal, attitudinal and structural factors in international relations. *Journal of Social Issues, 11*(1), 42–56.
  (Reprinted) In S. H. Hoffmann (Ed.), *Contemporary theory in international relations* (pp. 209–222). Englewood Cliffs, NJ: Prentice-Hall, 1960.
  (Reprinted) In E. Krippendorff (Ed.), *Political science: Amerikanische Beiträge zur Politikwissenschaft.* Tübingen, Germany: Mohr-Siebeck, 1966.
  (Reprinted) In C. G. Smith (Ed.), *Conflict resolution: Contributions of the behavioral sciences* (pp. 445–455). Notre Dame, IN: University of Notre Dame Press, 1971.
Kelman, H. C. Review of *Research for peace* by Quincy Wright et al. *Bulletin of the Research Exchange on the Prevention of War, 3,* 103–107.
Kelman, H. C., Barth, W., & Hefner, R. (Eds.). Research approaches to the study of war and peace. *Journal of Social Issues, 11*(1), 1–57.

1956

Kelman, H. C. *Compliance, identification, and internalization.* Monograph submitted to the American Association for the Advancement of Science and awarded the AAAS Socio-Psychological Prize. (Mimeo)
Kelman, H. C. Social influence and attitude change. In *The psychological approach to peaceful cooperation.* Paris: UNESCO. (Mimeo)
Kelman, H. C. Empathy is not enough. *Contemporary Psychology, 1,* 299–300.
Kelman, H. C. Review of *The sane society* by Erich Fromm. *Bulletin of the Research Exchange on the Prevention of War, 4,* 111–114.

1957

Kelman, H. C. Individual liberties and conformity. In *Social and economic issues—Past, present and future.* Washington, DC: American Association for University Women. (Mimeo)
Kelman, H. C. Security and federal employment: A recent case study. *SPSSI Newsletter,* February, pp. 1–4.
Kelman, H. C., & Parloff, M. B. Interrelations among three criteria of improvement in group therapy. *Journal of Abnormal and Social Psychology, 54,* 281–288.

1958

Kelman, H. C. Compliance, identification, and internalization: Three processes of attitude change. *Journal of Conflict Resolution, 2*(1), 51–60.

(Reprinted) In H. Proshansky & B. Seidenberg (Eds.), *Basic studies in social psychology* (pp. 140–148). New York: Holt, Rinehart & Winston, 1965.

(Reprinted) In J. D. Singer (Ed.), *Human behavior and international politics: Contributions from the social-psychological sciences* (pp. 232–242). Chicago: Rand McNally, 1965.

(Reprinted) In M. Fishbein (Ed.), *Readings in attitude theory and measurement* (pp. 469–476). New York: Wiley, 1967.

(Reprinted) In B. L. Hinton & H. J. Reitz (Eds.), *Groups and organizations*. Belmont, CA: Wadsworth, 1971.

(Reprinted) In D. R. Domm, R. N. Blakeney, M. T. Matteson, & R. Scofield (Eds.), *The individual and the organization*. Dubuque, IA: Kendall/Hunt, 1971.

(Reprinted) In S. Himmelfarb & A. H. Eagly (Eds.), *Readings in attitude change* (pp. 218–227). New York: Wiley, 1974.

(Translated into Hebrew) In A. Ben-Ami (Ed.), *Social psychology: Socialization-attitudes-groups*. Tel Aviv: Am Oved, 1974.

(Reprinted) In E. Krupat (Ed.), *Psychology is social: Readings and conversations in social psychology* (pp. 98–106). Glenview, IL: Scott, Foresman, 1975. (2nd ed., pp. 107–111, 1982)

Kelman, H. C. (Ed.). Studies on attitudes and communication. *Journal of Conflict Resolution, 2*(1), 1–105.

Kelman, H. C. Introduction. *Journal of Conflict Resolution, 2*(1), 1–7.

Kelman, H. C. Comments on susceptibility to influence and the "mature" personality. In *Changing attitudes in a changing world*. New York: Bank Street College of Education.

Kelman, H. C., Alexander, F., & Stein, M. I. *Some psychological correlates of six somatic disturbances*. Paper presented at the meeting of the American Psychological Association, Washington, DC, September.

1959

Kelman, H. C. Apprehension and academic freedom. *Public Opinion Quarterly, 23*, 181–188.

Kelman, H. C., & Cohler, J. *Reactions to persuasive communications as a function of cognitive needs and styles*. Paper presented at the meeting of the Eastern Psychological Association, Atlantic City, NJ, April.

Kelman, H. C., & Pettigrew, T. F. How to understand prejudice. *Commentary, 28*, 436–441.

1960

Kelman, H. C. The perceiving of persons. *Contemporary Psychology, 5*, 192–195.

Kelman, H. C. *Effects of role-orientation and value-orientation on the nature of attitude change*. Paper presented at the meeting of the Eastern Psychological Association, New York City, April.

1961

Kelman, H. C. Processes of opinion change. *Public Opinion Quarterly, 25*, 57–78.

(Reprinted) in W. G. Bennis, K. D. Benne, & R. Chin (Eds.), *The planning of change* (pp. 508–517). New York: Holt, 1961. (2nd ed., 1969)

(Reprinted) In E. P. Hollander & R. G. Hunt (Eds.), *Current perspectives in social psychology* (pp. 454–462). New York: Oxford University Press, 1963. (2nd ed., pp. 438–446, 1967; 3rd ed., 1971)

(Reprinted) In E. E. Sampson (Ed.), *Approaches, contexts and problems of social psychology: A book of readings*. Englewood Cliffs, NJ: Prentice-Hall, 1964.

(Reprinted) In M. Jahoda & N. Warren (Eds.), *Attitudes: Selected readings*. Baltimore: Penguin Books, 1966.

(Reprinted) In K. K. Sereno & C. D. Mortensen (Eds.), *Foundations of communication theory*. New York: Harper, 1969.

(Reprinted) In P. Suedfeld (Ed.), *Attitude change: The competing views* (pp. 205–233). Chicago: Aldine-Atherton, 1971.

(Reprinted) In W. Schramm & D. F. Roberts (Eds.), *The process and effects of mass communication* (rev. ed.). Urbana: University of Illinois Press, 1971.

(Reprinted) In T. D. Beisecker & D. W. Parsons (Eds.), *The process of social influence* (pp. 438–446). Englewood Cliffs, NJ: Prentice-Hall, 1972.

(Reprinted) In J. B. Cohen (Ed.), *Behavioral science foundations of consumer behavior*. New York: Free Press, 1972.

(Reprinted) In J. Blankenship (Ed.), *Selected readings in speech communication*. Encino, CA: Dickenson, 1974.

(Reprinted) In R. O. Carlson (Ed.), *Communications and public opinion* (pp. 228–249). New York: Praeger, 1975.

(Reprinted) In Associates, Office of Military Leadership, U. S. Military Academy (Eds.), *A study of organizational leadership*. Harrisburg, PA: Stackpole Books, 1976.

(Reprinted) In B. M. Staw (Ed.), *Psychological foundations of organizational behavior*. Santa Monica, CA: Goodyear, 1977.

(Reprinted) In *Bobbs-Merrill Reprint Series in the Social Sciences*, No. P-191.

Kelman, H. C. Blacky goes to war. *Contemporary Psychology, 6,* 123–124.

1962

Bailyn, L., & Kelman, H. C. The effects of a year's experience in America on the self-image of Scandinavians: A preliminary analysis of reactions to a new environment. *Journal of Social Issues, 18*(1), 30–40.

Kelman, H. C. Changing attitudes through international activities. *Journal of Social Issues, 18*(1), 68–87.

Kelman, H. C. The induction of action and attitude change. In S. Coopersmith (Ed.), *Personality research* (pp. 81–110). Copenhagen: Munksgaard.

(Reprinted) In C. W. Backman & P. F. Secord (Eds.), *Problems in social psychology* (pp. 141–152). New York: McGraw-Hill, 1966.

Kelman, H. C. Internationalizing military force. In W. Wright, W. M. Evan, & M. Deutsch (Eds.), *Preventing World War III* (pp. 106–122). New York: Simon & Schuster.

Kelman, H. C. Humanizing politics. *Contemporary Psychology, 7,* 332–333.

Kelman, H. C., & Bailyn, L. Effects of cross-cultural experience on national images: A study of Scandinavian students in America. *Journal of Conflict Resolution, 6,* 319–334.

1963

Kelman, H. C. The role of the group in the induction of therapeutic change. *International Journal of Group Psychotherapy, 13,* 399–432.

(Reprinted) In H. Wechsler, L. Solomon, & B. Kramer (Eds.), *Social psychology and mental health*. New York: Holt, 1970.

Kelman, H. C. Further comments. *International Journal of Group Psychotherapy, 13,* 445–451.

Kelman, H. C., & Barclay, J. The F scale as a measure of breadth of perspective. *Journal of Abnormal and Social Psychology, 67,* 608–615.

Kelman, H. C., with Steinitz, V. The reactions of participants in a foreign specialists seminar to their American experience. *Journal of Social Issues, 19*(3), 61–114.

1964

Katz, D., Kelman, H. C., & Flacks, R. The national role: Some hypotheses about the relation of individuals to nation in America today. *Peace Research Society (International) Papers, 1,* 113–127.

Kelman, H. C. Theoretische Grundlagen für Programme zur Einstellungsänderung. In K. D. Hartmann (Ed.), *Vorurteile: Ihre Erforschung und ihre Bekämpfung* (pp. 86–90). Frankfurt: Europäische Verlagsanstalt.

Kelman, H. C. Review of *Attitudes and social relations of foreign students in the United States* by Claire Selltiz et al. *American Anthropologist, 66,* 1461–1463.

Kelman, H. C. Statement [on research assumptions and needs]. In *Changing roles of youth in the developing nations* (pp. 18–27). Washington, DC: Bureau of Educational and Cultural Affairs, U.S. Department of State. (Mimeo)

Kelman, H. C., & Hollander, E. P. International cooperation in psychological research. *American Psychologist, 19,* 779–782.

1965

Kelman, H. C. (Ed.) *International behavior: A social-psychological analysis.* New York: Holt, Rinehart & Winston.

Kelman, H. C. Social-psychological approaches to the study of international relations: Definition of scope. In H. C. Kelman (Ed.), *International behavior* (pp. 3–39). New York: Holt, Rinehart & Winston.

    (Excerpted and translated into German) In H. Haftendorn (Ed.), *Theorie der internationalen Politik.* Hamburg: Hoffmann & Campe, 1975.

Kelman, H. C. Social-psychological approaches to the study of international relations: The question of relevance. In H. C. Kelman (Ed.), *International behavior* (pp. 565–607). New York: Holt, Rinehart & Winston.

Kelman, H. C. The effects of participation in a foreign specialists seminar on images of the host country and the professional field. *Journal of Applied Behavioral Science, 1,* 149–166.

Kelman, H. C. Manipulation of human behavior: An ethical dilemma for the social scientist. *Journal of Social Issues, 21*(2), 31–46.

    (Reprinted) In W. G. Bennis, K. D. Benne, & R. Chin (Eds.), *The planning of change* (2nd ed.), New York: Holt, 1969.

    (Reprinted) In G. A. Fargo, C. Behrns, & P. Nolen (Eds.), *Behavior modifications in the classroom.* Belmont, CA: Wadsworth, 1970.

    (Reprinted) In F. M. Trusty (Ed.), *Administering human resources: A behavioral approach to educational administration.* Berkeley, CA: McCutchan, 1971.

    (Reprinted) In G. Zaltman, P. Kotler, & I. Kaufman (Eds.), *Creating social change.* New York: Holt, 1972.

    (Translated into Spanish) In J. R. Torregrosa (Ed.), *Teoria e investigación en la psicología social actual.* Madrid: Instituto de la Opinión Publica, 1974.

    (Reprinted) In G. Levin, E. Trickett, & R. Hess (Eds.), *Ethical implications of primary prevention* (pp. 23–41). New York: Hawthorn Press, 1990.

Kelman, H. C. The social consequences of social research: A new social issue. *Journal of Social Issues, 21*(3), 21–40.

    (Reprinted) In U.S. House of Representatives Committee on Government Operations, *The use of research in federal domestic programs, Part III.* Washington, DC: U.S. Government Printing Office, 1967.

Kelman, H. C. From dystopia to utopia: An analysis of Huxley's *Island.* In R. E. Farson (Ed.), *Science and human affairs* (pp. 166–184). Palo Alto, CA: Science and Behavior Books.

Kelman, H. C. Foreword. In H. Proshansky & B. Seidenberg (Eds.), *Basic studies in social psychology* (pp. v–vi). New York: Holt, Rinehart & Winston.

Kelman, H. C. Foreword. In I. Steiner & M. Fishbein (Eds.) *Current studies in social psychology* (pp. v–vi). New York: Holt, Rinehart & Winston.

Kelman, H. C., & Eagly, A. H. Attitude toward the communicator, perception of communication content, and attitude change. *Journal of Personality and Social Psychology, 1,* 63–78.

(Reprinted) In S. Himmelfarb & A. H. Eagly (Eds.), *Readings in attitude change* (pp. 173–190). New York: Wiley, 1974.

1966

Converse, E., Kelman, H. C., & Vandenberg, E. L. (Eds.). *Alternative perspectives on Vietnam.* Ithaca, NY: Inter-University Committee for Debate on Foreign Policy.

Kelman, H. C. New departures in social action: The response of intellectuals to the Vietnam conflict. In E. Converse, H. C. Kelman, & E. L. Vandenberg (Eds.), *Alternative perspectives on Vietnam.* Ithaca, NY: Inter-University Committee for Debate on Foreign Policy.

(Translated into Japanese) *Tenbo,* 1966, No. 2, 72–83.

Kelman, H. C. Deception in social research. *Trans-action, 3*(5), 20–24.

(Reprinted) In L. Gorlow & W. Katkovsky (Eds.), *Readings in the psychology of adjustment* (2nd ed., pp. 534–541). New York: McGraw-Hill, 1968.

(Reprinted) In N. K. Denzin (Ed.), *The values of social science.* Chicago: Aldine-Atherton, 1970. (2nd ed., New Brunswick, NJ: Transaction Books, 1973)

(Reprinted) In I. L. Horowitz & M. S. Strong (Eds.), *Sociological realities: A guide to the study of society.* New York: Harper, 1971.

(Reprinted) In B. J. Franklin & H. W. Osborne (Eds.), *Research methods: Issues and insights.* Belmont, CA: Wadsworth, 1971.

Kelman, H. C. Sozialpsychologische Aspekte internationalen Verhaltens. In U. Nerlich (Ed.), *Krieg und Frieden im industriellen Zeitalter: Beiträge der Sozialwissenschaft I* (pp. 141–239). Gütersloh, Germany: Bertelsmann.

Kelman, H. C. Values for graduate education in psychology. *American Psychologist, 21,* 954–956.

Kelman, H. C. A proposal for internationalizing the "Domestic Peace Corps." *Background, 10,* 57–65.

Kelman, H. C. Notes on faculty activism. *Letter to Michigan Alumni,* pp. 2, 9–11.

1967

Kelman, H. C. Human use of human subjects: The problem of deception in social psychological experiments. *Psychological Bulletin, 67,* 1–11.

(Reprinted) In U.S. House of Representatives Committee on Government Operations. *The use of social research in federal domestic programs, Part IV.* Washington, DC: U.S. Government Printing Office, 1967.

(Reprinted) In P. Badia, A. Haber, & R. P. Runyon (Eds.), *Research problems in psychology.* Reading, MA: Addison-Wesley, 1970.

(Reprinted) In J. Jung (Ed.), *The experimenter's dilemma.* New York: Harper, 1971.

(Excerpted) In J. Katz (Ed.) *Experimentation with human beings* (pp. 357–358, 384, 406, 423–425). New York: Russell Sage Foundation, 1972.

(Reprinted) In A. G. Miller (Ed.), *The social psychology of psychological research* (pp. 163–178). New York: Free Press, 1972.

(Reprinted) In J. Brynner & K. M. Stribley (Eds.), *Social research: Principles and procedures.* New York: Longman, 1979.

(Reprinted) In W. A. Lesko (Ed.), *Readings in social psychology: General, classic and contemporary selections* (3rd ed.). Boston: Allyn & Bacon, 1996. (4th ed., 2000; 5th ed., 2002, pp. 9–19)

(Reprinted) In *Bobbs-Merrill Reprint Series in the Social Sciences,* No. P-657.

Kelman, H. C. Rigor versus vigor: Some dubious issues in the debate on research philosophy. *Revista Interamericana de Psicología, 1*(3), 205–222.

Kelman, H. C. Psychological research on social change: Some scientific and ethical issues. *International Journal of Psychology, 2,* 301–313.

(Translated into Spanish) In M. A. Escotet & R. Diaz-Guerrero (Eds.), *Cross-cultural research methodology*. Mexico City: Trillas.

Kelman, H. C. International cooperation and attitude change. In F. L. Ruch, *Psychology and life* (7th ed., section on "Frontiers in psychology," pp. 677–684). Chicago: Scott, Foresman.

Kelman, H. C. Social research and the triple revolution. *Focus/Midwest, 5*(37), 14–18.

Kelman, H. C. On civil disobedience, 1967: Civil disobedience is justified by Vietnam. *New York Times Magazine*, November 26, pp. 126–128.

1968

Kelman, H. C. *A time to speak: On human values and social research*. San Francisco: Jossey-Bass.

Kelman, H. C. International relations: Psychological aspects. In D. L. Sills (Ed.), *International encyclopedia of the social sciences* (Vol. 8, pp. 75–83). New York: Macmillan and Free Press.

Kelman, H. C. The use of university resources in foreign policy research. *International Studies Quarterly, 12*, 16–37.

Kelman, H. C. Education for the concept of a global society. *Social Education, 32*, 661–666.

Kelman, H. C. Socialization for independence: Notes on the training of social psychologists. In S. Lundstedt (Ed.), *Higher education in social psychology* (pp. 73–104). Cleveland, OH: Case Western Reserve University Press.

Kelman, H. C. Social psychology and national development: Background of the Ibadan Conference. *Journal of Social Issues, 24*(2), 9–20.

Kelman, H. C. The organization of research in developing countries: Introduction. *Journal of Social Issues, 24*(2), 211–215.

Kelman, H. C., & Baron, R. M. Inconsistency as a psychological signal. In R. P. Abelson et al. (Eds.), *Theories of cognitive consistency: A sourcebook* (pp. 331–336). Chicago: Rand McNally.

Kelman, H. C., & Baron, R. M. Determinants of modes of resolving inconsistency dilemmas: A functional analysis. In R. P. Abelson et al. (Eds.), *Theories of cognitive consistency: A sourcebook* (pp. 670–683). Chicago: Rand McNally.

1969

DeLamater, J., Katz, D., & Kelman, H. C. On the nature of national involvement: A preliminary study. *Journal of Conflict Resolution, 13*, 320–357.

Kelman, H. C. Patterns of personal involvement in the national system: A social-psychological analysis of political legitimacy. In J. N. Rosenau (Ed.), *International politics and foreign policy* (rev. ed., pp. 276–288). New York: Free Press.

Kelman, H. C. Is a new pattern of legitimacy emerging? (Comments on Richard Flacks's article, "Protest or conform: Some social psychological perspectives on legitimacy"). *Journal of Applied Behavioral Science, 5*, 156–160.

1970

Katz, D., Kelman, H. C., & Vassiliou, D. A comparative approach to the study of nationalism. *Peace Research Society (International) Papers, 14*, 1–13.

Kelman, H. C., & Ezekiel, R. S., with Kelman, R. B. *Cross-national encounters: The personal impact of an exchange program for broadcasters*. San Francisco: Jossey-Bass.

Kelman, H. C. The role of the individual in international relations: Some conceptual and methodological considerations. *Journal of International Affairs, 24*, 1–17.

(Reprinted) In F. A. Sondermann, W. C. Olson, & D. McLellan (Eds.), *The theory and practice of international relations*. Englewood Cliffs, NJ: Prentice-Hall, 1974.

Kelman, H. C. A social-psychological model of political legitimacy and its relevance to black and white student protest movements. *Psychiatry, 33*, 224–246.

Kelman, H. C. The relevance of social research to social issues: Promises and pitfalls. In P. Halmos (Ed.), *The sociology of sociology* (*The Sociological Review*, Monograph No. 16, 77–99).

Kelman, H. C. Horizons of research on the international civil service: II. *Public Administration Review, 30*, 247–251.

(Reprinted) In R. S. Jordan (Ed.), *Multinational cooperation*. New York: Oxford University Press, 1972.

Kelman, H. C. Comments on Wiesner's paper (J. B. Wiesner, "The need for social engineering"). In F. F. Korten, S. W. Cook, & J. I. Lacey (Eds.), *Psychology and the problems of society* (pp. 95–98). Washington, DC: American Psychological Association.

1971

Kelman, H. C. Language as an aid and barrier to involvement in the national system. In J. Rubin & B. H. Jernudd (Eds.), *Can language be planned? Sociolinguistic theory and practice for developing nations* (pp. 21–51). Honolulu: University Press of Hawaii.

(Reprinted) In J. A. Fishman (Ed.), *Advances in the sociology of language* (Vol. 2, pp. 185–212). The Hague, The Netherlands: Mouton, 1972.

Kelman, H. C. Three research foci. In S. N. Herman (Ed.), *The study of Jewish identity: Issues and approaches*. Jerusalem: Hebrew University, Institute of Contemporary Jewry.

1972

Kelman, H. C. The problem-solving workshop in conflict resolution. In R. L. Merritt (Ed.), *Communication in international politics* (pp. 168–204). Urbana: University of Illinois Press.

(Reprinted) In M. R. Berman & J. E. Johnson (Eds.), *Unofficial diplomats*. New York: Columbia University Press, 1977.

Kelman, H. C. The rights of the subject in social research: An analysis in terms of relative power and legitimacy. *American Psychologist, 27*, 989–1016.

(Reprinted) In *Mental Health Digest*, 1973, *5*(2), 32–41.

(Reprinted) In G. H. Lewis (Ed.), *Fist-fights in the kitchen: Manners and methods in social research*. Pacific Palisades, CA: Goodyear, 1975.

Kelman, H. C. Roles of the behavioral scientist in policy-oriented research. In G. V. Coelho & E. A. Rubinstein (Eds.), *Social change and human behavior* (pp. 193–209). Rockville, MD: National Institute of Mental Health.

Kelman, H. C. La influencia social y los nexos entre el individuo y el sistema social: Más sobre los procesos de sumisión, identificación e internalización. *Revista de Estudios Sociales*, No. 5, 11–38.

(Reprinted) In J. R. Torregrosa (Ed.), *Teoria e investigación en la psicología social actual*. Madrid: Instituto de la Opinión Publica, 1974.

Kelman, H. C. IQ and the *Atlantic Monthly:* Some issues raised by Herrnstein's article. *Massachusetts Psychological Association Newsletter, 15*(5), 5–7.

Kelman, H. C. The Kurt Lewin Memorial Award presentation by the Society for the Psychological Study of Social Issues to Jerome D. Frank. *Journal of Social Issues, 28*(4), 21–24.

Kelman, H. C., & Lawrence, L. H. (Hamilton, V. L.). Assignment of responsibility in the case of Lt. Calley: Preliminary report on a national survey. *Journal of Social Issues, 28*(1), 177–212.

(Reprinted) In *Warner Modular Publications*, No. R 710, 1973.

Kelman, H. C., & Lawrence, L. H. (Hamilton, V. L.). American response to the trial of Lt. William L. Calley. *Psychology Today*, June, pp. 41–45, 78–81.

(Translated into Japanese) In *President Magazine*, 1973.

1973

Kelman, H. C. Violence without moral restraint: Reflections on the dehumanization of victims and victimizers. *Journal of Social Issues, 29*(4), 25–61.

(Reprinted) In G. M. Kren & L. Rappoport (Eds.), *Varieties of psychohistory*. New York: Springer, 1976.

Kelman, H. C. The challenge of change. In J. L. Scheiber (Ed.), *America and the future of man*. Del Mar, CA: CRM Books.

Kelman, H. C. A sampler of nonviolent action—To whet the appetite (Review of *Exploring nonviolent alternatives* by Gene Sharp). *Contemporary Psychology, 18,* 336–337.

Kelman, H. C. Foreword. In J. A. Fishman, *Language and nationalism* (pp. vii–x). Rowley, MA: Newbury.

Kelman, H. C. POW issue: Still reason for concern? *APA Monitor,* May, p. 2.

Kelman, H. C., & Bloom, A. H. Assumptive frameworks in international politics. In J. N. Knutson (Ed.), *Handbook of political psychology* (pp. 261–295). San Francisco: Jossey-Bass.

Kelman, H. C., & Warwick, D. P. Bridging micro and macro approaches to social change: A social-psychological perspective. In G. Zaltman (Ed.), *Processes and phenomena of social change* (pp. 13–59). New York: Wiley.

Lawrence, L. H. (Hamilton, V. L.), & Kelman, H. C. Reactions to the Calley trial: Class and political authority. *Worldview, 16*(6), 34–40.

Warwick, D. P., & Kelman, H. C., Ethical issues in social intervention. In G. Zaltman (Ed.), *Processes and phenomena of social change* (pp. 377–417). New York: Wiley.

(Reprinted) In W. Bennis, K. Benne, R. Chin, & K. Corey (Eds.), *The planning of change* (3rd ed.). New York: Holt, 1976.

1974

Kelman, H. C. Attitudes are alive and well and gainfully employed in the sphere of action. *American Psychologist, 29,* 310–324.

(Reprinted) In M. Matthaei et al. (Eds.), *Reading about psychology and you*. Chicago: Scott, Foresman, 1979.

Kelman, H. C. Social influence and linkages between the individual and the social system: Further thoughts on the processes of compliance, identification, and internalization. In J. Tedeschi (Ed.), *Perspectives on social power* (pp. 125–171). Chicago: Aldine.

Kelman, H. C., & Baron, R. M. Moral and hedonic dissonance: A functional analysis of the relationship between discrepant action and attitude change. In S. Himmelfarb & A. H. Eagly (Eds.), *Readings in attitude change* (pp. 558–575). New York: Wiley.

Kelman, H. C., & Hamilton, V. L. Availability for violence: A study of U.S. public reactions to the trial of Lt. Calley. In J. D. Ben-Dak (Ed.), *The future of collective violence: Societal and international perspectives* (pp. 125–142). Lund, Sweden: Studentlitteratur.

Tapp, J. L., Kelman, H. C., Triandis, H. C., Wrightsman, L. S. & Coelho, G. V. Continuing concerns in cross-cultural ethics: A report. *International Journal of Psychology, 9,* 231–249.

1975

A conversation with Herbert C. Kelman. In E. Krupat (Ed.), *Psychology is social: Readings and conversations in social psychology* (pp. 88–96). Glenview, IL: Scott, Foresman.

(Reprinted) In E. Krupat (Ed.), *Psychology is social* (2nd ed., pp. 98–105). Dallas: Scott, Foresman, 1982.

(Excerpted) In T. Smoke (Ed.), *A writer's worlds: Exploration through readings*. New York: St. Martin's Press, 1989. (2nd ed., 1994)

Kelman, H. C. International interchanges: Some contributions from theories of attitude change. *Studies in Comparative International Development, 10*(1), 83–99.

(Reprinted) In W. D. Coplin & C. W. Kegley, Jr. (Eds.), *Analyzing international relations: A multimethod introduction*. New York: Praeger Publishers, 1975.

Kelman, H. C. Was deception justified—And was it necessary? Comments on "Self-control techniques as an alternative to pain medication. " *Journal of Abnormal Psychology, 84,* 172–174.

(Reprinted) In C. M. Franks & G. T. Wilson (Eds.), *Annual review of behavior therapy theory and practice 1976*. New York: Brunner/Mazel, 1976.

Kelman, H. C. War criminals and war resisters. *Society, 12*(4), 18–22.

1976

Kelman, H. C. Some reflections on authority, corruption, and punishment: The social-psychological context of Watergate. *Psychiatry, 39,* 303–317.

Kelman, H. C. Review of *Research on human subjects: Problems of social control in human experimentation* by Bernard Barber et al. *Social Forces, 55,* 540–542.

Kelman, H. C., & Cohen, S. P. The problem-solving workshop: A social-psychological contribution to the resolution of international conflicts. *Journal of Peace Research, 13,* 79–90.

1977

Cohen, S. P., Kelman, H. C., Miller, F. D., & Smith, B. L. Evolving intergroup techniques for conflict resolution: An Israeli–Palestinian pilot workshop. *Journal of Social Issues, 33*(1), 165–189.

Kelman, H. C. The conditions, criteria, and dialectics of human dignity: A transnational perspective. *International Studies Quarterly, 21,* 529–552.

Kelman, H. C. Privacy and research with human beings. *Journal of Social Issues, 33*(3), 169–195.

Kelman, H. C. The place of Jewish identity in the development of personal identity. In *Issues in Jewish education and Jewish identity* (pp. 1–27). New York: American Jewish Committee.

Kelman, H. C. Foreword. In S. N. Herman, *Jewish identity: A social psychological perspective* (pp. 9–12). Beverly Hills, CA: Sage. (2nd ed., pp. ix–xii, New Brunswick, NJ: Transaction Publishers, 1989)

1978

Bermant, G., Kelman, H. C., & Warwick, D. P. (Eds.), *The ethics of social intervention*. Washington, DC: Hemisphere Publishing Corporation..

Kelman, H. C. Research, behavioral. In W. T. Reich (Ed.), *Encyclopedia of bioethics* (Vol. 4, pp. 1470–1481). New York: Macmillan and Free Press.

Kelman, H. C. Israelis and Palestinians: Psychological prerequisites for mutual acceptance. *International Security, 3*(1), 162–186.

   (First published) In *Can an Israeli state and a Palestinian state co-exist?* New York: American Friends Service Committee, 1977.

Kelman, H. C. Attitude and behavior: A social-psychological problem. In M. Yinger & S. J. Cutler (Eds.), *Major social issues: A multi-disciplinary view* (pp. 412–420). New York: Free Press.

Kelman, H. C. The psychological impact of Sadat's visit on Israeli society. In *Sadat's historic initiative: Documents and analyses*. Cairo: Al-Ahram. (In Arabic)

Kelman, H. C., & Warwick, D. P. The ethics of social intervention: Goals, means, and consequences. In G. Bermant, H. C. Kelman, & D. P. Warwick (Eds.), *The ethics of social intervention* (pp. 3–33). Washington, DC: Hemisphere.

1979

Kelman, H. C. An interactional approach to conflict resolution and its application to Israeli–Palestinian relations. *International Interactions, 6*(2), 99–122.

   (Reprinted) In R. K. White (Ed.), *Psychology and the prevention of nuclear war* (pp. 171–193). New York: New York University Press, 1986.

Kelman, H. C. Fuentes de apego al estado nación: Una visión psico-social de las dimensiones del nacionalismo. In G. E. Finley & G. Marin (Eds.), *Avances en psicología contemporánea* (pp. 142–163). Mexico City: Trillas.

Kelman, H. C. U.S. gestures that could help in Iran. *Christian Science Monitor,* December 14, p. 23.

Kelman, H. C., & Cohen, S. P. Reduction of international conflict: An interactional approach. In W. Austin & S. Worchel (Eds.), *The social psychology of intergroup relations* (pp. 288–303). Monterey, CA: Brooks/Cole.

1980

Kelman, H. C. The role of action in attitude change. In H. E. Howe, Jr., & M. M. Page (Eds.), *Nebraska Symposium on Motivation, 1979: Attitudes, values, and beliefs* (pp. 117–194). Lincoln: University of Nebraska Press.

Kelman, H. C. Indigenous anthropology in non-Western countries: A further elaboration. *Current Anthropology, 21,* 655–661.

Kelman, H. C. Opposition to Daniel Heradstveit's doctoral thesis, "The Arab–Israeli conflict: Psychological obstacles to peace." *Internasjonal Politikk,* Supplement 1B, 209–219.

1981

Kelman, H. C. Reflections on the history and status of peace research. *Conflict Management and Peace Science, 5*(2), 95–110.

Winkler, J. D., Judd, C. M., & Kelman, H. C. Determinants of political participation in a Canadian and a United States city. *Political Psychology, 3*(3/4), 140–161.

1982

Kelman, H. C. Creating the conditions for Israeli–Palestinian negotiations. *Journal of Conflict Resolution, 26,* 39–75.

  (First published as) Working Paper No. 25, International Security Studies Program. Washington, DC: The Wilson Center, 1981.

  (Reprinted) In S. F. Wells, Jr., & M. A. Bruzonsky (Eds.), *Security in the Middle East: Prospects and problems in the 1980s* (pp. 139–157). Boulder, CO: Westview Press, 1987.

  (Excerpted and translated into Hebrew) Creating the conditions for negotiation. *Migvan,* January 1983, No. 77, 20–23.

Kelman, H. C. Talk with Arafat. *Foreign Policy,* No. 49, 119–139.

Kelman, H. C. A changing social science for a changing world: A social psychologist's perspective. In H. Fahim (Ed.), *Indigenous anthropology in non-Western countries* (pp. 269–283). Durham, NC: Carolina Academic Press.

Kelman, H. C. Ethical issues in different social science methods. In T. L. Beauchamp, R. R. Faden, R. J. Wallace, Jr., & L. Walters (Eds.), *Ethical issues in social science research* (pp. 40–98). Baltimore: Johns Hopkins University Press.

Kelman, H. C. Genocide as social policy. *Contemporary Psychology, 27,* 85–87.

Kelman, H. C. Resolving the Israel/Palestine conflict. *Harvard International Review, 5*(3), 54–55.

Kelman, H. C. Requirement for peace: Politically intact PLO. *The New York Times,* July 22, op-ed p. A23.

1983

Kelman, H. C. Conversations with Arafat: A social-psychological assessment of the prospects for Israeli–Palestinian peace. *American Psychologist, 38,* 203–216.

Kelman, H. C. *Understanding Arafat* (Discussion Paper No. 1). Tel Aviv: International Center for Peace in the Middle East.

Kelman, H. C. The Reagan plan and the peace process: Arab and Israeli perceptions. In W. G. Miller & P. H. Stoddard (Eds.), *Perspectives on the Middle East 1983* (pp. 120–140). Washington, DC: Middle East Institute.

Kelman, H. C. Nacionalismo e identidad nacional: Un analisis psicosocial. In J. R. Torregrosa & B. Sarabia (Eds.), *Perspectivas y contextos de la psicología social* (pp. 241–268). Barcelona: Editorial Hispano Europea.

Kelman, H. C. On social psychology and policy analysis. *American Psychologist, 38,* 1126–1127.

1984

Kelman, H. C. Protest movements. In *The phenomenon of change* (p. 38). New York: Cooper-Hewitt Museum.

Kelman, H. C. Foreword. In M. Banks (Ed.), *Conflict in world society: A new perspective on international relations* (pp. xvii–xx). Brighton, England: Wheatsheaf.

1985

Kelman, H. C. Overcoming the psychological barrier: An analysis of the Egyptian–Israeli peace process. *Negotiation Journal, 1*(3), 213–234.

(Also published) In S. P. Huntington & J. S. Nye, Jr. (Eds.), *Global dilemmas* (pp. 199–223). Cambridge, MA: Harvard Center for International Affairs.

1986

Kelman, H. C. Interactive problem solving: A social-psychological approach to conflict resolution. In W. Klassen (Ed.), *Dialogue toward interfaith understanding* (pp. 293–314). Tantur/Jerusalem: Ecumenical Institute for Theological Research.

(Translated into Spanish) La solucion interactiva de problemas: Un enfoque psicosocial a la resolucion de conflictos. *Revista de Psicología de El Salvador,* 1989, *8*(32), 115–133.

(Reprinted) In J. Burton & F. Dukes (Eds.), *Conflict: Readings in management and resolution* (pp. 199–215). New York: St. Martin's Press, 1990.

Kelman, H. C. Overcoming the barriers to negotiation of the Israeli–Palestinian conflict. *Journal of Palestine Studies, 16*(1), 13–28.

Kelman, H. C. Preface. In R. K. White (Ed.), *Psychology and the prevention of nuclear war* (pp. xi–xiii). New York: New York University Press.

Kelman, H. C. When scholars work with the CIA. *The New York Times,* March 5, op-ed p. A27.

Kelman, H. C., & Cohen, S. P. Resolution of international conflict: An interactional approach. In S. Worchel & W. G. Austin (Eds.), *Psychology of intergroup relations* (2nd ed., pp. 323–342). Chicago: Nelson-Hall.

1987

Kelman, H. C. The political psychology of the Israeli–Palestinian conflict: How can we overcome the barriers to a negotiated solution? *Political Psychology, 8*(3), 347–363.

(Translated into German) Wie Verhandlungsbereitschaft entstehen kann: Zur politischen Psychologie des israelisch–palästinensischen Konflikts. In R. Steinweg & C. Wellmann (Eds.),

Die vergessene Dimension internationaler Konflikte: Subjektivität (pp. 189–211). Frankfurt: Suhrkamp, 1990.

Kelman, H. C. Overcoming the barriers. *Fellowship, 53*(6), 16–18.

1988

Kelman, H. C. The Palestinianization of the Arab–Israeli conflict. *The Jerusalem Quarterly,* Spring, *46,* 3–15.

   (Also published) In Y. Lukacs & A. M. Battah (Eds.), *The Arab–Israeli conflict: Two decades of change* (pp. 332–343). Boulder, CO: Westview Press.

Kelman, H. C., with the Project "Preparedness for Peace." Social-psychological aspects of peace education: With a focus on interactive problem solving, redefining security, and fostering personal responsibility. *Reprints and Miniprints,* No. 626. Malmo, Sweden: School of Education.

1989

Kelman, H. C., & Hamilton, V. L. *Crimes of obedience: Toward a social psychology of authority and responsibility.* New Haven, CT: Yale University Press.

   (Translated into Spanish) *Crimenes de obediencia: Los límites de la autoridad y la responsabilidad.* Buenos Aires: Planeta, 1990.

   (Excerpted) Sanctioned massacres. In N. J. Kressel (Ed.), *Political psychology: Classic and contemporary readings* (pp. 232–240). New York: Paragon House, 1993.

   (Excerpted) The My Lai massacre. In J. M. Henslin (Ed.), *Down to earth sociology: Introductory readings* (9th ed., pp. 447–459). New York: Free Press, 1997.

   (Excerpted) The My Lai massacre. In D. M. Newman (Ed.), *Sociology: Exploring the architecture of everyday life* (pp. 17–28). New York: Free Press, 1997.

Kelman, H. C. The Nazi biomedical vision: Killing in the name of healing (Review of *The Nazi doctors* by R. J. Lifton). *Contemporary Psychology, 34,* 437–440.

Kelman, H. C. How the U.S. can advance Israeli–Palestinian peace. *Christian Science Monitor,* December 7, p. 19.

   (Reprinted) The U.S. role in Israeli–Palestinian peace. *New Outlook,* March 1990, *33*(1–2), 40–41.

1990

Kelman, H. C. Applying a human needs perspective to the practice of conflict resolution: The Israeli–Palestinian case. In J. Burton (Ed.), *Conflict: Human needs theory* (pp. 283–297). New York: St. Martin's Press.

Kelman, H. C. Now nobody's talking: How the U.S. and the PLO can get back to the table. *Christian Science Monitor,* July 2, p. 18.

1991

Hernandez de Frutos, T. Entrevista con Herbert Kelman: Reconsideraciones sobre los procesos de influencia social. *Interaccion Social, 1,* 187–205.

Kelman, H. C. A behavorial science perspective on the study of war and peace. In R. Jessor (Ed.), *Perspectives on behavorial science: The Colorado lectures* (pp. 245–275). Boulder, CO: Westview Press.

Kelman, H. C. Interactive problem-solving: The uses and limits of a therapeutic model for the resolution of international conflicts. In V. Volkan, J. V. Montville, & D. A. Julius (Eds.), *The psychodynamics of international relationships, Volume 2: Unofficial diplomacy at work* (pp. 145–160).
Lexington, MA: Heath/Lexington Books.

Kelman, H. C. On the history and development of peace research: Personal reflections. In J. W.
Nobel (Ed.), *The coming of age of peace research* (pp. 25–37). Groningen, The Netherlands:
STYX Publications.

Kelman, H. C. Existential fears and mutual reassurance in Israeli–Palestinian relations. *La Croix
L'Evenement,* August 3, p. 3.

Kelman, H. C. The Middle East Peace Conference. *Psychologists for Social Responsibility Newsletter, 10*(4), 1–2.

1992

Kelman, H. C. Informal mediation by the scholar/practitioner. In J. Bercovitch & J. Rubin (Eds.),
Mediation in international relations: Multiple approaches to conflict management (pp. 64–96).
New York: St. Martin's Press.
(Revised and reprinted) In E. Weiner (Ed.), *The handbook of interethnic coexistence* (pp. 310–
331). New York: Continuum, 1998.

Kelman, H. C. Acknowledging the other's nationhood: How to create a momentum for the Israeli–
Palestinian negotiations. *Journal of Palestine Studies, 22*(1), 18–38.

Kelman, H. C. Foreword. In S. Staub & P. Green (Eds.), *Psychology and social responsibility: Facing
global challenges* (pp. ix–xii). New York: New York University Press.

Kelman, H. C., & Hamilton, V. L. Comment on Sonia Lambert's review of "Crimes of Obedience."
Politics and the Individual, 2(1), 93–97.

1993

Kelman, H. C. Coalitions across conflict lines: The interplay of conflicts within and between the
Israeli and Palestinian communities. In S. Worchel & J. Simpson (Eds.), *Conflict between people and groups* (pp. 236–258). Chicago: Nelson-Hall.
(First published as) Working paper No. 91-9. Cambridge, MA: Harvard Center for International Affairs, 1991.

Kelman, H. C. The social context of torture: Policy process and authority structure. In R. D. Crelinsten & A. P. Schmid (Eds.), *The politics of pain: Torturers and their masters* (pp. 21–38).
Leiden, The Netherlands: COMT, University of Leiden.
(Reprinted) In R. D. Crelinsten & A. P. Schmid (Eds.), *The politics of pain: Torturers and their
masters* (U.S. ed., pp. 19–34). Boulder, CO: Westview Press, 1995.

Kelman, H. C. Conceptions of civic responsibility and the role of education in a multicultural world.
The Swarthmore Papers, 1(1), 33–49.

Kelman, H. C. Commentary on Part IV: The reaction of mass publics to the Gulf War. In S. A. Ren-
shon (Ed.), *The political psychology of the Gulf War: Leaders, publics, and the process of conflict* (pp. 251–265). Pittsburgh: University of Pittsburgh Press.

Kelman, H. C. Foreword. In D. J. D. Sandole & H. van der Merwe (Eds.), *Conflict resolution theory
and practice: Integration and application* (pp. ix–xii). Manchester and New York: Manchester
University Press.

1994

Kelman, H. C. Inoffizielle Diplomatie im Nahen Osten: Ein Forschungsprogramm zur Lösung
internationaler Konflikte. *Literarität,* November, No. 2, 36–45.

(Revised and reprinted) Inoffizielle Diplomatie—ihr Beitrag zur Lösung internationaler Konf-
   likte. In D. Senghaas (Ed.), *Frieden machen* (pp. 243–267). Frankfurt: Suhrkamp, 1997.
Kelman, H. C. Essay [on recent developments in the Middle East]. *Psychology International,*
   Spring, *5*(2), pp. 1, 6–7.
Kelman, H. C. Three steps to advance Israeli–Arab peace. *The Boston Globe,* March 8, op-ed p. 15.
Rouhana, N. N., & Kelman, H. C. Promoting joint thinking in international conflicts: An Israeli–
   Palestinian continuing workshop. *Journal of Social Issues, 50*(1), 157–178.

1995

Kelman, H. C. Contributions of an unofficial conflict resolution effort to the Israeli–Palestinian
   breakthrough. *Negotiation Journal, 11*(1), 19–27.
Kelman, H. C. Ignacio Martín-Baró: A personal remembrance of a martyred peace psychologist.
   Peace and Conflict: Journal of Peace Psychology, 1(1), 11–15.
Kelman, H. C. Decision making and public discourse in the Gulf War: An assessment of underlying
   psychological and moral assumptions. *Peace and Conflict: Journal of Peace Psychology, 1*(2),
   117–130.
Kelman, H. C. Discurso de aceptación. In *Discursos correspondientes a las Investiduras de doctor
   "honoris causa"* (pp. 111–117). Madrid: Universidad Complutense.

1996

Kelman, H. C. Negotiation as interactive problem solving. *International Negotiation: A Journal of
   Theory and Practice, 1*(1), 99–123.
Kelman, H. C. The interactive problem-solving approach. In C. A. Crocker & F. O. Hampson (Eds.),
   Managing global chaos: Sources of and responses to international conflict (pp. 501–519). Wash-
   ington: United States Institute of Peace.
Kelman, H. C. Foreword. In A. J. Kimmel, *Ethical issues in behavioral science* (pp. xiii–xv). Cam-
   bridge, MA, and Oxford: Blackwell Publishers.

1997

Kelman, H. C. Group processes in the resolution of international conflicts: Experiences from the
   Israeli–Palestinian case. *American Psychologist, 52,* 212–220.
   (Reprinted) In J. Garcia & K. A. Keough (Eds.), *Social psychology of gender, race, and ethnic-
      ity: Readings and projects.* Guilford, CT: McGraw-Hill, 1999.
Kelman, H. C. Negotiating national identity and self-determination in ethnic conflicts: The choice
   between pluralism and ethnic cleansing. *Negotiation Journal, 13*(4), 327–340.
Kelman, H. C. Some determinants of the Oslo breakthrough. *International Negotiation, 2*(2), 183–194.
   (Reprinted) In D. M. Kolb (Ed.), *Negotiation eclectics* (pp. 276–288). Cambridge, MA: PON
      Books, 1999.
Kelman, H. C. Social-psychological dimensions of international conflict. In I. W. Zartman &
   J. L. Rasmussen (Eds.), *Peacemaking in international conflict: Methods and techniques*
   (pp. 191–236). Washington, DC: United States Institute of Peace Press.
   (Excerpted and translated into Japanese) In Y. Araki & J. Kawada (Eds.), *Handbook of politi-
      cal psychology* (pp. 161–169). Tokyo: Hokuju, 2003.
   (Revised) In I. W. Zartman (Ed.*), Peacemaking in international conflict: Methods and tech-
      niques* (rev. ed.). Washington, DC: United States Institute of Peace Press, in press.

Kelman, H. C. Nationalism, patriotism, and national identity: Social-psychological dimensions. In D. Bar-Tal & E. Staub (Eds.), *Patriotism in the life of individuals and nations* (pp. 165–189). Chicago: Nelson-Hall.

Kelman, H. C. Settlers must leave Hebron or accept Palestinian authority, *The Boston Sunday Globe,* January 5, op-ed p. F7.

1998

Kelman, H. C. Interactive problem solving: An approach to conflict resolution and its application in the Middle East. *PS: Political Science and Politics, 31*(2), 190–198.

(Revised and reprinted) Interactive problem solving in the Middle East. In L. Reychler & T. Paffenholz (Eds.), *Peacebuilding: A field guide* (pp. 97–110). Boulder, CO, and London: Lynne Rienner, 2001.

Kelman, H. C. Social-psychological contributions to peacemaking and peacebuilding in the Middle East. *Applied Psychology: An International Review, 47*(1), 5–28.

(Reprinted) In G. Baechler (Ed.), *Promoting peace: The role of civilian conflict resolution* (pp. 61–82). Berne, Switzerland: Staempfli, 2002.

Kelman, H. C. Building a sustainable peace: The limits of pragmatism in the Israeli–Palestinian negotiations. *Journal of Palestine Studies, 28*(1), 36–50.

(Reprinted) In *Peace and Conflict: Journal of Peace Psychology,* 1999, *5*(2), 101–115.

(Reprinted) In J. Rourke (Ed.), *Taking sides: Clashing views on controversial issues in world politics* (9th ed.). Guilford, CT: Dushkin/McGraw-Hill, 1999. (10th ed., pp. 140–150, 2002)

Kelman, H. C. The place of ethnic identity in the development of personal identity: A challenge for the Jewish family. In P. Y. Medding (Ed.), *Coping with life and death: Jewish families in the twentieth century* (Vol. XIV of *Studies in Contemporary Jewry: An Annual,* pp. 3–26). New York and Oxford: Oxford University Press.

Kelman, H. C. Israel in transition from Zionism to post-Zionism. In G. Ben-Dor (Ed.), *Israel in transition* (Vol. 555 of *The Annals of the American Academy of Political and Social Science,* pp. 46–61). Thousand Oaks, CA: Sage.

Kelman, H. C. Creating sustainable peace in the Middle East. In D. Francis (Ed.), *Mediating deadly conflicts* (pp. 75–81). Cambridge, MA: World Peace Foundation.

1999

Kelman, H. C. Transforming the relationship between former enemies: A social-psychological analysis. In R. L. Rothstein (Ed.), *After the peace: Resistance and reconciliation* (pp. 193–205). Boulder, CO, and London: Lynne Rienner.

Kelman, H. C. The interdependence of Israeli and Palestinian national identities: The role of the other in existential conflicts. *Journal of Social Issues, 55,* 581–600.

Kelman, H. C. Experiences from 30 years of action research on the Israeli–Palestinian conflict. In K. P. Spillmann & A. Wenger (Eds.), *Zeitgeschichtliche Hintergründe aktueller Konflikte VII: Zürcher Beiträge zur Sicherheitspolitik und Konfliktforschung,* No. 54, 173–197.

Kelman, H. C. Interactive problem solving as a metaphor for international conflict resolution: Lessons for the policy process. *Peace and Conflict: Journal of Peace Psychology, 5,* 201–218.

Kelman, H. C. Scholars, practitioners, and scholar-practitioners: The complementary role of Track II diplomacy. *Centerpiece: Newsletter of the Weatherhead Center for International Affairs at Harvard University, 13*(3), 2–4, 5–6.

Kelman, H. C., & Rouhana, N. N. Introduction to J. Alpher, K. Shikaki, et al., Concept paper: The Palestinian refugee problem and the right of return. *Middle East Policy, 6*(1), 167–189.

(First published as) Working Paper No. 98-7. Cambridge, MA: Weatherhead Center for International Affairs, Harvard University, 1998.

Kelman, H. C., & Rouhana, N. N. Introduction to Joint Working Group on Israeli–Palestinian Relations, Document: General principles for the final Israeli–Palestinian agreement. *The Middle East Journal, 53*(1), 170–175.

> (First published as) PICAR (Program on International Conflict Analysis and Resolution) Working Paper. Cambridge, MA: Weatherhead Center for International Affairs, Harvard University, September 1998.

Ruggiero, K. M., & Kelman, H. C. (Eds.). Prejudice and intergroup relations: Papers in honor of Allport's centennial. *Journal of Social Issues, 55,* 404–600.

Ruggiero, K. M., & Kelman, H. C. Introduction to the issue. *Journal of Social Issues, 55,* 405–414.

2000

Kelman, H. C. The role of the scholar-practitioner in international conflict resolution. *International Studies Perspectives, 1,* 273–288.

Kelman, H. C. International conflict resolution. In G. Magerl, H. Rumpler, & C. Smekal (Eds.), *Wissenschaft und Zukunft: Beiträge der Wissenschaften zur Bewältigung globaler Krisen* (pp. 207–224). Vienna: Böhlau.

Kelman, H. C. Transcending the balance of power. *Middle East Insight, 15*(2), 51–53.

Kelman, H. C. The components of a "principled compromise." *The Boston Globe,* July 18, op-ed p. A13.

Kelman, H. C. The challenge for Arafat and Barak. *The Boston Globe,* September 7, op-ed p. A15.

Kelman, H. C. Israeli–Palestinian [case]. Contributed to H. H. Saunders, Interactive conflict resolution: A view for policy makers on making and building peace. In P. C. Stern & D. Druckman (Eds.), *International conflict resolution after the Cold War* (pp. 269–271). Washington, DC: National Academy Press.

Kelman, H. C. (Ed.) The future Israeli–Palestinian relationship: A concept paper by the Joint Working Group on Israeli–Palestinian Relations. *Middle East Policy, 7*(2), 90–112.

> (First published as) Working Paper No. 99-12. Cambridge, MA: Weatherhead Center for International Affairs, Harvard University, 1999.

2001

Kelman, H. C. The role of national identity in conflict resolution: Experiences from Israeli–Palestinian problem-solving workshops. In R. D. Ashmore, L. Jussim, & D. Wilder (Eds.), *Social identity, intergroup conflict, and conflict reduction* (pp. 187–212). Oxford and New York: Oxford University Press.

Kelman, H. C. Dignity and dehumanization: The impact of the Holocaust on central themes of my work. In P. Suedfeld (Ed.), *Light from the ashes: Social science careers of young Holocaust refugees and survivors* (pp. 197–220). Ann Arbor: University of Michigan Press.

Kelman, H. C. Reflections on the social and psychological processes of legitimization and delegitimization. In J. T. Jost & B. Major (Eds.), *The psychology of legitimacy: Emerging perspectives on ideology, justice, and intergroup relations* (pp. 54–73). Cambridge: Cambridge University Press.

Kelman, H. C. Ethical limits on the use of influence in hierarchical relationships. In J. M. Darley, D. Messick, & T. R. Tyler (Eds.), *Social influences on ethical behavior in organizations* (pp. 11–20). Mahwah, NJ, and London: Lawrence Erlbaum.

Kelman, H. C. How to renew Israeli–Palestinian peace process. *The Boston Globe,* August 6, op-ed p. A11.

Kelman, H. C. A vision for compromise. *The Boston Globe,* December 8, op-ed p. A19.

2002

Kelman, H. C. National identity and the role of the "other" in existential conflicts: The Israeli–Palestinian case. In G. Baechler & A. Wenger (Eds.). *Conflict and cooperation: The individual between ideal and reality (Festschrift in honor of Kurt R. Spillmann,* pp. 107–124). Zurich: Neue Zürcher Zeitung Publishing.

(Revised) In J. Bunzl (Ed.), *In God's name: On the political role of religions in the contemporary Middle East.* Gainesville: University Press of Florida, in press.

Kelman, H. C. Interactive problem solving as a tool for second track diplomacy. In J. Davies & E. Kaufman (Eds.), *Second track/citizens' diplomacy: Concepts and techniques for conflict transformation* (pp. 81–105). Lanham, MD: Rowman & Littlefield.

Kelman, H. C. Interactive problem solving: Informal mediation by the scholar-practitioner. In J. Bercovitch (Ed.), *Studies in international mediation: Essays in honor of Jeffrey Z. Rubin* (pp. 167–193). New York: Palgrave Macmillan.

Kelman, H. C. Needed: A manifesto for Mideast peace. *The Boston Globe,* March 14, op-ed p. A15.

2003

Kelman, H. C. The major roadblock on road map to peace. *The Boston Globe,* May 16, op-ed p. A19.

Kelman, H. C. Move Yasser Arafat up—not out. *The Boston Globe,* September 20, op-ed p. A11.

Kelman, H. C. Ein sozialpsychologischer Zugang zur Lösung internationaler Konflikte: Erfahrungen mit dem israelisch–palästinensischen Fall. In M. Hassler, M. Hautzinger, & J. Wertheimer (Eds.), *Frieden schaffen—aber wie?* (pp. 41–60). Tübingen, Germany: Stauffenburg Verlag.

Kelman, H. C. Foreword. In S. Cheldelin, D. Druckman, & L. Fast (Eds.), *Conflict: From analysis to intervention* (pp. vii–ix). New York: Continuum.

Kelman, H. C., & Fisher, R. J. Conflict analysis and resolution. In D. O. Sears, L. Huddy, & R. Jervis (Eds.), *Oxford handbook of political psychology* (pp. 315–353). Oxford, England: Oxford University Press.

In Press

Kelman, H. C. Continuity and change: My life as a social psychologist. In A. H. Eagly, R. M. Baron, & V. L. Hamilton (Eds.), *The social psychology of group identity and social conflict: Theory, application, and practice.* Washington, DC: American Psychological Association.

Kelman, H. C. The nature of international conflict: A social-psychological perspective. In H. Langholtz & C. E. Stout (Eds.), *The Psychology of diplomacy.* New York: Praeger Publishers.

Kelman, H. C. Reconciliation as identity change: A social-psychological perspective. In Y. Bar-Siman-Tov (Ed.), *From conflict resolution to reconciliation.* Oxford, England: Oxford University Press.

Kelman, H. C. Foreword. In J. H. Zalles, *Why is it so difficult to enter into dialogue and build consensus?* Bogota, Colombia: Editorial Norma.

Submitted for Publication

Kelman, H. C. The contributions of non-governmental organizations to the resolution of ethnonational conflict: An approach to evaluation. (Based on paper presented at the Carnegie Corporation Conference on the Role of International NGOs in Ethnic and Nationalist Conflicts, New York, November 1996.)

Kelman, H. C. The building stones of the Oslo agreement. (Based on lecture at Ben-Gurion University of the Negev, June 2001.)

Index

About the Editors

Alice H. Eagly, PhD, is a social psychologist who is professor of psychology at Northwestern University and Faculty Fellow in the Institute for Policy Research. She has served as president of the Midwestern Psychological Association, president of the Society of Personality and Social Psychology (Division 8) of the American Psychological Association (APA), chair of the Executive Committee of the Society of Experimental Social Psychology, and chair of the Board of Scientific Affairs of the APA. She received the Distinguished Scientist Award from the Society of Experimental Social Psychology, Donald Campbell Award for Distinguished Contribution to Social Psychology from the Society of Personality and Social Psychology, Gordon Allport Award from the Society for the Psychological Study of Social Issues, citation as Distinguished Leader for Women in Psychology from the Committee on Women in Psychology of the APA, Distinguished Publication Award of the Association for Women in Psychology, and Sabbatical Award from the James McKeen Cattell Fund. She has published many journal articles and book chapters. In addition, she has authored two books and edited two books and served as associate editor of the *Journal of Personality and Social Psychology*. She is particularly known for her work on attitudes, including the book *Psychology of Attitudes* that she wrote with Shelly Chaiken, her research on the psychology of gender, and her many articles implementing meta-analysis as well as other research methods.

Reuben M. Baron, PhD, is a social psychologist who is a research professor at the University of Connecticut. He has been an associate editor for the *Personality and Social Psychology Bulletin* and consulting editor for *Personality and Social Psychology Bulletin*, the *Journal of Social and Personality Psychology,* and *Developmental Psychology.* He has coedited a social psychology textbook and published many journal articles and book chapters including three articles in *Psychological Review.* His article with David Kenny in the *Journal of Personality and Social Psychology* on the moderator–mediator distinction received the third highest citation of any psychology article for a five-year period from 1985 to 1990. His research in social perception has been supported by the National Science Foundation. He is particularly known for applying models from other domains such as Gibson's ecological perception approach, complex dynamical systems, and an evolutionary perspective to areas in social psychology such as social perception, social relations, and small groups. He is currently engaged in research at the University of Connecticut on the emergence of cooperation in problem-solving contexts using a combination of ecological and dynamical systems models.

V. Lee Hamilton, PhD, is a social psychologist who has served as professor and chair of sociology at the University of Maryland. Recently, she has also been a visiting professor of psychology at the Chinese University of Hong Kong and of management at City University of Hong Kong. She has served on the review board for sociology for the National Science Foundation and on editorial boards of both theoretical and applied journals. Her research has been supported by the National Science Foundation programs in law and society and in sociology since 1975 and has resulted in three coauthored books, one coedited book, and more than 40 articles, in addition to the current volume. She has studied authority, responsibility, and justice throughout her career, both in the United States and across cultures; since the 1980s, she has also explored effects of downsizing on civilian and military populations. She has recently decided to take a "time-out" from her social psychological pursuits and will be enrolling in a master's of theological studies program in fall of 2003. Her primary focus will be care of those at the end of life and their families.